"The great value of Andrew Delbanco's interpretively edifying *The War Before the War* is in centering the cause of the great irrepressible conflict of 1860 in the many hearts and minds of otherwise indifferent, sympathetic, uncertain northern men and women who finally found enforced complicity in the South's 'peculiar institution' intolerable and a war for human ideals inescapable."

—*David Levering Lewis*, Pulitzer Prize–winning author of
W. E. B. Du Bois: A Biography

"Timely, incisive, deeply researched, *The War Before the War* tells the vital story of fugitive slaves, whose courageous defiance forced the young nation to reckon with its primal horror. Delbanco's swift-moving yet powerfully nuanced narrative offers insights into the institution of slavery and the political maneuvering that led up to the Civil War. This book is essential reading today, at a historical moment that demands unflinching reflection on founding truths."

—*Elizabeth D. Samet*, author of *Soldier's Heart* and editor of
The Annotated Memoirs of Ulysses S. Grant

"In *The War Before the War*, one of America's most eloquent scholars draws readers into the compelling story of how the North-South struggle over runaway slaves prepared the way for the Civil War. From the making of the Constitution to the bloodbath that began at Fort Sumter, Andrew Delbanco captures the experience of escaped slaves as they forced white Americans to confront the cruelties of slavery. This is a political, legal, and, above all, human story with powerful resonance today."

—*Dan T. Carter*, author of *Scottsboro: A Tragedy of the American South*

BY ANDREW DELBANCO

The

WAR BEFORE
the WAR

—

*Fugitive Slaves and the Struggle for America's Soul
from the Revolution to the Civil War*

—

ANDREW DELBANCO

PENGUIN PRESS
NEW YORK
2018

PENGUIN PRESS

An imprint of Penguin Random House LLC
penguinrandomhouse.com

Photograph and art credits appear on pages 393–395

ISBN: 9781594204050 (hardcover)
ISBN: 9780525560302 (ebook)

Printed in the United States of America
1   3   5   7   9   10   8   6   4   2

Designed by Amanda Dewey

To Ben and Raina, Yvonne and Emilia, and, always,

for Dawn

"To love and live beloved is the soul's paradise"

CONTENTS

——

INTRODUCTION

I N NOVEMBER 1863, Abraham Lincoln went to Gettysburg, Pennsylvania, to honor the thousands of men and boys who had died there four months before. In what became the most famous speech in American history, he consecrated the battlefield in the name of a nation "conceived in liberty, and dedicated to the proposition that all men are created equal." For most Americans, and for much of the world, those words have attained the status of scripture. They were, however, not strictly true, and Lincoln knew it.

Five years earlier, he had been more candid. Speaking in Chicago in the summer of 1858, he noted that when the Republic was founded, "we had slavery among us," and that "we could not get our constitution unless we permitted" slavery to persist in those parts of the nation where it was already entrenched. "We could not secure the good we did secure," he said, "if we grasped for more." The United States, in other words, could not have been created if the eradication of slavery had been a condition of its creation. Had Lincoln said at Gettysburg that the nation was conceived not in liberty but in compromise, the phrase would have been less memorable but more accurate.

The hard truth is that the United States was founded in an act of accommodation between two fundamentally different societies. As one southern-born antislavery activist later wrote, it was a "sad satire to call [the] States 'United,'" because in one-half of the country slavery was basic to its way of life while in the other it was fading or already gone. The founding fathers tried to stitch these two nations together with no idea how long the stitching would hold.

For nearly a century, the two halves of the so-called United States co-existed relatively peacefully. In its early decades, the young republic was little more than a business consortium dependent on interstate trade and central financing for infrastructure improvements. Countless transactions took place between North and South without incident. Southern planters supplied northern textile mills with slave-grown cotton, while northern banks supplied southern planters with financial capital. Inhabitants of one section regularly crossed over into the other. The sight of white southerners with their black maids or valets was common in the streets of northern cities and towns.

This book tells the story of how that composite nation came apart. There were many reasons for the unraveling, but one in particular exposed the idea of the "united" states as a lie. This was the fact that enslaved black people, against long odds, repeatedly risked their lives to flee their masters in the South in search of freedom in the North. Fugitives from slavery ripped open the screen behind which America tried to conceal the reality of life for black Americans, most of whom lived in the South, out of sight and out of mind for most people in the North. Fugitive slaves exposed the contradiction between the myth that slavery was a benign institution and the reality that a nation putatively based on the principle of human equality was actually a prison house in which millions of Americans had virtually no rights at all. By awakening northerners to this grim fact, and by enraging southerners who demanded the return of their "absconded" property, fugitive slaves pushed the nation toward confronting the truth about itself. They incited conflict in the streets, the courts, the press, the halls of Congress, and perhaps most important in the minds and hearts of Americans who had been oblivious to their plight. This manifold conflict—under way long before the first shots were fired in the Civil War—was the war before the war.

THE PROBLEM OF FUGITIVE slaves loomed over the Republic from the start. Many of the founding fathers were slave owners themselves, including Thomas Jefferson and George Washington, whose own slaves periodically ran away. The founders made an effort to solve the problem in Article 4, Section 2, Clause 3 of the Constitution, which came to be known (although it referred to indentured servants as well as to slaves) as the fugitive slave clause:

> No Person held to Service or Labour in one State, under the Laws thereof, escaping into another, shall, in Consequence of any Law or Regulation therein, be discharged from such Service or Labour, but shall be delivered up on Claim of the Party to whom such Service or Labour may be due.

But stating this principle proved to be much easier than carrying it out. Although from the southern point of view, law-abiding citizens were obliged to return a runaway slave just as if they had come upon stray cattle or stolen cash, the fugitive slave clause was erratically enforced. For the most part, slavery was left to the jurisdiction of the states. In 1793, Congress passed a law that tried to strengthen the constitutional requirement, but the federal government remained too weak to enforce it. Over the ensuing decades, northern states adopted "personal liberty" laws that put up further barriers to enforcement, including laws guaranteeing jury trials for accused fugitives and prohibiting state officials from assisting in returning them to the South.

In fact, most runaways never made it out of the South, where chronic offenders were sometimes mutilated—tendons cut, faces branded—as warnings not to try again, and to others not to try at all. But some who did get through to the North or to British Canada gave witness to the cruelties and indignities from which they had freed themselves in the South, and thereby presented a fateful challenge to the political fiction that the two American nations were one.

Southerners, blaming northerners for encouraging slaves to flee or revolt, demanded that the drain of their human property be stopped, while many northerners deplored the idea that human beings could be considered property at all. For some in the North, harboring a fugitive became a moral imperative dictated by the "higher law" that comes not from the Constitution or Congress but from God. By the late 1840s, the problem had become a political and moral crisis, and when Congress attempted to defuse it by passing a fugitive slave law intended to address the issue once and for all, it had the unintended effect of pushing the nation toward violent conflict with itself.

THE FINAL RECKONING was set in motion in 1846 with the outbreak of the Mexican War. With strong but not universal support in the South and against strong but not universal resistance in the North, both halves of the United States joined to wage a war of conquest. By the time the fighting ended two years later, the United States had seized a huge swath of land stretching from Texas to California, nearly equal in size to one-third of our present-day nation. This immense expansion of territory under control of the federal government brought back the old question of compromise in a new form. Would slavery be confined to states where it already existed, or would it be allowed to spread into the new territories, which would eventually become states? A growing number of northerners insisted on the former. White southerners, almost universally, demanded the latter. As Lincoln later put the matter, "One section of our country thinks slavery is *right,* and ought to be extended, while the other believes it is *wrong,* and ought not to be extended." The fragile political truce that had held the United States together was coming apart.

Then, in 1850, Congress attempted a resolution. The bargain it struck, which came to be known as the Compromise of 1850, belongs to the long history of compromise—beginning with the Constitution itself—by which white Americans advanced their interests at the expense of black Americans. In an intricate balancing act designed to prevent an irreparable rupture between the free states and the slave states, the compromise proposed to keep slavery out of some of the new territories while leaving its future in others to be decided by local referendum.

Many southerners considered the so-called peace measures heavily weighted toward the North, and so, as the price of their consent, they demanded something more: a new and stringent law that would put teeth into the fugitive slave clause of the Constitution and cut off asylum in the North once and for all. In September 1850, Congress sealed the deal by passing what became known as the Fugitive Slave Act. It was meant to be a remedy and salve, but it turned out to be an incendiary event that lit the fuse that led to civil war.

It was an act without mercy. To those arrested under its authority, it denied the most basic right enshrined in the Anglo-American legal tradition: habeas corpus—the right to challenge, in open court, the legality of their detention. It forbade defendants to testify in their own defense. It ruled out trial by jury. Except for proof of freedom such as emancipation papers signed by a former owner, the Fugitive Slave Act disallowed all forms of exonerating evidence, including evidence of beatings, rape, or other forms of abuse while the defendant had been enslaved. It criminalized the act of sheltering a fugitive and required local authorities to assist the claimant in recovering his lost human property. It put the power of extradition in the hands of "commissioners" appointed by the federal government and limited the disputed issue to confirming the identity of the person who had tried to flee to freedom. If the accused could be shown to have belonged to the claimant according to the laws of the state from which she had fled, she was ordered back to captivity. Everything about the Fugitive Slave Act favored the slave owners.

Even free black people in the North—including those who had never been enslaved—found their lives infused with the terror of being seized and deported on the pretext that they had once belonged to someone in the South. The Fugitive Slave Act forced them to live furtively in dread of every footstep on the stairs and every knock on the door. At any moment, they could be snatched off the street—and some were. As for the millions of slaves still held in the South, the Fugitive Slave Act deepened the despair of the already desperate.

One incensed citizen called it the "most disgraceful, atrocious, unjust, detestable, heathenish, barbarous, diabolical, man-degrading, woman-murdering, demon-pleasing, Heaven defying act ever perpetrated." Many northerners agreed but found the adjectives too mild. Meanwhile, hard-liners in the South, fearful that their slave-based culture was under mortal threat, considered the Fugitive Slave Act "the only tub thrown to the whale of the South out of the whole series of *compromise measures*" and warned that upon its "faithful execution depends our beloved Union."

On September 18, 1850, the president of the United States, Millard Fillmore, a New Yorker who disliked slavery, signed the legislation into law. Before the signing, a white clergyman in Fillmore's home state prayed that the hand holding the pen "might be palsied." In Ohio, a black minister who had escaped slavery twenty years earlier remarked that Satan could now "*rent out hell* and move to the United States," where he would feel more at home. When Massachusetts representative Horace Mann, attending a White House reception, was greeted by the president with hand outstretched, he refused to touch Fillmore's hand with his own. The leading intellectual of the North, Ralph Waldo Emerson, declared that "none that was not ready to go on all fours, would back this law."

EMERSON'S CLAIM has a satisfying clarity, and yet if it were wholly true, we would have to count among those crawling in the mud a good many people who despised slavery at least as much as he did—including Lincoln, who wrote to a friend in 1855, "I hate to see the poor creatures hunted down and sent back to their stripes, but I bite my lip and keep quiet."

Out of the gap between Emerson's righteous fury and Lincoln's reluctant acquiescence comes the driving question of this book: How could anyone who loathed slavery—in Lincoln's case, a man who built his political career on opposing it and eventually led the war that would destroy it—countenance such an odious law? Confronting this question takes us beyond a world where the line between good and evil is sharp and bright, into a gray confusion where navigation was soul-trying work. Understanding the moral ambiguities of the pre–Civil War years requires immersion in the particulars of the time when the fugitive slave problem preoccupied not only those whom it affected most directly—slaves and slave masters—but politicians, jurists, writers, activists, and some indeterminate portion of the silent public. It is a question about a particular historical era, but it recurs in one form or another whenever people must decide whether to submit to an unjust law or to resist it.

The choice may seem to have been a simple one, but nothing about antebellum America was simple. Some historians think that the fugitive slave crisis should be told as a story of bluffing and flinching—of white southerners not yet ready to secede and white northerners too ready to crush the hopes of refugees from slavery for the sake of preserving the Union. In this version of the story, the compromise was an act of abject appeasement of the South by the North.

Other historians prefer a story of political realists in the North who feared that an independent South released from federal constraint would grow into a slave-based empire not only incorporating territories won from Mexico but reaching to Cuba and into the Caribbean. In this version of the story, the compromise secured a decade of peace during which free states outstripped slave states in industrial development and a network of railroads linking producers in the West with consumers in the East came to rival the Mississippi and Missouri rivers as arteries of commerce. Given what we know from hindsight—that by the time compromise gave way to civil war, the North had achieved the requisite economic and political unity to overwhelm the South—the freedom-killing law proved to be ultimately an advance toward freedom.

In light of this confounding irony, how should the compromisers be judged? Should they be condemned for joining the long lineage of white Americans who have shown a "craven willingness to bargain on the backs of black people?" Were they knowingly complicit in a crime against humanity? Or should they be credited for buying time that eventually made emancipation possible? Was the compromise unconscionable? Or was it a concession necessary to avert something worse—the secession of the South, by which a new slave-based nation would be created and slavery released from all constraint?

However one answers these questions, the fugitive slave law was a vivid instance of the law of unintended consequences. It turned antebellum America upside down. In the North, after a fugitive was violently arrested in Boston and sent back to his master in Virginia, one New England industrialist, whose textile mills wove slave-grown cotton into cloth, remarked, "We went to bed one night old-fashioned, conservative, Compromise Union Whigs & waked up stark mad Abolitionists." In the South, unionists became prospective secessionists, as when one North Carolina newspaper announced, "Respect and Enforce the Fugitive Slave Law as it stands. If not, *we leave you!*"

Southerners who had insisted on states' rights now demanded federal intervention to enforce what they considered their property rights. Northerners who had once derided the South for its theory of "nullification"—John C. Calhoun's idea that acts of Congress require consent from each individual state before they can take effect within its borders—now became nullifiers themselves. The black abolitionist Martin Delany, who had once scorned the idea that blacks should leave the United States for Africa, Canada, or the Caribbean, now concluded that the fugitive slave law had created a situation so desperate that "emigration is absolutely necessary."

Intended to secure the Union, the fugitive slave law made it less secure. It clarified just how mutually hostile North and South had become. It broke the Democratic Party into northern and southern factions. It fractured the Whig Party into "Cotton Whigs" and "Conscience Whigs." It made the possibility of disunion, once an extremist idea, seem plausible. One eminent New Englander replied to the southern secessionist threat with a shrug of disgust: "If the Union be in any way dependent on an act so revolting in every regard, then it ought not to exist."

And yet vile as it was, the fugitive slave law was also, ironically, a gift to antislavery activists, both black and white, because wherever it was enforced, it allowed them to show off human beings dragged back to the hell whence they came—a more potent aid to the cause than any speech or pamphlet. It implicated northerners in the business of slavery in a way they had never felt before. It made visible the suffering of human beings who had been hitherto invisible. It forced northerners to choose between coming to their aid in defiance of the law or surrendering them under penalty of the law. Before the fugitive slave law, northerners could pretend that slavery had nothing to do with them. After the fugitive slave law, there was no evading their complicity. The most famous fugitive in America, Frederick Douglass, acknowledged as much when he said that "the fugitive slave bill has especially been of positive service to the anti-slavery movement."

Indeed, some of slavery's most ardent champions in the South were wary of the fugitive slave law. Jefferson Davis, future president of the Confederacy, not only suspected that "the law will be a dead letter in any State where the popular opinion is opposed to such rendition" but feared that it could have long-term consequences costly to the South. Because slave owners thought of themselves as a besieged "minority" vulnerable to the expansion of federal power, there was risk in allowing the federal government "to assume control over the slave property." The fugitive slave law might prove to be an "illusive triumph" because it granted unprecedented power to the federal government that could someday be turned against them. In ways beyond anything Davis could imagine, it would indeed come back to haunt the South when, after the Civil War, it was invoked in Congress as precedent for empowering the federal government to enforce the rights of black citizens in the former slave states.

The inconsistencies and paradoxes of the fugitive slave problem were by no means limited to the sphere of politics. Men and women from all walks of life were pulled into a maelstrom of contradiction as they tried to come to terms with it. It not only alienated neighbor from neighbor, friend from friend, but divided people within themselves. Some who had been slave owners came to abhor their former way of life. Ministers in the North who preached against slavery told their parishioners that sending fugitives back to the South was a civic duty. Judges who deplored slavery as a godless injustice nevertheless felt bound to enforce the law. One judge who sent fugitives back to their masters countenanced the harboring of runaways in his own home.

It is too simple to tell this tale as a fable of good versus evil, not because of any ambiguity about the evil of slavery itself but because—given the facts of antebellum politics, the compulsion of economic interests, and the constitutional protections slaveholders enjoyed—it was far from clear how the evil could be destroyed. "Humanity cries out against this vast enormity," Herman Melville wrote in 1849, "but not one man knows a prudent remedy." By "prudent" he meant some way of destroying slavery without destroying the union itself. Nor was this a matter of two competing goods: abolition on the one hand versus union on the other. There was reason to believe that destroying the union would actually strengthen slavery rather than weaken it. If the constitutional guarantee of the right of slave masters to recover their runaway slaves were to collapse, an outraged South might go its own way, emboldened to build a slave-based empire beyond the limits of the United States.

The story recounted in this book is therefore not a story in which, as one of the compromisers put it with justified doubt, "right may be distinguished from what is wrong with the precision of an algebraic equation." It is better told, as an antislavery minister living in a slave state wrote, as a story in which "right-minded men could hardly tell where the lines of right and wrong crossed each other" and "the complications of actions and motive, both right and wrong, were past finding out."

ONE REASON THE STORY of the fugitive slave law is worth telling is that it takes us back to a time when the public and the personal became indistinguishable, when the lives of some Americans were put at risk by a vote of Congress, and other Americans, rejecting the option of what Henry David Thoreau called "spectatordom," risked their reputations and sometimes their lives in response. It transformed the lives of both ordinary and eminent Americans and eventually touched virtually all.

For this story to be grasped in anything like its full complexity, it must be told from the multiple perspectives of northerners and southerners, black and white, whose lives were forced by the fugitive slave problem into unwanted convergence. It begins with the nation's founding because the founding fathers themselves were inextricably bound up in it. It has a large and varied cast of characters, starting with such architects of the Republic as James Madison, Alexander Hamilton, and Benjamin Franklin as well as Washington and Jefferson. The founders entrusted their constitutional compromise to successors such as Calhoun, Daniel Webster, and Henry Clay, who, in turn, handed it off to the generation of Stephen A. Douglas and Lincoln.

But there is much more to the story than the work of mainstream politicians. By the 1830s, a biracial antislavery movement was gaining strength outside electoral politics. Some of its leaders, including some who had escaped from bondage themselves, believed that slavery could be reasoned or preached out of existence, while others believed it could be defeated only by blood and fire. Writers—journalists, polemicists, poets, and novelists—attacked slavery with new passion. An obscure author named Harriet Beecher Stowe, who was living in Cincinnati near the Kentucky border in 1850, was so outraged by the fugitive slave law that she wrote a bestselling book, *Uncle Tom's Cabin*, whose most memorable scene made visible the terror of an enslaved mother leaping from ice floe to ice floe across the Ohio River with her baby in her arms, just ahead of a slave-catching posse.

At the center of the history that Stowe brought to life are, of course, the fugitives themselves, whose own writings—editorials, speeches, letters, memoirs—began to appear in print in significant numbers in the 1840s even before passage of the fugitive slave law. Their experiences are both imperative and impossible to recapture, in part because most slaves were kept illiterate by law or custom, and so their published accounts tended to be filtered through the minds of abolitionist editors. Even those who wrote and spoke without mediation knew that the ordeal of slavery—like combat, incarceration, or deadly illness—is something no one can grasp who has not gone through it. William Wells Brown, enslaved in Kentucky before escaping to Ohio, told a largely female audience in New England, "Were I about to tell you the evils of Slavery, I should wish to take you one at a time, and whisper it to you. Slavery has never been represented;

Slavery can never be represented." At the other end of the spectrum were the slave owners, whose experience is also difficult to imagine because their attitudes—ranging from racial contempt to a self-justifying sense of paternalistic responsibility for their slaves—now seem so far outside the bounds of decency that most people shut their ears to them.

And then there were those—perhaps a majority of white people in the North—who struggled to find a way, as one antislavery minister put it, "to obey the law while respecting themselves." Writing with a certain voyeuristic pleasure, Nathaniel Hawthorne described one New England politician oscillating between saying yes and saying no to the fugitive slave law, attempting "first to throw himself upon one side of the gulf, then on the other," until he "finally tumbled headlong into the bottomless depth between." In Boston, a U.S. marshal reluctantly obeyed a court order to send a fugitive back to slavery, then raised money to try to buy the same man's freedom and after the Civil War hired him to work as an employee of the federal government.

Through most of his career, Lincoln himself tried to walk the line between compliance and resistance to the fugitive slave law. Repulsed by the southern demand that "we must arrest and return their fugitive slaves with greedy pleasure," he nevertheless pledged to respect the law. Even after his election as president and well into the Civil War, he continued trying to reconcile his revulsion at slavery with his devotion to the Union. In that sense, he was the embodiment of America's long struggle to remake itself as a morally coherent nation. Under his leadership, the Civil War finally resolved the problem of fugitive slaves by destroying the institution from which they had fled. By the time of his death, some four million black Americans were no longer at risk of forcible return to their erstwhile masters. They had entered a limbo between the privations of their past and the future promise of American life—a transition that remains far from complete.

THERE IS AN APHORISM attributed to Mark Twain (though no evidence exists that he ever said it) that while history does not repeat itself, it does rhyme. The fugitive slave story is a rhyming story. It is impossible to follow it without hearing echoes in our own time. It is about the breakup of the two major political parties in antebellum America. It is about the rise of what might be called the first Black Lives Matter movement, as black people in the North protested the outrage of slavery and stormed the jails where runaway slaves were held. It is about the establishment of "sanctuary cities" where fugitives—the undocumented immigrants of their time—sought safe haven. It is about the transfer of the states' rights principle from the right to the left as a means of defense against a predatory central government. It is about a political realignment that culminated in the election of a president with a minority of the popular vote. It takes place at a time when insult and invective became the currency of public discourse. And most of all, it reminds us at every turn of how enduring the devastating effects of America's original accommodation with slavery were—and are—on the lives of black Americans.

Perhaps the strongest affinity between then and now was suggested by the great historian Richard Hofstadter more than a century after the fugitive slave crisis and half a century before our own time. Writing in that tumultuous year, 1968, about the ineffable sense of shared values by which a society sustains itself—which he called "comity"—Hofstadter made no reference to the struggle over slavery and no effort to predict when the next such crisis would arrive. Yet his words have a striking pertinence to America in the 1850s as well as an eerie currency today:

> Comity exists in a society to the degree that those enlisted in its contending interests have a basic minimal regard for each other: one party or interest seeks the defeat of an opposing interest on matters of policy, but at the same time seeks to avoid crushing the opposition, denying the legitimacy of its existence or its values, or inflicting upon it extreme and gratuitous humiliations beyond the substance of the gains that are being sought. The basic humanity of the opposition is not forgotten; civility is not abandoned; the sense that a community life must be carried on after the acerbic issues of the moment have been fought over and won is seldom very far out of mind; an

awareness that the opposition will someday be the government is always present. The reality and value of comity can best be appreciated when we contemplate a society in which it is almost completely lacking.

As Hofstadter suggests, comity is as fragile as it is precious. In America, in the 1850s, it collapsed. As one antebellum newspaper put it with considerable prescience, the congressional debates that concluded in the apparent truce of 1850 resembled "the maneuverings of two armies before an impending war."

Americans before the Civil War were, of course, living in circumstances and with beliefs very different from our own. But in trying to hold their country together amid the conflict over slavery, they were as fallible as we are, uncertain of when to make a stand and when to give way to fight another day. In that sense, the questions they faced were not so different from those we face. What to do when law comes into conflict with justice? How to choose when the "pursuit of one duty . . . involve[s] . . . the violation of others"? What are our obligations to human beings in flight from horrors that are, in part, of our own making? With whom should one seek compromise, and whom should one shun, even at risk of war?*

The problem of the 1850s—how (for southerners) to preserve slavery without destroying the Union, or (for northerners) how to destroy slavery while preserving the Union—was a political problem specific to a particular time and place. But the moral problem of how to reconcile irreconcilable values is a timeless one that, sooner or later, confronts us all.

---

*In October 2017, the retired general John Kelly, chief of staff to President Trump, caused a furor when he remarked that "a lack of an ability to compromise" led to the Civil War (Maggie Astor, "John Kelly Pins Civil War on a 'Lack of Ability to Compromise,'" *New York Times*, Oct. 31, 2017). As a statement of fact, the claim is, of course, true. The question Kelly failed to ask was whether, by adding to the long history of compromise, the war could have, or should have, been averted. His implication seemed to be yes.

Part One

THE LONG FUSE

One

THE PROBLEM

1.

In January 1850, when Senator James Mason of Virginia introduced the legislation that came to be known as the fugitive slave law, he described it as a procedural adjustment in law enforcement. "A bill," he called it, "to provide for the more effectual execution of the third clause of the second section fourth article of the Constitution of the United States." From the point of view of its proponents, it was a new attempt to solve an old problem: slavery is a condition from which the enslaved will seek to escape.

This was a problem the founding fathers knew well. In 1783, after the last shots had been fired in the war for independence from Great Britain, General George Washington worried that "Tories and Refugees" fleeing the country would take fugitive slaves with them, including "some of my own." It would be "fruitless to give to you their names," he wrote to the officer in charge of maritime traffic in and out of New York City, because "they are so easily changed." But "if by Chance, you should come of the knowledge of any of them, I will be much obliged by your securing them, so that I may obtain them again."

When the Father of our Country asked for help in tracking down his wayward slaves, the thirteen former colonies were linked only loosely by a cooperative agreement, the Articles of Confederation, adopted in 1781. The articles were a first step toward nationhood, but they left unclear the mutual obligations of the states in such matters as trade and commerce, the maintenance of a national army and navy, the conduct of foreign policy, and the consent each state owed to the laws of other states. It did not take long for the last of these questions—legal reciprocity among the states, or the principle of "comity"—to become acute, especially as it concerned the issue of slavery. Particularly troublesome was the question of whether a person enslaved in one state of the confederation could become free by crossing into another.

It was not a hypothetical question. Even before the close of the Revolutionary War, several states had moved to abolish slavery, which seemed, at least to some of the revolutionaries, an institution inconsistent with the ideals for which they were fighting. Between 1777 and 1784, Pennsylvania, Connecticut, Massachusetts, New Hampshire, and Rhode Island, as well as the Republic of Vermont (which entered the Union as the fourteenth state in 1791), put an end to it within their borders. Some ended it by legislation, others by judicial ruling, some did it immediately, others gradually, and more states seemed likely to follow. By the early 1780s, Thomas Jefferson—who decried slavery as a "moral evil" but never emancipated his own slaves—had come to believe that the "spirit of the master is abating, that of the slave rising from the dust."

With slavery apparently in retreat, slave owners grew alarmed about the security of their human property. Because the laws of the several states regarding slavery were, as James Madison put the matter, "uncharitable to one another," its presence in some states and absence from others presented a major obstacle for a confederation trying to make itself into a nation. What would be the status of slaves transported from a slave state to a free state, whether by their owner or by their own voluntary flight?

The same problem applied to the vast territories stretching south of British Canada, east of the Mississippi River, and north of the Ohio. Collectively known as the Northwest Territory, these lands had been apportioned by royal charter to the former colonies, now states, which ceded them after the Revolution to the new federal government. In July 1787, with the adoption of the Northwest Ordinance by the Congress of the

Confederation, slavery was banned from these territories, which were eventually organized into the states of Ohio, Indiana, Illinois, Michigan, and Wisconsin. The "free soil" North was starting to take form.

So it was in an already divided country that between May and September 1787, delegates from the states met at Philadelphia hoping to clarify their mutual obligations. Aware of the deficiencies of the Articles of Confederation in addressing the problem of comity, they produced a constitution that in some respects weakened the states and strengthened the central government. In order to persuade southern as well as northern state legislatures to ratify it, the authors of the new Constitution, led by Madison of Virginia and Alexander Hamilton of New York, understood the need to make "concession[s] to reconcile clashing interests."

Among those clashing interests, the most divisive was slavery, and the most fateful proved to be the constitutional guarantee (Article 4, Section 2, Clause 3) to slave owners of their right to reclaim escaped slaves. This was the clause, according to Senator Mason and his allies in 1850, in need of "more effectual execution":

> No Person held to Service or Labour in one State, under the Laws thereof, escaping into another, shall, in Consequence of any Law or Regulation therein, be discharged from such Service or Labour, but shall be delivered up on Claim of the Party to whom such Service or Labour may be due.

In fact, the fugitive slave clause of the Constitution was a weak directive. Phrased in the passive voice ("be discharged," "be delivered up"), it left wide open the matter of who was responsible for carrying it out. It made no distinction between indentured servants who worked under contract for a term of years and slaves whose bondage lasted from birth to death and was passed on to their children and to their children's children until the end of time. Its silence about this distinction registered the deepest irony of American history—that the word "slavery" does not appear anywhere in the U.S. Constitution until, after more than three-quarters of a century and four years of savage civil war, the Thirteenth Amendment* finally named the unnamed thing in order to destroy it.

2.

But if the words of Article 4, Section 2 were elliptical or even evasive, their intent was clear—clear enough, at any rate, for one southern delegate to declare victory on a point of great importance to the South. Speaking to constituents back home in Charleston, Charles Cotesworth Pinckney of South Carolina† told them, "We have obtained a right to recover our slaves in whatever part of America they may take refuge, which is a right we had not before."

Pinckney spoke too soon. Amid claims and counterclaims about the status of slaves crossing state borders, in particular the border between Virginia and Pennsylvania, southerners complained that while northerners paid lip service to the constitutional right of slave owners to recover their runaways, they were brazenly ignoring it. Years later, the Missouri senator Thomas Hart Benton would state the problem succinctly. The Constitution, he wrote, "allows the recovery of fugitive slaves," but "you cannot recover one without an act of Congress."

In 1792, Congress acted. It approved a bill empowering the "agent or attorney" of an aggrieved slave owner to seek rendition of his property in federal or state court. The bill also imposed a fine on anyone who "knowingly and willingly" obstructed the return of a runaway. On February 12, 1793, President Washington signed it into law.

But this law, too, proved insufficient. With the entry into the Union of new slave states (Kentucky [1792], Tennessee [1796], and Missouri [1821]) touching the borders of new free states (Ohio [1803], Indiana [1816], and

---

*Passed by the Senate on April 8, 1864, and by the House on January 31, 1865, the amendment was ratified by the required number of states on December 6, 1865, and confirmed as the law of the land by Secretary of State William Seward on December 18: "Neither slavery nor involuntary servitude, except as a punishment for crime whereof the party shall have been duly convicted, shall exist within the United States, or any place subject to their jurisdiction."

†The Reverend Clementa Pinckney, one of the victims of the mass murder that took place on June 17, 2015, in the Emanuel African Methodist Episcopal Church in Charleston, South Carolina, might have been a descendant of slaves owned by Charles Pinckney and possibly of Pinckney himself.

Illinois [1818]), the boundary between North and South became longer and more porous. As the growing domain of freedom in the North beckoned to unfree people in the South, it was increasingly evident that both the Constitution and the law of 1793—described by one irate Virginian as "inadequate to the object it proposed to effect"—raised more questions than they answered about how to deal with human beings fleeing from slavery to freedom in the "united" states.

What obligations, exactly, were prescribed by the phrase "shall be delivered up"? Delivered by whom? To what authority—local, state, or federal—did a slave owner have recourse if his slaves crossed the border onto free soil? Along with such theoretical and procedural questions, there were practical ones too. The new federal government simply did not have the resources to enforce the law. It had neither clear jurisdiction nor sufficient personnel to impose penalties on those who violated it, and so the interstate pursuit of fugitive slaves remained essentially a private business. But recovering slaves through private effort was easier said than done. Sending an agent on one's own to pursue a fugitive could be expensive, with no guarantee of success, and counting on citizens in a free state to volunteer for the work of human repossession was too much to expect, or, depending on one's view of the morality of the matter, too little.

In the first two decades of the nineteenth century, Congress made two further attempts, in 1801 and 1817, to strengthen the constitutional guarantee that runaways must be returned. Both failed. By the 1830s, cases involving "absconded" slaves were reaching the courts in growing numbers. The term "absconded" neatly expressed the slave owners' view that fugitive slaves were outlaws who had made off with someone else's property in the form of themselves. Another common term was "eloped" (already evolving into its modern sense of running off to marry without parental permission), as if runaway slaves were seeking forbidden intimacy with a missing part of themselves.

From the increasingly defensive pro-slavery point of view, a fugitive slave was the bad twin of a good slave—impetuous, gripped by illicit desire, in need of discipline and punishment. From the antislavery point of view, a fugitive was a sibling or spouse who had been forcibly separated from her natural partner—freedom—with whom reunion was long over-due. Some slaves who escaped to British Canada during the Revolution-ary War added "Liberty" or "Freedom" to the names they had been given by their masters as a way of declaring that they had found their long-lost partner at last.

As public debate intensified, growing numbers of conscientious people felt caught between the opposing factions, not necessarily because they countenanced slavery, but because they felt constrained by laws that clashed with their sense of justice. Faced with the legal question of whether to re-mand a fugitive to his or her owner, they fretted—in some cases agonized—over the conflict between their private beliefs and what they understood to be their public duty.

Among those caught in this way were attorneys and judges, including some who, despite personal antipathy to slavery, represented or ruled in favor of slave owners seeking return of their runaways. "God knows, no man in the country more regrets the black spot of slavery on our national escutcheon than I do," said one plaintiff's lawyer in an 1835 case of a Maryland man seeking return of an enslaved boy who had fled to Penn-sylvania, but "we must consider that we are acting, under the laws and constitution, in a legal manner, to obtain possession of property to which we have, in the amplest manner, proved our title." In explaining his ver-dict in favor of the plaintiff, the recorder of the city of Pittsburgh, who had judicial authority, expressed his struggle "not to let my feelings as a man interfere with my duties as a judge. In considering this case," he la-mented, "if any partiality remained on my mind, it was certainly in favour of this unfortunate negro boy. . . . Between *feeling* and *duty*, however, there is no medium."

But only a small fraction of incidents of flight and pursuit made it to court at all. Enforcement remained mostly extrajudicial, and "absconded" or "eloped" slaves were vulnerable to recapture by their owner or the own-er's agents virtually anywhere in America. "If a horse wandered away, and the owner found it," one scholar writes about life on the border between Maryland and Pennsylvania, "he could recover it without legal process, unless someone objected." The same was generally true for slaves. Farther

Newspaper ornaments from an 1840s printer's catalogue

south, on the frontier between the Mississippi Territory and the Creek Indian homelands, slave owners offered brandy, corn, salt, and silver to Indian tribal leaders in exchange for hunting down runaways and bringing them "home."

Newspaper advertisements offering rewards for runaways became so common that the historian Edward Baptist has called them the "tweets of the master class." Among the standard "ornaments" sold to printers by type manufacturers was a picture of a runaway slave, typically available for purchase for around $1.50, along with images of apothecaries, boots, and hats.

In 1841, when Charles Dickens came to the United States on a book-selling tour, he was struck by the many newspaper notices, "coolly read in families . . . as a part of the current news and small-talk," in which slave owners offered rewards for return of their runaways. Here is a sample of what he read in his New York City hotel over his morning toast and tea:

> Ran away, a negro woman and two children. A few days before she went off, I burnt her with a hot iron, on the left side of her face. I tried to make the letter "M."

Fifty dollars reward for the negro Jim Blake. Has a piece cut out of each ear, and the middle finger of the left hand cut off to the second joint.

Ran away, a negro named Arthur. Has a considerable scar across his breast and each arm, made by a knife; loves to talk much of the goodness of God.

We may stare in amazement at such descriptions of mutilated human beings, and wonder why, in a nation putatively dedicated to freedom, it took so long for passions over their fate to come to a boil. But given the horrors of our own time—millions of refugees abroad fleeing murderous violence only to drown or suffocate or be sold into sexual slavery; thousands in our own country held in jail or detention camps while awaiting deportation back to some form of servitude in the countries from which they fled—perhaps we ought also to ask this question of ourselves.*

3.

One reason why public dispute over the issue of fugitive slaves remained relatively subdued for so long is that they never amounted to more than a small fraction of the enslaved population. A survey conducted in 1850 put the number of slaves missing annually at about 1,000 in an enslaved population of over 3 million, or around 0.033 percent. In Maryland, which led the states in the number of fugitives, a total of 279 were counted in the year between June 1849 and June 1850. Census data suggest that between 1850 and 1860 the number of slaves in the United States emancipated by their masters exceeded the number who ran away by between 50 percent and 400 percent.

But surveys had limits. For one thing, only slaves who disappeared for

---

*While I was writing this book, the *New York Times* ran an article ("Three Days, 700 Deaths on Mediterranean as Migrant Crisis Flares," May 29, 2016) recounting the loss at sea of more refugees, by several multiples, than all the fugitive slaves recaptured under the Fugitive Slave Act of 1850. On one contemporary detention center in the United States, see Rhonda Brownstein, "The Corrections Corporation of America Is Blocking Immigrants from Seeing Their Lawyers at a Georgia Detention Center," *Huffington Post*, July 6, 2017.

long periods of time were usually counted, not those who went missing for a short while before they returned on their own or were recaptured. For another, acknowledging a problem of desertion to the census taker, who might be a neighbor or competitor, could make a slave master look incompetent or weak. It is hardly surprising that the subject elicited reactions ranging from voluble anger to mute indignation.

The prevalence of the problem varied, too, by region. In 1850, with grim plausibility, Daniel Webster estimated that "on an average, not one slave escapes in five years" from the cotton states of the lower South. In the border state of Missouri, on the other hand, the high number of runaway advertisements and the periodic toughening of local rendition laws have convinced one historian that "the sheer volume of absconding slaves was immense." The scale of escapes nationwide might indeed have been considerably higher than the conservative estimates. At the time the fugitive slave bill came up in Congress, contemporaries tended to put the total number of escaped slaves in the free states "upon whom this new fugitive slave law is intended to operate" at around 100,000. Some scholars since have suggested that as many as 50,000 slaves per year went missing temporarily, and perhaps 5,000 permanently, but as one authority puts it, all the figures are "guesses really."

Whatever the true count, a main reason more slaves did not take flight was their knowledge, acquired by personal experience or by witnessing failed attempts by others, that the odds were stacked heavily against them. Jefferson's expectation that slavery was "abating" proved to be one of the worst predictions in American history. Not only was it not shrinking; it was growing and spreading, resistance to it in the slave states was fading, and its center of gravity was shifting southward to a "carceral" world where the idea of deliverance was almost always a cruel fantasy.

No aspect of American history is more susceptible to an economic-determinist interpretation—to the view, that is, that material interests determine what people think and how they act—than the collapse of the antislavery movement in the antebellum South, which declined from a mainstream to a minority view in tandem with the rise of the cotton industry. In the early years of the Republic, leaders of the Methodist

Church—soon to become the largest denomination in the South—voted with regard to slavery "to extirpate this abomination among us." Slave owners who did not emancipate their slaves were to be expelled, along with slave dealers. But as the plantation system took hold and slaves poured into the lower South, churches that took a stand against slavery found their membership dwindling. Sanctions against slave owners softened into a "general rule" to which more and more exceptions were permitted until most antislavery clergy either censored themselves or left for churches in the North or the West. By the late 1830s, antislavery agitation in the South, where the idea of gradual emancipation had once attracted significant support, had largely subsided, and in the Deep South it had almost disappeared.

In descriptions of the effects of slavery on the American body politic, the metaphor of cancer is invoked so often that it has become a cliché— hackneyed, perhaps, but, like many clichés, substantially true. Slavery had a terrifying capacity to metastasize, and despite periodic announcements that a path to a cure had been found, no one before the Civil War had any idea how to put an end to it or even how to slow it down.

As demand for cotton rose from northern and European markets, so did investment in the cotton trade by northern and foreign banks. New technologies for harvesting and processing cotton transformed plantations into humming engines of production. Slavery became the "flywheel" driving not only the southern and American but also the global economy. As early as 1820, the United States overtook India as the world's largest cotton producer. At the time of the founding, cotton accounted for barely 7 percent of the new nation's exports; by the eve of the Civil War, that figure had risen to more than 60 percent. In 1844, as estimated by one antislavery newspaper, "twelve hundred million dollars worth of human beings" was held "by two hundred thousand slaveholders." Then, as now, great wealth was concentrated in relatively few hands, and then, as now, the have-nots (non-slaveholding southern whites) failed to mount an effective challenge to the haves, either by demanding a larger share of the wealth or by pulling down the system by which the wealth was created. By the 1850s, according to the historian Eric Foner, the economic value of enslaved "men, women, and children when considered as property exceeded the combined worth of all the banks, factories, and railroads in the United States."

Under the regime of "King Cotton," the need for involuntary labor grew so rapidly that supply could barely keep up with demand. Ever since 1808, when Congress banned American participation in the international slave trade (one of the constitutional compromises had been to postpone the ban for twenty years), slaves could no longer be imported directly from Africa, at least not legally.* Nor could the planters' need be met by "natural increase" among those already living in the United States. The result was a huge forced migration of slaves from the upper South to buyers in the lower South.

As early as 1811, one British visitor noted that as tobacco farming in Virginia and North Carolina became less profitable, "gangs of Negroes formerly engaged in it" were shipped farther south to cotton planters wishing to pursue their "operations with increasing vigour." In 1817, the Philadelphia physician Jesse Torrey, attending a session of Congress in Washington, found his attention arrested

> by the voice of a stammering boy, who, as he was coming into the house, from the street, exclaimed, "There goes the Ge-Ge-orgy men with a drove o' niggers chained together two and two." What's that, said I,—I must see,—and, going to the door, I just had a distant glimpse of a light covered wagon, followed by a procession of men, women and children, resembling that of a funeral. I followed them hastily; and as I approached so near as to discover that they were bound together in pairs, some with ropes, and some with iron chains, (which I had hitherto seen used only for restraining beasts,) the involuntary successive heavings of my bosom became irrepressible.

---

*Between the official end of the Atlantic slave trade in 1808 and the outbreak of the Civil War, some quarter of a million slaves were smuggled from Africa, Cuba, and elsewhere into the United States. See Andrew Wender Cohen, *Contraband: Smuggling and the Birth of the American Century* (New York: W. W. Norton, 2015), 65, who cites numerous authorities.

When Torrey asked one of the men prodding the slaves where they were going, "'To Georgia,' he replied. 'Have you not, said I, enough such people in that country yet?' 'Not quite enough,' he said."

Whether native or imported, slaves could not through "natural increase" keep up with rising demand for field laborers in the ever-expanding rice and cotton country, so there was unremitting need for more. Meanwhile, in parts of the upper South, where "slaves bred rather than died," there was pressure to reduce oversupply. To meet these complementary needs, vast numbers were forced southward—redistributed from a region where their lives were by some measures improving, to the "staple states," as Calhoun delicately called them, where the cultivation of cotton, as well as of rice and sugar, required backbreaking and soul-breaking work that no human being would do without coercion.

It was a terrible symmetry. In Maryland, where slaves were frequently "hired out," allowed to keep a portion of their wages, and sometimes to buy their freedom, the slave population leveled off or even declined. An estimated fifty thousand slaves were emancipated over three centuries, and by the eve of the Civil War roughly half the black population in Maryland was free. Meanwhile, in Mississippi, the slave population grew relentlessly.

The decline of slaves in the upper South as a proportion of the black population was also driven by sales of slaves to cotton planters whose female slaves were not bearing children fast enough to meet demand. In this respect, there was a convergence of interest between the Deep South plantation barons and the opponents of slavery in the upper South such as the Kentucky politician Cassius M. Clay, who, in the 1830s, proposed emancipating all slaves in his state when they reached age twenty-one. Clay promoted this policy to his supporters—who, by and large, were more interested in banishing slaves than in liberating them—on the grounds that it would motivate slave owners to sell their human property to out-of-state buyers before emancipation went into effect and they still had good title.

While living in Baltimore in the 1830s, the abolitionist William Lloyd Garrison declared that slave traders should be "sentenced to solitary confinement for life" and sent to "the lowest depths of perdition" in the afterlife—a remark that provoked a libel suit but did nothing to slow down slave sales. In 1839, a leading Baltimore slave dealer, Hope H. Slatter, who, by his own account, was "always purchasing for the New Orleans market," placed an advertisement in the *Baltimore Sun* for his escape-proof slave pen, "erected under his own inspection, without regard to price." Slatter described the building as if it were a luxury hotel, "planned and arranged upon the most approved principle, with an eye to comfort and convenience, not surpassed by any establishment of the kind in the United States." As if writing a brochure for prospective guests—"now ready to receive SLAVES"—he provided some enticing details:

> The male and female apartments are completely separate; the rooms for both are large, light and airy, and all above ground, with a firm large yard for exercise, with pure delightful water within doors. In erecting and planning this edifice, the subscriber had an eye to the health and cleanliness of the slaves, as well as the many other necessary conveniences.

Slatter's real audience, of course, was not the hotel guests but the buyers looking to acquire them after their restful residence:

> Having a wish to accommodate my Southern friends and others in the trade, I am determined to keep them on the lowest possible terms, at twenty-five cents per head a day, and furnish them with plenty of good and wholesome provisions. Such security and confidence I have in my building, that I hold myself bound to make good all jail breaking, or escape from my establishment. I also will receive, ship or forward to any place, at the request of the owner, and give it my personal attention.

With the help of merchants like Slatter, who also assured prospective sellers that he would pay "cash and the highest prices . . . for likely slaves of both sexes," slavery boomed in cotton country. The enslaved population in Georgia, which stood at around 35,000 in 1800, rose to half a million by the 1850s. In Mississippi, over the same period, the number soared from 3,000 to 400,000. Frederick Law Olmsted, who traveled through the South in the 1850s on commission for the *New York Times*, surmised that "the larger the body of negroes on a plantation or estate, the more completely are they treated as mere property." From coastal Georgia and South Carolina to the Mississippi delta and the Louisiana bayou, the degradation of men, women, and children into "mere property" was all but complete. Untold numbers of Americans of African ancestry were thus exported from a world where they might at least have dreamt of freedom into what was, in effect, a maximum-security prison where the "planters systematically sealed the exits."

4.

To wonder why flight from this prison was rare is rather like wondering why, in the next century, the Jews of Europe did not flee the concentration camps. Charles Ball, a Maryland slave sold south to work in the rice and cotton fields who somehow made it to Philadelphia after repeated escapes and re-enslavements, reported in a memoir dictated in 1836 that "no slave dare leave the plantation to which he belongs . . . without a written pass from the overseer or master" because "any white man who meets a slave off the plantation without a pass, has a right to take him up, and flog him at his discretion."

In fact, Ball understated the case. From Georgia and the Carolinas to Virginia and Tennessee, slave catchers were permitted by law to "moderately correct" slaves who, while "out of the house or plantation . . . refuse to submit to undergo the examination of any white person," and in cases where "such slave shall assault and strike such white person," the law prescribed that he "may be lawfully killed." Runaways resisting arrest—to which the only witness might be the killer himself—could be killed with impunity.

As for those captured alive, an overseer or master might require fellow slaves to witness what happened to them upon being returned "home." Forced to watch one such demonstration, Ball saw "flakes of flesh as long

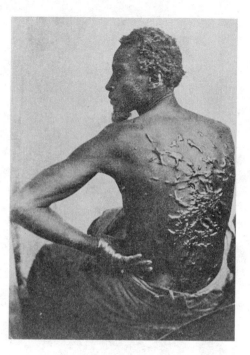

*Gordon, a Louisiana
slave who escaped
to Union lines,
photographed in 1863*

as my finger fall out of the gashes." Another fugitive, writing in the 1820s, compared the sight of a whipped slave's back to that of "a field lately ploughed" and proposed with scalding irony that "if it were not for the stripes on my back," he would bequeath his own skin to the government to be used as parchment wrapping for that "charter of American liberty," the U.S. Constitution.

In this sealed world, the hierarchy was clear. Regardless of temperamental differences among slave masters, or the relative severity or benignity of living conditions among slaves, everyone was either a guard or an inmate.

But the definition of "runaway" was less clear. A slave hoping to forestall or recover from a whipping or a rape might leave the plantation for a few hours or days and then, with nowhere to go, return in the hope that the perpetrator's rage or lust had passed at least for the moment. Others might go missing for weeks or months. Slave hunting became a kind of sport, not much different—for the hunter—from chasing fox or game, except that the thrill of pursuit could be greater, and so could the profit.

Illustration of a slave catcher by Miguel Covarrubias from a 1938 edition of Uncle Tom's Cabin. *Copyright María Elena Rico Covarrubias*

"Blood-hound trainers," explained Frederick Douglass, "placed advertisements . . . in the southern papers of the Union . . . offering to hunt down slaves at fifteen dollars apiece, recommending their hounds as the fleetest in the neighborhood." Slave catchers who "made a business of niggerhunting" kept "horses trained, as well as the dogs, to go over any common fence, or if they couldn't leap it, to break it down," and could expect to be paid up to two hundred dollars depending on how long it took to get the job done.

In a waterfront city like New Orleans, Mobile, or Savannah, a slave might dare to stow away on a ship bound for some northern port, but for the overwhelming majority of inland slaves there was no exit. Many plantation slaves lived in country surrounded by snake-infested swamps and accessible by roads traveled by thugs who were happy to hang a runaway and show off his corpse as an instructive example. But even for slaves who might once have fled into woods or swamps, the deforestation and draining of wetlands that advanced with the expansion of white settlement all but cut off their escape routes. Nor was there safety in what the slave master deemed good behavior. "The old doctrine," wrote Douglass, "that submission is the best cure for outrage and wrong, does not hold good on the slave plantation. He is whipped oftenest, who is whipped easiest." Nonviolent resistance was not an option.

As for those who tried against the odds to run away, repeat offenders might be rendered immobile by having their insteps split or Achilles tendons cut. Henry Bibb, who escaped from Kentucky in 1841, reports that after a previous escape attempt, an "iron collar [was] riveted on my neck with prongs extending above my head, on the end of which there was a small bell" designed to sound an alert if he strayed. In incorrigible cases, the offender might be stripped and beaten with a paddle specially designed with numerous small holes in order to raise blisters that could be shredded by a later beating or splashed with salt water to prolong the pain.

Slaves were subject not only to beatings by owners and overseers (black as well as white) but to fighting among themselves, sometimes goaded into it for the entertainment of onlookers who enjoyed betting on the outcome. In order to prepare himself for the next fight-on-demand, one former slave cut his hair short to prevent its being gripped and torn until his scalp bled, and in one particularly vicious encounter, to the delight of his audience, he bit off half his opponent's nose.

To witness this world through the eyes of a plantation master or mistress was to see it from a porched and columned house at the end of a gracious avenue lined with oaks or magnolias and, perhaps, copies of Roman statuary on whitewashed brick pedestals interspersed with pots of greenhouse plants. To view it through the eyes of the few plantation slaves who left a verbal record was to see a world patrolled by sentinels and spies, where the future replicates the past and all things beautiful are taunting reminders of how confining and impenetrable are the boundaries of one's life.

With rare exceptions like Ball—or Solomon Northup, a free black New Yorker kidnapped in 1841 in Washington, D.C., and rescued twelve years later from Louisiana by agents of the New York governor (Northup's story was published, in 1853, as *Twelve Years a Slave*)—running from this place was likely to end, in the words of the historian Walter Johnson, with being "run down and attacked by dogs, dragged through the woods on a noose attached to a horse, beaten with sticks, cut with whips, stapled to the floor of a cabin while a mob gathered outside" eager for a lynching. No wonder, as one slave catcher coolly remarked, that some runaways "would rather be shot than be took." Another hunter, proud of his proficiency, explained that his preference was to capture his quarry intact, but in the case of unruly fugitives "owners don't mind having them kind o' niggers tore a good deal; runaways ain't much account nohow, and it makes the rest more afraid to run away, when they see how they are sarved."

This kind of casual violence might have been less common in the upper South, but it was by no means unknown. In the Great Dismal Swamp of northeast North Carolina, dogs were trained as puppies to chase down any black person who was running or even walking fast. If one thinks forward to black movie actors consigned in the early sound-film era to playing shuffling servants, it seems a role straight out of the time when a sprinting or even striding black man was guilty unless proven otherwise— a time that is in many respects not yet over.

For a slave in, say, St. Louis or Baltimore, the proximity of free territory and the possibility of flight via river or bay—sometimes aided by free black sailors who were stopping in port—meant better prospects for escape than for her counterparts farther south. But the challenge was still daunting. Douglass, who beat the odds in 1838 by boarding a northbound train from Baltimore with identification papers given to him by a free black sailor, described what awaited any slave who dared to dream of freedom:

> We could see no spot this side of the ocean, where we could be free. We knew nothing about Canada. Our knowledge of the north did not extend farther than New York; and to go there, and be forever harassed with the frightful liability of being returned to slavery— with the certainty of being treated tenfold worse than before—the thought was truly a horrible one, and one which it was not easy to overcome. . . . At every gate through which we were to pass, we saw a

watchman—at every ferry a guard—on every bridge a sentinel—and in every wood a patrol. We were hemmed in on every side. . . . On the one hand, there stood slavery, a stern reality, glaring frightfully upon us. . . . On the other hand, away back in the dim distance, under the flickering light of the north star . . . stood a doubtful freedom—half frozen—beckoning us to come.

Even runaways who made it north remained at risk of recapture—not only, according to Douglass's fellow fugitive Henry Bibb, the light-skinned son of a slave mother and a Kentucky state senator, by white pursuers, but by "colored kidnappers" who, "under the pretext of being abolitionists, would find out all the fugitives they could" in return for a few dollars' reward. Slave owners sometimes sent loyal slaves north posing as fugitives in order to identify "safe houses" maintained by abolitionists who could then be reported to local authorities. Free blacks, too, were under constant threat in slave states or territories where slavery remained legal. As early as 1827, Congress decreed that any black person arrested as a runaway in the District of Columbia, whether or not he had ever been a slave, must pay his own legal fees and, if unable to do so, would be "liable to be sold into slavery" as a means of covering the cost of his detention.

For all these reasons—debilitating conditions, continual surveillance, brutal policing, betrayal by putative friends, infiltration of antislavery cells, oppressive laws—even such an enthusiast for all of the above as Senator James H. Hammond of South Carolina conceded with smug candor that the fugitive slave problem was "very small business."

5.

In a narrow numerical sense, Hammond was right. But in a broader sense, he could not have been more wrong. As the future of slavery became an issue of chronic contention between North and South, the felt significance of fugitive slaves grew far out of proportion to their numbers or the dollars they represented. In the grim work of tabulating the human cost of slavery, cold calculations never tell much about the heat of feeling.

For one thing, both sides had incentives to exaggerate the scale of what was happening. For enemies of slavery, fugitive slaves were eloquent evidence of an institution so cruel that it drove human beings to risk their lives—sometimes again and again—in the hope of escaping it. For friends of slavery, fugitives were evidence of a northern plot to dupe "Africa's poor sons and daughters, to lure them on to ruin and death of soul and body" in cities and factories where they would be used up as laborers cheaper and more reliably supine than their white counterparts. On each side, the appetite grew for arguments and stories that could be used to condemn the other side.

Among the enduring stories was that of the Underground Railroad—part truth, part myth. From one point of view, it was about brave citizens doing the godly work of sheltering fugitives en route to freedom. From another point of view, it was about "fanatics" doing the devil's work by "setting at defiance all laws, human and divine, the constitution of their country, all truth, all decency," in shocking disregard of their civil obligations.

Despite the implication of the metaphor, the "railroad"—or "liberty line," as it was sometimes called—had no settled routes, or schedules, or close coordination among its several branches. It ran between Kentucky and Ohio, or over the border from Maryland into Pennsylvania, or along the Eastern Seaboard, where some runaways—most famously, Frederick Douglass—did indeed travel by train as well as by foot, horse, carriage, or ship. It was a loose confederation of independent cells of which the membership was sometimes a single person making a snap decision to hide a runaway rather than turn him in. It was improvisational. It traversed cities and farming villages, mill towns as well as college towns such as Carlisle, Pennsylvania (Dickinson College), Lafayette, and Gettysburg, where students who called themselves the "Black Ducks" were known to create diversions to distract local authorities when runaways were rumored to be in the neighborhood.

After the Civil War, the complex reality of the Underground Railroad faded into an enveloping glow of myth. To read postwar accounts of the prewar years, one might think that every farmhouse in the North had

*Underground Railroad
monument at Oberlin
College, a center for aiding
fugitive slaves in the
1840s and 1850s*

been a station, everyone's father or grandfather had been a conductor, every home had had a secret pantry or attic where fugitives were sheltered while bounty hunters pounded on the door. Claiming to have served on the Underground Railroad became a way of laying claim to what the historian David Blight calls an "alternative veteranhood"—a way to satisfy the "yearning to bask in the glory of the old abolitionist generation." In fact, passengers were never safe. They encountered hostility not only from whites but from free blacks who feared that new arrivals, reduced to stealing crops or livestock in order to eat, would bring retribution on themselves.

Before the war, while northern papers described the horrors fugitives left behind in the South, southern papers recounted the miseries greeting them in the North. Often, the truth was somewhere in between. In 1850, one North Carolinian who declined to punish fugitives upon their (forcible or voluntary) return claimed he had heard that his own runaways were living as vagrants in New York City, begging and stealing in order to survive. "It would be some consolation to us," he wrote, "to learn that their condition was improved when they escape North, but not so." However disingenuous these words may sound to us today, there is no reason to doubt their sincerity at the time.

But whether it was sincere or strategic—most likely, some of both—the kind of concern this Carolina gentleman professed for his runaways was a quiet complaint compared with the loud outrage over what southerners regarded as northern collusion with their slaves. By the 1830s, many southern states had passed laws banning publication and distribution of any kind of antislavery writing. In Louisiana,

> any person using language in any public discourse, from the bar, bench, stage, or pulpit, or in any other place, or in any private conver-sation, or making use of any signs or actions having a tendency to produce discontent among the free colored population, or insubordi-nation among the slaves, or who shall be knowingly instrumental in bringing into the State any paper, book, or pamphlet, having the like tendency, shall, on conviction, be punished with imprisonment or death, at the discretion of the Court.

A small but tenacious cadre of clergy, mainly but not exclusively in the upper South, defied the prohibition. In up-country South Carolina, where Calhoun had been born half a century earlier, one Presbyterian minister who believed in preparing slaves for their coming emancipation protested that laws against teaching them to read were "a blot on the record of the state" and "offensive to God." Others continued to bring antislavery books into schools and churches attended by slave owners and sometimes slaves. They were the brave precursors of white southerners who, in the 1950s and 1960s, defied Jim Crow.

Prominent among the banned books were personal narratives by slaves who had somehow gotten away. Memoirs by former slaves such as Ball, Douglass, and Bibb appeared in growing numbers in the 1830s and 1840s as more and more fugitives in the North spoke and wrote publicly of what they had left behind in the South. Bibb reported that his master's wife insisted by day that he rock her in her rocking chair to keep off the flies and by night that he fan and rub her feet while she slept. "Too lazy to scratch her own head," this sweet Kentucky flower "would make me scratch and comb it for her" every morning upon awakening.

Stories like these were denounced in the slave states as slanders from well-rehearsed liars—Bibb, after all, confessed that "the only weapon of self-defence that I could use successfully was that of deception"—who not only violated the honor of the South but also drained its purse. To many whites in the South, the reproaches and open contempt expressed in the fugitive slave narratives were outrageously galling.

Meanwhile, southern newspapers published estimates of how much fugitives were costing the economy each year: $30,000 (Kentucky), $80,000 (Maryland), $100,000 (Virginia), amounts that translate, depending on which formula one chooses for adjusting monetary values over time, into many millions today. Some slave owners feared that fugitives flowing northward might even mean the beginning of the end of slavery itself—the opening wedge of a quasi-military strategy by which the North was planning to split the South by thinning its front lines through desertion and thereby exposing its interior to direct attack.

Many if not most slave masters claimed to believe, as one plantation mistress confided to her diary for no one's persuasion except her own, that "my own negroes are as happy as I am—happier." But if slavery was really a benign institution furnishing care for a simple people, why were the simpletons running away? It was a maddening question, and to read the attempts of antebellum southerners to answer it is to be reminded of the infinite human capacity for self-deception. Indeed, the literature of the pre–Civil War South constitutes an amazing documentation of moral insouciance, as when one lifelong slave owner celebrates the joys of retirement after years of labor—"Sweet is repose by labor earned / And safety won from perils past"—without the slightest acknowledgment of the millions who could never earn "repose" despite a lifetime of labor.

The eminent historian Kenneth Stampp once claimed that "in spite of their defense of the kind of slavery that existed among them and denial of its abuses, many [slave owners] . . . knew that their critics were essentially right." Whether or not this was widely true, at least some southerners

knew that northern lies and blandishments went only so far toward explaining why their slaves were running away.

Sometimes the slave owners' own words hinted unwittingly at the
truth, as when Pinckney of South Carolina praised the fugitive slave clause
of the Constitution for closing off "refuge" for runaways. Refuge from
what, one might ask, given all the talk about how happy slaves were?
Surely the goodness of slavery was a "strikingly peculiar" kind of goodness, because it is "the only good thing which no man ever seeks the good
of *for himself.*" The author of that tart comment was Abraham Lincoln.

Yet apologists for slavery never stopped blaming the runaway problem
on deceits propagated by white people in the North. At the same time,
they also attributed it to the inherent nature of black people in the South.
In 1851, a prominent Louisiana physician announced his discovery of a
disease peculiar to Negroes, to which he gave the name "drapetomania"—
a compound word that joined the Greek words for runaway (*drapetes*) and
madness (*mania*)—a mental disorder that "induces the negro to run away
from service." This condition, he wrote, "is as much a disease of the mind
as any other species of mental alienation, and much more curable, as a
general rule." The cure was simple enough: teach all slaves "the great primary truth, that a Negro is a slave by nature." Every slave owner must
continually remind his slaves of their slavishness and help them conform
to their own nature by keeping them away from stimulants such as in-
toxicating liquors or foolish ideas and by limiting their social contact even
with other slaves, lest their impressionable minds become infected with
childish fantasies of freedom.

The most powerful retort to this kind of pseudoscience was the eloquent courage of escaped slaves themselves. They pointed out, sometimes
with glee, that the slave owners' putatively stupid runaways were likely to
be their own children. In 1845, Douglass wrote almost perfunctorily that
"my father was a white man"—as if the point needed no elaboration given
how well known was the sexual exploitation of enslaved black women by
white masters.

When William Wells Brown, who spoke frequently throughout the

North after his escape from Kentucky to Ohio at the age of twenty in 1834, riffed on the theme of kinship (as reported in a New York antislavery newspaper, complete with notations of audience response), no one mistook his wit for good humor. He began with a satirical nod to the southern claim that slaves and slave masters are linked by bonds of affection. "Many of the free colored people of the North, especially the fugitive slaves," he said, are indeed "connected with the slaveholders of the South [by] . . . the tenderest ties of nature." As a matter of fact, when "they look into the Southern States . . . they see there their white relatives as slaveholders." Just yesterday, by chance,

> I met a good friend of mine . . . who came from the South about the time I did, and one of the first questions he asked me was, how my white relatives in Lexington prospered since I came away (laughter); and I asked after his white relatives. He wanted to know how my cousin William was, who is our Minister Plenipotentiary to the Court of Spain . . . (laughter). . . . My cousin Bob Wickliffe—the Wickliffe family is a very aristocratic family in Kentucky—died a few months since, worth, it is said, five millions.

Then Brown dialed back the mock pride and conveyed his resolve to see the whole slave system obliterated:

> Now . . . ladies and gentlemen, I do not look upon these white relatives of mine with as much pleasure as you would think, perhaps; but still, they are my relatives (laughter). Sometimes, you know, we find ourselves related to some people that we don't care much about (renewed laughter). But I say, here we are. We are connected with the slaves and the slaveholders by the tenderest ties of nature; and if this country wants me to run away and leave my white relatives, I can't do it (great merriment). If they want to drive me away from my black relatives, I shall stay here and labor for their emancipation (loud applause).

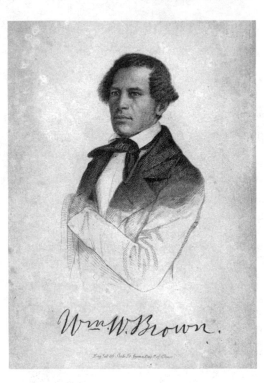

William Wells Brown
in 1849

By 1850, the fugitive slave issue had become much more than an irri-
tant between North and South. It had become, in Calhoun's words, "the
gravest and most vital of all questions, to us and the whole Union." For a
great many southerners, fugitives were thieves in the contorted sense that
they had stolen themselves. For a growing number of northerners, the real
thieves were slave owners and the agents whom they sent in pursuit. To
southerners, fugitive slaves proved that black people were inferior creatures requiring protection. To northerners, they proved their humanity,
which demanded liberation. Cutting to the heart of the matter, Lincoln
made the irrefutable point: "People of any color seldom run, unless there
be something to run from."

Two

SLAVERY AND THE FOUNDERS

1.

When delegates from the former colonies of Great Britain convened at Philadelphia in May 1787 with the aim of forming a common government, slavery had been an essential part of colonial life for nearly three hundred years. Between the first European settlements and the early nineteenth century, more than twelve million human beings were seized in Africa and shipped to the Spanish and Portuguese colonies of South and Central America, to the Dutch, British, and Danish colonies in the West Indies, and to French, Spanish, and British North America—under conditions that, despite the millions of words expended in trying to describe them, still defy comprehension.

In order to achieve maximum carrying capacity per vessel during the Middle Passage between capture in Africa and distribution in America, slave traders packed their human cargo onto racks with just enough space between them to accommodate a human body. Each man, woman, or child was confined by the press of bodies to less than a square yard, barely able to move during the inevitable bouts of vomiting and diarrhea.

Beneath the racks, or "platforms," the floor of the hold became so slippery with fluids and feces that, according to one eighteenth-century observer, the scene "resembled a slaughter house." Slave ships could be smelled from miles away. Over the course of the 1790s, one ship sailed

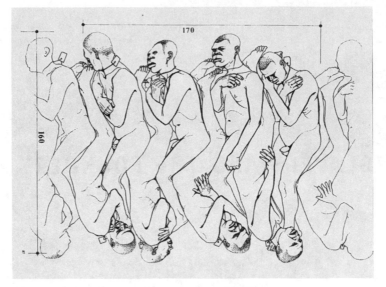

Slaves in "spoon" position aboard the French slave ship Aurore *(1784)*

every other day, on average, from Britain to Africa in order to pick up slaves and take them to the New World. State-of-the-art vessels were equipped with raised afterdecks to facilitate surveillance during periods when slaves were permitted in the open air, and with swivel guns in case they became unruly.

Uprisings occurred on roughly 10 percent of the voyages. Almost all failed. On at least one French ship, more than 90 percent of the "passengers" were children. In 1790, an English physician who had witnessed conditions at sea testified to the House of Commons about a slave woman who, having been flogged for some infraction, was flogged again for resisting the first flogging. After she died from her wounds, her flayed body was fed to the sharks. The same witness spoke of a young African man who tore at his own throat with his fingernails and bled to death. Despite incentives to deliver slaves in salable condition to auctioneers in the New World awaiting fresh shipments, at least a million human beings died en route from disease, suicide, beatings, and failed revolts, whereupon their corpses were tossed into the sea.

Over the centuries, most of the survivors were unloaded in South or Central America, but roughly half a million were delivered to British

North America. They came through such ports as Newport, New York, and Baltimore as well as Charleston and Savannah, from which the great majority were sent inland to work at planting, harvesting, and processing tobacco, cotton, sugar, rice, indigo, and other crops for the European and, later, the American markets. One reason that importing slaves remained profitable for so long was the calculation by slave owners that "replacement was cheaper than maintenance."

2.

More than 150 years after the first death ships arrived in Virginia, the eminent Virginian Thomas Jefferson sat in his rooms at Philadelphia drafting the document that has come to be known as the Declaration of Independence. He began with the stirring claim that all men are born equal, with an inalienable right to pursue happiness. But even as he announced the creation of a new nation devoted to those fine principles, more than half a million of its three million people were enslaved. In the five southern colonies (South Carolina, Georgia, North Carolina, Virginia, and Maryland), slaves accounted for two in every five persons. The slave population of the northern colonies was much smaller, ranging from twenty thousand in New York to barely two hundred in New Hampshire, but northern investors held large stakes in slave-produced commodities, and most slaves transported for sale along the southern coast were carried by northern ships. Slavery was a national institution before the creation of the nation.

It had not always been reserved for blacks. Half a century before the Revolution, Native tribal leaders sold so many captives from rival tribes to white settlers that Indians accounted for nearly a third of the slaves in South Carolina. But "unlike an imported slave or servant," as one historian points out, "the Indian was at home in the American forest and could survive in it. Consequently he was more likely to escape and had a better chance of succeeding." By comparison, Africans and their descendants proved to be more plentiful, easier to obtain, and, once they were distributed to buyers, a more secure form of human property.

Still, a slave of any origin presented what in a bail hearing is called a flight risk. At the height of the African slave trade, captives awaiting transport were fitted with spiked collars designed to snag in the underbrush if they tried to escape inland from the coast.

Such contrivances never fully solved the problem. As much as in Africa, slaves unwilling to remain enslaved were a persistent annoyance in America. South Carolina adopted its first "Act to Prevent Runaways" in 1683, limiting the mobility of servants as well as of slaves. That law was soon updated to authorize any sheriff "to raise a convenient party of men . . . to pursue, apprehend, and take . . . runaways, either alive or dead," at public expense. Sixty years later, the legislature was still working on the problem. A new law, adopted in 1751, prescribed a reward for the capture of an armed runaway who had been at large for more than six months. Even if the captor was himself a slave, he was eligible for compensation, though at half the amount paid to slave catchers who were free. In 1770, Georgia established a nightly slave patrol in its main port city that came to be known as the "Savannah Watch." In the waning years of British rule, colonial officials favored draining wetlands for the purpose not only of planting but of preventing "deserting slaves and wild beasts" from finding shelter in the swamps.

The end of imperial government did nothing to mitigate the problem. Shortly before drafting the Declaration of Independence, Thomas Jefferson offered a reward between forty shillings and ten pounds (depending on how far away the quarry was caught) for an "artful and knavish" runaway who had served him as a carpenter and shoemaker before making off with one of his horses along with shoe-making tools. To read the irritable prose in Jefferson's advertisement alongside the same writer's soaring calls for liberty in the Declaration is, to put it mildly, a startling experience.

The gift for casuistry—or, as some called it more bluntly, hypocrisy—evinced by Jefferson and his fellow revolutionaries did not go unnoticed at the time. "How is it," asked the English moralist Samuel Johnson in 1775, "that we hear the loudest yelps for liberty among the drivers of Negroes?" On the eve of the American Revolution, the French-born Quaker Anthony Benezet, who had immigrated to America as a young man, declared

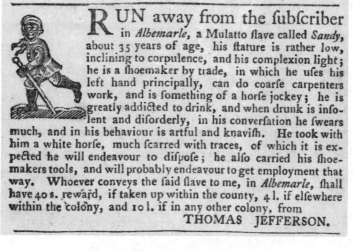

RUN away from the subscriber in *Albemarle*, a Mulatto slave called *Sandy*, about 35 years of age, his stature is rather low, inclining to corpulence, and his complexion light; he is a shoemaker by trade, in which he uses his left hand principally, can do coarse carpenters work, and is something of a horse jockey; he is greatly addicted to drink, and when drunk is insolent and disorderly, in his conversation he swears much, and in his behaviour is artful and knavish. He took with him a white horse, much scarred with traces, of which it is expected he will endeavour to dispose; he also carried his shoemakers tools, and will probably endeavour to get employment that way. Whoever conveys the said slave to me, in *Albemarle*, shall have 40 s. reward, if taken up within the county, 4 l. if elsewhere within the colony, and 10 l. if in any other colony, from
                                    THOMAS JEFFERSON.

From the Virginia Gazette, *1769*

with fearless lucidity that "no Christian can keep a slave . . . unless he is willing himself and posterity should be slaves." After war broke out with Britain, Abigail Adams, wife of Jefferson's rival from Massachusetts John Adams, wrote to her husband that it is "iniquitous . . . to fight for ourselves for what we are robbing and plundering from those who have as good a right to freedom as we have." Years later, Jefferson privately condemned his fellow southerners—somehow exempting himself—for being "zealous for their own liberties" while "trampling on those of others."

To make matters still more confounding, revolutionary leaders issued regular condemnations of slavery in the many broadsides and pamphlets through which they proclaimed their ideals to the world. Prominent among these was the original text of the declaration. At the request of a five-man committee charged by the Continental Congress with producing a public statement justifying the rebellion (the other members were Adams, Benjamin Franklin, Roger Sherman, and Robert Livingston), Jefferson composed the first draft.

With an ear for phrasing worthy of the musician he was, he opened with an arresting chord—the theme of equality—and then played variations on the theme of oppression. In the course of his composition, he accused the king, among other things, of maintaining an occupying army at the expense of his colonial subjects, appointing magistrates without popular consent, and imposing taxation without representation. To cap off the catalog of grievances, he charged the king with waging "cruel war against human nature itself, violating its most sacred rights of life and liberty in the persons of a distant people."

Jefferson would have liked to blame king and parliament for the "piratical warfare" by which Africans were stolen from their homes and to exonerate the colonists who received them. In this respect, he was more self-forgiving and less candid than his elder colleague Benjamin Franklin, who had levied the same charge against Britain six years earlier ("you bring the slaves to us and tempt us to purchase them") but concluded that *"the Receiver is as bad as the Thief."*

Jefferson's proposed attack on the slave trade never made it into the final draft of the declaration. By 1776, demand for slave labor was declining in Virginia but growing in Georgia and South Carolina. Like opponents of gun-control laws today, slave owners in the Deep South, whether or not they needed fresh supplies at the moment, were inclined to oppose any constraint of the trade lest it lead down a slippery slope toward curtailing their right to own slaves at all.

Jefferson's colleagues on the drafting committee were aware of these objections, and they also recognized the rhetorical weakness of condemning the slave trade while failing to condemn slavery itself. Another reason for excising the passage might have been to avoid antagonizing friends of the revolutionary cause in Britain, where parliament did not get around to outlawing the slave trade until 1807.* In the end, with a mixture of motives, the committee struck out the entire passage in an act of what its author called "mutilation" (Jefferson later claimed it was done "in complaisance to Georgia and South Carolina") as if the crescendo of his piece had been ripped out of the score.

---

*As a war measure, the Second Continental Congress, meeting in the fall of 1774, had imposed economic sanctions on Britain, including a ban on the slave trade, a measure reaffirmed in April 1776. But these proclamations were never officially enforced, though the trade was disrupted by the war itself. Following the war, the question of the slave trade was returned to the authority of the states. Don E. Fehrenbacher, *The Slaveholding Republic: An Account of the United States Government's Relations to Slavery*, ed. Ward M. McAfee (New York: Oxford University Press, 2001), 16.

A dozen years later, looking back at the debate as well as at the Constitutional Convention of 1787, when the issue of the slave trade came up again, Jefferson's Virginia neighbor James Madison asserted that "the southern states would not have entered into the union of America without" at least "the temporary permission of that trade." Yet northerners and southerners alike continued to invoke slavery as a synonym for evil itself. Frequently and fervently, they described the punitive policies imposed on them by Britain as tantamount to slavery.

"Those who are taxed without their own consent," wrote John Dickinson of Pennsylvania, "are slaves." According to Stephen Hopkins of Rhode Island, "they who have no property" are "reduced to the most abject slavery." John Witherspoon, the slave-owning president of Princeton—a favorite college for sons of the southern gentry—warned his students, including Madison (class of 1771), who was accompanied to college by his personal slave Sawney, that "to hesitate" in the struggle against Britain "is to consent to our own slavery." In these and many other cases, the word "slavery" became shorthand for the colonists' sense of being demeaned and despised by their British masters.

For anyone having trouble distinguishing between the metaphor and the real thing, Franklin was ready to help. "A slave," he explained in 1770,

is a human Creature, stolen, taken by Force, or bought of another or of himself, with Money; and who being so taken or bought, is compelled to serve the Taker, or Purchaser, during Pleasure or during Life. He may be sold again, or let for Hire, by his Master to another, and is then obliged to serve that other; he is one who is bound to obey, not only the Commands of his Master, but also the commands of the lowest Servant of that Master, when set over him; who must come when he is called, go when he is bid, and stay when he is ordered, though to the farthest Part of the World, and in the most unwholesome Climate; who must wear such Cloaths as his Master thinks fit to give him, and no other . . . and must be content with such Food or Subsistence as his Master thinks fit to order for him, or with such small Allowance in Money as shall be given him in lieu of Victuals or Clothing; who must never absent himself from his Master's Service without Leave; who is subject to severe Punishments for small Offences, to enormous Whippings, and even Death, for absconding from his Service, or for Disobedience to Orders.

But even as he offered this unsparing view of the matter, Franklin himself still owned at least two slaves. While living in London in the early 1760s, he had shared rooms with his son William, William's slave, King, who ran away in 1760, and his own slave, Peter, who was scheduled in Franklin's will to be emancipated upon his owner's death and who conducted himself "as well as I can expect. . . . So we rub on pretty comfortably." As a young newspaper editor, Franklin had accepted advertisements for human merchandise, one of which featured "a breeding Negro woman about twenty years of age." Another offered "a likely Negro wench about 15 years of age." ("Likely" referred to her prospects for bearing children.) An additional selling point in her case was that having "had the smallpox," she was unlikely to suffer a recurrence.

Admirers of "that great philosopher, Doctor Franklin," included George Washington, who, as a child of eleven, had inherited ten slaves from his father. By the 1770s, he owned over a hundred. From time to time, he added to the number by buying directly off slave ships in order to save the trouble (and the auctioneer's commission) of competing for them in public sales.

In short, regardless of what they said or wrote, America's founders were thoroughly implicated in the bloody business they decried. The schools and colleges they attended—from William and Mary in the South to Harvard in the North—were endowed with funds earned on the backs of slaves. Many of them, including some who denounced slavery, like George Mason of Virginia and James Wilson of Pennsylvania, were slave owners for much or all of their lives. Jefferson, we now know, fathered children by his enslaved mistress Sally Hemings. Washington, who claimed to possess slaves "very repugnantly to my own feelings" and only because "imperious necessity compels," used them not only to manage Mount Vernon but as laborers in a commercial distillery he acquired shortly before he died. Even in the case of those among the founders who disliked and condemned slavery, the banks and businesses to which they entrusted their personal assets were engaged directly or indirectly in slave-based commerce.

From the first days of the Republic, no one who personally owned slaves could be quite sure that transporting them from one state to another would not put his right of ownership at risk. Upon assuming the presidency in 1789, when the federal government was still located at Philadelphia, Washington sought confidential legal advice from Attorney General Edmund Randolph, who had lost some of his own slaves by failing to heed a 1780 Pennsylvania law granting freedom to slaves brought into Pennsylvania and residing there for more than six months.

Although the word "consecutive" or "continuous" did not appear in the statute, the exact meaning of the six-month provision was a matter of dispute, and so it remained for more than forty years. In one case (*Commonwealth v. Chambre*, 1794), the lawyer representing a group of slaves taken out of state by their owner after five months and three weeks made the inventive argument that they were legally free because their captivity spanned more than six *lunar* months. Not until 1821, with the case of *Butler v. Delaplaine* (in which counsel for the slave-owning plaintiff was Thaddeus Stevens, future leader of the radical antislavery faction of the Republican Party), was the law finally clarified to mean "continuous, day-to-day, residence for six calendar months," and slave owners were warned against "fraudulent shuffling backwards and forwards" into and out of the state in order to restart the clock.

Alert to these ambiguities, Washington had asked his personal secretary, Tobias Lear, to consult Attorney General Randolph for guidance. The advice he got back was that "if, before the expiration of six months," your slaves "could, upon any pretense whatever, be carried or sent out of the State, but for a single day, a new era would commence on their return, from whence the six months must be dated." Washington gratefully adopted this stratagem and asked Lear please to keep it private except for "yourself and Mrs. Washington," in whose company he sometimes dispatched his slaves out of state for short periods of time.

Among female slaves Washington had a taste for the "fat and lusty."

Among males he looked for "straight-limbed" specimens "with good teeth and good countenances." While president, he placed a newspaper advertisement seeking the return of a runaway "mulatto girl, much freckled," whose flight caught him so much by surprise that although he knew she had taken off with several changes of clothes, he could not recall exactly which ones. Convinced that she had been lured away by an unscrupulous Frenchman, he was still trying to get her back until almost the end of his life, in 1799, by which time she was living in Portsmouth, New Hampshire, as a free woman, married, with children.

For these and many other reasons, it remains no easy matter to come to terms with Samuel Johnson's question. How, indeed, did the founding fathers reconcile their complicity with slavery with their commitment to liberty? It is a compulsory question with no satisfactory answer.

3.

But there are partial answers. To begin with, the founders were born into a world in which slavery was widely regarded as a universal feature of human society. The more learned among them—Jefferson, Madison, Adams, John Jay—knew that Aristotle, king of philosophers, had declared it to be part of the natural order of things. "The lower sort are by nature slaves," Aristotle wrote in the *Politics,* and "it is better for them as for all inferiors that they should be under the rule of a master."

When they turned from classical to what would now be called Judeo-Christian authorities, the founders discovered warrant for slavery there too. The Hebrew Bible (Exodus 21:7; Leviticus 25:44–46) describes buying, selling, inheriting, and punishing slaves. It prescribes rules governing sexual relations between masters and slaves ("When a man sells his daughter as a slave [and] she does not please her master, who has designated her for himself . . . he shall have no right to sell her to a foreign people, since he has broken faith with her. If he designates her for his son, he shall deal with her as a daughter"), and in cases where a master has injured his slave, it stipulates when punishment or pardon is called for:

EXODUS 21:20–21: *If a man strikes his male or female slave with a rod and he dies at his hand, he shall be punished. If, however, he survives a day or two, no vengeance shall be taken; for he is his property.*

EXODUS 21:26–27: *If a man strikes the eye of his male or female slave, and destroys it, he shall let him go free on account of his eye. And if he knocks out a tooth of his male or female slave, he shall let him go free on account of his tooth.*

Nor did the coming of the Christian gospel banish slavery to the heathen darkness. Saint Paul (6 Ephesians; 1 Timothy) exhorts slaves to obey their masters, and in the letter to Philemon he says explicitly that fugitive slaves must be returned—a requirement sometimes known as the Pauline Mandate. Nor was the fact that Christ himself never spoke against slavery lost on southern slaveholders, who construed his silence on the subject as implicit affirmation. In 1819, for instance, the *National Intelligencer* (published in Washington) ran an article asking, "If domestic slavery had been deemed by Jesus Christ the atrocious crime which it is now represented to be, could it have been passed over without censure?"

Nevertheless, growing numbers of Christian clergy spoke out against slavery over the course of the eighteenth century. Some regarded it as incompatible with the general spirit of Christ's teachings, as when the Calvinist minister Samuel Hopkins declared that "the whole divine revelation" condemns slavery. Others cited specific scriptural passages that seemed to disapprove of it, such as Matthew 18:25–27, which recounts an incident in which a man is about to be sold along with his wife and children as satisfaction for unpaid debts—until "the lord of that slave felt compassion and released him and forgave him the debt."

Until the mid-nineteenth century, Christianity in the new nation was more or less synonymous with Protestantism. Among the relatively small number of Roman Catholics, few spoke or wrote on the subject of slavery. John Carroll (1735–1815), first American bishop and founder of Georgetown University—which was saved from financial ruin in 1838 when a group of Jesuit priests sold their slaves and directed the proceeds into the college treasury—encouraged manumission but never advocated a policy of general emancipation. Among early American Protestants, notable antislavery clergy included the Baptist John Leland, the Methodist Francis Asbury, and the Quakers John Woolman and Anthony Benezet, who regarded the French and Indian War (1754–1763) as a divine judgment on a slave-trading people.

Samuel Hopkins, once a slaveholder himself, preached against the institution in slave-trading Newport while leading merchants sat sullen in the pews. In the auspicious year 1776, Hopkins, who, long after his death became the subject of a laudatory novel by Harriet Beecher Stowe, published *A Dialogue Concerning the Slavery of the Africans, Showing It to Be the Duty and Interest of the American States to Emancipate All Their African Slaves*—a duty he regarded as consonant with, indeed required by, a revolution waged on behalf of the rights of man. Especially in New England, and to a lesser degree in the upper South, a significant minority of clergy across denominations denounced slavery as "one of the crying sins of the land."

But it would be a flattering exaggeration to say that in the years leading to the Revolution, American Christianity became broadly inimical to slavery. George Whitefield, the English itinerant preacher whose tour of the colonies in the 1740s helped spark the evangelical revival that became known as the Great Awakening, spoke forcefully against slavery—so much so that Phillis Wheatley, the celebrated black poet who had been sold out of Africa as a child and purchased by a Boston family, lamented upon Whitefield's death in 1770 that "we hear no more the music of thy tongue." But by the 1750s, Whitefield had decided that slavery was essential for the prosperity of Georgia, where he supported a school for white orphans financed in part by profits from a plantation he owned in South Carolina worked by black slaves.

Of Whitefield's famous contemporary (and Hopkins's mentor) Jonathan Edwards (1703–1758), who owned two slaves, it has been said that he "cared less about slaves than about 'bad books'"—a reference to a scandal that broke out in Edwards's church in Northampton, Massachusetts, when adolescent boys passed around illustrated anatomical textbooks as aids to sexual arousal. For most people in the eighteenth century—North and South, whether they were classicists, theologians, or laymen with only a smattering of formal learning—the question was not whether there should be masters and slaves in this world but how masters and slaves should behave toward each other in a world where there had always been both.

To face this fact is to encounter one of the most demanding challenges in thinking about history: explaining how people in the past could have failed to see what seems so clear to us in retrospect. This is an imperative task but also a delicate and exacting one. On the one hand, explanation can shade into excuse; on the other hand, passing judgment on the past can be a form of self-congratulation in the present. The hard fact is that in a world where "most men and nearly all women lived in some form of unfreedom, tied to one thing or another, to an indenture, an apprentice contract, land rent, a mill, work house or prison, a husband or father," slavery was an unremarkable form of human relations.

Just how unremarkable may be gleaned from a diary entry of May 22, 1712, recorded by a member of the nascent Virginia gentry, William Byrd. Along with what he ate and drank (hot chocolate was a favorite) and how his bowels were working, Byrd noted some of the uses to which he and his wife liked to put their slaves:

> My wife caused Prue to be whipped violently notwithstanding I desired not, which provoked me to have Anaka whipped likewise who had deserved it much more, on which my wife flew into such a passion that she hoped she would be revenged of me.

"Take that" (or something to that effect), says wife to husband, ordering the whipping of his pet slave, Prue. "Take that," says husband to wife, ordering her favorite, Anaka, to be whipped in recompense.

This was a human economy that fit perfectly with Aristotle's view that "the slave is a living tool, and the tool a lifeless slave." It was an early instance of the long unfinished history through which white people, in Martin Luther King Jr.'s appallingly accurate phrase, have found so many ways to inflict on black people a "degenerating sense of 'nobodiness.'" In the case of the Byrds—and, one suspects, in many cases before and since—beating blacks seems to have had an aphrodisiac effect. Even if master and mistress did not stay close enough to watch the lashings, they likely heard Prue's and Anaka's cries before, or while, settling their marital quarrel with a bout of sex, which the husband construed as a gift to his repentant spouse: "I was reconciled to my wife and gave her a flourish in token of it." Whether she consented or resisted is not recorded.

Some seventy years later, Jefferson—arguably the most sophisticated thinker in revolutionary America—declared that "those who labour in the earth are the chosen people of God, if ever he had a chosen people." The people he had in mind were white farmers, who, by working the land with their hard and honest labor, would be repositories of virtue in the new nation—a counterweight to the wheeling-dealing life of cities, where, Jefferson thought, people were liable to be drawn through the life of commerce into duplicity and greed.

How could a man of such formidable intellect write such a sentence without, apparently, looking up through his study window at those laboring in the earth on his behalf? Chosen people indeed! At his beck and call, subject to his wish and whim, they were chosen, like the Israelites of old, to bear the bitter burden of knowing they were owned. By the time Jefferson performed the dark magic of rendering slaves invisible, the disappearing trick had a long history, and it was a long way from over.

4.

Another reason that slavery failed to provoke focused outrage in early America was that the distinction between servitude for life and labor contracted for a term of years could be a formal distinction without much substantive difference. Beginning in the seventeenth century, thousands of indentured servants—men, women, and children whose transportation and upkeep were paid in exchange for a term of service—came to the New World from northern Europe, especially the British Isles. Their voyage was nothing like the Middle Passage endured by African slaves, but it was no pleasure cruise either. According to one eighteenth-century witness, it was an ordeal of "hunger, thirst, frost, heat, dampness, fear, misery, vexation, and lamentation" attended by "so many lice, especially on the sick people, that they have to be scraped off their bodies" so they might appear minimally presentable to buyers evaluating them as prospective workers once they arrived.

As for their pre-voyage experience, labor merchants in British or Continental port towns were able, in the words of the historian Richard Hofstadter,

> to lure children with sweets, to seize upon the weak or the gin-sodden and take them aboard ship, and to bedazzle the credulous or weak-minded by fabulous promises of an easy life in the New World. Often their victims were taken roughly in hand and, pending departure, held in imprisonment either on shipboard or in low-grade hostels or brothels.

In 1770, the surveyor of customs at Annapolis, having watched buyers at the pier inspecting shipments of immigrants with particular attention to their muscles and teeth, believed they were destined to "groan beneath a worse than Egyptian bondage"—worse, in other words, than what African-born slaves faced. He expected masters of bonded servants to extract every last ounce of labor during their years of indenture with no regard to effects on their health, while slaves, being lifelong property, had the advantage, he thought, that it was in the master's interest to extend the span of their working lives.

This hypothesis overestimated the rationality of the slave system and underestimated the irrationality of racial contempt, but it was not always groundless. Because some servants renewed their terms of compulsory service repeatedly until they stretched over a lifetime (average life expectancy in the late eighteenth century was around forty), indentured servitude was not inevitably a temporary condition. And because masters sometimes emancipated their slaves for reasons ranging from compassion to aggravation at having to maintain them past their useful years, slavery was not always a permanent condition.

And so servants and slaves, to whom William Byrd referred indistinguishably as "bondsmen," were often conflated, as they would be in Article 4, Section 2, Clause 3 of the U.S. Constitution—known too narrowly as the fugitive slave clause—which applied to both.

The day-to-day experience of a servant was not always markedly better than that of a slave. One Pennsylvania clergyman, writing in 1765, lamented the fate of a German immigrant girl whose contract binding her to a local family for six and a half years required that she be taught to read and write but who, upon completing her term, could "neither read a letter nor pray a single word" and had "been so completely debauched that she prefers to remain with her mistress because she is satisfied with her brutish life." By the time of the Revolution, the number of apprentices, servants, and slaves in Philadelphia was about the same as free wage laborers, and there is no telling the scale of exploitation—sexual and otherwise—to which they were subjected regardless of the distinction between servitude for a term and servitude for life. As late as 1835, former slaves freed by emancipation laws throughout the North feared, often with good reason, that if their children were to become indentured servants they would "be treated as they themselves have been while slaves."

"Absconding" was no less rampant among servants than slaves. The problem of "pirating"—enticing a bound servant away from his master with promises of pay or better working conditions or early release—became so widespread that criminal and civil penalties (whipping, consignment to the stocks) were often severe. Especially in the tobacco colonies, to provide food or shelter to a servant other than one's own was to risk punishment even if he had been abandoned by his master.

In a short story (1831) set in the revolutionary period, Nathaniel Hawthorne gives a glimpse of this penal world, in which wanted posters for runaway servants—as commonplace as "Don't Text and Drive" billboards today—were all but indistinguishable from those for runaway slaves. Hawthorne describes a flyer posted on a tavern wall that offers a reward for the capture of a "bounded servant" who had been wearing "when he went away, grey coat, leather breeches," and who, in an act of impudent thievery, absconded not only with himself but with his "master's third best hat."

Here is a typical newspaper notice from the third decade of the nineteenth century:

TEN DOLLARS REWARD

Ran away from the Subscriber, on the night of the 15th instant, two apprentice boys, legally bound, named WILLIAM and ANDREW JOHNSON. The former is of a dark complexion, black hair, eyes and habits. The latter is very fleshy, freckled face, light hair, and fair complexion. . . . I will pay the above Reward to any person who will deliver said Apprentices to me in Raleigh, or I will give the above reward for Andrew Johnson alone.

James J. Selby, Tailor
Raleigh Gazette
June 24, 1824

Because some jurisdictions added additional time in service for periods of unexcused absence, fugitive servants risked longer terms of servitude if apprehended, with habitual runaways facing extensions of as much as five years. Early America was a nation teeming with pursuers and pursued, and they were by no means only masters and slaves.

For "free" people as well as those enslaved, violence was routine. Corporal punishment was standard practice in families and schools. Public cages, stocks, and whipping posts were familiar sights in the squares and commons of villages and towns. Although by the late eighteenth century flogging came under attack as a barbarous practice, and new penal institutions—called penitentiaries—arose with the stated purpose of rehabilitation rather than retribution, beatings continued out of sight behind the walls. The "shower bath"—an early version of water boarding—was a favored means for disciplining unruly prisoners or those who, for one reason or another, displeased their jailers.* The pervasiveness of such "practices of unfreedom" leads one historian to conclude that "slavery and other forms of enforced labor did not seem all that different from free labor." A majority of early Americans—not only slaves and servants, but convicts, beggars, children, vagabonds, and virtually all women—lived at the mercy of those wielding power over them.

Slavery thus enjoyed a kind of camouflage. Today no reasonable person disputes that in the "hierarchy of dependencies" it was "the most base and dependent." But that conclusion was a long time coming. As late as 1850, Herman Melville—who detested slavery but knew other forms of subjection—asked, "Who aint a slave? Tell me that." It was a question to which Frederick Douglass reacted with earned exasperation:

> It is common in this country to distinguish every bad thing by the name of slavery. Intemperance is slavery; to be deprived of the right to vote is slavery, says one; to have to work hard is slavery, says another; and I do not know but that if we should let them go on, they would say that to eat when we are hungry, to walk when we desire to have exercise, or to minister to our necessities, or have necessities at all, is slavery.

Having fled from and fought against the real thing, Douglass had good reason for his scorn. As for our scorn toward those who owned or tolerated the owning of slaves, one might want to balance it with some self-interrogation. Calling out the moral failures of the past surely brings with it an obligation to confront one's own complicity with forms of "unfreedom" in the present. For many if not most Americans in the first decades of the Republic, slaves were out of sight or out of mind in much the same way that millions of incarcerated or impoverished people are today—until some shocking incident or anguished plea gives them a moment's visibility before they vanish again.

---

*For a harrowing account of how shower torture continues today, see Eyal Press, "Madness," *New Yorker*, May 2, 2016, 41, on inmate abuse in the Florida prison system.

5.

That slavery seemed so ordinary to so many for so long is all the more striking because it had two features that would seem to have made it conspicuous. The first was that except in cases of manumission, or of slaves who managed to buy their freedom, or in the relatively rare instances of successful escape, it was a life sentence. It was a closed system in which girls were circulated as breeders and boys as human machines for producing salable goods, including their own children, all of whom were doomed to repeat the cycle of coercion from which the only deliverance was death.

The second distinctive feature was that slavery selected its victims by color or "blood." Historians still debate whether the idea that black people were suited by nature to be slaves preceded or followed their enslavement—a debate that seems fair to call, in the pejorative sense of the word, academic. Whether racist ideas created the conditions for slavery or slavery was justified ex post facto by racist ideas made precious little difference to the enslaved. Either way, many if not most colonial Americans thought it as reasonable to enslave a black person as to train a dog or saddle a horse.

A favorite source for making the case was Genesis 9:18–25, in which Noah's son Ham, future patriarch of the Canaanites, comes upon his father "drunken [and] uncovered within his tent"—a sight he reports with salacious delight to his brothers, Shem and Japhet, who, in order to rescue the dignity that their brother had defiled, "took a garment, and laid it upon both their shoulders, and went backward, and covered the nakedness of their father." With eyes averted, Shem and Japhet withdrew from his presence and "saw not their father's nakedness." When "Noah awoke from his wine," he "knew what his younger son had done unto him. And he said, Cursed be Canaan; A servant of servants shall he be unto his brethren."

It may seem incredible that a foundation as flimsy as this story could support the enormous edifice of slavery for millennia to come. But through the work of medieval and early modern exegetes, a pernicious tradition developed that Ham's curse not only entailed exile and disgrace but also left him stigmatized by a darkened skin—a mark of shame to be passed on to his descendants. Thus Ham came to be identified as the founding father of black Africans.

In fact, skin color was no "criterion for categorizing humanity" in the ancient world, and slavery in classical times had no particular association with race. It was the price one paid for ending up on the losing side of a war, as it continues to be in some parts of the world today, especially for women and girls. Race-based slavery, by contrast, was a medieval invention that became a modern convention. With the forced influx of millions of African laborers into North America, it turned out to be a convenient convention indeed.

If religion furnished one pillar for the rationalization of New World slavery, science seemingly provided the other.* Learned naturalists claimed that surface distinctions in pigment and physiognomy signified deeper distinctions in mental capacity and character. In this respect, America's founding fathers were, to one extent or another, racists—not in the loose sense of the word as we use it today to signify bias, fear, contempt, or patronizing pity, but in a more technical sense.

They were impressed by so-called evidence ("preserved in most anatomical museums") that the feet, fingers, craniums, and genitals of black people proved that blacks were not fully human but an "intermediate species between the white man and the ape." Blacks were supposedly less reflective and less courageous than whites and, because of their relatively undeveloped nervous systems, had a higher threshold for pain and a less delicate sense of touch. And so it went—on and on. Long after the Civil War, in the anthropological museum of Harvard University, America's leading black intellectual, W. E. B. Du Bois, found himself confronted by an exhibit of "skeletons arranged from a little monkey to a tall well-developed white man, with a Negro barely outranking a chimpanzee." There was no great distance to travel between such ideas and what would

---

*In *Slave and Citizen: The Negro in the Americas* (New York: Knopf, 1946), Frank Tannenbaum points out that pseudoscientific arguments that blackness itself marked a human being as suitable for slavery were more prevalent in the United States and the British West Indies than in Latin America (65–69).

later become the ideology of Nazism, according to which intermarriage between Aryans and the lower races could only result, as Hitler wrote in *Mein Kampf,* in "monstrosities between man and ape."

Such notions infected Jefferson's *Notes on the State of Virginia,* a treatise on New World nature and culture written in response to queries put to him in 1780 by the secretary of the French delegation in Philadelphia. Much of that book is excruciating to read today, as when Jefferson asserts that the orangutan prefers "black women over those of his own species." At stake in Jefferson's mind was an emerging theory known as polygenesis, which posited that blacks and whites, having evolved through two distinct lines of descent rather than from common ancestors, were unsuited for interbreeding. According to this hypothesis, by which Jefferson was attracted but not entirely convinced, blacks were more naturally suited to mate with apes than with human males or females. It was a theory difficult to square with his own sexual practice—one reason, perhaps, that he remained wary of it.

It is always hard to know to what degree "advanced" thought converges with or diverges from popular opinion. With respect to racial attitudes in early America, we get a hint from James Mars, who was born a slave in New York in 1790 and remained enslaved, in Connecticut, until age twenty-five. In a memoir published in multiple editions between 1864 and 1876, Mars recalled from his childhood that slaves "at the North were admitted to be a species of the human family," and yet he also remembered being told as a boy "that slaves had no souls, and that they would never go to heaven, let them do ever so well." Racial contempt was not a regional phenomenon. It was nationwide.

Yet despite all such encouragements to believe that blacks were "naturally" inferior to whites, the founders hedged their bets. They proceeded with a certain nervous tentativeness, as when Jefferson described the supposition as a "conjecture" pending "further observation." One finds the same rhythm of proposition and retraction in a letter from Alexander Hamilton to John Jay, in which it is possible to watch rationality mitigate prejudice as Hamilton deletes the word "perhaps" and substitutes "probably." "Their natural faculties," he writes of blacks, "are ~~perhaps~~ probably as good as ours." In another instance of self-correction, Franklin, who had written in 1751 that slaves are thieves "by nature," converted that claim eighteen years later into the quite different point that slaves may be compelled "by the nature of slavery" to become thieves.

Perhaps the story of the founders on race is best summed up in a remark by Franklin (made in another context at his own expense): "so convenient a thing it is to be a *reasonable Creature*, since it enables one to find or make a Reason for everything one has a mind to do." On that view, all the high-flown theories that blacks are designated for slavery by Nature, God, History, Fate, or whatever force one prefers to credit or blame suddenly and utterly collapse. All the weighty reasons for tolerating slavery were actually nothing but rationalizations.

Patrick Henry, whose famous oath "Give me Liberty, or Give me Death!" became the battle cry of the Revolution, admitted as much. Writing in 1773 with a certain disarming candor to an antislavery activist, he confessed that while he shared his correspondent's antipathy to the institution, he found himself "drawn along" to keep his own slaves simply because he could not deny "the general Inconveniency of living here without them." Here was the long and the short of it: slavery served his interest. All other arguments on its behalf were bogus (a word the founders would not have recognized but whose meaning they well understood), and somewhere, in heart if not in head, they knew it.

Three

A COMPROMISED
CONSTITUTION

1.

Unlike human evolution or racial difference, interest was a subject the founders knew a lot about. Madison named the main obstacle that conflicting interests placed in the path toward nationhood when he wrote, in retrospect, that "the States were divided into different interests not by their difference of size, but by other circumstances, the most material of which resulted partly from climate, but principally from the effects of their having or not having slaves."

The facts bore him out. By the 1780s, the number of slaves in what was about to become the United States was approaching three-quarters of a million, with all but fifty thousand concentrated in the South. Within twenty years, every state north of Delaware was to take judicial or legislative steps to abolish slavery either immediately or on some schedule of future completion, and by the 1780s the process was well under way. In the nation's first capital city, Philadelphia, the number of slaves had declined since the 1760s from roughly fourteen hundred (in a city of some thirty thousand) to less than half that number by the time of the Revolution. The men who converged there in 1787 faced a daunting problem: how to consolidate a nation in which slavery was the bedrock of the economy and culture in one region but increasingly peripheral in the other.

If we could transport ourselves back to their time, we would be struck by corresponding contrasts between the southern and the northern delegates who came together to try to get the job done. Delegates from the South were accompanied by black valets, cooks, and housemaids, some of whom might have doubled as mistresses, while their northern counterparts traveled alone or perhaps with a free (by comparison) white servant or two. If a northern gentleman chided his southern counterpart for bringing along his slaves, it did not take much wit for the southerner to ask just how, given his scruples, the esteemed gentleman from, say, Connecticut or New Jersey could enjoy his morning molasses or evening smoke, or dress himself in slave-grown cotton, without aiming his revulsion at himself.

Sixty years later, a child's primer titled *The Anti-slavery Alphabet* made the point in rhyme:

> *S is the sugar, that the slave*
> *Is toiling hard to make,*
> *To put into your pie and tea,*
> *Your candy, and your cake.*

Here was the basic difference between South and North: not the presence or absence of slavery, but the fact that in the former it was visible everywhere while in the latter it was visible almost nowhere.

Of the fifty-five delegates, twenty-five owned slaves. Three—Franklin, Hamilton, and William Livingston—belonged to abolition societies, but only Livingston had no personal entanglement with slavery. Franklin denounced slavery in print but delayed the emancipation of his own slaves until after his death. Hamilton had married into a slave-owning family and might briefly have owned one or more household slaves himself. "The web of slavery," as the novelist James McBride puts it, "is sticky business. And at the end of the day, ain't nobody clear of it."

Knowing they would not extract themselves from the web anytime soon, the delegates also knew that if they were to agree on how to organize a nation, the dispute over slavery must somehow be deferred—or, to use the parliamentarian term, tabled. This was a challenge for which they were well prepared. Committed to the Aristotelian principle that "the intermediate state is in all things to be praised," they were natural deal makers. Compromise, as one might say today, was in their DNA.

In matters of religion, this meant they were tolerationists. Some were sincerely Christian, others nominally so, but all agreed—or at least professed to agree—with the political philosopher John Locke that "if men were better instructed themselves, they would be less imposing on others." They were acutely aware that in the Old World a toxic combination of established religion and suppression of dissent had produced endless strife. They doubted that any one creed had a monopoly on truth. From these convictions arose the novel American principle of separation of church and state.

In politics, they believed in what Jefferson called "temperate liberty"— the virtuous moderation required of a republican citizen, by which private wants are willingly subordinated to the public good. Yet if they credited human beings with a capacity for reason and sympathy, they were also inclined to believe that all people were liable to sink into rank selfishness. As a boy in Boston, Franklin had been impressed by the Puritan preacher Cotton Mather, who privately admonished him to "*stoop*" in humility "as you go through" the world rather than strut through it in pride. Madison, as a student at Princeton, had imbibed the neo-Calvinist theology of its late president Jonathan Edwards, who delivered what is still probably the most famous sermon in American history, "Sinners in the Hands of an Angry God," and whose books on will and virtue remained in Madison's personal library all his life.

The founders belonged to the secular Enlightenment, but they retained more than a trace of what Edwards called "the Great Christian Doctrine of Original Sin." They believed that a just and stable government must take account of the human propensity to coerce and exploit others. Such a government must be flexible enough to adapt to the ebb and flow of contesting passions. It must occupy a middle ground, even though the ground was always shifting. They believed, too, with the British philosopher and statesman Edmund Burke (who sympathized with the American Revolution) that "all government—indeed every human benefit and enjoyment, every virtue and every prudent act—is founded on compromise and barter." Hamilton had a shorter phrase for the same idea: he called it the "prudent mean."

This was the core idea of the Constitution. It underlay the concept of mixed government, in which power would be distributed among legislative, executive, and judicial branches—thereby, its authors hoped, blunting the inevitable quest for power by one faction over another. The national legislature would be bicameral, with the lower house based on the principle of proportional representation while the upper house (the Senate) gave each state equal voice regardless of the relative size of its population. The executive (the president) would stand apart from and above the legislature but would also be constrained by it. The Supreme Court would be independent—empowered to review both state and federal statutes to ensure their consistency with constitutional principles, and to do so, in theory at least, in a disinterested spirit.* And the Constitution even provided for its own revision by allowing for amendment through a process that was deliberately designed to be difficult and slow.

All these checks and balances were well and good, but how, on the question of slavery, could a "prudent mean" be achieved? In the decade since Jefferson had tried to inject a condemnation of the slave trade into the declaration, tension over slavery had only increased. Gouverneur Morris, a native New Yorker who represented Pennsylvania at the convention, declared that slavery was "the curse of heaven on the states where it prevailed." Two weeks later, Charles Pinckney of South Carolina, younger cousin of Charles Cotesworth Pinckney, retorted by estimating that "in all ages one half of mankind have been slaves" and called slavery a blessing "justified by the example of all the world."

As usual, the Virginians were caught in the cross fire. Washington, who chaired the convention, once confessed, "I wish from my soul that

---

*Although the Constitution did not explicitly empower the Court to review acts of Congress, Hamilton argued in Federalist No. 78 that in cases where law conflicts with constitutional principle, "the Constitution ought to be preferred to the statute" (*The Federalist*, ed. Jacob E. Cooke [Middletown, Conn.: Wesleyan University Press, 1961], 525). The principle of judicial review was established in 1803, when, in a unanimous ruling in the case of *Marbury v. Madison*, Chief Justice John Marshall declared that "the powers of the Legislature are defined and limited; and that those limits may not be mistaken, or forgotten, the Constitution is written."

the legislature of this state [Virginia] could see the policy of a gradual abolition," adding hopefully that such a policy "would prevent much future mischief." Jefferson (absent from the proceedings while serving as American minister in Paris) expressed deeper foreboding. "I tremble for my country," he wrote about slavery, "when I reflect that God is just: that his justice does not sleep forever."

In 1784, Jefferson attacked the Atlantic slave trade again in the form of a proposal for its prohibition to the Continental Congress (now known as the Confederation Congress), but the bill fell short of approval by one state. The South Carolinian Charles Cotesworth Pinckney dismissed that proposal as selfishness dressed up as altruism. "Virginia," he sneered, "will gain by stopping the importations. Her slaves will rise in value, & she has more than she wants." The question of the future of slavery pitted not only North against South but the South against itself.

Among the issues confronting the delegates at Philadelphia, one of the most pressing was how explicit—pro, con, or studiously neutral—the Constitution should be about slavery. Ultimately, the framers produced a text so filled with euphemism and circumlocution that politicians and historians have argued ever since about what its authors really intended to say on the subject. Although it has often been noted that the word "slavery" appears nowhere in the document, we are left with a "curious silence to explain: the refusal to mention the word." The fact that the word was used in the course of debate makes its absence from the final document all the more striking, and there has never been a consensus about why.*

Seventy years after the adoption of the Constitution, Abraham Lincoln gave his view on this question. By excluding the contested word, he said, the founders had "hid slavery away, in the constitution, just as an

---

*The delegates discussed whether or not to use the word "slavery." On August 25, Gouverneur Morris recommended that the clause prohibiting "Importation of such Persons as any of the States . . . shall think proper to admit" be revised to read "importation of slaves into N. Carolina, S— Carolina & Georgia," a change which he believed would make clear that the proposed prohibition had nothing to do with naturalization of European immigrants to those states. George Mason of Virginia expressed no objection to using the word "slaves" but worried that explicitly naming certain states might cause offense. See Max Farrand, ed., *The Records of the Federal Convention of 1787* (New Haven, Conn.: Yale University Press, 1937), 2:415.

afflicted man hides away a wen or a cancer, which he dares not cut out at once, lest he bleed to death; with the promise, nevertheless, that the cutting may begin at the end of a given time"—though they never disclosed a date for performing the operation. Frederick Douglass disagreed, aligning himself instead with his first political mentor, William Lloyd Garrison, who decried the Constitution for its tacit protection of slavery as a "covenant with death" (a phrase, as the scholar Manisha Sinha has recently discovered, that previously had been used by the black abolitionist James W. C. Pennington, who was, like Douglass, a fugitive from the South). But a few years later, Douglass broke with Garrison and adopted a view closer to Lincoln's and that of the new Republican Party. "If in its origin," he wrote in 1863, "slavery had any relation to the government, it was only as the scaffolding to the magnificent structure, to be removed as soon as the building was completed."

Whichever side one takes on the question of how the founders and their followers imagined the ultimate fate of slavery, the Constitution certainly protected it in several significant ways. Everyone understood what was intended by Article 1, Section 9, Clause 1: "The Migration or Importation of such Persons as any of the States now existing shall think proper to admit, shall not be prohibited by the Congress prior to the Year one thousand eight hundred and eight, but a tax or duty may be imposed on such Importation, not exceeding ten dollars for each Person."

Some delegates favored an immediate ban on the Atlantic slave traffic, while others opposed any ban at any time and swore they would "never receive the plan if it prohibits the slave-trade" now or ever. Even the planters of South Carolina, which had recently imposed a two-year pause in the importation of slaves in response to falling commodity and slave prices, were divided over whether to continue or curtail the trade. But by 1788, Charles Cotesworth Pinckney was warning that without a reliable supply of fresh slaves "South Carolina would soon be a desert waste."

Even though the Constitutional Convention reached a deal that would postpone prohibition for twenty years, howls of protest arose from Georgia as well as South Carolina that "Negroes were our wealth, yet behold how our kind friends in the north were determined soon to tie up our hands, and drain us of what we had!" James Wilson of Pennsylvania, recommending ratification of the Constitution to his state's legislature, singled out the slave-trade clause for special praise: "I consider this as laying the foundation for banishing slavery out of this country." Many years later, in a brief on behalf of a fugitive slave whom he was defending in court, John Jay's grandson remarked that "great was the disgust" of his grandfather's generation at permitting the Atlantic slave trade to continue even for a moment—yet, in the hope that compromise would prove to be a step toward slavery's extinction, they agreed to tolerate the trade for a limited time.

Meanwhile, if anything else was to get done, another question had to be settled: How should slaves be counted for the purpose of calculating the number of representatives from each state in the lower house of Congress and for computing taxes that might be levied by the federal government on the states, based on their population? It is often mistakenly said that the eventual answer—the notorious "three-fifths" compromise (Article 1, Section 2, Clause 3)—implied that a black slave was equivalent in some existential sense to three-fifths of a free white person:

> Representatives and direct Taxes shall be apportioned among the several States which may be included within this Union, according to their respective Numbers, which shall be determined by adding to the whole Number of free Persons, including those bound to Service for a Term of Years, and excluding Indians not taxed, three fifths of all other Persons.

In fact it would have been in the interest of slave states to count slaves as whole persons because the South would thereby have increased its number of seats in the House of Representatives. The North would have preferred to count each slave as a smaller fraction of a person (early in the negotiations one-half was proposed) or not at all, which would have reduced the number of southern seats in the House. Like the temporary proscription of action against the slave trade, the three-fifths rule was a compromise accepted with reluctance by both sides.* It was achieved in part because while slave states conceded that slaves were not full persons for the purpose of determining congressional representation, they bene-fited from a commensurate reduction in federal taxes that might be levied against them based on their total number of eligible inhabitants.

Both deals were instances of what Du Bois, in his remarkably even-handed account of the proceedings, called "log-rolling." The authors of the Constitution might have been, as Jefferson called them, an "assembly of demi-gods," but they were much more like the grousing gods of ancient Greece than the all-knowing god of Christianity. They performed their divine work not only in the Convention Hall but also over stew and grog in the proverbial smoke-filled rooms of hostelries and taverns. And as so often in American history, a political bargain struck by white people came at the expense of black people, for whom there was no seat at the table.

2.

Before a final text was settled on, one more issue concerning slaves re-mained to be decided: What was to be done with those who ran away?

This was a question to which the recent war had given new urgency. Even Great Britain, with all its military might, had found it no simple matter to wage war across the Atlantic. So in addition to payments for mercenaries and pardons for criminals at home in exchange for enlistment, a strategy was developed to turn the rebels' slaves against them.

The first official proclamation promising freedom to slaves in ex-change for deserting their masters and aiding the loyalist cause came in the summer of 1776 from Virginia's royal governor, Lord Dunmore, who, with mob violence breaking out against British officials, had fled to safety aboard a Royal Navy frigate off the coast from Norfolk. John André, a

---

*In 2013, the president of Emory University, James Wagner, set off a storm of controversy when he wrote in the campus magazine that the three-fifths compromise exemplified cooperation among people with different values and commitments in order to achieve "a common goal." Wagner later apologized for what he called his "clumsiness and insensitivity," but the controversy might have shortened his tenure as president. See Scott Jaschik, "Compromised Position," *Inside Higher Ed,* Feb. 18, 2013.

British officer of high social polish and higher self-esteem who would be hanged in 1780 as an accomplice of Benedict Arnold's in the plot to surrender West Point, was convinced that the emancipation strategy would be both easy and effective. "We need not seek" the rebels' human property, he believed, because "it flies to us" on its own accord, and once slave owners are left helpless to till their land and reap their crops, "famine follows."

Three years later, in June 1779, with the war going badly for the British, Sir Henry Clinton, commander of British forces in North America, extended the offer of freedom to all slaves except those owned by masters loyal to the crown. That these policies were more a matter of military strategy than moral conviction is attested to by the fact that in some areas where fugitives became too numerous for the British to manage, Clinton ordered them returned to their masters.

The scholar who pioneered the study of the Revolutionary War experience of African Americans, Benjamin Quarles, has remarked that "slaves had been running away a century and a half before the Revolution, but what in peacetime was a rivulet became in wartime a flood." As is often the case in the story of fugitive slaves, their flight had unforeseen consequences. Not only did slave enticement by the British prove insufficient to turn the tide of war, but by inflaming the colonists, it helped to snuff out "whatever loyalty there was" in the South and left a legacy of racial fear that lingered long after the war was over.

Some of the fear was deliberately stoked by the colonists themselves— and not only by southerners. Franklin, serving as ambassador to France in 1779, collaborated with the Marquis de Lafayette on designing a children's book (never published) intended to "impress the minds of Children and Posterity with a deep sense" of British barbarism. One of the planned illustrations was to depict

Dunmore's hiring the Negroes to murder their Master's Families.
    A large House
    Blacks arm'd with Guns and Hangers
    Master and his Sons on the Ground dead,

> Wife and Daughters lifted up in the Arms of the Negroes as
> they are carrying off.

According to Jefferson, some 70,000 slaves fled to British lines in search of freedom between the outbreak of hostilities in 1775 and the British surrender at Yorktown in 1781. Some modern historians put the number closer to 100,000. These estimates may be high, especially considering that many of the runaways were re-enslaved, but whatever the true number, the flight from slavery during the Revolutionary War has been plausibly described as "the largest unknown slave rebellion in American history." Along the coastal waterways of Maryland, Virginia, and the Carolinas, slaves cut boats loose from their moorings or stole them from untended barns, then sailed, rowed, or paddled to British naval vessels cruising close to shore. Farther inland, slaves caught in the chaos of battle, including some owned by signers of the Declaration of Independence, were pressed into service by British troops.*

Hundreds of miles to the north, New York City became "a haven for fugitive slaves" during the British occupation, which lasted from September 1776 until the end of the war. After defecting to the British, Benedict Arnold led a series of raids through Virginia in early 1781, dispatching his troops to ransack rebel plantations (including the Byrd family seat at Westover), after which one contemporary reported that "the infatuation" of the slaves "was amazing: they flocked to the Enemy from all quarters, even from very remote parts." With its "vast Concourse of runaway Negroes," the Revolution offered a shocking preview of what it would mean if the edifice of slavery were to collapse.

Removed as we are today from these events by nearly two and a half centuries, we tend to think of the Revolution as a sort of costume drama— a decorous affair conducted by men in three-cornered hats brandishing sabers or clumsy muskets at one another with little risk of mutual harm.

---

*Many slaves refused to abandon their masters. The historian Benjamin Quarles writes, "A few proprietors could speak proudly of the devotion of their black retainers." Quarles, *The Negro in the American Revolution* (Chapel Hill: University of North Carolina Press, 1961), 121.

In fact it was a bloody and brutal war. On the rebel side alone, some twenty-five thousand died during military service from wounds, disease, and starvation. And like all subsequent wars, it opened fissures not only between the enemies but among those who made the alliance by which the war was won. After the fighting was done, no question was more divisive among the victors than the future of slavery. One purpose of the postwar negotiations not only with Britain but also among the colonists themselves over the terms of their proposed Constitution was to put the genie of the runaway slave back in the bottle.

This was easier said than done. Could former owners hope to retrieve slaves who had fled to Canada, Newfoundland, or Nova Scotia? If so, how? George Washington, among others, doubted the former and threw up his hands at the latter. "Slaves which have absconded from their Masters," he lamented to another signer of the Declaration of Independence, Benjamin Harrison, "will never be restored to them," because there are too "many doors through which they can escape."

Washington's pessimism was well-founded. "Numberless difficulties" stood between identifying and apprehending escaped slaves, and the British, in no mood for reconciliation, were guilty, according to one Virginian, of "a glaring piece of injustice" in failing to honor the terms of the peace treaty signed in 1783. That treaty included a clause—added belatedly by the sole southern delegate to the negotiations, Henry Laurens of South Carolina—prohibiting imperial forces from "carrying away any negroes or other property of American inhabitants" in the course of their withdrawal. But "carrying away" was an ambiguous phrase, and because no one could draw a precise distinction between coerced defection and voluntary flight, it was an ambiguity of which the British took advantage.

When Sir Guy Carleton, commander in chief of His Majesty's forces in North America, made no serious effort to round up refugee slaves as part of the postwar settlement, the normally temperate James Madison condemned his inaction as "scandalous." Others among the founders took a different view—notably Alexander Hamilton, who had grown up on the West Indian "sugar island" of Nevis, where black slaves outnumbered

white colonists by eight to one.* Hamilton's mother, accused by her husband of committing multiple adulteries, had been incarcerated in a prison
to which blacks charged with crimes were taken for shackling and sometimes castration. As a child, Hamilton had seen teams of slaves lashed in
the streets as if they were horses whipped in order to quicken their trot.
During the war, he served as aide-de-camp to Washington and afterward
felt it would be unconscionable to re-enslave people who had been promised freedom, whether by the colonists or the British:

> In the interpretation of treaties, things odious or immoral are not to
> be presumed. The abandonment of negroes, who had been induced to
> quit their masters on the faith of official proclamations, promising
> them liberty, to fall again under the yoke of their masters and into
> slavery is as odious and immoral a thing as can be conceived. It is odi-
> ous not only as it imposes an act of perfidy on one of the contracting
> parties, but as it tends to bring back to servitude men once made free.

Congress tried nevertheless to induce the British to honor their stated
obligations or, if recovery of escaped slaves could not be accomplished, at
least to provide slave owners with some form of compensation. As postwar negotiations dragged on, the failure to resolve the issue sowed suspicion in the South not only toward the British but also toward the two
northern diplomats who had negotiated the postwar settlement—John
Jay, president of the New York Manumission Society, and John Adams of
Massachusetts—who, unlike their colleague Laurens, never had their
hearts in the business of slave reclamation.

Despite his personal feelings, Jay recognized that the question of wartime runaways created an ominous dilemma. In language close to Hamilton's, he reported to Congress in 1786 that it would be "cruelly perfidious"
to return slaves to their former masters—not only because, in his view,

---

*Hamilton's antislavery convictions have lately become well known through the immensely success-
ful musical inspired by his life. The truth was more complicated. Hamilton married into a slave-
owning family (the Schuylers) and benefited from their wealth and political connectedness, yet there
is evidence that his aversion to the institution ran deep. See Ron Chernow, *Alexander Hamilton* (New
York: Penguin Press, 2004), 128–37, 210.

slavery itself was a violation of human rights, but because recaptured slaves would be subject to vengeful punishment if forcibly returned to those from whom they had run. Notwithstanding these objections, Jay took the view that Britain was bound by the law of nations to uphold the treaty.

The result was a moral and political problem of which a variant would haunt the Republic for years to come: if escaped slaves were returned in accordance with the requirements of law (in this case the treaty with Britain), a "great wrong" would be done "to these Slaves, and yet" if justice prevailed over an unjust law, a wrong would be done "to their Masters." In a preview of many subsequent attempts—all of which failed—to find a middle way between law and justice, Jay suggested compensating slave masters for their losses. "No price can compensate a Man for bondage for life," he told Congress, "yet every Master may be compensated for a runaway Slave." Perhaps in principle it was a fair proposal, but given the British disinclination to act on it and the slave owners' fear that it would open the door to broader emancipation, it was, in practice, pointless.

3.

Memories of war were still fresh when the delegates to the Constitutional Convention turned directly to the fugitive slave issue in August 1787. That same summer another critical meeting was taking place one hundred miles north in New York, where the Confederation Congress had taken up the question of how to organize the immense territories northwest of the Ohio River. These lands had recently been ceded by the existing states to the federal government under the Articles of Confederation, and the time for decision about their governance was at hand.

On July 13, the Congress—which included some members, notably Madison and Hamilton, who shuttled between New York and Philadelphia to participate in both meetings—approved what came to be known as the Northwest Ordinance. This was a plan for creating new states, each of which would be eligible for admission to the Union once its population reached sixty thousand persons. In these future states, slavery was to be forbidden.

Although it was a representative from Massachusetts, Nathan Dane, who initially proposed to Congress that slavery be prohibited in the Northwest Territory, he met no significant opposition from southerners, who had reasons—wariness of competition in producing crops such as tobacco and indigo; eagerness to encourage settlement that would generate trade through southern ports—for favoring it. In one sense, a great principle was at stake, the principle that slavery had no place in "countries which have been talked of, which we have boasted of, as asylums for the oppressed of the earth." But this was also another instance of logrolling—a trade-off between keeping slaves out of territories assumed to be "principally for New England settlers," most of whom had no interest in slave owning, while permitting them in western lands recently ceded by North Carolina (eventually to become the state of Tennessee), where slavery was already established.

Nor was it the only trade-off within the larger territorial bargain. If the new territories and, subsequently, the states to be formed from them were to be closed to slavery, slave owners required assurance that their slaves could not gain freedom by taking themselves there. Excluding slavery from some parts of the nation must go hand in hand with providing means for the rendition of fugitive slaves to the parts where it still existed. In the language of the Northwest Ordinance,

> any person escaping in to the [free territories], from whom labor or service is lawfully claimed in any one of the original States, such fugitive may be lawfully reclaimed, and conveyed to the person claiming his or her service as aforesaid.

While Congress was dealing with the issue of fugitives in the Northwest Territory, the Constitutional Convention took up the related issue of persons accused of a crime in one state who fled to another. The Committee of Detail, charged with submitting draft language to the whole convention, proposed a clause that would require every state in the new republic to return persons to the state where such crimes had allegedly taken place:

Any person charged with treason, felony, or high misdemeanor in any State, who shall flee from Justice and shall be found in any other State, shall, on demand of the Executive Power of the State from which he fled, be delivered up and removed to the State having jurisdiction of the offence.

This was, in effect, an intra-national extradition treaty. But it was not strong enough to satisfy Charles Pinckney, who, most likely aware of what Congress had decided in New York, requested that "some provision should be included in favor of property in slaves" so that fugitives, whom he regarded as having stolen themselves from their owners, would be treated like any other thief or malefactor. Joining him was his cousin Charles Cotesworth Pinckney as well as his fellow South Carolinian Pierce Butler (Frederick Douglass later called the latter two a pair of "illustrious kidnappers"), who, on August 28, 1787, moved to add a phrase requiring "fugitive slaves and servants to be delivered up like criminals." At this, Roger Sherman of Connecticut protested that there was "no more propriety in the public seizing and surrendering a slave or servant than a horse." Wilson of Pennsylvania objected, too, on the ground that states where few citizens owned slaves should not be expected to provide protection for out-of-state slave owners at taxpayers' expense. With courteous alacrity, Butler withdrew his proposal in order to ponder a revision.

The next day he offered slightly modified language, and without further debate it was added as a separate clause to the wording previously submitted by the Committee of Detail:

If any Person bound to service or labor in any state of the United States shall escape into another State, He or She shall not be discharged from such service or labour in consequence of any regulations in the State to which they escape; but shall be delivered up to the person justly claiming their service or labor.

Thus the substance of what would become the fugitive slave clause was accepted without dissent.

In return, southern delegates gave up their insistence on a two-thirds majority in both House and Senate for passage of "navigation acts"—restrictions, that is, like those previously imposed by the British—which could limit trade to American ships and, by suppressing competition from carriers of other nations, would increase the cost of trade on which the South depended. The southern concession on this point (one historian counts it among "the Convention's most successful horse-trades") might have helped ease the way for new language aimed specifically at fugitive slaves. The earlier language concerning persons "charged in any State with Treason, Felony, or other Crime, who shall flee from Justice, and be found in another State" was retained as a separate clause (Article 4, Section 2, Clause 2) immediately preceding the new statement about persons "bound to service or labor."

By early September, the job was almost done. But before the finished text of the Constitution was put to a vote by the entire convention, the Committee of Style subjected the new clause to one more round of revision. The gender pronouns ("He or She shall not be discharged") were dropped, perhaps because it seemed unwise to call attention to the fact that women and girls would be vulnerable to forced rendition. The word "justly" was also struck out, perhaps because it invited challenges to the justice of a slave master's claim. And, as if to stress the presumed validity of such a claim, the word "due" was added:*

---

*In his 1860 pamphlet *The Constitution of the United States: Is It Pro-slavery or Anti-slavery?*, Frederick Douglass argued, in parodic emulation of pro-slavery "strict constructionists," that the so-called fugitive slave clause could not apply to slaves because the word "due" implied a contract and that slaves, by virtue of their non-personhood, could not make or be held to any contract. The clause, he wrote, "applies to indentured apprentices, and any other persons from whom service and labour may be due. The legal condition of the slave puts him beyond the operation of this provision. He is not described in it. He is a simple article of property. He does not owe and cannot owe service. He cannot even make a contract. It is impossible for him to do so. He can no more make such a contract than a horse or an ox can make one. This provision, then, only respects persons who owe service, and they only can owe service who can receive an equivalent and make a bargain. The slave cannot do that, and is therefore exempted from the operation of this fugitive provision. In all matters where laws are taught to be made the means of oppression, cruelty, and wickedness, I am for strict construction. I will concede nothing." Frederick Douglass, *The Constitution of the United States: Is It Pro-slavery or Anti-slavery? by Frederick Douglass; a Speech Delivered in Glasgow, March 26, 1860, in Reply to an Attack Made upon His Views by Mr. George Thompson* (Halifax: T. and W. Birtwhistle, 1860), 12.

No person held to service or labour in one state, under the laws thereof, escaping into another, shall, in consequence of any law or regulation therein, be discharged from such service or labour, but shall be delivered up on claim of the party to whom such service or labour may be due.

This final draft (Article 4, Section 2, Clause 3) seems to have been regarded as a commonsense clarification rather than a departure from precedent—so eminently sensible, in fact, that it "became a part of the Constitution with virtually no discussion of its exact meaning or potential application."

On September 17, thirty-nine of the original fifty-five delegates approved the finished document, including the thrice-revised fugitive slave clause. Among those who did not sign, most had left the convention for reasons of failing personal or family health. Among those still present, some declined to sign because they regarded the document as incomplete without a bill of rights. Others felt that the Constitution empowered the federal government excessively at the expense of the states. Of those who demurred, several came around to supporting it later, and among the stated reasons for refusing to sign, not a single objection to the fugitive slave clause was recorded.

Why did this part of the Constitution, which was to prove so incendiary and eventually explosive, pass without objection after barely a pause for "speedy, even collegial" debate? For one thing, there was a long line of precedents behind it, reaching back to the 1640s when the early New England colonies agreed that "if any servant run away from his master into any other of these confederated Jurisdictions," he "shall be delivered" to his master upon "due proof." More immediately, both pro- and anti-slavery delegates considered it a self-evident truth that if the new nation was to include states permitting slavery as well as states forbidding it, slave owners must have legal recourse should their human property flee from the one to the other.

Nearly twenty years later, John Adams went so far as to say that southerners consented to the Constitution because joining a nation whose states pledged allegiance to the laws of other states (Article 4, Section 1: "full faith and credit shall be given in each state to the public acts, records, and judicial proceedings of every other state") would actually improve the security of their slaves. From the southern point of view, a union in which fugitives from one state could not find refuge in another state marked an improvement over a loose confederation of semi-sovereign states with varying rules of extradition. The plain fact was that by joining the nation, slaveholders were more likely to get their runaways back. "Were they not restrained by their Negroes," Adams wrote to his son John Quincy Adams in 1805, "they would reject Us from their Union, within a Year." In short, the South chose to become part of the United States less out of desire to join the Union than out of fear of what might befall it if it remained outside.

Adams might have overstated the case, but his basic point was sound. In 1819, Pennsylvania's chief justice, William Tilghman (born in 1756), made much the same point as if it were obvious to anyone with personal memory of the founding. "Whatever may be our private opinions on the subject of slavery," he wrote, "it is well known that our southern brethren would not have consented to become parties to a Constitution . . . unless their property in slaves had been secured."

Looking back from the 1850s, the antislavery Virginian Edward Coles described what amounted to a coordinated compromise between the Congress in New York and the Constitutional Convention in Philadelphia. "The distracting question of slavery," he wrote in 1856,

> was agitating and retarding the labours of both, and led to conferences and inter-communications of the members, which resulted in a compromise by which the northern or anti-slavery portion of the country agreed to incorporate into the Ordinance and Constitution the provision to restore fugitive slaves; and this mutual and concurrent action was the cause of the similarity of the provision contained in both, and had its influence in creating the great unanimity by

which the Ordinance passed, and also making the constitution the
more acceptable to slaveholders.

Also writing in the 1850s about the Northwest Ordinance, Missouri's
senator Thomas Hart Benton, who had once favored slavery expansion
but now opposed it, agreed:

> The first clause prohibiting slavery in the Northwest territory, could
> not be obtained without the second, authorizing the recovery of slaves
> which should take refuge in that territory. It was a compromise be-
> tween the slave States and the free States, unanimously agreed to by
> both parties, and founded on a valuable consideration—one prevent-
> ing the spread of slavery over a vast extent of territory, the other re-
> taining the right of property in the slaves which might flee to it.

Without an accommodation for returning fugitive slaves, there would
have been no prohibition of slavery. The latter logically required the
former.

The same assurance was needed in Philadelphia—a need so clear to all
sides that opposition to the fugitive slave provision of the Constitution
never amounted to more than a few grumbles. In fact, by comparison to
the Northwest Ordinance, the constitutional guarantee offered to slave
owners concerning fugitives was stronger. Where the ordinance used the
language of permission ("may be lawfully reclaimed"), the Constitution
used the language of command ("shall be delivered up").

Benton, a close student of constitutional history, reiterated Coles's
point that the authors of the two documents had worked in concert:

> The right to recover fugitive slaves went into the constitution, as it
> went into the ordinance, simultaneously and unanimously; and it may
> be assumed upon the facts of the case, and all the evidence of the day,
> that the constitution, no more than the ordinance, could have been
> formed without the fugitive slave recovery clause contained in it. A

right to recover slaves is not only authorized by the constitution, but it is a right without which there would have been no constitution.

Neither Thomas Hart Benton nor Edward Coles was an entirely reliable source for what had happened or why. Benton, born in 1782, had been a child at the time of the founding. Coles, born in 1786, had been an infant. And like all historical writing, their versions of the past reflected their preoccupations in the present. At the time they were writing, in the 1850s, the fugitive slave question was again driving the sections apart. Coles, who had known several of the founders and was an admirer of Lincoln's, based his account on what he claimed were personal communications from Madison, whom he had once served as personal secretary and who lived until 1836. Benton, whose life also spanned the whole history of the nation, felt he was witnessing late in life a repeat of the nation's early history. He believed that resolution of the fugitive slave problem was less likely this time around, and while he supported the new fugitive slave law as part of the Compromise of 1850, he doubted it would work.

Looking back today at the nation's founding from our own vantage point, we can hardly know any better than Coles or Benton what would have happened if the southern demand for a fugitive slave clause had been refused during the drafting of the Constitution. We cannot know, as one historian puts it, whether the South was "really willing to take the risk of walking out of the Convention and remaining outside a union of American states. But we do know that the Northern delegates were not willing to call their bluff." Perhaps their unwillingness was cowardice, or perhaps it was prudence. In either case, it seemed clear to northerners and southerners alike that if there had been no provision for recovering fugitive slaves, there would have been no nation. So the deal was struck.

If ever there was a deal in which the devil was in the details, this was it. The resolution of the fugitive slave problem turned out to be no resolution at all because, on the details, the founders had nothing to say.

Four

THE FIRST TEST

1.

Although autumn had almost arrived by the time the convention adjourned on September 17, 1787, the remaining delegates—and not just those heading south—faced a hot trip home. As they scattered back to their respective states, a new challenge loomed: persuading their constituents to accept the charter whereby they hoped the nation would henceforth govern itself.

Pending ratification by the states, the deal was far from done. Skepticism or outright opposition existed in all thirteen states, but concern ran particularly high in the South about what exactly the proposed Constitution would mean for the future of slavery. Charles Cotesworth Pinckney, upon returning to his home state, conceded that "we would have made better if we could" but assured his fellow Carolinians that "considering all circumstances, we have made the best terms for the security of this species of property it was in our power to make." The Constitution would provide "a security that the general government can never emancipate our slaves."

Pinckney was articulating what has since been called "the federal consensus," the principle that the federal government—referred to at first, perhaps with a touch of disparagement, as the "general" government—had no authority to interfere with slavery where state law permitted it. Such, at least, was the widespread inference from Article 4, Section 1, which stated that "Full Faith and Credit shall be given in each State to the Public Acts, Records, and judicial Proceedings of every other State," a principle later to be amplified by the Tenth Amendment of the Bill of Rights: "The powers not delegated to the United States by the Constitution, nor prohibited by it to the States, are reserved to the States respectively, or to the people."

This principle was often restated in ensuing years and thus remained a legal obstacle to the abolition of slavery even as public opinion in the North turned against the institution. As the historian James Oakes remarks, "The biggest problem abolitionists faced was not a proslavery public but a Constitution that protected slavery in the states where it already existed." As early as June 1788, at the Virginia ratification convention, Madison asserted that "no power is given to the general government to interpose with respect to the property in slaves now held by the states." In 1790, in response to a petition for the abolition of slavery submitted by the Pennsylvania Abolition Society, Congress responded that it could not "interfere in the emancipation of slaves, or in the treatment of them within any of the States."

But despite provisions for property protection built into the Constitution, Pinckney's choices of phrase revealed an incomplete confidence that the protections would be strong enough. "Considering all the circumstances" had a note of defensiveness, and "this species of property" was a strained euphemism for human beings who, despite spurious arguments to the contrary, possessed as much reason and volition as their masters. The Constitution referred to them tellingly as persons because everyone knew that no matter how reasonable the slave owner or reticent the slave, every transaction between them entailed a contest of human wills.

Madison acknowledged as much in one of his contributions to the series of essays favoring ratification of the Constitution signed by "Publius" under the collective title *The Federalist*, written in collaboration with Hamilton and Jay between the fall of 1787 and the summer of 1788. He began by "deny[ing] the fact, that slaves are considered merely as property, and in no respect whatever as persons." In fact, he wrote, "the true state of the case is" more complicated, because "they partake of both these qualities: being considered by our laws, in some respects, as persons, and in other respects as property."

Madison went on to explain that "in being compelled to labor, not for himself, but for a master; in being vendible by one master to another master; and in being subject at all times to be restrained in his liberty and chastised in his body, by the capricious will of another, the slave may appear to be degraded from the human rank, and classed with those irrational animals which fall under the legal denomination of property." Yet "in being protected, on the other hand, in his life & in his limbs, against the violence of all others, even the master of his labor and his liberty; and in being punishable himself for all violence committed against others; the slave is no less evidently regarded by the law as a member of the society; not as a part of the irrational creation; as a moral person, not as a mere article of property." Here was a perverse version of the founders' vaunted ideal of the "prudent mean": the notion that slaves somehow occupied a middle ground between property and persons.

There was, of course, no equivalence between "this species of property" and any other. If a chair tipped over and injured its occupant, no one would think of prosecuting or punishing it, but if a slave struck his master, or a stranger, or another slave, the law held him just as accountable as if he were a free man. Except in cases where it could be shown that a master had commanded a slave to steal, assault, or commit some other crime, slave owners were not liable for the actions of their slaves—on the premise that despite their putative inferiority slaves were human beings fully capable of exercising free will.

In the period between the Revolution and the Civil War, most slave states permitted the killing of slaves as deemed necessary—a judgment left largely to the killer—for "dispersing unlawful Assemblies of rebel Slaves or Conspirators" or while apprehending resistant runaways. When it came to punishing slaves for criminal acts, which included running from one's master, vigilante violence appears to have been relatively rare in the early republic, at least compared with the horrors of the post-Reconstruction years, when mobs were free to lynch a black man without having to answer to a white man for destroying his personal property.

Toward the end of the eighteenth century, chiefly in order to protect human property from casual destruction, punishments for injuring or destroying a slave became more severe. This was the basis of Madison's claim that a slave was "protected . . . in his life and in his limbs, against the violence of all others." In one much-publicized case in 1791, a Virginia slave who killed his overseer was acquitted on grounds of self-defense. But despite such qualifications and exceptions, slave masters enjoyed wide latitude in punishing their own slaves, as well as exemption from laws designed to curb violence against a slave by anyone except his owner.

Perhaps the most outrageous feature of the law concerning slaves was its indifference to criminal sexual acts perpetrated against them. Women and girls were violated in untold numbers by masters and overseers as well as by other slaves, and yet, because the concept of rape was essentially absent from the slave codes, virtually no records exist of men brought to trial for committing sexual assault on a slave. As late as 1855, a female slave in Missouri charged with killing her master was convicted and hanged in the face of compelling evidence that he had repeatedly raped her and that she was defending not only her honor but her life. Because black females (slave or free) were said to be chronically wanton—enslaved, in effect, to their own lusts—they were granted no protection from laws that shielded white women from being "defiled . . . by force, menace, or duress." An enslaved woman was credited with a culpable will if she was accused of committing a crime, but when a sexual crime was committed against her, she was regarded, in the words of the scholar Saidiya Hartman, as "will-less and always willing." She was treated as a person when she transgressed but as property when she was transgressed against.

2.

Where, then, in a slave, did the line between humanity and property begin and end? To hear Madison parse this question is like hearing a physician describe a patient as if she were a laboratory specimen rather than a sentient being. Madison had a good deal to say about the subject but no apparent interest in what the subject might say for herself. Still, cold and clinical as he may sound to us now, he was taking a significant step toward acknowledging the contradiction within slavery that would ultimately destroy it. In private notes that he kept during the Constitutional Convention (not published until after his death), he stated the matter directly: "It would be wrong to admit in the Constitution the idea that there could be property in men."

Coming from a man who, twenty years later, was to take a contingent of his own slaves to the White House upon becoming president, this statement may seem brazen hypocrisy, or simply preposterous. To distinguish between slavery in principle and slavery in practice was to make a distinction without a difference, at least as far as people who were enslaved were concerned. But in the context of his time, Madison's objection to allowing the concept of human property into the federal constitution was coherent and consequential.

He was speaking from within a tradition of English jurisprudence that acknowledged slavery as a legitimate form of human relations if and where "the positive enactments of legislatures or other human agencies" deemed it so. But that same tradition, as represented by John Locke's immensely influential *Second Treatise of Government,* first published in 1689, asserted that the "*municipal laws of countries* . . . are only so far right, as they are founded on the law of nature." Because slavery, in the words of the English jurist William Blackstone, was "repugnant to reason, and the principles of natural law," more and more clergy, reformers, and, eventually, politicians became convinced that any statute (positive law) supporting slavery was rendered null and void by the manifest truth (natural law) that it is an unconscionable evil.

A major statement of the conflict between positive and natural law came in 1772, with lasting reverberations. Late in the previous year, Britain's chief justice, Lord Mansfield, was called upon to decide the case of James Somerset, an African-born man who had been enslaved in Virginia. Somerset had been brought by his owner to England, where he escaped, was recaptured, and was about to be shipped for sale in Jamaica. But before he could be returned to captivity, he was released to the Court of King's Bench on a writ of habeas corpus obtained by the antislavery activist Granville Sharp, who challenged the legality of his detention.

Mansfield tried to confine himself to the narrow question of whether Somerset's owner had the right to "compel the slave to go into a foreign country." But the language in which he delivered his decision—that the owner had no such right—was widely understood to mean that because slavery had never been authorized by statute or common law in England, the laws of the Virginia colony had no authority in the home country. Mansfield then went beyond the legalities of the case to express disgust not only at the enslavement of one man but at slavery itself:

> The state of slavery is of such a nature that it is incapable of being introduced on any reasons, moral or political, but only by positive law, which preserves its force long after the reasons, occasions, and time itself from whence it was created, is erased from memory. It is so odious, that nothing can be suffered to support it, but positive law. Whatever inconveniences, therefore, may follow from the decision, I cannot say this case is allowed or approved by the law of England; and therefore the black must be discharged.

In other words, a slave removed from a jurisdiction where slavery is permitted by positive law to one where it is forbidden in compliance with natural law becomes free by the very act of transit. The slave's former owner has no legal recourse to get him back. Somerset was released to live as a free man in England, and the case became a touchstone for the antislavery movement on both sides of the Atlantic.

One effect of Mansfield's ruling in Britain was to advance the emancipation of the relatively small number of slaves who had been brought to the homeland from the colonies—about fifteen thousand in a total population of ten million. It also marked a step toward the eradication of slavery throughout the empire. Although the chief justice was later to recall that "there had been no determination that [slaves] were free," and that his "judgment (meaning the case of Somerset) went no further than to determine the master had no right to compel the slave to go into a foreign country," he had sounded, however intentionally, what was heard as a clear call for freedom. While visiting London in 1773, one Virginia slave owner wrote to a correspondent back home that the high court's decision was "generally felt as putting a negative on the existence of slavery" in Great Britain. In 1785, the poet William Cowper spoke for many when he burst out in patriotic exultation:

Slaves cannot breathe in England; if their lungs
Receive our air, that moment they are free;
They touch our country, and their shackles fall.

Cowper's ebullience was premature, given that several thousand blacks in Britain continued to be treated as slaves in fact if not in name, and slavery would not be formally abolished in the British Empire until 1833. Soon after Mansfield's decision, Benjamin Franklin referred to the "Hypocrisy" of Great Britain "for promoting the [slave] Trade, while it piqu'd itself on its Virtue[,] Love of Liberty, and the Equity in its Courts in setting free a single Negro."

Nonetheless, in America, for decades to come, the *Somerset* decision would shine a bright light—or, from the southern point of view, cast a long shadow—over the question of whether a slave remains enslaved if he flees or is taken to a free state or territory. For slave owners, the answer was an emphatic yes because the Constitution said so. When, in 1804, South Carolina's senator Pierce Butler, living in Philadelphia with his slave Ben, was served with a writ of habeas corpus demanding Ben's release on the grounds that their residency in the city had exceeded six months, his reply was quick and short. "I am a citizen of South Carolina," he said. "The laws of Pennsylvania have nothing to do with me."

Here was a reminder that the so-called United States was nothing more than a loosely linked group of semi-sovereign states, each of which resisted federal incursion into its autonomy. It was a would-be nation in which the problem of comity—the constitutional principle of deference owed by one state to the laws of another—was a long way from being resolved. Southerners like Butler seemed to regard comity as a one-way street: Pennsylvania must respect the South Carolina laws by which he owned his slave without limit, but he need not respect the Pennsylvania law that freed any slave brought to the state after a residency of more than six months. Butler's retort implied that citizenship was conferred by one's home state, not by the nation, and that it was the home state that defined each citizen's rights and obligations.*

In more recent times, our own society was roiled by a similar question of comity: If two persons of the same sex living in a state where the law permits them to marry move to another state where the law forbids them to do so, what is the status of their marriage? Where is it valid, and where is it void? This question was answered on June 26, 2015, when the U.S. Supreme Court ruled that gay marriage is a constitutional right that cannot be abridged in any state of the nation. In antebellum America, the analogous (in a jurisdictional if not a substantive sense) problem of whether "residence on free soil made a man free, or whether those states were bound to give judicial recognition to the status created by the laws of the slave states" proved impossible to resolve until the Civil War settled it once and for all.

In effect, slave owners such as Butler were saying that the *Somerset* principle—that slavery may exist only where local laws allow it—could not be applied within the American union because to do so would be to deny them their property rights whenever they took their human property from a slave state to a free state. But the *Somerset* precedent went further: it also validated the idea that slavery was an offense against natural law, sometimes called the "higher law," or the law of nature inscribed in the human heart. This idea found especially warm adherents in New England, which had been settled in the preceding century by stringent

---

*This concept of state-based citizenship would hold essentially intact until after the Civil War and persists at least in residual form to this day. In *Reconstruction: America's Unfinished Revolution, 1863–1877* (New York: Harper & Row, 1988), Eric Foner describes the "state-building process born of the Civil War" by which "the primacy of a national citizenship" was established. The Fourteenth Amendment, ratified on July 9, 1868, secured citizenship rights for "all persons born or naturalized in the United States," explicitly protecting those rights from infringement by any state government. Citizenship was thus effectively redefined as national citizenship (258).

John Quincy Adams c. 1843

English Protestants (Puritans) who believed, in the words of one of their leading ministers, that "we have an oracle in our breasts, which if we would but rub up, would reveal all things to us." To their descendants—some of whom, bearing names of Puritan pedigree like Higginson, Beecher, Adams, and Weld, became leaders of the abolitionist movement—one of the things revealed was that whatever its status according to the laws of man, slavery was a heinous sin in the eyes of God.

As this conviction took hold in what has been called the "New England Conscience," it grew, in the minds of slaveholders, from an aggravation into an affront. Massachusetts, especially, was regarded by southerners as an "asylum" for fugitive slaves and its citizens seemed drenched in moralistic self-delight. When the South Carolina Whig William Grayson sat in Congress in the 1830s behind the neo-Puritan John Quincy Adams of Massachusetts, he made a habit of watching for a "tinge of crimson" to appear on Adams's "singularly bald" scalp. He knew that when Adams's head turned red, it was an infallible sign that he was about to launch another tirade against the sinful South. One correspondent to the

Richmond Enquirer improbably compared the cerebral Adams to a "hyena in human shape."

By the eve of the Civil War, southerners blamed the imminent breakup of the nation on what one Georgia planter called the "intolerant and turbulent spirit" of the "New England race," which had always believed itself exclusively privy to the will of God. During the war, when a captured Confederate soldier charged that "Emerson and Beecher, as well as Grant and Sherman, and their followers" were "sacrilegious enough to believe themselves a portion of the Deity," he was expressing a long-established view that Yankees were a people dripping with self-righteousness and self-love.

But invoking God against the sin of slavery was by no means unique to New England. In 1776, the Scottish founder of free-market economics, Adam Smith, who professed no strong religious faith, wrote that "the property which every man has in his own labour, as it is the original foundation of all other property, so it is the most sacred and inviolable." Such words—"sacred," "inviolable"—were deployed with increasing frequency from what Melville was later to call—at the start of the fugitive slave crisis in the 1850s—the "warm halls of the heart" against heartless rulings issued from the "cold courts."

With attacks mounting on slavery as a violation of "what law should be, but wasn't," significant numbers of people in the early republic, including a good many slave owners, expected that over time positive law would catch up with natural law until, like other unnatural practices such as cannibalism and human sacrifice, slavery would be a thing of the past. This expectation was embedded in the Declaration of Independence, in which Jefferson invoked "nature's God" as an approving witness to the power of the Revolution—a word that retained its root meaning of turning or revolving—to advance mankind along the arc of moral progress.

Both the declaration and the Constitution were filled with phrases of aspiration ("pursuit of happiness," "to form a more perfect union") not only for America but for the world. When Oliver Ellsworth, representing Connecticut at the Constitutional Convention, predicted that "slavery in time will not be a speck in our country," his words sounded credible to many in the room even if the nods of northerners were met by glares from their southern counterparts.

Cynical as one tends to be today about politics and politicians, it is tempting to hear such words as empty rhetoric. And knowing what we know—that slavery was to last almost another eighty years, to be destroyed not by moral consensus but by a war that consumed nearly a million lives— those confident predictions by the founding fathers of its demise may now sound foolish and glib.

But for at least a moment, the Revolution had seemed to bring the prospect of universal emancipation to the verge of fulfillment. When Jefferson reflected that God's "justice does not sleep forever," he was giving voice to the hope—mixed, for slave owners, with fear—that the end of slavery was drawing near. Even the deletion from the Declaration of Independence of Jefferson's attack on the slave trade, and the deferral, in the Constitution, of its prohibition for twenty years, did not confute the prevailing view that slavery was on the wrong side of history. "There were probably few members of the Convention," Du Bois wrote more than a century later in his history of the Atlantic slave trade, "who did not believe that the foundations of slavery had been sapped merely by putting the abolition of the slave-trade in the hands of Congress twenty years hence."

3.

Part of the reason was that the war itself had shaken its foundations. Even as some slave owners reviled the British for their policy of "stealing" slaves, others urged the colonists to do precisely what the British were doing: offer freedom to slaves in exchange for military service. In 1780, the Virginian Joseph Jones suggested to Madison that in order to encourage enlistment in the Continental army, which was chronically short of manpower, "a Negro not younger than ten or older than 40 years" should be provided "for each Recruit"—to be obtained from large-scale slave owners and paid for by the new national government. In reply, Madison wondered whether there might not be a simpler and better way. "Would it not be as well to liberate and make soldiers at once of the blacks themselves as to make them instruments for enlisting white Soldiers?" After all, he added, "it would certainly be more consonant to the principles of liberty which ought never to be lost sight of in a contest for liberty." Then, anticipating Jones's shock at such a radical suggestion, Madison assured him that "no imaginable danger could be feared from" liberated slaves even if guns were handed out to them.

It was a daring idea but not a new one. As early as June 1775, one of John Adams's Virginia correspondents had suggested that the Continental Congress "proclaim instant freedom to all the Servants that will join in the Defence of America." In 1778, Benedict Arnold, before he went over to the British side of the conflict, had proposed a joint attack with French naval forces against the British colonies of Barbados and Bermuda, where the invaders would "engage in the marine service of the united states about 5 or 6 hundred black and Mulatto Slaves who are employed as mariners in coasting vessels, by giving to them the pay and privileges of American Seamen, and assuring them of the[ir] freedom after the war, or three years Service."

John Laurens (son of Henry Laurens, who, before and after his diplomatic career, ran a thriving slave-trading business) repeatedly proposed that slaves who fought for the cause of independence should be rewarded with freedom. Such a plan was actually approved in 1779, when Congress authorized payments of up to a thousand dollars per slave to masters who would relinquish them to join the fight. But greeted by "contemptuous huzzas" in the South Carolina legislature and elsewhere, the scheme was never implemented. "We are much disgusted here," wrote one of its opponents, "at the Congress recommending we arm our slaves."

General Washington shared the concern. In a March 1779 letter to Henry Laurens, he worried that arming some portion of the slaves would cause "much discontent" among the rest, though he confessed that he had not thought the matter through:

The policy of our arming Slaves is, in my opinion, a moot point, unless the enemy set the example; for should we begin to form Battalions of them, I have not the smallest doubt (if the War is to be prosecuted) of their following us in it, and justifying the measure upon our own ground; the upshot then must be, who can arm fastest, and where are our Arms? Besides, I am not clear that a discrimination will not render Slavery more irksome to those who remain in it; most of the good and evil things of this life are judged of by comparison; and I fear a comparison in this case will be productive of much discontent in those who are held in servitude; but as this is a subject that has never employed much of my thoughts, these are no more than the first crude Ideas that have struck me upon the occasion.

Notably, the slave-owning Washington applied his view of human psychology ("the good and evil things of this life are judged of by comparison") to all persons without distinction between blacks and whites.

Like most if not all of the founders, he realized that the new nation, having assumed, in the language of the Declaration of Independence, "a separate and equal station . . . among the powers of the earth," now stood in a fundamentally changed relation to slavery as both an idea and an institution. Before the Revolution, proponents and opponents of slavery could speak of it as an unsought inheritance from their imperial masters. After the war, both were obliged, as one might say today, to "take ownership." What had been an imposition was now a choice—a choice, some historians have suggested, that left southerners "at least subconsciously aware" of the contradiction between their loyalty to slavery and their professed love of liberty.

Delving into the subconscious of people in the present, even those we know intimately, is hard enough. To do so for people in the past, whom we know only through writings by or about them, would seem to be all but impossible. And given their cavalier use of the slavery metaphor to express political grievance—first against the crown, later against the North—it would seem that self-knowledge among slave owners must have been buried deep if it was there at all. Yet the euphemistic language ("correction" for "whipping"; "sending" for "selling") with which they spoke of their slaves suggests that at least some could not bear to speak the truth even to themselves.

Defending slavery in postrevolutionary America on any but prudential grounds required a mental contortionist. This was increasingly obvious as the pseudoscientific racialism to which Jefferson was drawn and that others fully embraced began to lose its grip on educated people. In 1797, the distinguished Philadelphia physician Benjamin Rush presented a paper to the American Philosophical Society arguing "that the black color (as it is called) of the Negroes is the effect of a disease in the skin of the leprous kind." Today this statement sounds patently outrageous, but in its time it was a rebuke to popular prejudice. Whiteness, for Rush, was still the norm, and blackness a pathology, but skin color had no more implication for character or mental capacity than a boil or a rash. The idea that some people were "naturally" suited for slavery and unsuited for freedom was becoming intellectually disreputable.*

There were also strategic reasons to reject it. Just as, a century and a half later, racial segregation would become a liability for America's ideological struggle with the Soviet Union, slavery was becoming an international embarrassment for the young republic in the wake of its separation from Britain. "A slaveholding nation," as David Brion Davis has remarked, "could not serve the world as a model of freedom"—a point that became an enduring theme from the Revolution to the eve of the Civil War, when Lincoln said of slavery, "I hate it because it deprives our republican example of its just influence in the world."

Religious sentiment, too, was building against it. In 1784, the Methodist Church, soon to be the largest denomination in the South, resolved "to extirpate this abomination among us" by expelling members who did not emancipate their slaves, as well as anyone who bought or sold slaves except for the purpose of liberating them. And if science and religion were changing, so was the law. The highest court in Britain had declared slavery an "odious" form of barbarism that had lingered too long at the

---

*While Rush wrote that "the inferences" from his research "will be in favor of treating [black people] with humanity, and justice," he also evidently saw those inferences as confirming the need for "keeping up the existing prejudices against matrimonial connexions with them." Even for the most "advanced" thinkers of the time, the racial barrier remained impermeable.

periphery of the empire and had no place at the imperial center. That some of the former North American colonies were moving to abolish it while others retained it meant that every time a slave owner took his slaves across the internal American border between slavery and freedom, the putative unity of the new nation was exposed as a lie.

4.

Madison knew all this not only as a political or legal matter but from personal experience. In the summer of 1783, traveling to Philadelphia for a session of Congress, he took with him his slave Billey, whom he had owned since both were children. According to Pennsylvania's recently adopted Gradual Emancipation Act, a nonresident slave owner could retain his slave while on "sojourn" in the state, and when his business was concluded, as long as it consumed less than six months, he could take him home just like any other piece of movable property.

As a member of Congress, Madison was exempt from the six-month limit, but—possibly because Billey had attempted to escape or had grown restless while living in antislavery Philadelphia—he decided that rather than bring his slave back to Virginia, he would relinquish him locally, at a price less than his worth, to a Quaker merchant for a term of service as an indentured servant. After completing his term, Billey would be free.

Madison explained himself in a letter to his father, who, as a county judge, had once sentenced a slave to death for stealing twenty-five cents' worth of goods from a storehouse. The younger Madison's letter was a marvel of self-contradiction. On the one hand, he wrote approvingly that Billey yearned for the freedom due to any man by virtue of his humanity. On the other hand, perhaps to mollify his father, he wrote disapprovingly that Billey's yearning "tainted" him, so that if he were to return to Virginia, he would foment discontent among other slaves and pose a risk of spreading sedition. Having tasted freedom, Billey was no longer fit to live among those whom he might inspire to seek it for themselves:

I have judged it most prudent not to force Billey back to Virginia even if it could be done; and have accordingly taken measures for his final separation from me. I am persuaded his mind is too thoroughly tainted to be a fit companion for fellow slaves in Virginia. The laws here do not admit of his being sold for more than 7 years. I do not expect to get near the worth of him; but cannot think of punishing him by transportation merely for coveting that liberty for which we have paid the price of so much blood, and have proclaimed so often to be the right, & worthy pursuit, of every human being.

Here was a case of what F. Scott Fitzgerald was to describe many years later as "the ability to hold two opposed ideas in the mind at the same time, and still retain the ability to function." Fitzgerald associated this talent with "a first-rate intelligence," but the phrase could just as easily describe what is nowadays called compartmentalization, the habit of holding separately in mind irreconcilable commitments—a trick at which the founders were adept, especially the Virginians. In Madison's case, the opposed ideas were the universal right to freedom and the legitimacy of slavery as sanctioned by local law. When the British abolitionist Harriet Martineau traveled to Montpelier to visit him late in his life, she was amazed by his ability to hold forth at the dinner table on the evils of slavery while being waited on by his slaves.

Madison's experience with Billey—or, more accurately, with the distinction between how Billey was regarded in Virginia and Pennsylvania—pointed to the same division within the nation as within himself. The Constitution, of which he was chief architect, tried to bridge the difference. But it took no position on the fundamental question of positive versus natural law—on, that is, the rightness or wrongness of slavery itself. Instead, through the fugitive slave clause, it tried to reconcile the irreconcilable laws of a partitioned nation in which each side of the slavery dispute, for the sake of the nation's survival, conceded the sovereignty of the other side. Runaway slaves and those who pursued them thus found themselves in a borderland between two nations pretending to be one—a pretense that would soon be put to the test.

Portrait of James Madison
by Asher B. Durand, 1833

5.

The first test came even before ratification of the Constitution was complete. Shortly before the Revolution, a Maryland slave owner named Davis had moved to what he might have thought was then northwest Virginia, taking with him a slave named John, who, in keeping with custom, bore his master's surname. In 1779, however, the region where they had moved was absorbed into Washington County, Pennsylvania. One year later Pennsylvania adopted its Gradual Emancipation Act, which prohibited further importation of slaves and emancipated all children born thereafter in the state.

As for slaves already born, their masters could pay a registration fee before November 1, 1780, and thereby retain them.* But many slave owners simply ignored this requirement, especially those living near the Virginia border, which was not formally settled until 1784. Among them was John Davis's master, who continued to treat John as his personal property

---

*The deadline was later extended to January 1, 1783.

and in 1788 took him to Ohio County, Virginia, where he hired him out as his slave, collecting the main part of his wages for himself.

Thus began the shuttling of John Davis back and forth between the two states. Soon after his removal to Virginia, several abolitionists, knowing he had been sent away against his will, located him and returned him to Pennsylvania as a free man on the grounds that his owner had never registered him as a slave. A few months later, the man to whom he had been rented in Virginia, fearful of being held liable for his replacement value, hired a team of three bounty hunters to hunt him down and return him to Virginia and to slavery. They tracked him to his old neighborhood, where, according to the Pennsylvania Abolition Society, they "assaulted, seized, imprisoned, bound, and carried" him back against his will. In November 1788, a Pennsylvania grand jury indicted them for the crimes of kidnapping and assault.

Not surprisingly at a time when the authority of one state's laws over citizens of another state was unsettled, the accused men never showed up to face the charges. More than two years later, the governor of Pennsylvania requested their extradition in an effort to bring them to trial. When Virginia's governor refused, his Pennsylvania counterpart wrote to President Washington requesting federal help in arresting the three accused Virginia men as fugitives from justice. Technically, therefore, this "first interstate conflict over the rendition of fugitives from justice" centered not on the rights of a fugitive slave but on one state's right to prosecute persons from another state who had crossed its border for the purpose of enslaving a man who, under its laws, was free.

Washington turned first for advice to Jefferson, who passed the problem on to Attorney General Randolph, the man who had recently coached the president on how to skirt Pennsylvania's abolition law. Randolph, in turn, found both governors at fault. The Pennsylvanian, he thought, had failed to provide "an authenticated copy" of the state law in question and had also failed to provide sufficient evidence that the accused had in fact "fled from . . . justice." Randolph faulted the Virginia governor as well, who, on advice of his own attorney general, had tried to minimize the gravity of the crime by treating it as an act of "trespass" rather than felonious assault and kidnapping. On Randolph's advice, Washington asked both governors for more information—in the hope (vain, as it turned out) that they would work things out between them. Instead, the case grew more vexed as aggrieved Virginians accused Pennsylvania abolitionists of a campaign to "seduce" slaves into Pennsylvania—which, they thought, put the seizure of "fugitives" like John Davis in an innocent light as the retrieval of stolen property.

By the fall of 1791, with the dispute heating up, Washington decided to ask the House of Representatives to clarify the mutual obligations of states in cases where accused criminals—a category that included both kidnappers and fugitive slaves—fled from one state to another. The result—composed by a committee of three, two from Massachusetts, one from Virginia—was a draft bill according to which claimants were to apply for an arrest warrant to the governor in the state where the fugitive from justice was known to be hiding. In cases involving criminal defendants, such a warrant could be granted only upon presentation of evidence persuasive to a judge or grand jury. In fugitive slave cases, warrants could be issued on the strength of depositions from "two credible persons." In neither case was there any provision for the accused to contest extradition, presumably because it was assumed that criminal defendants would be granted due process in the state to which they were returned for trial. As for fugitive slaves, having been identified as such, they would simply be returned to their masters as if they were poached livestock—except that they had poached themselves.

Before the bill came to a vote, it had already become clear that it was aggravating more than alleviating tensions between pro- and antislavery factions, so the House suspended work on it. Among other problems, it made a jumble of state and federal authority by, on the one hand, defining reclamation as a state responsibility while, on the other hand, prescribing fines to be imposed by federal courts on state officials who failed to comply with valid warrants. The effort now shifted to the Senate, where, between March 1792 and January 1793, multiple attempts were made to shape a bill that could command support from southern as well as northern members.

One version provided compensation for slave masters based on how many days a fugitive was delayed from returning to "service." Another required only a deposition from the claimant in order to initiate pursuit of an accused runaway, while still another required submission of oral testimony or affidavits from at least two persons to a duly empowered magistrate before rendition could be lawfully ordered. Yet another draft proposed a statute of limitations (how long an interval between flight and attempted reclamation was never defined) that would protect persons who might once have been enslaved but who had lived for years in a free community. Through it all, debate went round and round over whether someone helping a fugitive evade arrest must be shown to have done so "knowingly," "willingly," or "willfully" in order for the offense to rise to the level of a punishable crime, as well as over how, or by whom, such fine discriminations of intent were to be made.

After almost a year of wrangling, the Senate sent a bill back to the House, which, on February 5, 1793, approved it. It stipulated that the governor of the state from which a fugitive has escaped must provide a certified copy of the indictment to his counterpart in the state to which the slave has fled. Slave owners or their agents were then authorized to seize him, take him before a federal judge or state officer in the sanctuary state, and, by "oral testimony or affidavit," seek a certificate of removal before taking him back. And while earlier draft language was removed that would have required local officials to do the work of seizure themselves, the bill prescribed a fine of five hundred dollars—an onerous sum at the time—for anyone "who shall knowingly and willingly obstruct or hinder such claimant, his agent, or attorney, in so seizing or arresting such fugitive from labor, or shall rescue such fugitive from such claimant, his agent or attorney."

Along the way to a final text, the many revisions and deletions had both hardened and softened it. For some northerners, the result was pure poison. Particularly offensive was the deletion of language forbidding removal to slavery of persons who had been born or had lived for a long period of time in a free state. The proposed bill also failed to ensure the right to legal counsel for fugitives, or to speak in their own defense, or to be tried by a

Kidnapping scene from Jesse Torrey's A Portraiture of Domestic Slavery, in the United States, *1817*

jury. By imposing fines on anyone who would "obstruct or hinder" their capture, it penalized northerners for refusing to perform the morally dubious duty of acquiescence. And it left free black persons vulnerable to kidnapping on the pretext that they had once been somebody's slave.

For many southerners, however, the bill was not strong enough. It stopped short of requiring northerners to take an active role in the chase and capture—although as the legal scholar Paul Finkelman, who has studied the intricacies of fugitive slave law more closely than anyone else, points out, it was a "blessing" for slave owners because it did not leave them dependent on northerners for help in recovering their slaves. Once authorized by the governor of the state from which the fugitive had fled, they or their agents had free rein to travel north and do it themselves.

Whatever its strengths or weaknesses, the 1793 law marked a new chapter in the history of efforts to regulate the fugitive slave problem: it criminalized behavior that had hitherto been largely outside legal constraints. It turned slave owners into outlaws if, as many were accustomed to do, they or their agents ventured north to seize a fugitive without submitting to a cumbersome judicial process. And it turned northerners into outlaws if they refused to cooperate with that process or actively resisted it. Intended to tighten the link between North and South, it had the effect of pushing them further apart, though the extent of the estrangement would not become fully evident for years to come. On February 12, 1793, President Washington signed the bill into law.

In the ensuing decades, as the weakness of the law became evident, two fruitless attempts were made in Congress to strengthen it. In 1801, led by a representative from Maryland, a bill was nearly passed that would have fined an employer for hiring any black person who could not produce a legal certificate proving his freedom. Employers would also have been required to advertise descriptions of newly hired black workers so that slave owners could scrutinize the newspapers to ensure that their absconded property was not among them. In 1817, another failed bill proposed immunizing bounty hunters from prosecution for any crime short of "mayhem or murder" in the state that they invaded in pursuit of runaways.*

For fifty-seven years, the law of 1793 remained the only federal effort to enforce Article 4, Section 2, Clause 3 of the U.S. Constitution. It turned out to have no effect on the fate of John Davis, who, as far as is known, remained enslaved in Virginia for the rest of his life, nor on the three men who forced him there, who were never prosecuted. By the time the second fugitive slave bill was signed into law in 1850, the first federal attempt to manage the problem had come to be regarded in the South as a dismal failure and in the North as a shameful precedent. It was, said Emerson, an effort to affirm "an intimate union between two countries, one civilized & Christian & the other barbarous." Over the intervening years, a good deal of evidence accumulated to support his contention that there were indeed two countries where the law of the land pretended there was only one.

---

*The proposed 1817 bill also would have curtailed the rights of accused fugitives by limiting the force of any writ of habeas corpus that might be issued on their behalf. Judges were enjoined from construing the writ as granting defendants the right to trial. Both the House and the Senate passed versions of the new bill, but the differences between them were never reconciled, so the effort fizzled and nothing was sent to President James Monroe for his signature. See Thomas D. Morris, *Free Men All: The Personal Liberty Laws of the North, 1780–1861* (Baltimore: Johns Hopkins University Press, 1974), 35–41. See also Fehrenbacher, *Slaveholding Republic*, 214.

Five

CAUGHT

1.

Of all the evidence supporting Emerson's claim that the American nation was in fact two nations, most compelling was the exodus of slaves from one to the other. A very few such as Douglass, who escaped from Maryland under his slave name, Fred Bailey, in 1838, or James W. C. Pennington, also enslaved in Maryland, under the name Jim Pembroke until he escaped in 1826, or Jermain Loguen, called Jarm Logue in Tennessee, from which he fled in 1834, or William Wells Brown, who got out of Kentucky in the same year, became public figures whose lives were substantially recorded.* Others less prominent, such as Charles Ball, who escaped from Georgia sometime in the 1830s, told their stories to witnesses who retold them for good, gain, or both. For the great majority, however, evidence of their lives is sparse.

Scholars have tried to piece together a picture of the typical runaway, but the individual inevitably gets lost in the composite. More than 80 percent of fugitives appear to have been male. His age was somewhere between the late teens and mid-thirties. He was likely to have been sold,

---

*Pennington became a minister in Brooklyn and officiated at the marriage ceremony for Douglass and his bride, Anna Murray, a free black woman from Maryland, on September 15, 1838. Douglass transcribes the certificate of marriage in his *Narrative* (Cambridge, Mass.: Harvard University Press, 1960), 146.

sometimes repeatedly. In the case of slaves who were hired out (in Virginia, on the eve of the Civil War, some 10 percent of its 250,000 slaves were hired out), he might have chafed against the requirement that he relinquish most of what he earned. Probably he lived in or near a town or city, knew other slaves who had fled, and might have faced the impending sale of family, friends, or himself.

For slave owners, losing a slave was of course a financial loss, though in cases of flight by horseback (rare but not unknown) the reward for returning the horse could be higher than for recovering the rider. The great majority of runaways made it only a few miles on foot before returning in discouragement or shackles. Even most who got farther remained nameless and faceless, known from newspaper descriptions ("yellow complexion, has a scar on his forehead . . . a little bald, very humble") or, if the advertiser was willing to pay for an illustration, from a stock image of a boy fleeing with his satchel or a girl running in silhouette—human versions of the proverbial tree falling in the woods with no one near enough to hear it fall.

It is almost impossible to conceive of the lives of the fallen. In his widely read book *Between the World and Me,* Ta-Nehisi Coates imagines one slave's inner life:

> Slavery is not an indefinable mass of flesh. It is a particular, specific enslaved woman, whose mind is active as your own, whose range of feeling is as vast as your own; who prefers the way the light falls in one particular spot in the woods, who enjoys fishing where the water eddies in a nearby stream, who loves her mother in her own complicated way, thinks her sister talks too loud, has a favorite cousin, a favorite season, who excels at dress-making and knows, inside herself, that she is as intelligent and capable as anyone.

Coates does not say if this woman tried to escape. If she did, anonymity might have been for her a bitter blessing. She might have gone north and contracted herself as a servant to a white family who, like many employers of illegal immigrants today, preferred to ask no questions. Or, if she served on a plantation in the Deep South, she might have hidden away—for days, months, in some cases years—in the borderland between cleared ground and the swamp or forest beyond, sneaking back by night to planted fields or outbuildings to scavenge for food. Or, especially before deforestation and draining of marshland became widespread, she might have joined a nomadic community of "maroons" living beyond reach of the slave patrols.

Or perhaps she managed to take herself, alone or in a group, all the way to Florida, a thinly populated outpost of the Spanish Empire until it became a U.S. territory in 1821, and which remained a haven for fugitive slaves for another twenty years until most Seminole Indians, among whom fugitives found shelter, had been killed or driven west by U.S. troops. Or she could have traveled north to Ontario, from which family and friends might never have heard from her again. Some runaways wrote to their masters—or prevailed upon someone to write on their behalf—to say that they had reached Canada while, in fact, they had gone underground in a nearby southern town or city to which they had fled or where they had been hired out.

"Most people," as the twentieth-century writer John Bartlow Martin remarked, "seldom realize how much protection we derive from society simply because it is organized. If we disappear we are missed by relatives, friends, employers, many others." In this respect, the experience of fugitive slaves was an inversion of most people's experience: they *wanted* to disappear. There were opportunities. By 1800, the population of free blacks in Philadelphia had risen to more than six thousand, in New York to some thirty-five hundred, and in Washington, D.C., where slavery remained legal until 1862, to roughly one thousand—numbers that made it possible, if always perilous, for a fugitive to seek cover.

Still, the eyes of every stranger felt intrusive. Today, when a young African American man, feeling conspicuous among whites, lowers his gaze, walks in the shadows, suppresses his rage if frisked by police or cursed by passersby, he relives in some measure the demeaning—or deadly—experience of his forebears.

2.

Adopting a phrase first used to describe the decline of partisan rancor following the War of 1812, historians have named the immediate postwar period the "Era of Good Feelings." Applied to the issue of slavery, the claim is a stretch. Most incidents of flight and pursuit involving fugitive slaves took place, as the phrase goes, under the radar, but they were becoming sufficiently visible to spark what has been called a border war.

Fighting was initially light and sporadic, certainly compared with what was to come in the 1830s, when mobs attacked free blacks and white abolitionists with stones and fire, or in the 1850s, when Free-Soilers and proslavery settlers fought pitched battles in what turned out to be a rehearsal for civil war. But even before the War of 1812, vigilantism was already serious enough to make clear that the 1793 fugitive slave law—intended to prescribe legal means for the recovery of runaways—was not working.

In 1806, in Dayton, Ohio, local whites organized the rescue of a formerly enslaved black couple who had been seized by armed men intending to return them to Kentucky. In 1810, also in Ohio, a group of armed black men intercepted a pair of Kentucky slave hunters carrying bowie knives and pistols who had seized a black family with the same intent. Because recorded incidents were doubtless a small fraction of those that went unrecorded, we may assume there were many more.

While the undeclared internal border war continued, the declared War of 1812 pitted the United States against its old enemy, Britain. Aiming to undermine the economy of their former subjects just as they had done in trying to suppress the rebellion thirty years earlier, the British resumed enticing slaves with promises of freedom. They even assembled special battalions of fugitives (known as the Black Corps), who, they hoped, would have incentive to fight and none to desert because the enemy was likely to re-enslave them. In April 1814, Admiral Alexander Cochrane issued a carefully phrased statement (he never used the word "slaves") proclaiming that "all those who may be disposed to emigrate from the United States" would be received by British naval vessels and given the choice of joining British forces or sent as "FREE settlers to the British Possessions in North America or the West Indies, where they will meet with all due encouragement."

The British secretary of war, however, instructed his subordinates that they must "on no account give encouragement to any disposition which may be manifested by the Negroes to rise against their Masters" and should encourage enlistment only by slaves who, having already assisted British forces, may be exposed "to the vengeance of their Masters." Because enticement never became official policy, slaves seeking a new life beyond British lines were at the mercy of individual field commanders. According to one officer who marched in the British advance upon Washington in August 1814, the British general Robert Ross, determined to protect "private property of every description," turned away scores of slaves "who implored us to take them along with us, offering to serve either as soldiers or sailors."

Nonetheless, from Virginia and Maryland alone, more than three thousand slaves fled to British naval vessels close enough to be reached by raft or rowboat. After being armed and trained, hundreds returned ashore as night raiders.* Nearly fifty years later, during the Civil War, Lincoln would speculate that "the bare sight of fifty thousand armed, and drilled black soldiers on the banks of the Mississippi, would end the rebellion at once." While the number of black fighters on the British side in the War of 1812 never approached that many (during the Civil War, some 200,000 would fight for the Union), they were numerous enough to make for uneasy sleep among plantation masters short of dependable sentries at night.

As in other times of mass dislocation when endangered people must decide between running or huddling in place, young people led the way in choosing action over acquiescence. In her remarkable book *The Warmth of Other Suns*, Isabel Wilkerson describes the great migration in the twentieth century by which millions of southern blacks sought a better life in the North. "To the old folks who stayed," she writes, "the young people looked to be going in circles, chasing a wish." So, perhaps, it has always been: the

---

*Some slaves, by choice or coercion, fought on the American side, including Charles Ball, who complained that white soldiers in his militia unit "ran like sheep chased by dogs." *Fifty Years in Chains* (1837), ed. Philip S. Foner (Mineola, N.Y.: Dover, 1970), 298.

young readier than their elders to throw aside the known for the unknown. As British troops advanced into slave country, older slaves were more inclined to stay with the enemy they already knew than to take their chances with a self-professed new friend.

Among those who did flee, some took with them spouses, children, and even persuadable parents. Following the Revolution, the old-world tradition of primogeniture—the right of the firstborn son to inherit his father's whole estate—had come under attack as a vestige of feudalism unsuited to a republic. Georgia abolished primogeniture in 1777, South Carolina in 1791. Inheritable property, including slave families, could now be broken up and distributed among multiple heirs, leaving plantation slaves in a new kind of jeopardy. If a slave-owning patriarch died intestate, his assets no longer passed intact to his eldest son, and even if a legal will existed, there might be room for sons to bargain not only over who got what portion of the acreage and silverware but also over the strongest farmhands and the prettiest slave girls. As chances went down for enslaved family members to stay together after the death of their owner, motivation to flee went up.

Through the collaborative efforts of free blacks and antislavery whites, the network of escape routes that came to be known as the Underground Railroad began to develop. Among the first "conductors" were Philadelphia Quakers who specialized in slowing down rendition cases in local courts by using tactics (presenting a writ of habeas corpus, for example, to a sympathetic judge) whereby a captive could be released from detention while safe passage farther north was arranged before the plaintiff could reclaim him. Another hub was central North Carolina, where as early as the second decade of the nineteenth century runaways were taken along by families (also often Quakers) immigrating through the Cumberland Gap to the free Northwest.

Like generations of illegal immigrants since, fugitive slaves were both dependent on and exploited by those who aided them. Some who helped were true Samaritans motivated by hatred of slavery and sympathy for its victims; others traded aid for money, labor, or sex. The white man, for example, who assisted four slaves to escape from Richmond in 1848—including Henry "Box" Brown, who became famous for having himself shipped north in a ventilated crate—charged dearly for his services and has been described as "not so much an abolitionist emissary as an opportunistic peddler." Even when there was no quid pro quo, the house, wagon, or makeshift shelter in which a fugitive was concealed was subject to sudden search by authorities looking for runaways or by gangs "of ruffians, moved by the prospect of . . . large reward" if they could scare one up.

Whether in peacetime or wartime, it is impossible to know how many slaves felt desperate enough to take the risks. According to no less an authority than Frederick Douglass, under slavery chronic fear sapped the will to imagine a different life:

> The people of the north, and free people generally, I think, have less attachment to the places where they are born and brought up than have the slaves. Their freedom to go and come, to be here and there, as they list, prevents any extravagant attachment to any one particular place, in their case. On the other hand, the slave is a fixture; he has no choice, no goal, no destination; but is pegged down to a single spot, and must take root here, or nowhere. The idea of removal elsewhere, comes, generally, in the shape of a threat, and in punishment of crime. It is, therefore, attended with fear and dread . . . like [that of] a living man going into the tomb, who, with open eyes, sees himself buried out of sight and hearing of wife, children and friends of kindred tie.

But sometimes fear gave way to desperation. In 1817, the Philadelphian Jesse Torrey published a compilation of stories—about black people kidnapped, or chained in groups trudging south, or displayed on the auction block—titled *A Portraiture of Domestic Slavery in the United States*. One of the most devastating stories was of Anna, a mother enslaved in Delaware until she was moved to a Washington tavern that doubled as a slave pen, from which she was scheduled to be sold. Upon learning that she would be separated from her children, she leaped from a third-floor

From Jesse Torrey's
A Portraiture of Domestic
Slavery, in the United States,
1817

window, shattering her arms and breaking her back. It was unclear
whether survival was, to her, a curse or a blessing.

Anna's story became, as the historian Edward Baptist has called it, "a
media scandal"—one of the first eruptions of the human cost of slavery
into the national consciousness. It was accompanied in Torrey's book by a
striking engraving that rendered Anna less as a tumbling body than as a
levitating angel floating above what looks to modern eyes like a scene
from a film noir with dark doorways and ominous shadows sweeping
across the cobblestone street.

In the subtitle of his book, Torrey captured the fundamental problem
that, despite the best efforts by the best legal minds, could never be resolved: "Reflections on the Practicability of Restoring the Moral Rights
of the Slave, Without Impairing the Legal Privileges of the Possessor."

One who was stopped by the impasse was the Virginia congressman
John Randolph. An orator of great power, Randolph was outraged by the

cruelty that drove Anna to madness—if that is what it was—and railed against slave drivers who pushed mothers beyond endurance. He owned over four hundred slaves, whom he emancipated in his will (much to the dismay of relatives hoping to inherit them) and provided funds for their resettlement in Ohio. Among the first to call for an end to the slave trade in the nation's capital, he promised personally to "ferret out" its villainous practitioners from "their holes and corners." There is a plausible story that upon seeing a woman sewing garments to be sent abroad to fighters in the Greek revolution—a popular cause for northerners and southerners alike—he called her attention to a passing group of ill-clad slaves and said, "Madam, the Greeks are at your door."

Yet if ever anyone perfected the art of self-contradiction, it was Randolph. Whenever he spoke at length in the House, which was often, he was attended for his refreshment by a slave boy carrying a jug of ale. After a swallow or two, he would launch into lamenting his "misfortune to be, and to have been born, a slaveholder" while warning at the same time that abuses such as those that tormented Anna would someday persuade Congress to use war as a pretext to abolish slavery altogether. It would be done, he predicted, on grounds of military necessity, just as Madison and the younger Laurens had contemplated during the Revolution, except that next time emancipation would be forced upon the slave owners without compensation.

Randolph thus joined a long line of Virginians, including Patrick Henry, who worried that the federal government would someday invoke its war powers in order to "pronounce all slaves free." Apart from the fact that when wartime emancipation finally did arrive, on January 1, 1863, it would come not by an act of Congress but by presidential proclamation. He turned out to be impressively prophetic.

In his ability to attack and defend slavery simultaneously, Randolph was a descendant of Jefferson and Madison, but in his fear of federal intervention he foreshadowed Calhoun. He could have been the subject of one of Mark Twain's wicked riffs (Twain was born in Missouri in 1835) on the universal human talent for moral incoherence. Here, writing

John Randolph in 1831

ostensibly about a "native Australasian" whom he encountered on his Pacific travels, Twain captures—perhaps as only a southern writer could—the self-division of which Randolph was an early exemplar:

> He takes his reluctant bride by force, he courts her with a club, then loves her faithfully through a long life—it is of record. He gathers to himself another wife by the same processes, beats and bangs her as a daily diversion, and by and by lays down his life in defending her from some outside harm—it is of record. He will face a hundred hostiles to rescue one of his children, and will kill another of his children because the family is large enough without it. His delicate stomach turns, at certain details of the white man's food; but he likes over-ripe fish, and brazed dog, and cat, and rat, and will eat his own uncle with relish. He is a sociable animal, yet he turns aside and hides behind his shield when his mother-in-law goes by.

John Randolph had no wife to beat and therefore no mother-in-law to fear, nor did he, presumably, eat rat, dog, or his uncle, but it is of record that he defended and denounced slavery with equal indignation. Like Jefferson and Madison, he reminded anyone who needed reminding that slavery drove slave owners—at least the reflective ones—into a labyrinth of contradictions.

3.

Runaway slaves had always posed a particular problem for conflicted slave owners: they exposed the gap between myth (the inferiority of slaves, the benignity of masters) and reality (the courage it took to run away, the risk of retribution). Now, as they moved from the periphery toward the center of public awareness, their determination to seek freedom became more and more alarming to one side of the national divide and encouraging to the other.

During the 1820s, American diplomats made repeated appeals to Britain seeking return of fugitive slaves who had fled to British Canada during the War of 1812. As late as 1826, Secretary of State Henry Clay was still urging the American minister in London, Albert Gallatin, to press the case for returning fugitive slaves who had found sanctuary in Britain's North American territories. Two years later, Gallatin's successor, James Barbour, continued to seek British cooperation on the grounds that every successful "attempt at elopement" constituted "a strong allurement" for other slaves "to abscond." As had been the case after the Revolution, all these efforts got nowhere—rebuffed with curt reminders that on the *Somerset* precedent the British government would not "depart from the principle recognized by the British courts, that every man is free who reaches British ground."*

When it came to dealing with Spain—a much weaker power than Britain—diplomacy was a cursory preface to military action. In the spring

---

*Abolitionists, black and white, cited the exchange between Clay and Gallatin in arguing for the universality of the *Somerset* principle. *Freedom's Journal,* for example, the African American newspaper founded by John B. Russwurm and Samuel E. Cornish, paraphrased Gallatin's response in its January 9, 1829, edition as evidence that there existed "no regulation by which [fugitive slaves] can be surrendered to their masters" (321).

of 1816, with slaves fleeing in alarming numbers from coastal Georgia to the Spanish colony of Florida, the Spanish fort at Pensacola had become, according to one American naval officer, a "rendezvous for runaway slaves . . . an asylum where they found arms and ammunition to protect themselves against their owners and the government." General Andrew Jackson, hero of the last battle of the War of 1812, at New Orleans, regarded these fugitives as nothing more than "lawless banditti" and issued a perfunctory demand that the Spanish governor give them up. In the absence of a satisfactory response, Jackson's subordinates sent an artillery assault of "red-hot shot" into the fort's magazine. Writing some twenty years later about the attack, William Jay (grandson of John Jay) claimed that more than two hundred men, women, and children died in the ensuing explosion.

Within the borders of the United States, tension over the fugitive problem continued to increase. In 1820, the Maryland legislature complained that Pennsylvanians were resorting to force in order to thwart recovery of fugitives by their legal owners. From Louisiana, in 1827, came denunciation of "self-styled philanthropists" in the North who "think themselves justified in the use of every possible means by which they can rob a southern master of a slave." And as always, some people figured out how to make money from misery: in 1835, a group of investors in Richmond organized the Virginia Slave Insurance Company "with power and authority to make insurance upon slaves absconding from their owners."

Slave states tried to crack down. Throughout the South, black people—free as well as enslaved—were banned from riverboats and vessels capable of travel by sea. Free black sailors on ships berthed in southern ports were jailed in order to prevent them from smuggling slaves aboard for embarkation to the North. Slave patrols were fortified to make flight by land more difficult. Shoes, issued to reduce the chance of foot injury or infection by the hookworm parasite (a common route of infection was through the bare sole) that could sideline a slave from work, were collected at night to reduce the chance of escape. An 1822 statute in Missouri prescribed a 9:00 p.m. curfew requiring that any slave out after dark be returned to his master for compulsory whipping. If the owner failed to comply, a fine was imposed. Also in danger were white people suspected of encouraging slaves to run away. In 1819, a white Methodist elder in Maryland was indicted for preaching antislavery sermons intended, according to his accusers, to incite slaves to flee.

The scarcity of similar court cases in the ensuing years suggests how completely the South closed ranks. Antislavery agitation was moving in inverse proportion to the size of the local slave population: it subsided in the South, while it gathered force in the North. In mid-century Mississippi, where the number of slaves was approaching 400,000, organized antislavery activity was all but over. Meanwhile, Concord, Massachusetts, where free blacks accounted for roughly 1 percent of the population and where there were of course no slaves at all, became a hub of abolitionism.

One result of this asymmetry was that whites charged in southern courts with sedition on behalf of slaves were increasingly likely to be transplanted northerners who ran afoul of local laws. While living in Baltimore in 1829, the northern abolitionist William Lloyd Garrison, for example, published an article in a local antislavery paper (edited by a New Jersey–born Quaker, Benjamin Lundy) calling for slave traders to be "sentenced to solitary confinement for life" and sent to "the lowest depths of perdition" in the afterlife. He took particular aim at a fellow New Englander, Francis Todd, a shipowner born in Garrison's native town of Newburyport, Massachusetts, who hired out his vessel for transporting slaves from Maryland to New Orleans. Having excoriated Todd as a sordid illustration of "New-England humanity and morality" who deserved "thick infamy," Garrison was convicted for libel and jailed for nearly two months until the wealthy New York abolitionist Arthur Tappan paid his fine.

Two years later, the Connecticut-born physician Reuben Crandall (brother of the well-known abolitionist Prudence Crandall) was tried in Washington, D.C., for distributing antislavery pamphlets. Although ultimately acquitted, Crandall became a symbol of abolitionist incursion into the South at a time when antislavery activity had shifted almost entirely to the North. The prosecutor in the Crandall case, District Attorney Francis Scott Key, was destined to become famous as the author of "The Star-Spangled Banner," which includes a (rarely sung) verse blaming the

British for using fugitive servants or slaves as mercenaries during the War of 1812: "No refuge could save the hireling and slave / From the terror of flight or the gloom of the grave." Like John Randolph, Key was a man bristling with contradictions. He regarded abolitionists as fanatics who, by calling for a quick end to slavery, risked destroying white America by opening the way to racial amalgamation. Because the "great moral and political evil amongst us" was not slavery but "the whole colored race" itself, a better way to deal with the slavery problem would be to purify the nation by sending the slaves back to Africa. Nonetheless, Key was sufficiently moved by the plight of a slave mother facing the prospect of being sold away from her children that he helped to raise money to buy her and her children's freedom.

Outside the courts, southerners continued to accuse northerners of colluding with "slave stealers," while northerners accused southerners of sending thugs across the border to abduct not just fugitive slaves but any human prey that might fetch a good price in the flesh market back home. It is impossible to know how many or how often free blacks were kidnapped for the purpose of sale into slavery, but it happened often enough to become an inflammatory issue. The original name of the Pennsylvania Abolition Society, founded in 1775, was the Society for the Relief of Free Negroes Unlawfully Held in Bondage. Writing in 1817, Jesse Torrey reported the case of a Philadelphia black man who made a practice of marrying black women, then selling them across the border in Maryland or Virginia. As late as 1836, in New Hampshire, a destitute black boy was sold to an Alabama slave owner by the local white man with whom the child had been lodged by the overseers of the poor. The following year, the antislavery paper *National Enquirer and Constitutional Advocate of Universal Liberty* reported a surge in kidnapping, including a free black woman along with her six children.

Light complexion was no sure protection. Because centuries of interracial sexual relations had made skin color an unreliable standard by which to distinguish black from white, race came to be defined less as a matter of color than of "blood." Slave states established elaborate legal taxonomies by which people were characterized as "quadroons" or "octoroons" (typical was an 1822 Virginia law classifying any person with one Negro grandparent as a "mulatto") depending on how tainted with "black blood" they were deemed to be.

Some persons defined by genealogy as black thus found themselves "separated from the white race by a line of division so faint that it can only be traced by the keen eye of prejudice." Not only fugitive slaves, but also anyone of low social standing, including vagabonds, migrant laborers, and petty criminals who might have been physically indistinguishable from free whites, was vulnerable to being seized, bought, and sold as a slave. In 1841, the Ohio legislature threatened war against Virginia for its failure to extradite four Virginians who had kidnapped three white men in Ohio to be sold in Kentucky. Kidnapping was also a threat to white abolitionists. In 1838, an Ohio man was seized and taken to Virginia, where he was tarred and feathered. In 1845, three Ohioans accused of aiding fugitive slaves were jailed in Virginia until Ohio's governor stepped in to have them released.

Women and children were particularly vulnerable to abduction. Writing in the *Philanthropist* in 1836, James G. Birney called for strengthening anti-kidnapping laws in order to reduce the risk of white women's being captured and sold into sex slavery. "There are in the South, already," he wrote, "slaves as white as any of us, who have in our veins the purest Saxon blood. . . . The whiter the slave—especially if it be a female—the more extravagant the price—the more desirable the victim." A columnist for the *Western Citizen*, writing in 1845, agreed. "Without legal security against kidnapping, the whitest and best known free child in the city" of Chicago would be subject to capture and enslavement. His alarm was not baseless. In the late 1850s, a fifteen-year-old girl who had escaped from the man who had bought her at a New Orleans slave auction sued for her freedom on the grounds that she was white. Her lawyers claimed that her whiteness was "on view" not only in her blue eyes and blond hair but in her modest behavior, impossible to emulate even by a light mulatto, which the defense claimed her to be.

However common or rare were the kidnapping incidents, the specter of "white slavery" was one factor behind the rash of personal liberty laws adopted in the 1830s and 1840s by northern states seeking to throw up legal obstacles blocking out-of-state agents from seizing persons accused of being fugitives from slavery. In 1835, Gerrit Smith announced with strategic exaggeration that "the question now is not merely, nor mainly, whether the blacks of the South shall remain slaves, but whether the whites at the North shall become slaves also." No doubt Smith was speaking metaphorically, but his metaphor touched a nerve. That slavery posed a menace not only to blacks but also to whites became a keynote in stump speeches by antislavery politicians, including, eventually, Lincoln, who warned in the 1850s that no one, regardless of color, was safe from the Slave Power.

4.

Poets and fiction writers were ahead of the politicians in understanding that tales of white slaves had a horror-story fascination. As early as 1797, the Boston author Royall Tyler, in a novel titled *The Algerine Captive,* told the story of a white physician who serves as a surgeon on a slave ship before falling into slavery himself at the hands of Algerian captors. In 1835, the French writer Gustave de Beaumont, who had traveled in America with Alexis de Tocqueville, published an essay on race in the form of a novel, *Marie; or, Slavery in the United States*—the story of a young Frenchman and his American bride, whose admixture of African blood provokes such ostracism that the couple is driven into exile among Cherokee Indians, who give them shelter. The following year saw the first full-scale literary treatment of the "tragic mulatto" theme, Richard Hildreth's novel *The Slave; or, Memoirs of Archy Moore.*

Hildreth was a scholarly Bostonian who for reasons of health had spent several months on a Florida plantation. Described by one newspaper as "an abolitionist pamphlet in the guise of a stirring and interesting work of fiction," his book was composed in the first-person voice and published pseudonymously as if Archy had written it himself. It told the tale of the son of a slave owner and his concubine, whose "trace of African blood, by which her veins were contaminated . . . imparted to her complexion . . . a peculiar richness," and whose "flashing . . . dark eyes completed a picture which might perhaps be matched in Spain or Italy, but for which, it would be in vain to seek a rival among the pale-faced, languid beauties of eastern Virginia."

Archy, child of this mixed-blood beauty and her white master's son, is tormented in boyhood by his racial ambiguity and, upon achieving manhood, encounters rapacious planters who regard his own alluring light-skinned wife as a luxury to be passed around like a good cognac. After he is impressed into the British navy, his pent-up rage explodes, and he fights in the War of 1812 for the crown. At a time when many bookshops, in the North as well as the South, refused to stock abolition tracts as if they were a form of pornography, Hildreth's book helped make the subject respectable, appearing in subsequent editions under his own name and with a more explicit title—*Archy Moore, the White Slave.*

The fact of racial mixing revealed a reality that slave owners preferred, of course, to suppress. "Every lady," wrote one straight-talking mistress of a South Carolina plantation, "tells you who is the father of all the mulatto children in everybody's household, but those in her own she seems to think drop from the clouds."

The sordid truth was that once a slave girl reached puberty—doubtless sometimes sooner—she became the object of white men's demands and could never draw a clear line between coercion and consent. While visiting the South in the 1840s, the British naturalist Charles Lyell was struck that "the female slave is proud of her connection with a white man, and thinks it is an honor to have a mulatto, hoping it will be better provided for than a black child." Years later, Harriet Jacobs provided some personal context for that remark. Looking back to her adolescence (she was born in 1813), she recalled that "when she is fourteen or fifteen," an enslaved girl's "owner or his sons or the overseers, or perhaps all of them, begin to bribe her with presents." If she did not respond willingly, she could expect to be initiated into what amounted to a lifetime of serial rape.

More and more writers took up the theme. A play of unknown authorship, *The Kidnapped Clergyman* (probably never performed, but evidently known to antislavery activists in its printed version), appeared in 1839, about a pompous white minister who, in the midst of congratulating himself for preaching against abolitionists, is kidnapped by a slave trader and sold as a runaway, but not before being forced to watch his daughter carried off by a buyer who pays well for her carnal services. In 1842, in the abolitionist annual *The Liberty Bell*, Lydia Maria Child's story "The Quadroons" told the tale of two beautiful mixed-race women in Georgia, mother and daughter, who are seduced (when they resisted, "threats took the place of persuasion"), then abandoned by white men who move on to other pleasures.

That same year, in "The Quadroon Girl," America's unofficial poet laureate, Henry Wadsworth Longfellow, portrayed a planter under financial duress who overcomes his scruples ("the voice of nature was too weak / He took the glittering gold!") and sells his honey-hued daughter for use by the buyer as a sex slave:

> *Her eyes were, like a falcon's, gray,*
> *Her arms and neck were bare;*
> *No garment she wore save a kirtle gay,*
> *And her own long, raven hair.*
> . . .
> *Then pale as death grew the maiden's cheek,*
> *Her hands as icy cold.*
>
> *The Slaver led her from the door,*
> *He led her by the hand,*
> *To be his slave and paramour*
> *In a strange and distant land!*

The shock that fugitives encountered in the North at the idea of "white slavery" was both an opportunity and an offense. It was an opportunity because the image of the enslaved white woman made slavery feel closer to northern whites. It was an offense because white outrage seemed reserved for cases where slavery ensnared one of their own. One British visitor, upon inspecting Hope Slatter's infamous Baltimore slave pen, was stunned to find imprisoned there two women "whose complexion was so near white as to attract peculiar attention" and was even more astonished to learn that they "were sisters, and the children of their master!"

In 1843, when the Ohio Methodist minister Calvin Fairbank raised funds from Levi Coffin, Salmon P. Chase, and other antislavery leaders in order to buy a light-skinned girl at a Kentucky auction, he was moved to rescue her because she was said to be only one sixty-fourth black—below what he deemed a reasonable threshold for enslavement. After unbuttoning her dress to exhibit "her superb neck and breast," the auctioneer, by Fairbank's account, was dissatisfied with the bids, and so, "lifting her skirts, laid bare her beautiful, symmetrical body, from her feet to her waist, and with his brutal, sacrilegious hand smote her white flesh, exclaiming: 'Ah! gentlemen, who is going to be the winner of this prize? Whose is the next bid?'"

Then came the moral of the story: there was a line that decent people—southerners no less than northerners—would not cross. "'Shame! shame!' they cried; and Boston and New Orleans shed tears, wept, side by side." This kind of writing had the character of an antipornography tract that invites the reader to disapprove publicly while privately savoring the evidence. There would have been less shame if her flesh had been less white.

Trading in slaves of fair complexion involved risk intermingled with excitement. On the one hand, a light-skinned "fancy girl" deemed suitable as a sexual servant commanded a premium price. On the other hand, she posed a constant risk of slipping away and melting into the white world. "Too white to keep" became a term of the trade.

In the North, light-skinned slaves traveling with their masters provoked astonishment as if they were circus animals run amok. Others were ogled. When the fair-skinned Harriet Powell, as elegant as she was voluptuous, fled her Mississippi master in 1839 during a trip to Syracuse, New York, the former slave Jermain Loguen remarked with sardonic amusement that she "awakened curiosity and indignation among some who had no objection to black slavery." Having never seen "a woman so white and attractive . . . held as property," crowds of "citizens and strangers, caught by her attractions, turned to look at her" as she passed by.

The Greek Slave

A decade later, when the white marble figure *The Greek Slave*—created in 1843 by the Vermont-born sculptor Hiram Powers—went on tour in the North, it triggered a flood of editorials, essays, and poems. By the 1850s numerous copies had been made and were touring Britain and the United States, and mass-produced souvenir statuettes proved enormously popular.

Who can know what proportions of prurience and sympathy drew crowds to this ravishing nude in chains? Modeled after well-known classical versions of Venus in a pose of modesty, the sculpture must have shocked nineteenth-century viewers with the incongruity of the goddess in chains. Somewhere beyond her is an unseen man holding the key to the lock, to whom, we know, the girl must yield once he arrives. Through her posture—provisionally at rest, head and eyes averted from the viewer-voyeur, one hand helping to support her body's weight, the other partially screening her genitals—the sculptor conveys her anxious shame while implicating the viewer in the excitement of watching and waiting. For some, she doubtless provided a certain sadistic pleasure in imagining her sexual degradation, while others felt the uneasy gratitude expressed in the proverb "there, but for the grace of God, go I."* No doubt more than a few viewers felt a combination of both.

5.

Yet even as literature and art began to grapple one way or another with the problem of slavery, political institutions stayed remarkably inert. Some sixty years after adoption of the Constitution, the states, in Tocqueville's words, remained "twenty-four little sovereign nations" and Congress little more than a periodic gathering of independent emissaries. The "united" in "United States" was still a gross exaggeration.

In May 1836, in one of the true ostrich moments in American history, Congress tried to shut down discussion of slavery altogether. Hoping to restore "tranquility to the public mind," the House of Representatives resolved that all petitions demanding action against slavery be tabled immediately upon receipt without debate. The "gag rule"—as the moratorium came to be known after John Quincy Adams, protesting the violation of his First Amendment rights, demanded to know "Am I gagged, or am I not?"—was reaffirmed annually for almost a decade, until party discipline among southern and northern Democrats broke down and the rule was rescinded in December 1844. As much as it may seem in retrospect a rash act of suppression, the gag rule was seen as a rational, or at least a comprehensible, response to the increasingly manifest fact that the question of slavery had become impervious to compromise.

Most accounts of the antebellum years stress the growing divide between North and South, but on the matter of racial animus it is a mistake to draw too bright a dividing line. By and large, northerners wanted to stop the inflow of runaways as much as southerners wanted to stop the

---

*Perhaps a paraphrase of 1 Corinthians 15:8–10 ("By the grace of God I am what I am"), the phrase is sometimes traced to the sixteenth-century English Protestant reformer John Bradford, who is said to have spoken it while watching a group of prisoners being led to their execution: "There but for the grace of God, goes John Bradford."

outflow. As early as 1803, within a year after Ohio achieved statehood, its General Assembly passed "An Act to Regulate Black and Mulatto Persons," decreeing that "No Negro or Mulatto should be allowed to settle in the state unless he could furnish a certificate from some court . . . of his actual freedom" and that "Blacks already living in the state must register . . . with the county clerk." Illinois, to which Lincoln moved from Indiana in 1830, had passed a law eleven years earlier requiring blacks entering the state to post a thousand-dollar bond guaranteeing good behavior—a law designed to ensure that the state would "not become a retreat for runaway slaves." In 1820, the legislature of Missouri—a slave-state peninsula jutting into free territory—approved a constitution forbidding "free negroes and mulattoes from coming to and settling in this State."

Black Americans were thus caught between one region that wished to keep them as slave laborers and another that did not want them at all. Connecticut restricted the franchise to white males in 1818, a year earlier than Alabama. In 1838, Pennsylvania revoked the voting rights of black men. In 1844, the provisional government of the Oregon Country passed a law banning slavery while prescribing whipping and expulsion for former slaves who did not leave the state upon their emancipation. Even in Massachusetts, from which slavery was long gone, many whites "loathed slavery and feared emancipation" at the same time.

It was a contradiction with a long history. As early as 1700, the jurist Samuel Sewall (best known for his role in hanging "witches" at Salem) conceded that New England was "culpable in forcing the *Africans* to become Slaves among ourselves," yet declared that black people could never grow "up into orderly Families" or coexist with whites in civilized society. Without some scheme for colonizing them out of the country, he feared, they would "remain in our Body Politick as a kind of extravasat Blood"—blood, that is, that leaks through its vessels and seeps into the body as a slow poison.

A century later, not much had changed. In 1795, John Adams noted the depth of popular hostility in his home state toward slaves as well as slave owners. "If the gentlemen had been permitted to hold slaves," he wrote, "the common white people would have put the slaves to death, and their masters too, perhaps." Adams was a careful writer who knew exactly what he was doing when he gave the benefit of the "perhaps" only to the masters.

Adams's son John Quincy Adams sincerely believed that nothing could "be more false and heartless than this doctrine which makes the first and holiest rights of humanity to depend upon the color of the skin." Nevertheless, he found himself disgusted by Desdemona's passion in *Othello* for a "rude, unbleached African soldier," and declared that "the great moral lesson" of Shakespeare's play is "that black and white blood cannot be intermingled in marriage without a gross outrage upon the law of Nature."

Writing in the same year, Tocqueville reported that "race prejudice seems stronger in those states that have abolished slavery than in those where it still exists." Nearly twenty years later, in 1854, William J. Watkins, born to free black parents in Baltimore, described racial animus among white northerners as "more virulent" than anything he had encountered in the South. Also in the 1850s, one medical "authority," who has been described as "perhaps the first professional racist in American history," answered the pesky question of how it could be that a "negro child, in some respects, at the same age, is more intelligent than the white child" by likening black children to "domestic animals" whose development at first outpaces that of human infants but are soon enough overtaken by the more advanced species. These observations appear in a book titled *Negroes and Negro "Slavery": The First an Inferior Race; the Latter Its Normal Condition*, written in New York, not New Orleans.

Not only was northern racism rampant, but it was generous in scope. In 1837, before he began speaking out publicly against slavery, Emerson confided to his notebook that "it cannot be maintained by any candid person that the African race have ever occupied or do promise ever to occupy any very high place in the human family. Their present condition is the strongest proof that they cannot. The Irish cannot; the American Indian cannot; the Chinese cannot. Before the energy of the Caucasian race all the other races have quailed and done obeisance." Even Theodore Parker, the Massachusetts clergyman who was an early and passionate abolitionist, considered Africans "at the bottom . . . in respect to *power of* civilization," though he thought they might rise in the ranks. Whatever the relative intensity of racist feeling in free states and slave states, very few whites anywhere in America were free from what Emerson called "natural colorphobia," which, he was honest enough to admit, he "controlled" in his own case "only by moral conviction."

In 1844, the antislavery activist Gerrit Smith—a notable exception to the "colorphobia" rule—summed up what fugitives from the slave South faced in the so-called free North. "The laws and usages," he wrote, "by which the free people of color in the northern States are vexed, hampered, outraged, crushed, constitute so gratuitous, so wantonly wicked a chiming with the slaveholding policy of the South, and so indispensable a prop of this policy, as to make them not less guilty than her bloodiest slave codes."

Every fugitive knew the "usages." Aboard ship on Long Island Sound, Douglass was forced to sleep on the freezing deck and, while traveling by railroad through New England, was "dragged from the cars for the crime of being colored." When another refugee from Maryland, Henry Highland Garnet, who had escaped as a child with his family in 1824, was admitted to the Noyes Academy in New Hampshire in 1835, local farmers hitched a team of oxen to a campus building and pulled it down. Later that night, shots were fired into the house where Garnet, his friend Alexander Crummell, and other black students boarded. Speaking in England in 1849, William Wells Brown told his audience that "the slave is just as much a slave in the city of Boston . . . as he is in Charleston, South Carolina: he is just as much a slave in any of the Eastern States as he is in the Southern States."

After fleeing from North Carolina in 1842, Harriet Jacobs found employment with a family in New York City, where one of her duties was to take their daughter to and from the studio of an artist hired to paint the girl's portrait. Because streetcars were closed to black passengers, she had to make the six-mile trek on foot unless the conductor was moved to relent by the beseeching eyes of a white child clutching her black nursemaid's hand. Upon discovering that "prejudice against color is stronger north than south" (Douglass's words), fugitives from slavery found themselves living as strangers in a not-so-strange land. And yet by 1840 more than a thousand antislavery societies had sprung up in the free states, many of which included former slaves.

How could racial animosity and antislavery sentiment coexist so cordially? Part of the answer is that even as moral outrage at slavery rose among whites, so did fear of blacks. "Opposing slavery and hating its victims," Douglass observed, "has come to be a very common form of abolitionism." White people of strong antislavery feeling (including such luminaries as Harriet Beecher Stowe and, for a time, Lincoln) kept company with slave owners like Henry Clay in favoring the colonization of former slaves somewhere outside the country, at a safe remove in Africa, the Caribbean, Central America, or Canada. Others proposed "colonization" within the United States itself. Even as sympathetic an advocate as Gerrit Smith, who donated 120,000 acres of land in upstate New York to poor blacks for the purposes of their settlement, seemed to recognize that for the foreseeable future the prospect of fully integrating free blacks or former slaves into white society was remote. With few exceptions, such as Charles Sumner, who argued for integrating the public schools of Boston, opponents of slavery were not necessarily committed to the dignity, much less the political or social equality, of its victims.* The same newspapers that published sympathetic stories about Harriet Powell's flight to freedom carried advertisements for minstrel shows.

Another part of the answer is that American society—North and South—has never been uniform in mood or sentiment, and its internal

---

*In *Roberts v. City of Boston* (1850), Sumner argued for the right of the plaintiff, a five-year-old black girl named Sarah Roberts, to attend an all-white school in Boston on the grounds that "the law contemplates not only that [children] shall all be taught, but that they shall be taught all together. They are not only to receive equal quantities of knowledge, but all are to receive it in the same way." Sumner's impassioned speech attacked segregation on both constitutional and moral grounds, arguing that it led to a "caste system" like that of India. "You have already banished slavery from this Commonwealth," he told the court. "I call upon you now to obliterate the last of its footprints." (Argument of Charles Sumner, Esq. Against the Constitutionality of Separate Colored Schools in the Case of Sarah C. Roberts vs. the City of Boston, Argued Before the Supreme Court of Massachusetts, Dec. 4, 1849 [Boston: B. F. Roberts, 1849], 30–31). The court, led by Justice Lemuel Shaw, decided in favor of the defense. Though segregation was legally banned in Boston public schools in 1855, the *Roberts* decision was cited in *Plessy v. Ferguson* (1896) as a precedent for the constitutionality of the "separate but equal" doctrine and would only be overturned by the Warren Court in *Brown v. Board of Education* (1954).

divisions have never fallen neatly along geographic dividing lines. In Pennsylvania, even as black men were denied the franchise, the "self-emancipating department" of the antislavery movement was booming as hundreds of fugitives, attracting "deep interest manifested by the inhabitants in their success and safety," were "continually passing through the central part of the State, on their way to the North." By the fourth decade of the century, it was unremarkable for an African American shopkeeper in Boston to conduct a profitable business serving white clients. Yet when a successful black store owner bought a pew in the Park Street Church, his "appearance and that of his family in that fashionable house of worship," according to the abolitionist Oliver Johnson, "was accounted by all of Boston as an outrage scarcely less flagrant than the use of a pew as a pigpen."

The compatibility of racial contempt with antislavery conviction was something northern politicians well understood. During his rise to power, Lincoln was not above appealing to both, as when he opposed the expansion of slavery on the grounds that the best "preventive of amalgamation" between blacks and whites would be "to keep them apart." He regarded the "forced concubinage" of enslaved women as morally reprehensible, but he also objected on the grounds that it accounted for "nine tenths of all the mulattoes—all the mixing of blood in the nation." When Ohio senator Thomas Corwin opposed the introduction of slaves into the West, it was not on their behalf but because the slave has brought trouble "wherever he has set down his black foot!"

Southerners tried using this argument—that blacks are irredeemably primitive—as a way to convince northerners that it was in their own interest to close their borders to runaways. Sensible people, wrote Edgar Allan Poe in 1845, should shut their ears to "negrophilic old ladies of the north" who, he noted in a swipe at a literary rival, "form so large a part of Mr. Longfellow's friends" and who wail and moan on behalf of subhuman people they know nothing about.

On this view, slave hunters were not hired thugs but public-spirited citizens doing northerners a favor by keeping the wretches out. If slavery was an asset to the South, it was also a burden, and northerners should be grateful to their southern brethren for bearing it! Besides, once slaves in the South came to understand that they were not wanted in the North, the flow of fugitives would slow, and sooner or later it would stop.

This was nonsense, of course, as today's migrants from the Middle East to western Europe, or from Latin America to the United States, should remind us. No amount of hatred or hostility on the receiving end will prevent refugees from coming if the conditions from which they seek refuge are desperate enough.

Chapter Six

WAR OF WORDS

1.

By the second third of the century, the struggle by and for fugitive slaves had opened a new front in which the weapons were words. With no solution to the problem of comity even remotely in sight, America's internal slave traffic—many thousands moving south within the slave states against their will, many fewer moving north out of the slave states by strength of will—was becoming ever more visible.

Between 1800 and 1830, the number of newspapers in the United States rose from around two hundred to nearly a thousand. By 1840, in New York City alone, some thirty thousand copies of antislavery publications were being printed every month. Ten years later, visiting the offices of Horace Greeley's *New-York Tribune*, Richard Henry Dana Jr., author of the bestselling memoir *Two Years Before the Mast* (1840), realized he was witnessing "the great enginery of the 19th century, steam engines in every part of the huge building, & four editors at humble tables, with pen & scissors in hand, preparing for 100,000 readers & more, with telegraphic despatches every hour, from all parts of the Union." As this new world came into being, slave hunters and their allies might still hope for public indifference, but they could no longer count on public ignorance.

In 1836, a black steamboat worker in St. Louis was under pursuit by police—perhaps because he had been involved in a fight with another sailor—when a free man of mixed race named Francis McIntosh who worked as a cook on another steamboat was arrested for failing to heed the officers' call to aid them. Told that his offense would land him in prison for five years, he drew a knife, wounding one of the officers and killing the other. After being hauled off to jail, McIntosh was "taken from prison by a mob," then "chained to a tree at the corner of Seventh and Chestnut. Chests, barrels and lumber were piled about him. This was then lit, and the unfortunate man was slowly roasted to death" while he begged for someone in the crowd to shoot him.

Such stories were now much more likely to spread beyond the sight and smell of the fire. The St. Louis incident became so widely known that more than a year later Abraham Lincoln, just stepping out into the public sphere, told an audience in Springfield, Illinois, that a "mulatto man" had been "seized in the street" in the major city of a neighboring state, "dragged to the suburbs of the city, chained to a tree, and actually burned to death; and all within a single hour from the time he had been a freeman, attending to his own business, and at peace with the world."

Two months before Lincoln spoke, a pro-slavery mob assembled across the river from St. Louis in the Illinois town of Alton, set fire to the house of the abolitionist newspaper editor Elijah Lovejoy, shot him to death, and threw his printing press into the river. John Quincy Adams called it "the most atrocious case of mob rioting which ever disgraced this Country." Lincoln feared that the United States was sliding toward anarchy.

Part of what was happening was that abolitionism, once a fringe movement, was gaining strength, and so was the reaction against it. In Washington, under "the dark and threatening cloud of abolition," senators and representatives fell into mutual recrimination. This was as true in some state legislatures as it was in Congress. In Virginia, where small farmers in the Piedmont and mountainous west resented the slave-owning elite concentrated in the tidewater east, the last substantive debate over emancipation took place during the legislative session of 1831–1832, ending with the nondecision that we must "await a more definite development of public opinion." If nineteenth-century Virginians had known Samuel

Beckett's twentieth-century play, they might as well have said they were waiting for Godot.

One effect of the political paralysis was to force antislavery into new channels. Among them was a new kind of writing: personal accounts by and about slaves who ran from slavery. At first white writers presumed to tell their stories for them on the assumption that the poor creatures were incapable of speaking for themselves. Self-appointed spokesmen included estimable authors with stately three-part names—John Greenleaf Whittier, James Russell Lowell, Henry Wadsworth Longfellow—known for specializing in safe subjects like the serenities of nature or the pleasures of holiday hayrides. Their rolling rhythms and memory-assisting rhymes made for poetry that parents could recite around the hearth to their children.

But now the "Fireside Poets" took up darker themes, as in Whittier's "Hunters of Men," published in 1835:

> *HAVE ye heard of our hunting, o'er mountain and glen,*
> *Through cane-brake and forest,—the hunting of men?*
> *The lords of our land to this hunting have gone,*
> *As the fox-hunter follows the sound of the horn;*
> *Hark! the cheer and the hallo! the crack of the whip,*
> *And the yell of the hound as he fastens his grip!*
> *All blithe are our hunters, and noble their match,*
> *Though hundreds are caught, there are millions to catch.*

Like Bible verse in a good Protestant home, this kind of writing was meant to be read aloud as an aid to moral reflection. Children had many questions. Who were these mounted men? What prey were they chasing? How could their grisly work be a "noble" adventure?

Garrison himself, who had published Whittier's first poem in 1826 (about an Irish emigrant longing for his native land), tried his hand at child's verse on the premise that the struggle against slavery must begin with young minds "untainted" by the poison of race prejudice. In his *Juvenile Poems, for the Use of Free American Children, of Every Complexion,* also published in 1835, he addressed one of his short poems to a plate of sugarplums:

For the poor slaves have labored, far down in the south,
To make you so sweet, and so nice for my mouth;
But I want no slaves toiling for me in the sun,
Driven on with the whip, till the long day is done.

The point of such writing was to make slavery vivid to the mind's eye—to help readers, especially the young, see the desperate "whip-scarred" runaways until no one could "look upon [slavery] as mere abstraction." Like Whittier, Garrison hoped to evoke images in the minds of his readers, and in his case he supplemented his words with actual pictures:

"*Female Cruelty*" *from Garrison's* Juvenile Poems

Visual representations of slaves and those who hunted them did not stop with book illustrations. They were imprinted on porcelain plates, carved in the handles of silverware, sewn into quilts, embossed on window blinds, so that the mundane activities of daily life—setting the table, making the bed, screening out sunlight by day and darkness by night—would not hide what went on beyond the glass: "runaways hunted with blood-hounds into swamps and hills." The phrase came from Emerson, who caustically remarked, in 1844, that when New Englanders sat down to tea and crumpets, they found that "the sugar is excellent" and "nobody tasted blood" in the treats.

2.

The work of rescuing fugitive slaves from invisibility was becoming a transatlantic literary project. In England, Elizabeth Barrett Browning joined the cause with "The Runaway Slave at Pilgrim's Point," about an enslaved woman who strangles her "too white" child conceived in rape by her master—a poem so dark that the editors of *The Liberty Bell* took two years to ponder it between its submission in 1846 and its publication in 1848.

Meanwhile, in America, the escaped slave was already a stock literary character. In *The Fugitives* (1841), an amateur theatrical performed in the hope that dramatizing the lives of runaways would do more for the cause than lectures or sermons could do, a fugitive mother watches her daughter while she sleeps:

> *How I love to look upon her as she*
> *Breathes so gently:—now she sighs, poor thing!*
> *No doubt her womanish heart is shaken*
> *By sad dreams, the fear that we may never*
> *Reach that stream, which crossed, will give us Freedom.*

In "The Fugitive Slave's Apostrophe to the North Star," written in 1839, the Connecticut poet John Pierpont imagined a plantation slave plotting his escape while hiding from his overseer in a treetop:

> *In the dark top of southern pines*
> *I nestled, when the driver's horn*
> *Called to the field, in lengthening lines,*

My fellows at the break of morn.
And there I lay, till thy sweet face
Looked in upon "my hiding-place."

Then, we are left to imagine, he moved on, looking up to the North Star
to guide him by night.

All these writers were making a good-faith effort to redress the problem, in the words of Wendell Phillips, of having "been left long enough to
gather the character of slaves from the involuntary evidence of the masters." But on the literary evidence, it was not always much preferable to
turn the task over to white writers striving to imagine what they were
writing about. In 1842, John Collins, secretary of the Massachusetts
Anti-slavery Society, made the salient point. "The public," he wrote to
Garrison, "have itching ears to hear a colored man speak, and particularly
a *slave*." In Frederick Douglass they found their man.

Born in 1818 in Talbot County, Maryland, Douglass was owned from
age eight to eighteen by a merchant named Thomas Auld, who had inherited the boy from his father-in-law, Aaron Anthony, who might also have
been Frederick's father by one of his slaves, Harriet Bailey. Young Frederick Bailey (he took the name Douglass years later, from a swashbuckling
character in a poem by Sir Walter Scott) was traded back and forth between the rural household of Thomas and Lucretia Anthony Auld and that
of Thomas's brother Hugh, in Baltimore, where Hugh's wife, Sophia,
instructed the precocious child in the rudiments of reading. Although
Maryland was among the few slave states where teaching literacy to slaves
was not illegal, Hugh put a stop to it on the grounds (in Douglass's recollection) that "if you give a nigger an inch, he will take an ell." By observ-
ing white children at their lessons, the boy continued his education
surreptitiously.

With a reputation for truculence as well as great intelligence, Douglass
was treated sometimes as a family servant, sometimes as an adoptive son,
and sometimes as a piece of equipment to be rented out for cash. In an
incident about which he spoke and wrote often in later life, he fought off
a brutal slave breaker to whom Thomas Auld had sent him and who tried

to beat him for his insolence before retreating in terror from the young man's fury. In 1836, barely eighteen, Douglass joined a plot to flee to the North, but when his co-conspirators lost their nerve, the plan fell apart.

In September 1838, he tried again, and this time he succeeded. Having acquired identification papers from a free black seaman (whether by purchase or as a gift is unclear), he traveled, in sailor's garb, via train, steamboat, and ferry through Delaware and Pennsylvania to New York City, where he was sheltered by members of the Underground Railroad. But New York proved to be only a temporary haven. Even "black people in New York were not to be trusted," he later recalled, and some, "for a few dollars, would betray me into the hands of the slave-catchers."

He stayed just long enough to be married—by James Pennington, also a Maryland runaway, now a Presbyterian minister in Brooklyn—to Anna Murray, a free black woman whom he had known in Baltimore and who had journeyed north to join him. Finding it too dangerous to go "on the wharves to work, or to a boarding-house to board," lest word get out that his capture might yield a handsome reward, he moved with his wife to Massachusetts, where, in the seaport towns of New Bedford and Lynn, he "sawed wood, shoveled coal, dug cellars, moved rubbish . . . , loaded and unloaded vessels, and scoured their cabins."

It was his first taste of self-reliance. But what Douglass found in "the grand old commonwealth of Massachusetts" was more than compensated work. He found his calling. Having begun to "whisper in private, among the white laborers on the wharves . . . the truths which burned in my heart," he ventured, in the spring of 1839, to an antislavery meeting where Garrison spoke, and felt his "heart bounding at every true utterance against the slave system."

Two years later, at the invitation of another member of the abolitionist aristocracy, William C. Coffin, he joined an antislavery gathering on Nantucket, with Garrison again presiding. In the Quaker spirit of that meeting, he rose spontaneously to speak—an event he later described, using the language of religious conversion, as the moment when there "opened upon me a new life—a life for which I had had no preparation." His hearers were stunned by his eloquence. "Urgently solicited to become

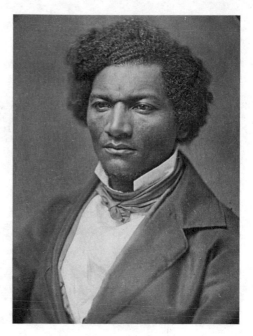

*Frederick Douglass
in 1843*

an agent" of the Massachusetts Anti-slavery Society, he was sent on a
speaking tour through New England, New York, and as far west as Ohio
and Indiana.

One can only imagine what it was like to hear him. As a child in
Maryland, he might have picked up a New England intonation from white
playmates who were being trained in elocution by a tutor from Massachusetts. Now, on the stump in the North, he found that "people doubted if I
had ever been a slave . . . [because] I did not talk like a slave, look like a
slave, nor act like a slave," so his managers advised him to adopt "a little of
the plantation manner of speech." An imposing man with leonine hair, he
had a booming voice and seemed always on the verge of exploding. "Fred
Douglass," according to one acquaintance, "was a tornado in a forest."

Other speakers in demand included Josiah Henson (escaped from
Maryland, in 1830), William Wells Brown* (from Kentucky, in 1834),

---

*Brown had been hired out briefly in St. Louis to the antislavery newspaper editor Elijah Lovejoy, for
whom he worked "mainly in the printing office." After Lovejoy was murdered, Brown wrote of him
that he was "a very good man, and decidedly the best master that I ever had. I am chiefly indebted to
him . . . for what little learning I obtained while in slavery." *Narrative of William W. Brown, a Fugitive*

Henry Bibb (also from Kentucky, in 1842), Ellen and William Craft (from Georgia, in 1848), and Sojourner Truth, born in upstate New York as Isabella Baumfree, who had left her master in 1826 just before New York's emancipation law took effect ("I did not run off, for I thought that wicked, but I walked off, believing that to be all right") to become an itinerant evangelist, first for women's rights, then for abolition. The antislavery meeting—especially in New England and across the evangelized districts of upstate New York—was becoming a secular communion in which the sacramental moment arrives when a flesh-and-blood runaway stands before the congregation as a living crucifix and begins to speak.

3.

But it was one thing for a community to affirm its faith to itself and quite another to attract new converts. If fugitive slaves and their allies were to advance the work, in Bibb's words, of "abolitionizing the free States," they would have to turn some significant portion of northern whites from indifference to commitment.

More daunting still, even if northerners could be warmed to the cause, there could be no final victory over slavery until it was repudiated by its practitioners in the South. Former slaves were thus recruited to campaign for "moral suasion"—the long, slow process of persuading slaveholders, one by one, soul by soul, to repent.

To modern ears, such a strategy will sound hopelessly naive. Anyone who has lived through the second half of the twentieth century is accustomed to thinking first of government—courts, Congress, presidents—as agents of change. Change the law, we want to believe, and hearts and minds will follow. Through the application of federal power, we have indeed witnessed the destruction or at least the modification of social norms that not so long ago seemed intractable—de jure segregation, laws against miscegenation, formal barriers to equal rights for gay people, stigmatization of abortion.

Slave. Written by Himself (Boston, 1847; repr., *Slave Narratives*, ed. William L. Andrews and Henry Louis Gates Jr. [New York: Library of America, 2000]), 383.

But in antebellum America, the case was entirely different. Slavery could not be legislated away by Congress or ruled out of existence by the Supreme Court. The "slavocracy" (the derisive name applied to the southern ruling class by its enemies) held an effective veto in the federal government, and even if northern influence were to grow over Congress, the Court, and the presidency, as Calhoun and others feared, federal jurisdiction over slavery was foreclosed by the Constitution, which guaranteed to the states the right to control their internal institutions.

It was therefore quite possible to hate slavery while believing that the only route to abolition was through the spiritual conversion of those who owned slaves. Despite efforts to censor abolitionist speech and writing, the South could no more seal its borders against incoming words than against outgoing slaves. Writings by and about fugitive slaves were thus deployed in the hope of touching the slave owners' hearts. In this sense, these writings were literary precursors of the televised images broadcast a century later during the civil rights movement—police dogs unleashed on protesters, white adults spitting at black schoolchildren—on the premise that decent people everywhere would recoil from what they saw.

In 1838, the argument for moral suasion was made by Edward Beecher, brother of Harriet Beecher Stowe and friend of the murdered Elijah Lovejoy. Beecher described slavery as an "organic sin," by which he meant a sin that permeates the body politic so completely that it cannot be cured by targeted excision but must be overwhelmed with an infusion of love. He had no illusion about how soon the cure would come. "Organic sins," he wrote, "are the most difficult of all to reform, because before they can be reformed, there must be disseminated through the body politic such an amount of knowledge and moral principle, as shall induce a whole community, or at least a majority of them, to concur in abolishing by law the sinful system." To this end, the words that fugitives spoke on the stage had to be moved to the page. And so one way to trace the growth of the antislavery movement is to follow the rising arc of autobiographical slave narratives published as books—four in the 1820s, nine in the 1830s, twenty-five in the 1840s, thirty-three in the 1850s.

Stories by and about fugitive slaves also appeared in the antislavery press. Early instances included the *Genius of Universal Emancipation*, published briefly first in Tennessee, then, beginning in 1824, for fifteen years in Baltimore by the Quaker Benjamin Lundy, assisted by Garrison, who publicized whippings and lynchings in a column called the "Black List." The first African American newspaper, *Freedom's Journal*, appeared in New York, in 1827, edited by Samuel Cornish, a Delaware-born free black man and founding member of the American Anti-slavery Society, and John Russwurm, born in Jamaica to an enslaved mother and an English father, who supported the American Colonization Society and moved in 1829 to what was to become Liberia. Like all papers in its time, it functioned in part as a news-gathering service for local readers, reprinting articles from other papers and excerpting speeches by public figures on issues of the day, notably the fugitive slave question.

By the 1830s, the antislavery press, led by Garrison's *Liberator* (founded in 1831), was spreading throughout the free states and had even established outposts in the upper South. As the number of papers devoted to the cause rose, violence against them grew apace. In 1835, the *Standard and Democrat*, published at Utica, New York, was attacked by a mob. In 1838, the Philadelphia office of the *Pennsylvania Freeman*, edited by Whittier, was trashed and burned. Upon leaving Philadelphia, Whittier took up the editorship of the *Middlesex Standard*, published at Lowell, Massachusetts, which ran many stories about runaways, including one who stowed away aboard a vessel carrying cotton from Mobile to Providence, until, upon being discovered, he threw himself into the sea.

In 1845, pro-slavery thugs drove the *True American*, edited by Cassius Clay in Lexington, Kentucky, out of the state despite his having fortified the office with a cache of rifles and gunpowder. Before Elijah Lovejoy moved the *Observer* in 1837 from St. Louis to the illusory safety of Alton, Illinois, it had already been attacked three times. When the mob made a fourth assault, it was Lovejoy's death, not the death of the paper, that made the event national news.

In an age when part of an editor's job was to spit vitriol at his competitors, violence—most of it having nothing to do with slavery—was routine. Duels over personal insults were so common that the editors of the *Vicksburg Sentinel* fought four before the Civil War. It was not unusual for aggrieved readers to storm the offices of papers by which they were offended, in order to conduct "censorship by cudgel and horsewhip."

Writing just a step beyond credibility, Mark Twain caught the tone of the times in a sketch (written after the Civil War) of a Tennessee newspaperman who, having shot one of his detractors, leaves a note of advice for his successor before skipping town:

> Jones will be here at three—cowhide him. Gillespie will call earlier, perhaps—throw him out of the window. Ferguson will be along about four—kill him. That is all for today, I believe. If you have any odd time, you may write a blistering article on the police. The cowhides are under the table, weapons in the drawer, ammunition there in the corner, lint and bandages up there in the pigeon-holes. In case of accident, go to Lancet, the surgeon, downstairs. He advertises; we take it out in trade.

Most disputes were petty and local, but it was the abolitionist editors who spread offense quicker and farther than anyone else. Although the *Liberator* was edited and published in Massachusetts, Garrison was indicted for "felonious acts" as far away as North Carolina. In South Carolina, rewards were posted for the arrest of anyone distributing his paper.

Among the regular features of antislavery papers were stories of fugitives living in the North under threat of recapture. The *African Observer*, published in Philadelphia (1827–1828), called attention to protections that had been furnished to fugitives in the ancient world by the Mosaic law, pointing out that the Israelites "themselves were fugitive slaves (Exodus, 14:5)." Published in New York from 1833 to 1834, the *American Antislavery Reporter* devoted a pages-long "Chronicle of Kidnappings in New York" to former slaves who, having lived peacefully in the city for years, were seized and thrown into "cells about 7 feet by 3½ with no light but that which straggles through a grating in the door" before being returned to their states of origin, where they were beaten until they named other runaways after whom slave catchers could be dispatched.

The antislavery press also publicized incidents in which blacks who had never been enslaved were seized by kidnappers on the pretext that they were runaways. These papers included the *Mirror of Liberty,* edited by David Ruggles, leader of the New York City Vigilance Committee, which tried to disrupt abduction attempts by hired thugs who did not much care if they seized a confirmed fugitive or any black person suitable for sale in the slave market back home. Also in New York, the *National Anti-slavery Standard* ran regular notices about slave escapes throughout the country while remaining prudently reticent about the local network— just then coming to be known as the Underground Railroad—that was helping them travel farther north to New England or Canada. In Boston, Garrison's *Liberator* continued publication all the way until the Civil War, running more than two hundred narrative sketches of slave escapes over three decades.

One often hears it said that among the dark novelties of our own time is our easy recourse via some favorite website, or TV news network, or radio talk show to an "echo chamber" where there is nothing to hear but amplified validations of what we already believe. In fact, the case in antebellum America was not so different. There was no such concept as journalistic "balance." Newspapers did not run Op-Eds with alternative points of view. With rare exceptions such as James Gordon Bennett's *New York Herald*—which, like Page Six of today's *New York Post,* dispensed gossip and slander with little regard for the political allegiance of its targets— virtually every paper was, first and last, a party organ.

The same array of party alignments was evident among the more intellectually ambitious periodicals. The moderate pro-slavery position—held by people who considered slavery beneficial for both races but who were willing to acknowledge its susceptibility to abuse—could be found in the *Southern Quarterly Review,* edited in Charleston by a transplanted New Englander. For those convinced of the natural justice of slavery, the journal of choice was *DeBow's Review,* published in New Orleans, which gave strident voice to the Calhoun wing of the Democratic Party.

Conservative northerners who disapproved privately of slavery but refrained from denouncing it publicly for fear of disturbing the delicate balance between North and South could subscribe to the *North American Review*. For intellectuals outraged by slavery but with no practical plan for terminating it, there was the *Dial*, edited by Margaret Fuller, who, in the summer of 1843, declared that "freedom and equality have been proclaimed" in the United States "only to leave room for a monstrous display of slave dealing and slave keeping."

4.

For anyone anywhere on the spectrum of antislavery opinion, the first challenge was to refute the idea that slavery was a benevolent institution. Hard as it may be for us to fathom, decades after the Revolution, in a republic founded in the name of human rights, there was no consensus that slavery was outrageous or even anomalous. Speaking in Congress in 1820, Senator Nathaniel Macon of North Carolina made the amiable suggestion that all doubts about its benignity could be dispelled if only his northern colleagues "would go home with me, or some other southern member, and witness the meeting between the slaves and the owner, and see the glad faces and the hearty shaking of hands."

Through the 1830s, this kind of treacle was avidly consumed, promoted in such pastoral idylls as *Swallow Barn*, a bestselling book about plantation life by the Maryland Whig John Pendleton Kennedy, published in Philadelphia in 1832. Kennedy, who eventually came to favor compensated emancipation, portrayed the South—at least the upper South—as populated by carefree slave boys whose "predominant love of sunshine" keeps them outside until after dark, always playing, never working, eager for visits from their kindly master, whom they hail "with pleasure" whenever he drops by "to add to their comforts or relieve their wants." The same picturesque fantasy persisted to and beyond *Gone with the Wind* (1936), and no doubt lingers today in the minds of people unwilling to admit that they still believe it.

So when former slaves stepped forward to dispute it in person, or in

The Interesting Narrative of the Life of Olaudah Equiano, *published in
London in 1789 and reprinted thirty-six times before 1850, bore a
frontispiece showing the author holding the Bible open to the book of Acts
(chapter 4, verse 12): "Neither is there salvation in any other, for there is none
other name under heaven given among men whereby we must be saved."*

newspapers, periodicals, or books, they were challenging a deeply entrenched myth. In this respect, they were following in the footsteps of
British abolitionists who, over the course of the eighteenth century, had
sponsored memoirs by former slaves in an effort to convince the nation
that enslaved Africans were capable of becoming good English Christians. It was in England that the slave narrative as we now recognize it
first took form.

When the genre moved to America, it remained generally true that
"the slavery of sin received much more condemnation than the sin of slavery." In his 1825 memoir, Solomon Bayley, a slave born in Delaware who
managed to buy freedom for himself, his wife, and his children, opened
his narrative with this confession of faith:

Having lived some months in continual expectation of death, I have felt uneasy in mind about leaving the world, without leaving behind me some account of the kindness and mercy of God towards me. But when I go to tell of his favours, I am struck with wonder at the exceeding riches of his grace. O! that all people would come to admire him for his goodness, and declare his wonders which he doth for the children of men. The Lord tried to teach me his fear when I was a little boy; but I delighted in vanity and foolishness, and went astray. But the Lord found out a way to overcome me, and to cause me to desire his favour, and his great help; and although I thought no one could be more unworthy of his favour, yet he did look on me, and pitied me in my great distress.

Although recent precedents for this kind of writing could be found in eighteenth-century Britain, its roots reached much further back through the long history of Christian confession all the way to such tracts as Thomas à Kempis's *Imitatio Christi* (1427), which called sinners to emulate Christ in penitent humility, and John Foxe's *Acts and Monuments* (1559) (better known as Foxe's *Book of Martyrs*), which recounted the sufferings of believers for whom the price of fidelity was pain and death. Virtually all early American slave narrators prescribed to their readers a strong dose of Christian piety, with only a few declining to fill the prescription for themselves.

One notable dissenter was William Grimes, who, in his *Life of William Grimes, the Runaway Slave, Written by Himself* (1825)—a book little read in its own time, and still too little known in our own—was as tough on his fellow slaves as he was on his masters. The book seems to have been the unassisted work of Grimes himself, whose sentences no editor would have left unrevised because of both what he said and how he said it. "I have been so hungry for meat," he wrote, "that I could have eat my mother."

From his time in Virginia, he recalled how another slave fouled their master's morning coffee by mixing the grinds with bitter herbs in order to get Grimes—also assigned to kitchen work—blamed and banished to the fields, thereby opening up a house position for her own son. From his time in Georgia, he recalled the "witch" who shared his sleeping space located directly below their master's. She would "ride" him (he claims she visited his bed only in dreams she sent to him as spells in the night), forcing from him involuntary "noise like one apparently choking or strangling" until his master is provoked to wrath—whether out of disgust, or irritation at being awakened, or jealousy over what was going on in the bed beneath him, he does not say.

Grimes ended his slave career in the possession of a Savannah merchant who, while on holiday with his family in his native Bermuda, allowed him to earn what he could on the wharves and, except for three dollars a week to be collected upon his master's return, to keep his wages. During those months of quasi-freedom, he was befriended by sailors who took him aboard the brig *Casket*, where he created a hiding place by cutting a hole within a group of cotton bales that had been lashed together. Having supplied himself with survival provisions—"bread, water, dried beef"—he was confined in this puffy pocket except for nighttime forays onto the open deck until the ship made landfall at Staten Island, whence he made his way to New Haven, Connecticut.

There Grimes embarked on a new life that turned out to be barely better than the life he had left behind. Yale students, pretending to befriend him, plied him with drink in order to amuse themselves with his slurring and stumbling until, his dignity destroyed, he "took the floor and lay there speechless some hours."* This was a far cry from the standard tale of deliverance to "northern regions, / Where smiles all that is glorious, aye, all / That is beautiful." As Grimes's modern editor remarks, "The more he reveals about his life in the North, the more ironically pointless his flight to freedom seems." His was an early and fearless account of how limited "freedom" in the North could be.

---

*As historian Craig Steven Wilder points out, "college boys felt particularly entitled to terrorize slaves and servants" and enjoyed such diversions as watching a black man "smash his head with wooden boards and barrels." See his *Ebony and Ivy: Race, Slavery, and the Troubled History of America's Universities* (New York: Bloomsbury, 2013), 142.

5.

But Grimes, in his candor, was exceptional. By the 1830s, the slave narrative—factual, fictional, or a hybrid of both—was settling into the formula that would define it for decades to come: a pilgrimage story of rising from darkness to light. Most of Grimes's contemporaries stuck faithfully to the script of what has been called the "liberty plot," describing the gauntlet of horrors they had been forced to endure—beatings, broken promises, separation of parents from children, enforced illiteracy, sexual abuse—always careful to expunge any trace of bitterness at what had been done to them. Writing in 1837, Moses Roper (whose memoir went through ten editions in twenty years) explained, "I bear no enmity even to the slave-holders but regret their delusions." In the 1849 book that helped to inspire Harriet Beecher Stowe to write *Uncle Tom's Cabin,* Josiah Henson writes that upon learning that he was to be sold to a New Orleans buyer, he was tempted to kill his master's son before conscience checked his rage and subdued it into Christian forgiveness. The slave's self-restraint became a sentimental convention, reaching its apotheosis in the fictional figure of Uncle Tom.

Every teller of a chase-and-escape story knows that all but the most heartless reader will root, at least half-consciously, for the prey to get away. So it was with the slave narratives. They tapped into that place in the human psyche from which dreams arise of being stalked to the verge of disaster—toward the edge of a precipice, into the jaws of some ravenous animal or the clutches of some human brute—just before we wake to the delicious relief of knowing it was all a dream. We want the pursuers to take a wrong turn, to blow a tire, to run out of gas. Think of the harrowing manhunt in Richard Wright's novel *Native Son* as police close in on a black teen who has strangled a white girl in a moment of panic, or Fritz Lang's film *M,* about a frenzied hunt for a child killer, or any number of films by Alfred Hitchcock (*North by Northwest; The Wrong Man; Frenzy*), in which the fugitive's guilt or innocence has little bearing on our allegiance. Whether by luck, or guts, or God's favor, we want the pursued to get away no matter what set him to running in the first place.

But if runaways had an intrinsic advantage in telling their stories, it was quite another matter to convince the public that they were telling the truth. Most southerners and not a few northerners suspected that the relation between sponsor and fugitive was a form of puppetry. Virtually every published work by a black antebellum writer was a collaboration with a white editor. When Douglass took his story into print in 1845, he had been reciting it at public meetings for the better part of four years, during which he was coached as if he were a novice courtroom witness. "'Tell your story, Frederick,' would whisper my revered friend Garrison," he wrote late in life, investing that word "revered" with something like a sneer. Garrison's deputy John Collins chimed in with this piece of patronizing advice: "Give us the facts, we will take care of the philosophy." Yet when the spontaneity of speech gave way to the fixity of print, the facts themselves came into dispute.

Not all slave narratives were edited by committed abolitionists. David Wilson, the lawyer who helped Solomon Northup write *Twelve Years a Slave* (1853), seems to have been more interested in making money than in advancing the cause. Samuel Eliot, who worked on the first edition of Josiah Henson's 1849 narrative, entered Congress the following year and promptly voted in favor of the fugitive slave law. But regardless of the political allegiance of the editor, it was obvious that most memoirs by fugitive slaves had been to one degree or another sanitized. For one thing, they were reticent about the fact that slave catchers could get assistance from other slaves swayed by threats of reprisal if they refused to help, or by hope for a reward, or by a grudge against the escapee.

And if the substance of the narratives was trimmed and shaped by their editors, so was their style. Most had a formality that brought the first-person voice into conformity with prevailing norms of literary diction. They alluded to writers unlikely to be known to someone who had struggled to gain literacy (Henson did not learn to read until the age of forty-two) and employed phrases that echo or anticipate other works by the same editor. They lacked the unrehearsed immediacy of oral histories like that of one runaway who, in an interview with William Still, leader of the Philadelphia Vigilance Committee, described his master as "a *speckled-faced—pretty large stomach man,* but . . . not very abuseful." This sort of freewheeling language was rare in the published narratives, which tended to have a certain forced propriety as if a friendly censor had cleaned up the infelicities and gaffes. When Lydia Maria Child, who guided Harriet Jacobs's *Incidents in the Life of a Slave Girl* (1861) into print, assured readers that "with trifling exceptions both the ideas and the language" were the author's own, the claim itself seemed a trifle defensive.

One text that seemed especially dubious was the *Narrative of James Williams,* published by the American Anti-slavery Society in March 1838 with a preface by Whittier. As lurid as anything in Quentin Tarantino's film *Django Unchained* (2012), the book described the Alabama from which Williams escaped as a bloodbath world in which fugitives are tracked and torn by vicious dogs. After finishing their murderous work, the proud hounds trot back, "jaws, heads, and feet" dripping red, eager to lead their handlers to what's left of the prey, whose "entrails [are] clinging to the old and broken cane" through which the victim has made his frantic run.

It turned out that Williams had changed locations and names (including his own), conflated places and dates, and laced his story with exaggerations and outright fabrications. It was all done, no doubt, from a mix of motives: to please his interviewers, to protect himself from slave owners' agents posing as Underground Railroad conductors (a common practice), and, perhaps, to achieve renown that could be translated into money. Southerners, led by J. B. Rittenhouse, editor of the Birmingham *Alabama Beacon,* leaped to attack the book with alliterative fury as a "foul fester of falsehood." In October 1838, seven months after it had been published, the American Anti-slavery Society disavowed it.

We now know that despite his embellishments and use of false names, most of what Williams wrote was substantially true. Like all fugitives, once he arrived in the North, he had every reason to be anxious, bewildered, and uncertain of whom to trust. He was held in semi-voluntary detention in a New York City safe house, where he was interrogated by a trio of antislavery luminaries—Whittier, the Boston Unitarian Charles Follen, and James Birney, a former Alabama slaveholder who had left the South to become an outspoken abolitionist in the North. His hosts—sometimes they must have seemed to him not so different from captors—checked and rechecked his stories against maps, against the letter of introduction sent ahead of his arrival by the Underground Railroad conductor who had sheltered him near Philadelphia, and against Birney's personal knowledge of the terrain over which Williams claimed to have fled.

Even when news arrived that slave catchers were on their way, accompanied by a black man who could identify him, the interrogation continued—giving him every reason to tell his questioners what they wanted to hear. As Renata Adler has remarked about refugees fleeing today's Middle East, "questions of identity, national origin, even date of birth" are bound to provoke "an instinct, perhaps common to all refugees from dangerous situations, to lie." Fugitives have always had reason to fear that telling the truth and nothing but the truth raises their risk of deportation.

6.

It was Douglass who broke through to a new level of public trust. With prefaces by Garrison and Phillips, his *Narrative of the Life of Frederick Douglass, an American Slave, Written by Himself,* was published by the American Anti-slavery Society in 1845. At first, its veracity, too, was questioned, notably by a neighbor of Thomas Auld's, A. C. C. Thompson (short for his rather ungainly full name, Absalom Christopher Columbus Americus Vespucius Thompson), who, in a letter to the *Delaware Republican,* denounced Douglass's book as a pack of lies.

In fact, by defending the honor of principal figures in Douglass's *Narrative* while confirming their identities, Thompson unwittingly enhanced its credibility, for which Douglass thanked him in the *Liberator.** "You, sir," Douglass wrote, "have relieved me. I now stand before both the American and British public, endorsed by you as being just what I have

---

*Ironically, Thompson's letter, intended to challenge Douglass's credibility, was reprinted in Garrison's *Liberator* with the editorial conclusion that "this attempt to invalidate the Narrative of Frederick Douglass, only confirms its correctness, as Mr. Thompson admits every thing but the cruelty described by Douglass—and on that point the latter speaks from experience and knowledge." *Liberator,* Dec. 12, 1845, 1. Douglass's note of mock appreciation appeared a little more than two months later, on Feb. 27, 1846.

represented myself to be—to wit, an *American slave. . . .* You thus brush away the miserable insinuations of my Northern pro-slavery enemies, that I have used fictitious, not real names." Meanwhile, the book was commended by, among others, Margaret Fuller, who praised it in Horace Greeley's *New-York Tribune* in June 1845, and within five years it had sold some thirty thousand copies, making its author nationally and internationally famous.

But fame, for a fugitive slave, was a dangerous thing. It made him an enticing target for slave catchers. Still legally the property of a Maryland slave owner, Douglass accepted advice from friends that he seek "refuge in monarchical England from the dangers of republican slavery." In Britain, he found himself still more in demand, and discovering that "it is quite an advantage to be a 'nigger' here," he promised, with due mordancy, that lest he not be "black enough for the british taste," he would keep his "hair as wooly as possible."

Going abroad did not close the gap between what his audiences wanted and what he wanted to give them. "Accounts of floggings," as his biographer William McFeely has remarked, were among "the most sought-after forms of nineteenth-century pornography (disguised in the plain wrapper of a call to virtuous antislavery action)." Douglass recoiled from this kind of prurience but nevertheless took advantage of it. "I do not wish to dwell at length upon . . . the physical evils of slavery," he said. "I will not dwell at length upon these cruelties"—yet he never stopped speaking and writing of "the whip, the chain, the gag, the thumb-screw, the blood-hound, the stocks, and all the other bloody paraphernalia of the slave system."

As his fame grew, he became less a scripted witness and more his own man—a man to whom antislavery activists and, eventually, mainstream politicians turned for advice and for the sheer prestige of his affiliation. In the enlarged version of his memoir published in 1855 as *My Bondage and My Freedom,* he wrote, "It was slavery, not its mere incidents—that I hated." There was, of course, nothing "mere" about the physical abuses he had witnessed and endured, but he bristled at being regarded as a freak survivor whose intellect was doubted even by those who swooned at his afflictions.

In November 1846, while Douglass was in Britain, Thomas Auld sold him in absentia, for unclear reasons, to his brother Hugh for $100. Within a month, Hugh accepted an offer of 150 pounds sterling (more than $1,000 in nineteenth-century dollars) from Douglass's English friends, who had raised the funds to buy his freedom. In December 1846, Auld filed a deed of manumission in the Baltimore County courthouse. In an early sign of the tension with Garrison that would soon become estrangement, Douglass discovered upon his return to the United States that some of his "uncompromising antislavery friends" disapproved of his having allowed his liberty to be paid for, thereby, they thought, consenting to have his freedom bought as if it were a house or a horse rather than the stolen birthright of a man.

Publication of the *Narrative* made Frederick Douglass, as one scholar writes with stinging accuracy, "the most famous black exhibit of the nineteenth century." Whenever he appeared on a speakers program, crowds poured out to hear him, including large numbers of women, at whom he took special aim. Beginning his book with the piteous confession that he could barely remember his own mother, he told how she was forced to live miles away, traveling on foot by night to visit her child under threat of flogging if she should fail to return to work in the fields by sunrise. "I do not recollect of ever seeing my mother by the light of day. She was with me in the night. She would lie down with me, and get me to sleep, but long before I waked she was gone."

Here was a version of what the literary scholar Northrop Frye has called the "theme of the hunted mother." A figure in Western literature from medieval romance to the nineteenth-century novel, she appears in one form or another in almost all the slave narratives, reaching her American apotheosis in *Uncle Tom's Cabin* when Eliza flees the slave catchers with her child clasped to her breast. Hers is the story of Anna's failed suicide as told by Jesse Torrey in 1817. Twenty years later, she appears in the diary of John Quincy Adams, who describes the anguish of Dorcas Allen, awaiting sale in a slave pen in Alexandria, who killed two of her four children because "if they had lived she did not know what would become of them." We meet her again in Margaret Garner (the model for

Sethe in Toni Morrison's novel *Beloved*), who, in 1856, cut the throat of her daughter as slave catchers closed in on them.

Douglass's treatment of the theme was both heartfelt and deft. "Never having enjoyed . . . her soothing presence," he writes of his own mother, "I received the tidings of her death with much the same emotions I should have probably felt at the death of a stranger." The message was clear. Slavery robs mothers of their motherhood and thereby stunts the souls of their sons. It turns motherless black boys into heartless black men. Beware of the dark millions headed toward manhood: they will grow into potency with no sense of empathy or love. Slavery is a factory for manufacturing monsters. For your own sake, Dear Reader, you had better curtail production!

But if Douglass portrayed himself as a force to be feared, he was also shrewdly pacifying. He told his life as a quintessentially American boy-makes-good story—an inspirational tale of beating the odds, of rising from low circumstances to high station. Even as he recalled such radicals as David Walker—who, in his *Appeal to the Coloured Citizens of the World* (1829), had urged slaves to rise up against their masters—he wrapped himself in the mantle of revered patriots like Ben Franklin, who, in his own memoir, had recounted his life as a journey from servitude to independence. "In coming to a fixed determination to run away," Douglass declared, "we did more than Patrick Henry, when he resolved upon liberty or death." I'm not looking for vengeance, he seems to say, but—just like you, my fellow Americans—I'm looking for opportunity. No work is too low for me as long as it is paid work. "I found employment, the third day after my arrival" in New Bedford,

> in stowing a sloop with a load of oil. It was new, dirty, and hard work for me; but I went at it with a glad heart and a willing hand. I was now my own master. It was a happy moment, the rapture of which can be understood only by those who have been slaves.

Douglass played with the fire of fear, but his message was ultimately palliative: white people will have less reason to fear black people if slavery is abolished than if it is perpetuated. And like so many of his predecessors, he cast his story as a "glorious resurrection . . . from the tomb of slavery, to the heaven of freedom." In all these respects, he presented himself, as his friend James McCune Smith remarked, as a "Representative American man—a type of his countrymen."

7.

In 1845, the same year that saw the publication of Douglass's memoir, the antislavery clergyman Theodore Parker, who had been reading slave narratives as they rolled off the presses, declared them "the one portion of our permanent literature . . . which is wholly indigenous and original." America's distinctive institution, slavery, had at last inspired a distinctively American literary form.

Parker was writing at a time when American writers were defensively sensitive to the charge that even their best efforts were weak imitations of British models. It was a time, as Melville complained, of "literary flunkeyism towards England." In this sense, Parker was right that the slave narrators were stepping into a literary void.

There was another sense, too, in which he was right—and shockingly so. Most of the white antebellum writers who have since achieved the status of classics—Hawthorne, Poe, Dickinson, Emerson, and Whitman (until the 1850s)—were amazingly adept at averting their eyes from what Theodore Weld, in a compendium of damning facts published in 1839, called *American Slavery as It Is*. One must strain to find a single line referring to slavery in all of Dickinson's poetry. When Whitman wrote about slavery, he treated it essentially as a white man's problem. Hawthorne reacted to it as if, catching a whiff of some unpleasant odor while out on a stroll, he pauses for a clearing breeze before proceeding on his way. Slavery, to his mind, was "one of those evils which divine Providence does not leave to be remedied by human contrivances, but which, in its own good time, by some means impossible to be anticipated, but of the simplest and easiest operation, when all its uses shall have been fulfilled, it causes to vanish like a dream." There is a long, straight line between this genial call for patience in 1862 and Martin Luther King's great speech of 1965 delivered after marching from Selma to Montgomery, Alabama, in which he asks white America, "How long . . . ? How long?"

Writing contemporaneously with King, one literary scholar called it "the shame of American literature" that "our authors of the 1830s and 1840s kept silent during the rising storm of debate on the slavery issue." He, too, was right. Anyone hoping to learn about antebellum America by reading America's classic white authors must read very closely to notice that slavery existed at all. In Hawthorne's fiction, the closest thing to a black person was an edible treat displayed in a shopwindow: a gingerbread cookie in the shape of Jim Crow.

Among the major antebellum white writers, only Melville acknowledged the scope and horror of slavery, and even he wrote of it obliquely. In *Moby-Dick* (1851), after a boat pursuing a harpooned whale abandons the chase in order to pluck from the sea the black cabin boy, Pip, who has fallen overboard, he is warned that he won't be rescued a second time, because "a whale would sell for thirty times what you would, Pip, in Alabama."* Not until his 1855 novella, *Benito Cereno*, about a shipboard slave revolt, did Melville confront slavery directly, and then he did so with exceptional literary tact—refusing to presume that he could write from within the unknowable experience of a black African shipped to his doom. So he tells the story from the naive point of view of a white seaman and leaves the ringleader of the insurrection "voiceless" to the end.

In giving voice to people long silenced, the fugitive slave narratives were therefore exactly what Parker said they were: "wholly indigenous and original." They did, moreover, what literature rarely does: they moved public opinion. At the very least, they made it more difficult to browse through the runaway newspaper ads without recognizing them for what

---

*Moby-Dick, chap. 93. In his 1849 novel, *Redburn*, the narrator gazes at the Liverpool monument to Lord Nelson with its four figures (meant to represent "Nelson's principal victories") cowering at the admiral's feet and is "involuntarily reminded of four African slaves in the marketplace." Melville also addressed slavery in his collection of Civil War poems, *Battle-Pieces*, published in 1866, notably in "Formerly a Slave," a response to a portrait of an emancipated woman by the painter Elihu Vedder in which Melville saw the sorrow of "too late deliverance" but hope for "her children's children," who shall know "the good withheld from her."

they were: "an ever-rolling, self-generating flood of evidence, which damned the slave owners out of their own mouths."

It should not be surprising that these books have lost the urgency they had for antebellum readers. They were written at a time of emergency. Today they are history books. When they were written, they were constrained within the seemly norms of nineteenth-century expression. Today they must compete with such films as Tarantino's *Django,* or Steve McQueen's adaptation of Solomon Northup's *Twelve Years a Slave,* in which we see every gash in glistening color and hear every smack of the lash in Dolby sound. When they were first published, they were weapons in a war just begun. Today they belong to a vast literature devoted to every aspect of the slave system—proof, in one sense, of how far we have come, but evidence, too, of the impassable gulf between antebellum readers whom they shocked by revealing a hidden world and current readers, for whom they are archival records of a world long gone. Consigned to college reading lists, the slave narratives, which were once urgent calls to action, now furnish occasions for competitive grieving in the safety of retrospect.

Perhaps the sense in which they remain most alive is in their capacity for literary provocation. Twain's great novel *The Adventures of Huckleberry Finn* (1884) is in large part the story of a fugitive slave, Jim, fleeing in the company of a white boy conflicted over whether to protect or betray him. Writers today continue to turn to the slave narratives—some in a spirit of somber emulation (Toni Morrison, *Beloved* [1987]), others with inventive exuberance (Charles Johnson, *Oxherding Tale* [1982], Colson Whitehead, *The Underground Railroad* [2016]). Consider, among the latter, James McBride's rollicking novel *The Good Lord Bird* (2013), in which Douglass is a randy badass who can't keep his hands off a fugitive slave boy posing—apparently convincingly—as a girl in order to elude the slave catchers. Fooled by the cross-dressing boy (Henry now calls himself Henrietta), the great man sidles up to him, commencing a slow grope while whispering, "My friends call me Fred," then rising into a speech in which seduction takes the guise of instruction:

They know not you, Henrietta. They know you as property. They know not the spirit inside you that gives you your humanity. They care not about the pounding of your silent and lustful heart, thirsting for freedom; your carnal nature, craving the wide, open spaces that they have procured for themselves. You're but chattel to them, stolen property, to be squeezed, used, savaged, and occupied.

Now the boy starts to worry:

Well, all that tinkering and squeezing and savaging made me right nervous, 'specially since he was doing it his own self, squeezing and savaging my arse, working his hand down toward my mechanicals as he spoke the last, with his eyes all dewy, so I hopped to my feet.

This kind of writing defies the dictates of martyrology by which the antebellum slave narratives were controlled and confined. Perhaps the fact that a black writer today can write about a black icon like Douglass with such jaunty irreverence is a sign that we are finally getting past the squeamish pieties that are another form of the condescension he faced, from allies as well as enemies, in his own time.

The Douglass of the memoirs is a paragon. There is little trace in him of the man who must sometimes have been petty, impulsive, and vain—not a piece of property to be utilized in one way or another but, as one putative friend complained, a "haughty" and "self-possessed" man with the low as well as exalted desires that constitute freedom. To pretend otherwise is to treat him once again as less than human.

Surely, then, there are grounds for dissent from Parker's judgment that the slave narratives marked the first maturity of America's literature. No one can doubt the power with which they testified against the inhuman institution. But no one can say that they dove deep into the contradictions of the human heart. They were truncated stories of impossibly virtuous victims. They were more than propaganda but less than literature. They were populated by stock types—the decent but weak master, the jealous

Runaway
advertisement,
1857

Jan. 9th   HEDRICK & RYAN.

NOTICE.

FIFTY DOLLARS REWARD will be paid by the subscriber, for the apprehension and delivery to me, or confinement in any jail in the State, so that I can get her again, of my servant HANNAH. Said Hannah is a bright mulatto, very likely, and is about twenty years old. She is about the common height, stout built, and weighs about 130 pounds; has small flat feet, and a small scar near the centr of her forehead—no other particular marks or scars recollected. Said girl was raised near Smithville, by Robert McKackan, and has many acquaintances in that vicinity and on Federal Point; she has also acquaintances in Wilmington, and may try to get there and thence to a free State.

Jan 31—124-4t-23-tf.   DAVID GILBERT.

COFFEE! COFFEE!!

mistress, the self-hating house slave, the vicious overseer (forerunner of Simon Legree) who knows that he stands in the social hierarchy barely above the slaves he despises. As one sympathetic critic has said, they "rather breathlessly review the subject's life from a single unchanged perspective, that of a condition known as Freedom."

In fact, they tend to stop with the attainment of freedom, before human problems—love unrequited, desire thwarted or sated, fear of oneself as well as of others—begin. In this sense they were not so far from the stock newspaper images they were meant to refute, brilliantly echoed by Kara Walker in her featureless silhouettes:

Alabama Loyalists
Greeting the Federal
Gun-Boats, *Kara Walker,*
2005

Of course there were exceptions. In William Wells Brown's memoir, we encounter his shame at colluding with slave dealers when, compelled to prepare older men for sale, he shaves them and applies boot black to their graying stubble in order to make prospective buyers think they are younger than they really are. Brown, who cautioned that "slavery can never be represented," found ways to convey the pitiless indignity to which it subjected all who came within its reach:

> I was ordered to have the old men's whiskers shaved off, and the grey hairs plucked out, where they were not too numerous, in which case [the slave owner] had a preparation of blacking to color it, and with a blacking-brush we would put it on. . . . After going through the blacking process, they looked ten or fifteen years younger; and I am sure that some of those who purchased slaves . . . were dreadfully cheated, especially in the ages of the slaves which they bought.

In Solomon Northup's *Twelve Years a Slave,* there is a heartrending account of his master ordering him to whip a slave girl for whom the master feels a toxic combination of rage and lust:

> Turning to me, he ordered four stakes to be driven into the ground, pointing with the toe of his boot to the places where he wanted them. When the stakes were driven down, he ordered her to be stripped of every article of dress. Ropes were then brought, and the naked girl was laid upon her face, her wrists and feet each tied firmly to a stake. Stepping to the piazza, he took down a heavy whip, and placing it in my hands, commanded me to lash her.

After endangering himself by hesitating, Northup lays into her with what seems a good imitation of his master's zeal, forcing us beyond the position of a spectator watching cruelties that we cannot imagine perpetrating or suffering, into wondering how we would behave—surely, we know the ugly answer—if compelled to choose between doing the master's bidding and diverting the master's wrath to ourselves.

Such moments, foreign yet familiar, are literary moments because, as much as they are about the men and women who wrote them, they are also about us.

Seven

INTO THE COURTS

1.

In 1849, inspired by Henry Bibb's memoir, the mathematician and militant abolitionist Elizur Wright predicted that "this fugitive slave literature is destined to be a powerful lever . . . an infallible means of abolitionizing the free states." The reason, he wrote, is that unlike speeches and even sermons, the "narratives of slaves go right to the hearts of men." If only one could "put a dozen copies of this book into every school district or neighborhood in the Free States," stories like Bibb's would "sweep the whole north on a thorough going Liberty Platform for abolishing slavery, everywhere and every how."

Whatever their differences in tone or style, all the slave narratives of the 1830s and 1840s had a common purpose: to arouse sympathy for runaways and revulsion at the horrors from which they fled. They were written in impassioned language intended to make them painful and thrilling to read.

But in those same years, the dispute over slavery was proceeding on a parallel track in an entirely different kind of language—the dispassionate language of the law. "In the warm halls of the heart," Herman Melville was soon to write, "memory's spark" can "enkindle such a blaze of evidence, that all the corners of conviction are as suddenly lighted up as a midnight city by a burning building." But "in the cold courts of justice" there are only "oaths" and "proofs."

Every judge in every court had sworn an oath to uphold the Constitution. This was not an oath that could be selectively applied. "You know full well," as Supreme Court justice Joseph Story wrote to a friend in 1842, "that I have ever been opposed to slavery. But I take my standard of duty *as a Judge* from the Constitution." However repugnant he might find slavery and the props that supported it, he had sworn fidelity to Article 4, Section 2, Clause 3 of the Constitution as much as to any of its other provisions. The "object" of that clause, as Story put it, "was to secure to the citizens of the slave-holding states the complete right and title of ownership in their slaves, in every state of the Union, into which they might escape."*

As for the proofs, the Constitution was mute. And so it was up to Congress to determine which proofs would count. Congress had tried to meet this challenge by stipulating in the fugitive slave law of 1793 that an affidavit or oral testimony "taken before and certified by a magistrate" of the state to which a runaway had escaped was proof enough to send him back. Presented with such evidence, any judge charged with deciding the fate of any accused fugitive was expected, as today's idiom would have it, to check his personal beliefs at the courthouse door.

Most did their best to do so. In an 1834 trial of a slave whose Louisiana mistress had tracked him to New York, Judge Samuel Nelson of the New York Supreme Court turned his courtroom into a classroom for instructing the public about what the Constitution said about runaways, and why:

> At the adoption of the constitution, a small minority of the states had abolished slavery within their limits. . . . It was natural for [the southern] portion of the Union to fear that the latter states might, under the influence of this unhappy and exciting subject, be tempted to adopt a course of legislation that would embarrass the owners pursuing their fugitive slaves, if not discharge them from service, and invite escape by affording a place of refuge.

After concluding this history lesson, Nelson denied a writ of *homine replegiando* (personal replevin), which would have granted the defendant

---

*As early as 1819, Story expressed revulsion at the hypocrisy of "boast[ing] of our noble struggle against the encroachments of tyranny [while] there are men among us who think it no wrong to condemn the shivering negro to perpetual slavery." *Life and Letters of Joseph Story,* ed. William W. Story (Boston: Little, Brown, 1851), 1:340.

trial by jury, and ordered him into the custody of the Louisiana woman so she could take him back. "The right of the owner," Judge Nelson said, "to reclaim the fugitive in the state to which he fled has been yielded up to him by the states," and "it cannot be doubted, that under the provision of the constitution and laws, the right to this species of service is protected without regard to the residence of the owner."

In a fugitive slave case ten years later, Judge Nathaniel Read of the Ohio Supreme Court distinguished, to the same effect, between the higher law of nature and the positive law of the land:

> It being my duty to declare the law, not to make it, the question is not, what conforms to the great principles of natural right and universal freedom—but what do the positive law and institutions which we, as members of the government under which we live, are bound to recognize and obey, command and direct.

The Constitution, as Frederick Douglass put the matter, was a "living, breathing fact, exerting a mighty power over the nation of which it is the bond of Union." For anyone who wondered just how mighty, Article 6, the so-called supremacy clause, spelled out the answer:

> This Constitution, and the laws of the United States which shall be made in pursuance thereof . . . shall be the supreme law of the land; and the judges in every state shall be bound thereby, anything in the Constitution or laws of any State to the contrary notwithstanding.*

These words would seem to have settled the matter once and for all: failure to return a fugitive upon presentation of due evidence of ownership was a violation of the slave owner's constitutional rights. By swearing loyalty to the Constitution, every judge in every court had sworn to send the runaways back.

---

*An earlier version of the supremacy principle had appeared in Article 13 of the Articles of Confederation: "Every state shall abide by the determination of the United States in Congress Assembled, on all questions which by this confederation are submitted to them."

2.

To the extent that they were committed to working within the law, anti-slavery activists were therefore left with two options: obey the Constitution or alter it. But Article 5 set out a daunting process for making even the slightest change: an amendment must be proposed by a two-thirds majority of both houses of Congress (or by a convention called by two-thirds of the state legislatures) and then ratified by three-quarters of the states. Given the intransigence of the slave states on the fugitive slave question, this was plainly impossible. Writing in 1832, William Lloyd Garrison offered his view of a Constitution that not only protected slavery but, by blocking its own revision, protected itself:

> A sacred compact, forsooth! . . . It was a compact formed at the sacrifice of the bodies and souls of millions of our race, for the sake of achieving a political object—an unblushing and monstrous coalition to do evil that good might come. Such a compact was, in the nature of things and according to the law of God, null and void from the beginning.

Some years later, the black activist Charles Lenox Remond amplified Garrison's point. "It does very well," he wrote in the *National Anti-slavery Standard* in 1844, "for nine-tenths of the people of the United States, to speak of the awe and reverence they feel as they contemplate the Constitution, but there are those who look upon it with a very different feeling, for they are in a very different position." White Americans might regard it as a sacred document, but from the point of view of black Americans "slavery was in the understanding that framed" the Constitution, and "slavery is in the will that administers it."

On this view, abolitionists of the Garrisonian stripe saw no choice for the free states but to secede and form a purified union of their own under a new constitution that would ban slavery altogether. Others, clinging to the hope that time would solve the problem, tried to convince themselves that the fugitive slave clause of the existing Constitution was a provisional

Charles Lenox Remond

necessity, a patch on a wound that would heal as the slave states slowly gave way under "moral suasion" to the higher law. Until such time as the patch could be removed without rupturing the wound, the right to recapture runaway slaves would remain in force.

These ideas, far removed from the actual experience of enslaved men and women, had a certain cerebral abstraction, as if they were debating points. But when it came to flesh-and-blood fugitives whose fate depended on a proceeding in court, neither radicals who disavowed the Constitution nor conservatives who waited for a sea change in the national culture were of much use. There were, however, others in the antislavery movement—some of them gifted lawyers—who were neither ready to see the nation dissolved nor inclined to wait for the slave states to repent. Their strategy was to probe the internal contradictions of the Constitution in the hope of opening up some legal space through which at least a few fugitives might slip.

They pinned their hopes on the fact that while the Constitution required return of fugitive slaves, it also included—thanks, ironically, to slave owners such as Jefferson and Madison—a bill of rights designed to protect individual liberties against government intrusion. The pertinent words were those of the Fifth Amendment, which stated that "no person . . . shall be deprived of life, liberty, or property without due process of law." Like everything else in the Constitution, these words were of course open to interpretation, and so antislavery lawyers set to work.

The courts were their battleground, and the issue at stake was whether slave owners could pursue runaways without constraint. The words of the fugitive slave clause—"shall be delivered up on claim of the party to whom such service or labor may be due"—sounded clear enough, but how could the rendition requirement be reconciled with the requirement for "due process"? Did the founders really mean to grant unchecked power for seizing a person on the bald claim that someone owned him?

The law of 1793 had attempted to answer these questions, but in fact it only raised more questions. Soon after it was passed by Congress, one Massachusetts representative protested on the floor of the House that it was an invitation for kidnappers to seize anyone they fancied on the pretext that they were acting on behalf of a slave owner exercising his property rights. "The person may be a freeman," he pointed out, "for it would not be easy to know whether the evidence was good, at a distance from the State; the poor man is then sent to his State in slavery." By the turn of the century, northern legislatures were responding to what they regarded as a dangerous federal law by passing state laws intended to provide protection against it.

These laws came to be known as "personal liberty" laws. In the first four decades of the nineteenth century, such laws were adopted throughout the free states, from Ohio to Vermont, with the cumulative effect of making it more difficult to extradite an accused runaway to a slave state. The most stringent was Pennsylvania's 1826 "Act to Give Effect to the Provisions of the Constitution of the United States, Relative to Fugitives from Labor, for the Protection of Free People of Color, and to Prevent Kidnapping," provoked in part by a notorious abduction of several black boys from the Philadelphia docks, where they were lured aboard ship and taken to Georgia and Mississippi as slaves. Pennsylvania was a common destination for fugitives from Maryland, Virginia, and points south, and among all the free states bordering on slave states (Iowa, Indiana, Illinois, Ohio, Pennsylvania, and New Jersey), it went furthest in protecting free blacks born or living for years in the state, as well as in making it difficult to retrieve recent runaways. By excluding testimony from the slave owner himself, the Pennsylvania law forced him to prove his "claim to a runaway by informed and impartial witnesses"—presumably men from his home state for whose time and travel expenses he would have to pay.

In the minds of supporters, personal liberty laws such as the Pennsylvania law of 1826 embodied a cardinal principle of American jurisprudence: even at risk of acquitting guilty persons (in this case, guilt meant fleeing for freedom), innocent persons, namely free blacks in the North claimed as runaways by whites in the South, must be afforded such basic rights as trial by jury and immunity against self-incrimination. For opponents, the personal liberty laws had nothing to do with protecting free citizens. The real aim of these laws was to obstruct slave owners by dragging them into a bureaucratic nightmare if they tried to reclaim property to which they had legitimate title. And so the personal liberty laws became another flash point between North and South.

Still, when it came to the constitutional principle that a slave could not achieve freedom by moving from South to North, the personal liberty laws only nibbled at the edges. Then, in 1836, the Massachusetts Supreme Court took a bite.

3.

Mary Slater, a resident of New Orleans, had come to Boston to visit her father, Thomas Aves. She brought with her a slave named Med, a girl of about six years old who belonged, according to the laws of Louisiana, to her husband. When Mrs. Slater became ill, she left the child with her father under his protection—or, from the point of view of antislavery Bostonians—in detention. When news reached members of the Boston Female Anti-slavery Society that a slave girl was being held in the heart of their city, they sought a writ of habeas corpus challenging Aves's right to keep her. He responded that he was acting as agent for his son-in-law, the girl's legal owner, until such time as the child could return to Louisiana in the company of Mrs. Slater or some other responsible party. In August 1836, the case reached the Massachusetts Supreme Court, presided over by Chief Justice Lemuel Shaw.*

The substantive issue facing the court was whether an enslaved person from another state could be forcibly returned from Massachusetts into slavery. This was not quite the same question Judge Nelson had faced in the New York case of 1834, because the defendant in that case had been charged as a fugitive. In the Aves case, the little girl had been brought into the state by an agent of her master (his wife), and no one accused her of having run away. Massachusetts also had a distinctive history with slavery. New York had been late in abolishing it (its last slaves were not emancipated until 1827), and slave owners who brought human property into the state were still granted a nine-month grace period before any such slave could claim freedom. In Massachusetts, where slavery had been illegal since 1783, there was no law prescribing one way or another the status of a slave brought in from another state.

Now, thanks to the interest of the Boston Female Anti-slavery Society in a six-year-old girl, that issue would have to be faced. Was the fact of her presence in Massachusetts reason enough to free her? Or, as Judge Nelson had ruled, was it true that to a "qualified extent slavery may be said still to exist in a state, however effectually it may have been denounced by her constitution and laws"—to a sufficient extent, that is, that a slave remained enslaved while traveling to a free state in the company of her master?

Benjamin R. Curtis, the attorney for Aves, answered this question in the affirmative. He argued on the principle of "voluntary comity" that Massachusetts owed deference to the laws of Louisiana, regardless of what feelings those laws might affront. The attorney for the plaintiffs, Ellis Gray Loring, countered that the principle of comity did not apply. There had been no

---

*Future father-in-law of Herman Melville.

slaves in Massachusetts for over fifty years, so the very idea of comity was a farce. Besides, Louisiana was known for throwing into jail black sailors who arrived in one of its ports aboard Massachusetts-registered ships. According to the principle of comity, should Massachusetts reciprocate by jailing citizens of Louisiana upon their arrival in Boston Harbor?

To the consternation of some northern conservatives, and to the horror of many in the South, Judge Lemuel Shaw came down on Loring's side of the argument. Comity, he ruled, applied "only to those commodities which are everywhere and by all nations, treated and deemed subjects of property." People were not recognized as property in Massachusetts. Med was removed from the custody of Mr. Aves and released.

She was given over for protection to members of the Boston Female Anti-slavery Society, who assigned her a new name, Maria Somerset, in dual honor of their founder Maria Weston Chapman and the liberated slave in the famous *Somerset* case. Perhaps Shaw expected that someone in the society would adopt her. Instead, she was sent to an orphanage. Whether this was because of the limits of Boston charity or because the child's bewilderment at being kept from her family in Louisiana made her frantic and unmanageable is not known.

The *Aves* case set an important precedent. Over the next few years, many northern states followed it by granting freedom to slaves belonging to masters who voluntarily brought them into the state. Even historically slow New York repealed its statute granting slave owners a nine-month reprieve before their slaves were declared free. Nevertheless, one can feel Shaw straining, almost squirming, as he took pains to deny that a slave, simply by being carried to a free state, is released in any metaphysical sense from his status as a slave:

> Although such persons have been slaves, they become free, not so much because any alteration is made in their *status*, or condition, as because there is no law which will warrant, but there are laws, if they choose to avail themselves of them, which prohibit, their forcible detention or forcible removal.

But the basic problem of the legal status of *fugitive* slaves remained, and Shaw knew it. According to the Constitution, which was the supreme law of the land, fugitives who had run from their masters were exempt from any prohibition placed by state law against "detention or forcible removal." In Shaw's mind, therefore, the whole case turned on the meaning of "escaping." "The claimant of a slave, to avail himself of the provisions of the constitution and laws of the United States," he said, "must bring himself within their plain and obvious meaning," which "in the constitution is confined to the case of a slave escaping from one state and fleeing to another."

By this logic, if Med had run into the arms of the Female Anti-slavery Society begging for sanctuary, Shaw might well have regarded her as a fugitive and returned her to slavery. But because she was not guilty of escaping, and remained entirely passive—carried into the state like a package, and docile once she got there—he set her free.

4.

Suddenly Lemuel Shaw was a hero to the antislavery movement. Garrison, not exactly known for respecting jurists, called him "rational, just," and even "noble." Yet as a legal precedent, the *Aves* case proved to be a diversion from the more contentious problem of how the law should deal with slaves who had run from their masters.

In most such cases, the masters prevailed. Few judges concurred (though they might have wished to) with Judge Theophilus Harrington of Vermont, who was reputed to have said back in 1807 when presented with documents purporting to prove the identity of a fugitive, "If the master could show a bill of sale, or grant, from the Almighty, then his title to him would be complete: otherwise it would not." Throughout the 1830s and 1840s, convictions were the norm, though judges often handed them down in language tinged with resignation and regret.

Even lawyers for the plaintiffs sometimes gave voice to the "alas my hands are tied by the Constitution" theme. In Pittsburgh, not long before the *Aves* case, a fugitive named Charles Brown was apprehended by agents for his Maryland owner, who had advertised for his return, making little distinction between the goods ("blue cloth coat," "white fur hat") with which Brown had absconded and Brown himself:

> Stop the thief—50 dollars reward.—Ran away from the subscriber's farm, near Williamsport, on Saturday night last, a negro boy, who calls himself Charles Brown, 18 years old, about 5 feet 9 or 10 inches high, not stout, but well proportioned; of a dark complexion, and good countenance. Had on and took with him, one fine blue cloth coat, half worn, white fur hat . . . one pair new drab corduroy pantaloons, one black silk vest, one fine muslin shirt, . . . one light drab home-made cloth short coat, one or two pair of double threaded cotton pantaloons, one pair white cotton drilling . . . fine shoes, stockings, and other articles not remembered. He rode away a sorrel mare, about 15 years old, with white blaze in the face, both hind feet believed to be white; paces and trots, and when pacing, throws one of her feet a little out, as if stiff in the joint.

Arguing that Brown must be restored to his master, the slave owner's attorney tried to soften his argument with expressions of lament ("God knows no man . . . more regrets the black spot of slavery on our national escutcheon than I do") before turning to the judge to say that he, too, must defer to mind over heart:

> And you, sir, certainly, acting under oath, will not yield to your abhorrence of the curse of slavery, in deciding a question which comes directly to your conscience, acting under oath; nor strain a point to deprive one of your fellow-citizens, of Maryland, wrongfully of his lawful property.

Two years later, in an 1837 case that gained national attention, a young enslaved woman named Matilda had been brought from Missouri to Ohio by her owner—who was also her father—a man named Larkin Lawrence. After he refused to grant her freedom, she fled and was hired as a household servant by James Birney, the Kentucky-born slave owner turned abolitionist, who was living in Cincinnati. It is not clear whether Birney, who had once owned a cotton plantation in Alabama but was now publishing an antislavery newspaper, the *Philanthropist,* knew she was a fugitive. In any case, when Lawrence's agents found her in his charge, Birney surrendered her, and she was brought to court.

Matilda was represented by Salmon P. Chase—the future Ohio senator and governor, later secretary of the Treasury and chief justice of the United States. Raising his sights heavenward, Chase noted that slavery would never survive a weighing in "the golden scales of justice . . . on high." Then, lowering his gaze, he conceded that "the right to hold a man is a naked legal right"—a right, that is, defined not by God in heaven but by legislatures and courts on earth. Still, as Judge Shaw had ruled in the *Aves* case, this right was not unlimited. "It is a right which, in its own nature, can have no existence beyond the territorial limits of the state which sanctions it, except in other states where positive law recognizes and protects it. It vanishes when the master and the slave meet in a state where positive law interdicts slavery." But because Matilda had run from her owner, Chase still had to find a way to save her from the constitutional demand that runaways be returned. On the principle that "the moment the slave comes within such a state, he acquires the legal right to freedom," he tried to convince the court that Matilda was not a fugitive at all because she had been brought to Ohio by her master and only upon reaching free soil had she attempted to escape.

Justice John McLean of the U.S. Supreme Court (serving on the western circuit at the time) was unconvinced. He admonished the jury to suppress its feelings and observed that

in the course of this discussion, much has been said of the laws of nature, of conscience, and the rights of conscience. This monitor, under great excitement, may mislead, and always does mislead, when it urges anyone to violate the law. I have read to you the Constitution and the acts of congress. They form the only guides in the administration of justice in this case.

Salmon P. Chase

The law was the law. Divine justice was something else. Matilda was re-moved to the custody of her owner. What became of her is unknown.

And so it went in case after case. Under the suffocating precedent of the Constitution, antislavery lawyers fought for breathing room, but they seldom found it. Five years later, in the spring of 1842, also in Ohio, a pi-ous antislavery man named John Van Zandt, who had once been a slave owner in Kentucky (he became the model for the virtuous John Van Trompe in *Uncle Tom's Cabin*), encountered a group of nine slaves on the run from his home state. He hid them in his wagon, where they were discovered by slave catchers hired by their owner. Eight were returned to Kentucky; one escaped.

Obliged under Kentucky law to pay the slave catchers a monetary re-ward for their services, and deprived of the slave who had successfully fled, the slave owner sued Van Zandt for damages totaling twelve hun-dred dollars. The case was eventually heard in 1847 by the U.S. Supreme Court, where Salmon P. Chase—assisted by William H. Seward—was once again counsel for the defense.

This time he tried some novel arguments. The law of 1793 penalized anyone who "shall harbor or conceal" any "person after notice that he or she was a fugitive from labor," but Chase claimed that Van Zandt had been unaware that the people whom he had treated with Christian charity were fugitives, and therefore he should not be convicted of having harbored them. Chase then launched into a lengthy disquisition on the etymology and definition of the word "harbor," citing Samuel Johnson's *Dictionary* and Shakespeare's *King John,* to which Seward later added the name of the French port city of Le Havre in order to make the case that "the idea of motion, progress, flight, or escape is absolutely excluded" from the meaning of the word. Therefore Van Zandt could not possibly be guilty of harboring anyone. In another act of intellectual contortion, Chase even claimed that the law of 1793 and the constitutional clause itself applied only to the original thirteen states in existence at the time they were written, and because Ohio did not enter the Union until 1803, Ohioans were exempt. These were all extravagant arguments. Writing for the Court, Justice Levi Woodbury of New Hampshire rejected them, and Van Zandt's conviction was upheld.

5.

Because of the stranglehold of the Constitution, everyone in the antislavery movement understood that runaways and their accomplices faced long odds in court no matter how ingenious their lawyers might be. And so the more militant among them tried to save them from coming to court at all. "Vigilance committees" formed throughout the North—groups of citizens, black and white, in Boston, New York, Philadelphia, and Albany, all the way to Pittsburgh and Detroit, committed to aiding and sheltering fugitives, to spreading the word when slave catchers showed up, sometimes even to breaking captives out of detention and getting them out of town. Still, the legal machine ground on. Then in 1842 came the first decision concerning the fugitive slave problem ever to be rendered by the U.S. Supreme Court—with larger implications than any previous ruling in any fugitive slave case.

A collision between the federal fugitive slave law of 1793 and the

Pennsylvania personal liberty law of 1826 had long been brewing. One purpose of the federal law had been to spare slave owners from delays and burdensome expenses. But the Pennsylvania law, by requiring a warrant from a Pennsylvania judge before an accused person could be arrested, made delay not only likely but long enough for vigilant citizens to hide him or help him to flee farther north. The Pennsylvania law also provided, regardless of the outcome of the case, that slave owners could be charged with court expenses. And while federal law allowed for penalties to be imposed on persons hindering the return of fugitives, the Pennsylvania law granted slave owners only the right to pursue damages, which would entail yet more court proceedings, more time, and more expense. In short, it was designed to make things as difficult as possible for slave owners to retrieve their runaways.

It was under these circumstances that a woman enslaved in Maryland named Margaret Morgan fled, in 1832, to Pennsylvania, where she joined her free black husband and, over the ensuing years, gave birth to several children. In 1837, a Maryland white woman who, under Maryland law, had inherited Margaret as well as her children hired an attorney named Edward Prigg "to seize and arrest the said negro woman" as her rightful property. Prigg attempted to obtain a warrant from a Pennsylvania justice of the peace, who refused. He then decided to sidestep the legal process and brought Margaret Morgan and her children back to Maryland by force. Prigg was charged in a Pennsylvania court and convicted of kidnapping, a judgment affirmed by the Pennsylvania Supreme Court—at which point he appealed to the Supreme Court of the United States. It was the first time a fugitive slave case reached the nation's highest court.

Writing for the high court on March 1, 1842, Justice Joseph Story found the 1826 Pennsylvania personal liberty law unconstitutional. Like other judges before him, he supplemented his verdict with a history lesson, pointing out that if the founders had not agreed on a constitution requiring the return of fugitive slaves—odious as that might be to lovers of freedom— every free state could "have declared free all runaway slaves coming within its limits" and would thereby have created "animosities" so "bitter" that "the Union could not have been formed." Story went on to declare that "any state

Joseph Story c. 1844

law or state regulation, which interrupts, limits, delays, or postpones the right of the owner to the immediate possession of the slave, and the immediate command of his service and labour" was invalid.

It was a bombshell. The Court had effectively struck down all legislative efforts by northern states to impede the fugitive slave clause of the Constitution. All protections for accused runaways had been swept away, including provisions for due process set out in the personal liberty laws. "One-half of the nation," as one historian puts it, "must sacrifice its presumption of freedom to the other half's presumption of slavery."

And yet Story gave something to the antislavery side too. Even as he upheld the constitutionality of the 1793 federal fugitive slave law by striking down state laws designed to interfere with it, he gave implicit permission to states to invent new ways to weaken or even render it useless. His decision left room for states to deny the use of state officials and facilities— justices of the peace, police officers, jails—for enforcing the federal law, and thereby to leave the work entirely up to federal authority. "The provisions of the act of 12th February, 1793, relative to fugitive slaves," Story wrote, "is clearly constitutional in all its leading provisions, and, indeed, with the exception of that part which confers authority on state magistrates, is free from reasonable doubt or difficulty." Then he noted a momentous exception:

> As to the authority so conferred on state magistrates, while a difference of opinion exists, and may exist on this point in different States, whether state magistrates are bound to act under it, none is entertained by the Court that state magistrates may, if they choose, exercise the authority unless prohibited by state legislation.

In short, while no state law may impede the claimant in a fugitive slave case, and state officials may aid the process of arrest and rendition "if they choose," they are not obliged to do so.

With five words—"unless prohibited by state legislation"—Story had unleashed, perhaps unwittingly, what would become a second wave of personal liberty laws. Over the next few years, states throughout the North passed new laws forbidding state officials to cooperate in the rendition of fugitives. The federal government at the time had few resources to make its laws stick, and so what the states were saying to the government in Washington was essentially, "Do your own dirty work. We won't help."* In a memoir of his father published in 1851, Justice Story's son looked back at the *Prigg* decision with filial pride and called it a "triumph of freedom."

Even before the rise of the new personal liberty laws, the *Prigg* decision was put to the test. The first test came in October 1842, once again in a Massachusetts courtroom presided over by Judge Shaw. A Boston police constable, armed with a warrant obtained from the Boston Police Court by a Virginia slave owner, arrested a young black man named George Latimer and held him in the Leverett Street jail. Word quickly spread, and concerned Bostonians petitioned Judge Shaw for a writ of habeas corpus. The writ was granted and the prisoner was brought before

---

*There is an analogy to disputes today over whether states or municipalities are obliged to assist federal Immigration and Customs Enforcement officers in arresting undocumented immigrants. In the 1840s, the federal government had much smaller means for enforcing federal law than it has now.

the state supreme court for a hearing to determine if he could be released on bail pending a hearing on his case in federal court.

This time, in the eyes of abolitionists, Shaw did not emerge a hero. He was firm in regarding the case as a federal matter and ruled that under the act of 1793, recently upheld in *Prigg v. Pennsylvania*, the slave owner and his agents had due authority to have the prisoner held as a suspected runaway until a federal court ruled on his fate. While transferring Latimer back to the city jail, officers of the court were attacked by a mob, with at least one person seriously hurt. Latimer remained in detention pending a rendition hearing before the federal judge—who happened to be Justice Story, on circuit duty—to whom Latimer's putative owner would presumably present proof of ownership.

In the interim, abolitionists tried various strategies to get the prisoner released. Among them was a writ of personal replevin—the same legal instrument presented to Judge Nelson in the 1834 New York case, which, if accepted, would have required trial by jury. When they took the matter again to Judge Shaw, his response was summarized by William Lloyd Garrison, who was present in the courtroom:

> He probably felt as much sympathy for the person in custody as others; but this was a case in which an appeal to natural rights and the paramount law of liberty was not pertinent! It was decided by the Constitution of the United States, and by the law of Congress, under that instrument, relating to fugitive slaves. These were to be obeyed, however disagreeable to our own natural sympathies. . . . He repeatedly said, that on no other terms could a union have been formed between the North and the South.

Soon thereafter, Garrison, who had once praised Shaw for his wisdom and probity, excoriated him for playing "the part of Pilate in the Crucifixion of the Son of God."

The Latimer case drove Boston into a fury. "Fire and bloodshed," according to one observer, "threatened in every direction." Petitions with over sixty-five thousand signatures and weighing more than 150 pounds were delivered in a barrel to the Massachusetts State Senate demanding a new law prohibiting cooperation by state authorities in any fugitive slave case. Another barrel of petitions beseeching Congress "to pass such laws and to propose such amendments to the Constitution of the United States as shall forever separate the people of Massachusetts from all connection with slavery" was sent to seventy-five-year-old John Quincy Adams, who attempted to present them in the House but was rebuffed on authority of the gag rule. Asked to serve as counsel for Latimer, Adams declined on the grounds that his legal skills were out of practice,* but he agreed to advise Latimer's attorneys "subject to my bounden duty of fidelity to the Constitution of the United States."

Abolitionists published a broadside called the *Latimer Journal and North Star,* in which they reported the latest events three times a week. "The slave shall never leave Boston," they said, "even if to gain that end the streets pour with blood." Meanwhile, the hearing in federal court had been delayed, possibly because Justice Story was ill or because he wished to grant the slave owner sufficient time to obtain proof of ownership from his home state.

---

*Adams had resisted, but finally accepted, similar entreaties two years earlier to join the defense team on behalf of a group of Africans who had revolted aboard the Spanish slave ship *Amistad,* killing the captain and another member of the crew. Like Britain and the United States, Spain had outlawed participation in the Atlantic slave trade, but Spanish slave dealers flouted the ban, seizing Africans for shipment to the Spanish colony of Cuba, where they were provided with false papers claiming they were Cuban-born. The *Amistad* had been transporting a group of some fifty such slaves along the Cuban coast from Havana to buyers who had purchased them with the intent of putting them to work in the sugar fields. After taking over the ship, the slaves tried to compel the Spanish crew to sail them back to Africa, but by turning by night toward the northwest, the Spaniards managed to steer the *Amistad* into Long Island Sound, where a U.S. Coast Guard cutter seized the vessel. The Africans were imprisoned in New Haven, Connecticut, pending resolution of their fate by U.S. courts.

Spain demanded return of the slaves and the U.S. government agreed, but antislavery attorneys, led by Roger Baldwin of Connecticut, intervened. After lower courts ordered the Africans released on the grounds that Spain had violated the ban on the international slave trade, the U.S. government appealed to the Supreme Court, and Adams joined the defense. In the winter of 1841, for more than eight hours over more than two days, he argued on grounds of natural law that the case against the slaves was a travesty of justice. The high court sustained the lower courts, and the slaves were released, but although Justice Story called Adams's performance "extraordinary," the ruling was a narrow one, confirming the claim by the defense that identification papers issued to the slaves were false and that they had been kidnapped, transported, and sold in violation of an international agreement banning the slave trade. In other words, they had never been legally slaves. (For a brief and clear account of the case, see William J. Cooper, *The Lost Founding Father: John Quincy Adams and the Transformation of American Politics* [New York: Liveright, 2017], 362–68.)

During the wait, pressure mounted on city authorities to release the prisoner to the custody of the claimant because holding Latimer much longer seemed likely to precipitate a riot. On November 18, the sheriff of Boston ordered that he be turned over to the Virginian—a nervous stranger in a hostile city—who now feared less for his property than for himself. When a group of abolitionists raised four hundred dollars to buy Latimer's freedom, he accepted the offer and the case was closed.

But not quite. On March 24, 1843, Massachusetts legislators walked through the door that Justice Story had opened. The legislature passed what became known as the "Latimer law," prohibiting state officials from detaining anyone charged under the 1793 fugitive slave law and from using any state facility for that purpose. Over the next few years, similar statutes were adopted in Pennsylvania, Connecticut, New York, and Rhode Island. Bostonians were proud to have taken the lead. John Greenleaf Whittier (echoing the English poet William Cowper's celebration of the *Somerset* verdict some sixty years earlier) exulted:

> *No slave-hunt in our borders,—no pirate on our strand!*
> *No fetters in the Bay State,—no slave upon our land!*

6.

But the legal battles were by no means over. Four years after the Latimer case, and three months after the Van Zandt conviction was upheld by the Supreme Court, another fugitive slave case made national news by proving the potency of the new personal liberty laws.

In June 1847, a pair of Maryland slave owners traveled to the town of Shippensburg, in Cumberland County, Pennsylvania, searching for three fugitive slaves rumored to have fled there—a man and a girl of about ten (possibly father and daughter), as well as an adult woman married to a free black man living nearby. The Maryland men forced their way into the house where the runaways were harbored, brought them to the county seat, Carlisle, and presented their claim of ownership to the local justice of the peace, who jailed the fugitives and, under the fugitive slave law of 1793, granted a certificate authorizing their return to Maryland.

But before the slave catchers could complete their mission, they ran into legal complications. The Cumberland County judge was presumably aware of the *Prigg* decision, including its stipulation that state authorities may assist in the rendition of fugitives "*unless prohibited by state legislation,*" but when a local lawyer presented him with a writ of habeas corpus on behalf of the prisoners, it became clear that the judge was unaware of the new personal liberty law passed two months earlier by the Pennsylvania legislature forbidding the use of "any jail or prison for the detention of anyone claimed as a fugitive." When a theology professor from nearby Dickinson College showed him a copy of the statute, which was modeled on the Massachusetts "Latimer law" of 1843, the judge allowed rendition of the runaways to proceed but voided the authority of the local sheriff to hold them in custody pending their return to Maryland. In short, the slave catchers would be allowed to complete their business, but as for holding and transporting their captives, they were on their own.

This was just the sort of hairsplitting that southerners had feared ever since the *Prigg* decision. One Maryland newspaper lamented that the new Pennsylvania law was intended "to destroy the force of the law of congress of 1793." To all intents and purposes, it did.

As the dispute inside the Carlisle courthouse heated up, so did the racially mixed crowd gathered outside. Whites mostly clamored for the slaves to be sent back to slave country, while blacks (roughly three hundred free black citizens lived in Carlisle and environs, of whom scores had shown up at the courthouse) demanded their release. When the captives were finally brought out onto the courthouse steps, dozens of black men, "seeing their fellows about to be carried away into interminable bondage," suddenly "made a rush, and carried off the woman and child." During the melee, one of the Maryland men was trampled and severely injured. A few days later he died. Thirty-four local black residents, including nine women, were arrested on charges ranging from assault to murder, and the Dickinson College professor was charged with inciting the riot.

Two months later, a jury convicted thirteen black defendants and acquitted the white professor. The Cumberland County judge, who had wanted to see the whole lot locked up, denounced what he regarded as the weakness of the verdict and sentenced eleven of the convicted men to three years' solitary confinement in the Eastern State Penitentiary. The following spring, the Pennsylvania Supreme Court reviewed the case, released all the defendants, and, in a rebuke of the judge, noted that three-quarters of a year spent in the penitentiary was more than enough punishment for their putative crimes.

News of these events spread far and wide. Moncure Conway, a Dickinson student from Virginia who was soon to join other conscientious objectors to slavery in the South such as James Birney and Angelina Grimké by exiling himself to the North, recalled years later that there was "probably not an abolitionist among the students, and most of us perhaps were from the slave States." Yet most came to the defense of their professor in a series of resolutions that were published in national antislavery newspapers.

Some local papers (reflecting not only racial animus but also, perhaps, a degree of "town-gown" hostility) took a different tack, declaring that the root problem behind the case was the fact that too many black people—slave and free—were entering Pennsylvania. Referring to the death of the Maryland man, one paper proclaimed that "the Abolition fanatics can now witness the first and choice fruits of their maddened zeal" and went on to

question whether it was a sound policy to permit blacks of all descriptions and characters such unrestricted liberty to come and settle among us. We appear to be the Botany Bay* for the African race. Every runaway negro finds a home in Pennsylvania. Is not this evil becoming a crying one? Should it not be remedied? . . . It is not to be denied that a large portion of the time of our Criminal Courts are taken up in trying worthless vagabond negroes, for almost every species of crime at a great expense to the public. They fill our poor houses and jails and this alarming evil is on the increase.

---

*Botany Bay was the nineteenth-century name for Australia, which had been populated in large part by convicts deported from Britain.

In short, lax immigration laws were to blame for rising crime rates. As we lately have been reminded, this facile explanation has perennial appeal.

The full implications of the Supreme Court decision in *Prigg v. Pennsylvania* were becoming evident. On the one hand, it reaffirmed the basic principle of the Constitution and the law of 1793—that slave masters had the right to retrieve their slaves from wherever within the United States they had fled. On the other hand, because state legislatures could forbid state authorities to assist them in exercising that right, it had become merely a nominal right—a paper privilege with little value in the real world.

Perhaps the largest consequence of the court battles leading to and flowing from the *Prigg* decision was that people on both right and left were losing faith in the legitimacy of legal and political institutions. John C. Calhoun deemed the personal liberty laws "one of the most fatal blows ever received by the South and the Union." For William Lloyd Garrison, the spectacle of judges upholding the right of slave owners to retrieve their slaves, however much the personal liberty laws might retard the process, only confirmed that "villainy is still villainy though it be pronounced equity in the statute book."

Senator Thomas Hart Benton of Missouri, an astute student not only of constitutional history but of political reality, summed up the impact of the *Prigg* decision: "This decision of the Supreme Court—so clear and full—was further valuable in making visible to the legislative authority"—namely, Congress—"what was wanting to give efficacy to the act of 1793; it was nothing but to substitute federal commissioners for the State officers forbidden to act under it." Sooner or later, in other words, the federal government would have to step in by creating a class of "commissioners" to do what state officials were refusing to do. The path forward—or backward—was clear, but it would be three more years before Congress would embark on it.

Part Two

THE FUSE IS LIT

Eight

TO THE BRINK

1.

Sectional tension had waxed and waned ever since the founding. But by the 1840s, with rancor rising in the courts, antislavery articles pouring from the northern press, and demand growing for personal testimony from former slaves, it reached unprecedented intensity. In the second half of the decade, it came to a boiling point—spurred by events in the far Southwest.

Mexico had won its independence from Spain in 1821. Eight years later, slavery, which had supplied labor under the Spaniards for mining gold and silver as well as for planting, harvesting, and processing sugar, was legally abolished. Meanwhile, settlement by "Anglos," many of them slave owners, was nevertheless tolerated and even encouraged in the area north of the Nueces River known as Tejas—a huge expanse of prairie, canyon, scrubland, and forest that was home to Comanche Indians and beyond effective control from Mexico City hundreds of miles away. The "open door" policy of the fledgling Mexican government was its acknowledgment that there was no way the door could be closed.

Through the 1820s and into the 1830s, Americans came riding and rolling in. Some came with the intention to settle, others as agents of absentee land speculators. By 1830, they outnumbered Spanish-speaking Tejanos two to one. Five years later, the ratio had risen to ten to one, and by 1845 there were roughly 125,000 English-speaking emigrants in the region now known to Americans by the anglicized name Texas, of whom more than a quarter were enslaved. The slave population was growing faster than the population as a whole.

Meanwhile, according to one satiric account of life on the frontier, it was getting difficult in the states from which the new arrivals mainly came—Louisiana, Mississippi, and Alabama—to "put an inch or two of knife in a fellow" over some property dispute or affair of honor without having to deal with "*Law, law, law*" in the persons of lawyers, jurors, and judges. Texas, by contrast, was wild and wide open—a place "whar a man [need] not be interfered with in his private consarns." One man's anarchy was another man's liberty, and Texas, to the latter, looked like the place to be.

It was only a matter of time before conflict broke out between the newcomers and those who had preceded them—Spanish Creoles as well as indigenous Indians who allied with one side or the other or tried to stay neutral. By late 1835, sporadic fighting had turned into organized warfare. From the point of view of white English-speaking Texans and their advocates in the United States, the conflict with Tejanos was a glorious reprise of America's own war of independence—waged by people, in the words of Mississippi senator Robert J. Walker, who "are imitating . . . our own revolution" by fighting a faraway government that would tax and oppress them. But it was also a slaveholders' rebellion against a regime hostile to slavery—or, more accurately, "a race war against a *mestizo* nation."

The fighting was savage. Early in 1836, some two hundred Americans were massacred at a former Spanish mission called the Alamo, where three times as many Mexicans died before the American defenders, including the former Tennessee congressman Davy Crockett, were overwhelmed and slaughtered. Texans regrouped under the leadership of Sam Houston, a twice-wounded veteran of the War of 1812 and former governor of Tennessee, and the tide of war turned. More bloody encounters followed, with summary executions of men on both sides while they were trying to surrender, until Texans finally prevailed at the Battle of San Jacinto in April 1836. Five months later, they declared themselves citizens of an independent republic.

Although its troops had been expelled from the province of Tejas, Mexico did not formally renounce the state of war and had no intention of recognizing a new sovereign nation immediately to its north. With border disputes continuing, the issue of whether Texas would remain independent or join the United States as a new slave state became an incendiary question, especially as rumors arose that Britain might assume its debts in return for emancipation of its slaves.

The prospect of British interference was not entirely fanciful. Since 1807, when Britain formally ended its participation in the international slave trade and tried, by means of its navy, to force other nations to do the same, its policy had been to undermine slavery wherever it could. For reasons both principled and calculated, slavery was abolished throughout the empire in 1833. Public revulsion played a part, but so did public concern that colonial slave owners had been bringing too many blacks into the British homeland as laborers and servants. Also at work was the idea that pressuring slavery out of existence throughout the colonized world was a way for Britain to improve its competitive position in the production of sugar, cotton, and rice. By the spring of 1844, the prospect of British intervention in Texas was sufficiently alarming that Andrew Jackson, weak and withered but still a commanding figure for many Americans, roused himself to warn that an "abolitionized" Texas could become "an asylum for all runaway slaves."

And so for a range of discordant reasons—greed, idealism, strategic prudence—the annexation of Texas became a popular cause in the United States, especially in the South. Its rallying cry was "Manifest Destiny"— the destiny, that is, of America "to overspread the continent allotted by Providence for the free development of our yearly multiplying millions." However illogical the logic—that freedom would be served by adding to the Union another slave state—many Americans, North as well as South, found it compelling. "The cry of Free Men," Frederick Douglass remarked with scathing accuracy, "was raised, not for the extension of liberty to the black man, but for the protection of the liberty of the white."

Believers in racially exclusive liberty were ideologically diverse. They included slave owners in want of more land as they contended with the

Andrew Jackson in 1845

problem of soil exhaustion (in order to grow cotton profitably, crops had to be rotated or fields fertilized at high expense), real estate speculators looking to buy low and sell high, immigrants from Europe hoping to move on from the crowded cities of the seaboard states, and many others with their eyes on the West as a vista of opportunity. Walt Whitman, celebrated today as a great poet of individual freedom, gave voice to the expansionist euphoria when he wrote in his poem "Song of Myself," "I skirt sierras, my palms cover continents, I am afoot with my vision," but his vision largely excluded black people from the panorama of liberty. Writing in approval of laws barring free blacks from the Oregon Territory, which Britain ceded to the United States in 1846, Whitman asked a rhetorical question, "Is not America for the Whites?" to which he gave an affirmative answer that pleased most if not all of his readers. In this respect, he was correct that "the proof of a poet is that his country absorbs him as affectionately as he has absorbed it."

But there were disbelievers too. A growing faction of northern and western Whigs—later to form the nucleus of the Republican Party—regarded the Democrats as a slavery party that "masked its intentions with

ANTI-TEXAS MEETING
AT FANEUIL HALL!

Friends of Freedom!

A proposition has been made, and will soon come up for consideration in the United States Senate, to annex Texas to the Union. This territory has been wrested from Mexico by violence and fraud. Such is the character of the leaders in this enterprise that the country has been aptly termed "that valley of rascals." It is large enough to make *nine* or *ten* States as large as Massachusetts. It was, under Mexico, a free territory. The freebooters have made it a slave territory. The design is to annex it, with its load of infamy and oppression, to the Union. The immediate result may be a war with Mexico—the ultimate result *will be* some 18 or 20 more slaveholders in the Senate of the United States, a still larger number in the House of Representatives, and the balance of power in the hands of the South! And if, when in a minority in Congress, slaveholders browbeat the North, demand the passage of gag laws, trample on the Right of Petition, and threaten, in defiance of the General Government, to hang every man, caught at the South, who dares to speak against their "domestic institutions," what limits shall be set to their intolerant demands and high handed usurpations, when they are in the majority?

All opposed to this scheme, of whatever sect or party, are invited to attend the meeting at the Old Cradle of Liberty, to-morrow, (Thursday Jan. 25,) at 10 o'clock, A. M., at which time addresses are expected from several able speakers.

Bostonians! Friends of Freedom!! Let your voices be heard in loud remonstrance against this scheme, fraught with such ruin to yourselves and such infamy to your country.
January 24, 1838.

Advertisement for an anti-annexation meeting in Boston, 1838

propaganda about freedom." From this point of view, the seizure of Texas was nothing but a land grab by slaveholders for whom the rest of Mexico would be next, and then "Cuba and Central America to be annexed as slave states." Protests broke out across the North denouncing the prospective acquisition of lands for the United States that had been "wrested from Mexico by violence and fraud."

Opponents of annexation also included pragmatic politicians such as Henry Clay of Kentucky (Whig) and Martin Van Buren of New York (Democrat), who for decades had held together a North-South coalition in their respective parties by deflecting the slavery question (they both supported the gag rule) and who feared that granting admission to Texas would open new fissures not only in the parties but in the Union itself.

As for the annexationists, if some of their arguments now seem repugnant to us, others sound downright bizarre. Senator Walker of Mississippi, who had been born in Pennsylvania and would end up supporting the Union in the Civil War, envisioned a new state of Texas as a "funnel through which the slave population could move into Mexico." Alarmed by the flood of slaves into his adopted state of Mississippi, he joined other southern whites in urging their "diffusion" by sending as many slaves as possible to Texas, whence they would be absorbed by Mexico, a nation where racial "amalgamation" was already far advanced and where, according to one former slave speaking long after the Civil War, no one cared "what color you was, black, white, yellow, or blue."

Whether Walker really believed in his plan for solving America's surplus slave problem, or he "had ceased to distinguish between the impressions made upon his mind by what came *from* it, and what came *to* it," is hard to say. However deluded he might have been, the idea that Texas would somehow siphon off America's excess slaves to Mexico affords a glimpse into the deepening impasse over slavery and the growing desperation to find some way out.

2.

Fear—sheer, chronic, irrepressible fear—had always been endemic to slave culture, and with slaves "crowding into the far South and increasing faster than the whites," it was growing fast on both sides of the color line. It is hideously expressed in artifacts from the penal world in which slaves were confined not only by law and custom but by shackles, manacles, and chains.

Slaves in the Deep South were at the mercy of virtually unregulated cruelty, and slaves farther north were not necessarily better off. In St. Louis, ladies and gentlemen strolled in their finery past the "Negro pens in the middle of the city" unfazed by the howls of slaves in transit to the auction house. Alexis de Tocqueville, touring America in 1831, was shocked by the sight of a Maryland slave beaten by a gentleman wielding a walking stick while a mixed black and white crowd looked on in apparent indifference, as if they had seen it all before and fully expected to see it again. Anywhere in the South, a slave could be whipped for any infraction ranging from theft or flight to failure to pound the hominy long

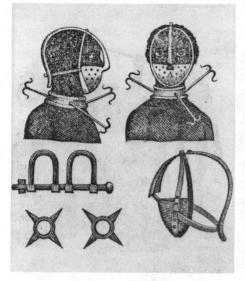

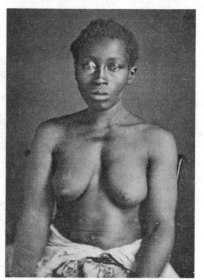

Iron mask, collar, leg shackles, and spurs used to restrict slaves

Delia, a slave in South Carolina, forced in 1850 to pose half-naked for a daguerreotype commissioned by Harvard ethnologist Louis Agassiz

enough to make grits soft enough to please her master or mistress at breakfast. In the few surviving photographic portraits of slaves, fear is visible in their eyes.

Whites, too, lived in fear—periodic, manageable, often based on next to nothing—but enervating nevertheless. From time to time, their fear was heightened by news of slave revolts. The terrifying precedent was the revolution in Haiti, where, between 1791 and 1804, the island had been periodically convulsed by black-against-white violence, including torture, rape, and murder of thousands of slave masters and their families—sometimes systematic, sometimes anarchic. There were domestic incidents too. In 1826, as a "coffle" of seventy-five slaves was being sent by flatboat down the Ohio River from Kentucky for sale in Mississippi or Louisiana, several of the slaves rose up, killed the slave traders, sank their bodies in the river with weights, and fled north into Indiana, where they were captured and returned south and the ringleaders hanged. That same year, one of America's first black college graduates, John Russwurm, who went on to co-edit the newspaper *Freedom's Journal,* justified the violence in Haiti in a commencement speech to faculty and students at Bowdoin College as "retaliatory measures" against slave owners.

While living in Boston in 1829, David Walker, the son of an enslaved father and free mother, published a pamphlet in which he warned

> that one good black man can put to death six white men, the reason is, the blacks, once you get them started, they glory in death. The whites have had us under them for more than three centuries, murdering, and treating us like brutes; and . . . there is an unconquerable disposition in the breasts of the blacks, which, when it is fully awakened and put in motion, will be subdued, only with the destruction of the animal existence. Get the blacks started, and if you do not have a gang of tigers and lions to deal with, I am a deceiver of the blacks and of the whites.

A decade later, Frederick Douglass urged America's slaves and their allies to "reach the slaveholder's conscience through his fear of personal danger. We must make him feel that there is death in the air about him, that there is death in the pot before him, that there is death all around him."

Among domestic insurrections, most infamous was the 1831 uprising in Southampton County, Virginia, led by a pious and literate slave named Nat Turner, in which some fifty whites died before at least two hundred blacks were beaten and killed in reprisal. The frequency of such events was small, but their psychological effects were large. Using Turner's full name as a mark of respect, Douglass recalled that "the insurrection of Nathaniel Turner had been quelled, but the alarm and terror had not subsided"—good reason, he later added, to "rejoice in every uprising." In 1841, aboard the slave ship *Creole,* which was transporting more than a hundred slaves from Richmond to New Orleans for sale, some number rebelled and, according to an account published in newspapers around the nation, attacked one of the owners "with clubs, handspikes, and knives," stabbing him to death "in not less than twenty places."

In an effort to prevent such horrors, laws were imposed throughout the

South making it a crime to teach slaves—or, for that matter, free blacks—
to read or write, lest they learn and spread seditious ideas about rebelling
or running away. In Georgia, as early as the 1820s, anyone caught teaching
a slave faced imprisonment or a five-hundred-dollar fine. Fathers could be
flogged for teaching their own children. In the early 1830s, although there
were only about one hundred slaves, mostly house servants, in the city of
St. Louis, it was "forbidden on pain of heavy penalty to teach a slave to read
or write." In North Carolina, patrols searched "every negro house for books
or prints of any kind," and if any were found, including "Bibles or hymn
books," the offender was subject to "whipping . . . until he *informed who*
gave them to him." Every "slaveholding community," Douglass observed,
had "a peculiar taste for ferreting out offenses against the slave system."

Not all whites complied. At risk of incurring her husband's ire, the
wife of Douglass's own master taught him to read. Charles Colcock Jones,
a Congregational pastor who ministered to blacks as well as whites on the
Georgia coast, protested that to deny "knowledge of letters to the Negroes" was to violate the core belief of every true Protestant: that all God's
children, whatever their earthly condition, must have "access to the Scrip-
tures" unmediated by ecclesiastical authority. This meant literacy for all so
all could read God's word for themselves.

In a more mischievous but kindred spirit, Angelina Grimké, daughter
of a wealthy slave-owning Charleston family, recalled that as a young girl
in the 1820s she

> took an almost malicious satisfaction in teaching my little
> waiting-maid at night, when she was supposed to be occupied in
> combing and brushing my long locks. The light was put out, the key-
> hole screened, and flat on our stomachs, before the fire, with the
> spelling book under our eyes, we defied the laws of South Carolina.

Among her favorite scriptural passages was Deuteronomy 23:15–16: "Thou
shalt not deliver unto his master the servant that is escaped from his master
unto thee." She read these words—presumably sometimes aloud in the
company of slaves—as God's indictment of the constitutional mandate by

which "not *one* city of refuge for the poor runaway fugitive" was permitted to exist in the United States. Before she was thirty, she left the South to take up the antislavery cause in the North, where she married the prominent abolitionist Theodore Weld.

Looking back after the Civil War, one of Grimké's fellow exiles from the South remarked that "two terrors were constantly before the minds of Southern families—fire and poison . . . the two weapons that slaves had in their hands." By rumor, report, or family lore, most if not all white southerners had heard of slaves using one or the other. Slave masters were warned not to free their slaves in their wills because "servants knowing that the period of their Emancipation depended upon the *Death of a person* whom they might possess the means of secretly destroying" would be tempted to hasten the day of liberty by hastening their owner's death. Floride Calhoun, wife of the senior South Carolina senator, was convinced that slaves on her childhood plantation had tried to poison her father (not that he had any intention of freeing them), and for the rest of her life she lived in fear of being burned or stabbed in the night. Arson, suspected in every fire, was assumed to be a favored stratagem of discontented slaves, so little distinction was made throughout the South between the militia and the Fire Guard. A slave's "impudence," as one scholar writes, "was thought a prelude to insurgency."

And why would whites living among black slaves not think so? Although slave rebellions were rare, quickly suppressed, and punished severely, fear of rebellion was common and constant. Today, after all, we live amid checkpoints and security cameras and bomb-sniffing dogs, yet news of any terrorist attack, no matter how far away, fills us with fear that next time it will happen in *our* neighborhood, in *our* home. So it was for slaveholders. Every moment seemed pregnant with danger. No wonder that the leading southern writer of the day, Edgar Allan Poe, was an expert on the subject. In Poe's novella of 1838, *The Narrative of Arthur Gordon Pym*, the narrator and his companion fear at one time or another that they will drown, starve, die of thirst, or be cannibalized by their shipmates, but the ultimate terror arrives when, having survived shipwreck and finding themselves outnumbered ashore by black-skinned "savages," the narrator (a sort of alter ego for Poe) exclaims, "We were the only living *white* men upon the island."

Poe's readers needed no elaboration. Black violence was always lurking—at least in the white mind. And no matter how much whites wanted to think that blacks were passive under the putatively benign regime of slavery, fugitives and rebels continually disproved this belief. Slave owners feared that if slaves did not run, they would fight. As the black physician, writer, and activist Martin Delany (son of a slave) put it, "Whatever liberty is worth to the whites, it is worth to the blacks; therefore, whatever it cost the whites to obtain it, the blacks would be willing and ready to pay." As early as the 1780s, Jefferson had feared an outbreak of slave rebellion that would mean the "extirpation" of their masters. The most astute foreign student of American life, Alexis de Tocqueville, after traveling through the slave states in 1831, envisioned the whole South engulfed in "the most horrible of civil wars" destined to end "in the extermination of one or the other of the two races."

And yet until Texas forced them to confront it, Americans were amazingly adept at dodging the question of the future of slavery. Beginning with the compromises that made possible the Constitution, they found ways again and again to defer it. They deferred it in 1820 through the Missouri Compromise, which ruled out slavery (except in Missouri itself) north of the 36°30′ parallel but permitted it below the demarcation line. That compromise garnered support from expansionists like Calhoun, who warned that excluding slavery entirely from the western territories would lead the South to secede and make alliance with Britain (which, despite its professed antipathy to slavery, had close commercial relations with the cotton-growing South), as well as from anti-expansionists like John Quincy Adams, who acceded because of his "extreme unwillingness to put the Union at hazard." Between 1836 and 1844, the issue was deflected again by the gag rule, whereby petitions sent to Congress demanding action against slavery were automatically tabled without debate. Yet the question of slavery's future proved irrepressible. Was it an anachronism that would fade away, or was it poised for a new surge of growth? In the summer of 1845, Texas delivered its answer.

3.

On the portentous date of July 4, 1845, a convention of elected delegates meeting at San Antonio voted to apply to the United States for statehood. After five months of raucous debate, the U.S. Congress formally approved the request, and in December 1845, Texas became the twenty-eighth state of the Union and the sixteenth slave state. The danger—or hope—that it would become a sanctuary for fugitive slaves had passed, and Mexico's border dispute with Texas was now a dispute with the United States.

Prospects for peaceful resolution were dim. Under Mexican rule, the southern border of the province of Tejas had been the Nueces River, and while the short-lived Republic of Texas had officially accepted that boundary, popular sentiment regarded the Rio Grande, 150 miles to the south, as the real and natural dividing line. Already in the summer of 1845, six months before annexation was enacted by Congress, James K. Polk, the expansion-minded Tennessee Democrat who had barely defeated Clay for the presidency a few months before (aided by the defection of antislavery votes to the abolitionist candidate James G. Birney), ordered General Zachary Taylor to lead a contingent of U.S. soldiers into Texas and to take up positions "as near the boundary line, the Rio Grande, as prudence will dictate." Taylor, aware that the order amounted to a provocation, interpreted it conservatively and advanced no farther than Corpus Christi, at the mouth of the Nueces.

For much of the ensuing year, the United States attempted to pressure Mexico into more territorial concessions, including not only more land to the south but also the grand prize to the northwest, California. After negotiations backed by the threat of force failed to get Polk what he wanted, he ordered Taylor to advance to the Rio Grande. The American president portrayed the movement of troops as a defensive deployment. Mexico, of course, regarded it as an invasion.

The Mexican-American war, which began in April 1846, lasted nearly two years and cost almost twenty thousand lives on the American side alone. Even some of slavery's most loyal friends opposed it, including Calhoun, who had pushed for annexation but whom Polk now considered not merely "mischievous, but wicked" for refusing to endorse the president's wish for further expansion. Calhoun feared that new territorial acquisitions from Mexico would only inflame sectional conflict at home—a conflict, he believed, in which the South would ultimately come out the loser.

Another southern dissident, who shared Calhoun's doubts about both the morality and the strategy of territorial conquest, was the slave-owning Georgia congressman Alexander Stephens. In a speech on the floor of the House delivered several months into the war, Stephens condemned it with words that could have been delivered in the twenty-first century by an opponent of the second Iraq war launched by George W. Bush:

> It is to be doubted whether any man, save the President and his Cabinet, knows the real and secret designs that provoked [the war]. To suppress inquiry, and silence all opposition to conduct so monstrous, an executive ukase* has been sent forth, strongly intimating, if not clearly threatening, the charge of treason, against all who may dare to call in question the wisdom or propriety of his measures.

A year later, when Stephens spoke again to the same effect, his fellow Whig Abraham Lincoln described his remarks as "the best speech, of an hour's length, I have ever heard." Tempers ran so hot that one Alabama Democrat accused Stephens, the future vice president of the Confederacy, of having "joined the contemptible hordes of abolitionists in this hall."

Like other wars yet to come, the Mexican War pitted Americans against each other in furious expressions of reciprocal contempt. Supporters saw it as advancing America's sacred mission to spread itself from sea to shining sea. Opponents saw it as jingoism dressed up in fancy talk about democracy and freedom. At the start of the war, Frederick Douglass was in England speaking to packed halls about the horrors of American

---

*An edict issued by a tyrant.

Frederick Douglass in 1856

slavery. After abolitionist allies raised funds to buy his freedom, he returned to the United States and took full advantage of it. Now he spoke and wrote without restraint, declaring in 1849, "I would not care if, tomorrow, I should hear of the death of every man who engaged in that bloody war in Mexico, and that every man had met the fate he went there to perpetrate upon unoffending Mexicans." To some, such statements smacked of treason, but that was a hard charge to make stick when the accused had been denied citizenship in his own country.

To anyone who remembers the Vietnam years, the bitter exchanges between pro-war and antiwar camps of the late 1840s will sound eerily familiar, but unlike the debacle in Vietnam the Mexican War ended with an American victory. Once that victory was formalized by the Treaty of Guadalupe Hidalgo in February 1848, the lands over which the United States claimed sovereignty had been extended over an area almost twice as large as the Northwest Territory—a staggering expansion that amounts to some 30 percent of our present-day nation.

4.

But military success—as it often does—created a political problem. How could the new territories be organized in a way that would satisfy both North and South? Emerson predicted that "Mexico will poison us." Because both North and South had contributed blood and treasure to the war effort, each demanded a share of the spoils, and, just as Clay and Van Buren had feared, the slavery question came back with a vengeance. It might once have been true, according to a novelist who had tried but failed in the 1830s to interest readers in his Mexican themes, that most Americans "know and care as little about Mexico as they do about the moon," but now, in the words of Senator Benton, it became impossible not to care because "the large acquisition of new territory was fiercely lighting up the fires of a slavery controversy."

Among those trying to tamp down the flames was Zachary Taylor, who, having fought off a superior Mexican force at a strategic mountain pass known as Buena Vista, came out of the war with a big reputation. Born in Virginia to a family with roots in New England, Taylor had moved as a boy to Kentucky, and in addition to extensive properties there he owned plantations and slaves in Louisiana and Mississippi, so he had a certain national provenance. By 1848, "Old Zack" was being talked about as a potential presidential candidate. Like General Eisenhower a hundred years later, he played coy about his party affiliation, but in the end he went with the Whigs. During the Mexican conflict, Taylor's combination of reluctance and resolve won him admiration on both sides of the slavery divide, and on the political questions of the day he kept his convictions to himself—or, more likely, he did not quite know what they were.

Although at heart a military man, Taylor had a politician's talent for seeming to answer a question without actually answering it. When one southern planter, boasting that a lifetime of hard work had earned him enough to buy a hundred slaves, wrote to candidate Taylor with a straightforward question—"Before I vote, I want to know how you stand on the

*Zachary Taylor during
the Mexican War*

slavery question?"—he got a cryptic answer. "Sir," Taylor replied, "I too
have worked faithfully these many years, and the end product remaining
to me is a plantation with *three* hundred negroes. Yours truly." Apparently
impressed, the planter gave him his support, and so did enough other voters that in November 1848, despite his party's choice of the mildly antislavery New Yorker Millard Fillmore as its vice presidential candidate,
Taylor was elected.

Hard-line southerners who suspected the new president of being soft
on defending slavery turned out to be at least partly right. He did not support the unconditional right of slave owners to take their human property
into the territories from which the Missouri Compromise had excluded it.
Nor did he join northerners who sought prohibition of slavery from the
new territories on the precedent of the Northwest Ordinance. The latter
view had been introduced in Congress in August 1846 by an obscure
Pennsylvania congressman, David Wilmot, who proposed a rider on a
military appropriations bill banning slavery in any territory that might be
won from Mexico. After passing the House, the "Wilmot Proviso" failed

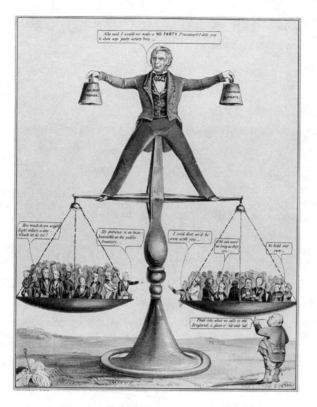

"Congressional Scales, a True Balance"

in the Senate, but not before setting off an uproar between pro- and anti-slavery factions in both parties.* Taylor, trying to mediate, favored extending to the Pacific some version of the boundary line established by the Missouri Compromise of 1820.

With Congress now less a forum for debate than "a cockpit in which rival groups could match their best fighters against one another," a momentous shift was under way in American political culture. The very idea of compromise on which the nation had been built was falling into ill repute, even ridicule, as in a cartoon published by Currier and Ives showing Taylor straddling a pair of scales with "Wilmot Proviso" in one hand and

---

*Wilmot referred to his plan as the "White Man's Proviso," by which he made clear that his purpose was to keep slaves out of the new territories and preserve them for white settlement.

"Southern Rights" in the other. The president's reward for attempting the balancing act was to be skewered in the crotch.

5.

Considering the victory they had achieved with the annexation of Texas and their ravenous appetite for more ("the slave power must go on in its career of exactions," Douglass said, "give, give will be its cry"), the notion of a vulnerable South at the mercy of a merciless North may be difficult to take seriously. The antebellum South was proficient at suppressing dissent by means of censorship, surveillance, and, when it came to its slaves, violence and terror. In many respects, it fit the definition of what we would call a police state. It held disproportionate (to its voting population) power in the national legislature. More often than not, its candidates, or candidates sympathetic to its interests, prevailed in presidential elections, and by mid-century the dozen richest counties in the United States were located below the Mason-Dixon Line. The leading producer of a commodity in worldwide demand, it has been aptly described as the "Saudi Arabia of the early nineteenth century." To sympathize with grievances emanating from this global powerhouse seems something like sympathizing with the Nazis' quest for Lebensraum.

And then there is the problem of hindsight: we know what happened next. We know that in 1854, during yet another territorial dispute, Congress passed the Kansas-Nebraska Act by which the Missouri Compromise was effectively repealed, and the prospect grew that slavery would spread still farther. We know, too, that in 1857 the Supreme Court repudiated the *Somerset* principle by ruling, in the case of Dred Scott—a slave who sued for freedom on the grounds that his master had taken him into free territory—not only that any slave owner could take his human property anywhere he liked but also that no black man, slave or free, had any "rights that the white man is bound to respect," including the right to sue in court. To many people in the North, slavery before the Civil War looked like an institution not in retreat but on the march. In 1858, Lincoln warned the citizens of Illinois that they might one day "*lie down* pleasantly dreaming" but "*awake* to the *reality* . . . that the *Supreme* Court has made *Illinois* a *slave* State."

But "living up here in 'futurity,'" we know what those living before the Civil War could not know. We know which predictions were right and which were wrong. To recover some sense of how it felt for Americans to live through those years requires an effort to imagine their ignorance of what was to come. To southerners in the 1840s, the political winds seemed to be blowing not for but against them. They felt imperiled. Slaves running north were a continual reminder that the border between slavery and freedom was growing weaker as it grew longer, while militant northerners called for arming fugitive slaves so they could defend themselves against anyone coming after them.

Even deep in cotton country slave owners feared that sooner or later the slave-owning border states would follow the North into abolition, raising the pace of slave escapes in their own states and triggering a cascade of panic sales until the value of slave property collapsed. "The North appeared to be growing more hostile," writes one historian, while "the Border South" was becoming "more disposed to debate its southernness" in the sense of contemplating the mass expulsion of blacks to the lower South. When slave owners looked north, they saw a free-soil enemy with proliferating cities and industries as well as railroads and canals for cross-country transport—a rapidly growing power by which they were treated as quasi-colonials whose main function was to send raw materials up to feed the hungry giant. They knew, moreover, that "the day when slavery can no longer extend itself, is the day of its doom." If the cotton economy were to prosper, it had to expand—no less in good times than in bad. When the price of cotton rose, so did the incentive to increase production in order to lift profits. When the price fell, the planter's motive to raise production was even stronger because cotton was the main collateral for his loans. Either way, there was no end to the need for more land and for more slaves to work it.

Yet as the scope of free soil grew, slave owners found themselves running out of places to go. "Confined to prescribed limits," as the incensed governor of Virginia put the matter in 1849, not only was the cotton economy starved for growing room, but future prospects for the exertion of southern power in national politics looked dim. To make matters worse, as each new free state entered the Union, it would add two senators and a contingent of representatives to bolster the northern voting bloc in Congress. The balance of power in the Senate would be destroyed, and control of the presidency and consequently of the Supreme Court would pass to the North, which, as Calhoun was soon to warn, was gaining "predominance in every department of government."

Benton, who had once favored slavery expansion but now—to Calhoun's fury—opposed it, cut to the heart of what was at stake in the struggle over the Mexican cession. He saw that southern anger over the fugitive slave issue was really a proxy for the larger fear that slavery itself was doomed. "Ostensibly," he wrote, "the complaint [of the South] was that the emigrant from the slave State was not allowed to carry his slave with him: in reality it was that he was not allowed to carry the State law along with him to protect his slave." In the short run, everyone knew that human property "carried" to free soil became insecure property, and many suspected that in the long run the boundary line between slave and free soil would not hold.

It was less and less clear whether a slave rented to an out-of-state employer or taken on "sojourn" into free territory continued, in the eyes of the law, to be the possession of her master. From the southern point of view, the *Aves* case in Massachusetts had set a dangerous precedent. It was followed in 1837 by a case in which the Connecticut Supreme Court granted a slave her freedom after two years of residency in the state under the "protection" of her master, who had brought her there from Georgia. And by the mid-1840s, courts throughout the North were ruling in one case or another that slaves brought into any free state were free regardless of how long they had lived there.

Early abolition measures such as the Pennsylvania law of 1780 had been written with an eye toward reassuring slave owners that excluding slavery from one state "shall not give any relief or shelter to any absconding or runaway Negro or Mulatto slave or servant, who has absented himself or shall absent himself from his or her owner, master or mistress residing in any other state." But such reassurances sounded increasingly hollow. No matter what the law said, when a slave ran for freedom, it was less and less sure that he could be caught and returned. Depending on time of residence or the disposition of local sheriffs and judges, all sorts of means could be used to obstruct rendition. A deed of ownership could be demanded from the claimant, and if produced, it could be contested. The identity of the accused fugitive could be disputed. Enemies of slavery who came to be known as conductors on the Underground Railroad might intervene to shelter a threatened runaway and send her farther north or even out of the country.

As early as 1827, one Louisiana jurist conceded the uncomfortable (to slave owners) truth that had loomed ever since the *Somerset* decision of 1772:

> By the laws of this country, slavery is permitted, and the rights of the master can be enforced. [But] suppose the individual subject to it is carried to England or Massachusetts;—would their courts sustain the argument that this state or condition was fixed by the laws of his domicile of origin? We know, they would not.

By the 1830s and 1840s, this prediction had been borne out in many northern states. Southerners were enraged by the rash of personal liberty laws guaranteeing jury trials for accused fugitives and forbidding state authorities throughout the North to cooperate in recapturing fugitives. What seemed in the North a defense of human rights seemed in the South brazen defiance of the law of the land and of the principle of comity itself.

Meanwhile, from outside the circle of slavery, abolitionist "agitation," as southerners called it, was becoming so routine that even the normally punctilious Massachusetts representative Horace Mann took to the floor of the House to say, "Better disunion, better a civil or a servile war— better anything that God in his providence shall send than an extension of the boundaries of slavery." From our point of view, he was speaking an obvious and overdue truth. But from the point of view of antebellum white southerners, to speak of "servile war" was to call upon slaves to rise up and murder them and their families. To say that southern whites felt insecure amid unceasing attacks on their "peculiar institution" is an understatement. The historian Matthew Karp, in documenting the outsize influence of antebellum southerners over American foreign policy (ten of the first sixteen secretaries of state were from slave states), writes of "the paradox of the 1850s," by which he means "slaveholders growing more confident abroad but becoming more beleaguered at home."

"Evils which are patiently endured when they seem inevitable," Tocqueville wrote, "become intolerable when once the idea of escape from them is suggested." He was referring not to slavery in the New World but to revolution in the Old World, which broke out in his native France not when the poor and dispossessed had fallen into despair but when their hopes were rising. In the same sense, American slave owners lived in dread of a "revolution of rising expectations" among their slaves. Sooner or later, they feared, the drumbeat from northerners urging them to flee their masters or to rise up in violence against them would be answered by action.

Given the gulf between their time and ours, and—one dares to hope—between prevailing racial attitudes then and now, it is difficult to see the world through the eyes of antebellum white southerners. One modern writer who managed to do so, not exactly with sympathy but with an unusual degree of understanding, was the twentieth-century scholar Barrington Moore Jr. Writing at the height of the cold war, when Americans felt themselves living within striking distance of an enemy both potent and reckless, Moore made an analogy with the "bitterness and anxiety" white southerners had felt a century earlier:

> To grasp how a Southern planter must have felt, a twentieth-century Northerner has to make an effort. He would do well to ask how a solid American businessman of the 1960s might feel if the Soviet Union existed where Canada does on the map and were obviously growing stronger day by day. Let him further imagine that the communist giant spouted self-righteousness at the seams (while the government denied that these statements reflected true policy) and continually sent insults and agents across the border.

Whatever we may think of their morals, the anxiety of southerners was real, and by the late 1840s the figure of the fugitive slave had become its leading symbol.

6.

Whether or not the pace of slave escapes actually rose through the 1840s, mutual recrimination between North and South was certainly growing louder. From Florida to Iowa and just about everywhere in between, incidents involving slave escapes were "agitating our country from Washington to the most distant borders."

In some cases, disputants continued to take recourse to the courts. In 1844, a Massachusetts shipowner operating in Florida (which joined the Union as the twenty-seventh state in the following year) was convicted of helping local slaves escape to the British Bahamas. In addition to incurring a fine, he was sentenced to time in the pillory, then jailed and branded "SS" on one hand—marking him forever as having committed the heinous crime of slave stealing.

In 1845, in Ohio, a Virginia slave owner traveling by steamboat on the Ohio River with his slave found his human property standing on the dock during a stopover in Cincinnati and took him before a justice of the peace with proof of ownership in case any meddlesome abolitionist should challenge it. Salmon P. Chase did just that, obtaining a writ of habeas corpus to prevent the slave owner from repossessing his slave. The case was heard by Ohio Supreme Court justice Nathaniel Read, who ruled that despite having entered Ohio, the slave remained the property of his Virginia master because to "deny the right to navigate the Ohio with a slave" would be an affront to the citizens of a "sister state."

Two years later, in Illinois, another telling piece of evidence emerged that the law regarding fugitive slaves remained unsettled. This was the case of Robert Matson, a Kentuckian who owned land in southern Illinois and brought some of his slaves there to work his Illinois farm. Matson was careful to send them back to Kentucky periodically and to replace them with others so he would not run afoul of Illinois laws granting freedom in cases of prolonged residency. One of his male slaves, however, with Matson's consent, remained in Illinois long enough to obtain papers certifying his freedom and continued to work as Matson's foreman. He was joined by his wife, who eventually filed suit for her own freedom based on her extended residency in a free state. Matson contested the suit with the help of two local lawyers, one of whom was none other than Abraham Lincoln. Lincoln's "business" at the time, one biographer contends, "was law, not morality."

Perhaps his experience with the *Matson* case—which he might have taken on for financial reasons, or to fulfill what he considered his duty to represent clients regardless of his personal feelings about the extralegal merits of their cases—contributed to his growing antipathy to slavery. In any event, Lincoln tried to counter the suit on the grounds that Matson had brought his slaves into Illinois temporarily and therefore retained ownership rights. But ever since the *Aves* case of 1834, northern courts had been inclined to reject the "sojourn" defense. The Illinois judge proved to be no exception. He ruled against the slave owner in a case that would be forgotten by now except for the fact that Abraham Lincoln was the losing counsel.

In 1848, nine slaves escaped into Iowa from their owner in Missouri, who put up a reward for their recapture. Pursuing both the slaves and the reward, two white men crossed the state line and found the fugitives in hiding. Before they could take them back, a crowd intervened and hauled the slave hunters before a local justice of the peace who dismissed their claim on the grounds that without a document signed by the slave owner, they had failed to meet the requirements of the 1793 fugitive slave law. Undeterred, the slave catchers returned with reinforcements and went on a search from house to house, at one of which they focused their attention on a ladder leading up to a loft. Here is what the owner of the house is reputed to have said, with discouraging effect:

> You may go up if you wish, gentlemen. There are three negroes hidden away in that loft. But mind you, it is a risky business to make an attempt to carry out the search. The first man who touches a rung of

that ladder is in danger of his life. I am armed, gentlemen, with
enough of these little instruments [bullets] to make just thirteen holes
in your flesh.

In the end, none of the runaways were returned to Missouri. Their aggrieved owner successfully sued six Iowans for financial damages equivalent to their market value.

The upset caused by the Florida, Ohio, Illinois, and Iowa cases, among
many others, never rose to the level of uproar. But in 1848 an incident took
place with much larger reverberations because of its scale and location.
That spring, the nation's capital was a scene of celebration. The White
House was festooned with flags and bunting; marching bands and citizens
formed spontaneous parades converging on Lafayette Square, where
speakers cheered the recent expulsion of King Louis-Philippe from France
and the establishment of the Second French Republic. Senator Henry
Foote of Mississippi spoke of universal human brotherhood, rejoicing that
"the age of tyrants and of slavery" was drawing to a close and would soon
be followed by the "universal emancipation of man from the fetters of civic
oppression."

The grotesque irony of these remarks was not lost on everyone in the
crowd. Washington had been created in 1791 by the cession of land from
two slave states (Virginia and Maryland), and slavery continued to thrive
in the city despite all the talk of liberty and the rights of man. It was home
as well to a substantial population of free blacks, some of whom attended the
celebrations that day. Washington's black population also included fugitives whose siblings, parents, and children remained enslaved in neighboring
states and who feared for their own safety in a town that was prime hunting ground for slave catchers. A few weeks earlier, the president of the
Philadelphia Anti-slavery Society had been informed by a "gentleman of
Washington" of "two or three slave cases there of great distress—females
who for months have been concealed by humane families to prevent them
being sold"—and told "that it was extremely desirous that they should soon
be got off" to safety in the North. In the intervening weeks, the "two or
three" cases ballooned to several dozen, and on April 15, 1848, more than

seventy slaves, after preconcerted planning with the help of free blacks and white abolitionists, made their way through the night to the schooner *Pearl*, docked on the Potomac under the command of Daniel Drayton.

Drayton, who was badly in need of money, was somewhere between a moralist and an opportunist. A few weeks earlier, while in Philadelphia, he had been approached by a stranger with an offer to pay him to smuggle a group of slaves out of Washington. The plan was to sail the *Pearl* downriver into the Chesapeake Bay and then turn toward some northern port. On Sunday morning, a good number of Washington's slave owners were shocked to find their slaves gone. "Breakfasts were not ready, babies were not dressed, horses and chickens were going hungry; nobody was performing the morning tasks expected of urban slaves."

The runaways did not get far. Slowed by unfavorable tide and wind, the *Pearl* was forced to drop anchor about 150 miles out of Washington, where, news of the escape having spread, it was boarded by an armed party that had followed by steamer. The fugitives were seized and the ship towed back to Washington, where an angry pro-slavery mob waited. The crowd warmed up by hurling stones at the offices of the antislavery newspaper the *National Era*. After the white crew and black passengers arrived in port under guard by the men who had seized the ship, they were marched through the streets to shouts and screams for a mass lynching. Drayton and two white accomplices were eventually convicted and imprisoned, despite the best efforts of their defense attorney, Horace Mann, until President Fillmore pardoned them in 1852.

In a half-organized attempt to extract information about how and by whom the plot had been hatched, slaves as well as free blacks were assaulted and beaten throughout the city. When Senator John P. Hale of New Hampshire proposed that authorities within the District of Columbia be held liable for property damage due to "any riotous or tumultuous assemblage of people," Senator Henry Foote invited Hale to visit Mississippi, where he would soon "grace one of the tallest trees of the forest, with a rope around his neck."

Some fifty of the slaves who had attempted to flee were taken off by train to the Baltimore auction house operated by that ever-resourceful slave dealer Hope Slatter, who was eager to groom them for sale. Slatter, whom William Lloyd Garrison described as a "double-distilled devil," had rushed to Washington as soon as he got wind of the *Pearl* affair to see what money could be made. Just as he had hoped, some Washington slave owners were in a mood to dispose of their disloyal slaves, and so Slatter was soon seen at the train depot with a trove of human loot. He was assisted by men armed with canes who prodded the captives to get aboard while fending off relatives hoping to give them a last embrace.

7.

The bold but failed escape down the Potomac and the ensuing pro-slavery riot in Washington seemed the capstone events of a decade during which the nation moved closer and closer to a decisive confrontation with itself. Then, in the spring of 1849, there occurred perhaps the most spectacular slave escape yet. On March 23, Henry Brown, an enslaved Virginia tobacco worker, had himself shipped from Richmond to the office of the Pennsylvania Anti-slavery Society in Philadelphia in a twelve-cubic-foot crate labeled "dry goods," from which he emerged after twenty-six hours of confinement.

Henry "Box" Brown became an instant celebrity. He toured New England as a speaker and singer specializing in hymns of thanksgiving, his story was published as a book ghostwritten by the abolitionist Charles Stearns, and he was featured in a painted panorama depicting slavery scenes that opened to public view in several northern cities.*

By the time President Zachary Taylor delivered his annual message to Congress on December 4, 1849, all these fugitive slave incidents, which in isolation might have flared out, had combined to take the territorial crisis to the verge of combustion. Earlier that fall, at what pro-slavery southerners considered a rogue convention, Californians wanting to skip the territorial stage during which Congress would have authority to determine the status of slavery had petitioned for immediate entry into the Union as

---

*After passage of the new fugitive slave law in 1850, Brown was badly beaten in Providence, Rhode Island, and fled to England, where he continued his public performances and remained until 1875.

The "unboxing" of Henry "Box" Brown at Philadelphia

a free state. Word was out that the president would welcome the same request from New Mexico. The discovery of gold in California was luring scores of thousands of migrants from all over the country, and although some in California objected to slavery on moral grounds, much of the opposition came from whites wary of competition from black slaves for mining jobs. Whites were fearful that once slave-owning gold prospectors had found—or failed to find—the treasure they were looking for, they would simply abandon their slaves to beg and steal on the streets. For many immigrants to California—as for many whites who opposed slavery in the established states of the East and the old Northwest—there was no difference between wanting to keep slaves out of their state and wanting to keep out blacks.

Amid all the contention, Taylor sounded like a well-meaning uncle who walks in on a family quarrel and tries to calm everyone with genial chatter. He counseled patience while the new territories sorted out their preferences. He promised that "all causes of uneasiness may be avoided, and confidence and kind feeling preserved. With the view of maintaining the harmony and tranquillity so dear to all, we should abstain from the introduction of those exciting topics of a sectional character which have hitherto produced painful apprehensions in the public mind."

But sectional rancor had long passed the point where it could be dispelled by this kind of "now, now, children" scolding. The president had alienated southern supporters by, among other things, relying for advice on the antislavery senator from New York William Seward, who supported personal liberty laws guaranteeing jury trials to accused fugitives and requiring district attorneys to provide them with legal counsel at public expense. Some fellow southerners considered Taylor, in his unwillingness to confront "disquieting issues, such as fugitive slaves," a traitor to the South.

The day after the president's message to Congress, Alexander Stephens wrote to his brother that "the feeling among the Southern members for a dissolution of the Union" was stronger than ever. Within the week, Calhoun noted that more and more southern members of Congress "avow themselves disunionists," and according to Calhoun's South Carolina colleague James Hammond, "The value of the Union is now calculated hourly in every corner of the South." Richard Crallé, a Virginia confidant of Calhoun's, confirmed that "many men here speak openly in favor of *dissolution;* for the course of the northern States has goaded them on to this."

All semblance of order in Congress was breaking down. Free-soil independents in the House stalled the election of a Speaker by demanding adoption of the Wilmot Proviso as the price of their votes. After multiple ballots failed to produce a majority for any candidate, Representative Richard Meade of Virginia predicted that if a bargain were reached that included the Wilmot Proviso, whoever was elected would be the last Speaker of the House because Congress would never meet again. When the sergeant at arms tried to restore order, he was mocked and hissed. Between December 1849 and March 1850, meetings were called in South Carolina, Mississippi, Georgia, Texas, and Virginia to prepare responses to northern "aggression." To consider next steps, a gathering of delegates from all across the South was planned for the spring in Nashville.

Meanwhile, talk of secession was spreading north. New Hampshire's senator John P. Hale declared that "if this Union . . . has no other cement than the blood of human slavery, let it perish." Later that year, the intensity of secessionist sentiment in both North and South disturbed Henry Wadsworth Longfellow so much that he tried to tamp it down with a poem, "The Building of the Ship," about a majestic sailing vessel named *Union*. Lest anyone miss the point, he built his ship out of "Cedar of Maine and Georgia pine":

> *Thou too, sail on, O Ship of State!*
> *Sail on, O Union, strong and great!*
> *Humanity with all its fears,*
> *With all the hopes of future years,*
> *Is hanging breathless on thy fate!*
> . . .
>
> *In spite of rock and tempest's roar,*
> *In spite of false lights on the shore,*
> *Sail on, nor fear to breast the sea!*
> *Our hearts, our hopes, are all with thee,*
> *Our hearts, our hopes, our prayers, our tears,*
> *Our faith triumphant o'er our fears,*
> *Are all with thee,—are all with thee!*

The poet's reward, despite his well-known antislavery convictions, was to be attacked for toadying to the slave drivers of the South. A storm of abolitionist contempt broke over him for having "prostituted his fine genius in praise of that which is crushing the Slave population to the earth," namely, the "Union . . . formed in utter derogation of all the principles of justice, humanity and righteousness—solely by the immolation of one-sixth portion of the population on the altar of Slavery—and through the most guilty compromises." At a meeting of the Massachusetts Anti-slavery Society, Garrison called yet again, but this time with some prospect of success, for "IMMEDIATE DISSOLUTION OF THE AMERICAN UNION—a Union based on the prostrate bodies of three millions of the people, and cemented with their blood." Its "overthrow," he proclaimed, "would inevitably burst asunder the chain of every bondman." How exactly disunion would break the chains of slavery he did not say.

Orations, editorials, pamphlets, poems, even sermons, sank to a level of personal invective unmatched before or since. It became standard practice for politicians to call each other devils and whores. With dripping irony, the Massachusetts Anti-slavery Society praised the "Cotton Whig" Robert C. Winthrop—a Boston blue blood allied with local banks involved in financing the slave-dependent textile industry—for selling himself to the Slave Power and flaunting his "wages insolently and without shame" like a streetwalker flashing her baubles. By comparison with antebellum politics, our politics, even in the age of Trump, are a model of decorum.

On December 13, 1849, Representative Robert Toombs of Georgia, who had a reputation for moderation, issued a warning from the floor of the House:

> I do not hesitate to avow before this House and the Country, and in the presence of the living God, that if, by your legislation, you seek to drive us from the territories of California and New Mexico, purchased by the common blood and treasure of the whole people, and to abolish slavery in this District, thereby attempting to fix a national degradation upon half the states of this Confederacy, *I am for disunion.*

Two months later, Democratic senator Lewis Cass of Michigan made the rueful—and prophetic—observation that "we talk flippantly of breaking up this Union as we talk about dividing a township."

Nine

STATE OF THE UNION

1.

When the Thirty-first Congress convened in December 1849, sentiment for disunion had been building for years, and in some parts of the South it was reaching fever pitch. In retrospect, it is impossible to say how much of the secession talk was serious and how much was bluster. Some historians think mainly the latter—partly, no doubt, because we know in hindsight that no state actually left the Union in 1850, and partly, perhaps, because in our own time the idea of secession has been reduced to a grumble that bubbles up now and then from, say, Texas (Lone Star Republic!) or California (Calexit!) over some unpopular tilt of federal policy to left or right. It is something we associate with failed states like "the former Yugoslavia" or hybrid states like Belgium, where French and Flemish speakers threaten each other with divorce without ever quite getting around to it. In today's United States, a call for secession is a crank call.

This was far from the case in antebellum America. Not only was secession conceivable; it was by no means clear that the Constitution did not permit it, and the Declaration of Independence was often invoked, especially in the South, as justifying it. As late as 1850, some Americans—the relatively few who had lived into their seventies and eighties—could still remember the violent break from Britain by which the nation had created itself. Many more could remember a father's or grandfather's stories about Bunker Hill, or Yorktown, or some siege or battle in between. Lincoln, speaking in 1838, described the Revolution as "living history." Whether the memories were first- or secondhand, everyone knew that the nation owed its existence to what has been called "a secessionist ethos"—the conviction that the ultimate recourse for an aggrieved people is to rise up and throw off the government by which they feel oppressed. John C. Calhoun ominously reminded his colleagues in Congress that George Washington himself, "who was born and grew up to manhood" in a union between Britain and its colonies, "did not hesitate," once he concluded that it had ceased to be a blessing and had become a curse, "to draw his sword and head the great movement by which that union was forever severed."

When, at the Constitutional Convention chaired by Washington, the founders declared that they sought "a more perfect Union," they skirted the issue of whether perfection meant perpetuity. Was "perpetuity . . . implied, if not expressed," as Lincoln was later to claim in his first inaugural address? Was the new Union divisible or indivisible? Was it ephemeral or eternal? Did states reserve the right to withdraw if their interests came into conflict with those of other states? Because every state harbored some degree of doubt about joining the new nation, it would have been bad politics to give too clear an answer to these questions. And so—like the closely related question of the future of slavery—they were deferred for future generations to decide.

Under the Articles of Confederation, threats to leave the Union had been neither extraordinary nor especially unusual. In 1783, after a Massachusetts judge ordered a group of fugitive slaves released from a captured pirate ship, the governor of South Carolina threatened secession if the runaways were not returned to their masters. The early state of the Union was like an impetuous marriage in which the partners kept having second thoughts.

Ratification of the Constitution did not end their doubts. Long after the experiment in nationhood formally commenced in 1788, northerners as well as southerners, enemies of slavery as well as its friends, continued to reconsider their mutual commitment. "I love the Union as I love my wife," John Quincy Adams wrote in 1801. "But if my wife should ask for and insist upon a separation, she should have it though it broke my heart."

The first serious threat of a breakup came not from the South but from New England, following President Jefferson's imposition, in 1807, of a trade embargo that crippled shipping and commercial farming from Maine to Connecticut.* During the War of 1812, representatives of the New England states, meeting at Hartford, considered negotiating a separate peace with Britain, which would have been tantamount to seceding from the Union. One organizer of that gathering, Timothy Pickering of Massachusetts, a former secretary of state, found "no magic in the sound of Union" and "no Terrors" in the prospect of its dissolution. A few years later, during debate over the extension of slavery into the Missouri Territory, Adams anticipated that "if the Union must be dissolved, slavery is precisely the question upon which it ought to break."

In 1824, John Randolph reminded his congressional colleagues that "this government is the breath of the nostrils of the States"—by which he meant that the states were the heart and lungs from which the breath of life flowed to the central government, not the other way around. "This government cannot go on one day without a mutual understanding and deference between the state and general governments." The Union, in other words, was a provisional alliance of independent states—"isolatoes . . . federated along one keel," as Melville was to allude to them years later in a book that ends in shipwreck, *Moby-Dick*.

In the later 1820s, the prospect of breaking up arose again, this time led by South Carolina, which threatened to "nullify," that is, to ignore, what it considered a punitive import tariff imposed by the federal

---

*There had been an earlier rumbling of secession, in 1790, from the northern states, which favored Hamilton's proposal that the federal government should assume the debts of the states incurred during the Revolutionary War. Speculators stood to profit by buying depreciated state debt at a fraction of its face value and then selling it back to the federal government. The dispute was resolved when southern states allowed the assumption bill to pass in exchange for northern support for moving the national capital from New York to Washington, D.C. A second threat of secession, centered on New England, arose in 1804 over the Louisiana Purchase, which New England federalists regarded as a reckless expansion that would diminish their own political power.

government in 1828. Describing the tariff as a subsidy for northern industry, Calhoun, already a major figure on the national scene, believed that it raised a fundamental constitutional question: Did government have the "right to impose burdens on the capital and industry of one portion of the country, not with a view to revenue, but to benefit another"? His answer was an emphatic no, and he set no limit on the right to resist, by force if necessary, anyone who answered yes. Although the "tariff of abominations," as its self-styled victims called it, was modified in 1832, opposition remained intense enough to convince one South Carolinian that "a miracle of mercy alone will prevent the disunion of our country."

As the nullification crisis heated up, the last of the surviving founders tried to cool it down. Late in the summer of 1830, writing from his home in Virginia, James Madison—now nearly eighty—sent a lengthy letter to Edward Everett of Massachusetts, intended for publication in the *North American Review*. In that letter, Madison reiterated his view that at the time of the founding there was no such thing as conditional ratification— that joining the United States was akin to entering a marriage from which there could be no exit by annulment or divorce:

> It was formed, not by the Governments of the component States, as the [Articles of Confederation] for which it was substituted was formed; nor was it formed by a majority of the people of the U.S. as a single community in the manner of a consolidated Government.
>
> It was formed by the States—that is by the people in each of the States, acting in their highest sovereign capacity; and formed, consequently by the same authority which formed the State Constitutions.
>
> Being thus derived from the same source as the Constitutions of the States, it has within each State, the same authority as the Constitution of the State . . . but with this obvious and essential difference, that being a compact among the States in their highest sovereign capacity, and constituting the people thereof one people for certain purposes, it cannot be altered or annulled at the will of the

States individually, as the Constitution of a State may be at its individual will.

Madison conceded that if all legal means, including attempts to amend the Constitution, should fail, the people did have one ultimate recourse:

> And in the event of a failure of every constitutional resort, and an accumulation of usurpations & abuses, rendering passive obedience & non-resistance a greater evil than resistance & revolution, there can remain but one resort, the last of all, an appeal from the cancelled obligations of the constitutional compact, to original rights and the law of self preservation.

What Madison called resistance and revolution, Lincoln was later to call "treasonable" and "the essence of anarchy." Yet even Lincoln, speaking in 1848 of the revolt by Texas against Mexico, once asserted that "any people anywhere . . . have the *right* to rise up, and shake off the existing government, and form a new one that suits them better." It was a statement that would come back to haunt him.

2.

The Congress that opened for business on December 3, 1849, was a mirror of the fractious nation. In the House, Democrats outnumbered Whigs by a narrow margin, 112 to 105, with the balance made up by members of the Free-Soil Party, founded in 1848 on the platform of keeping slavery out of the territories. In the sixty-member Senate, Democrats enjoyed a ten-vote majority, 34–24, over the Whigs, with the remaining two seats held by the Free-Soilers Salmon P. Chase of Ohio and John P. Hale of New Hampshire. But because both major parties were splintering along regional lines, party unity could no longer be presumed on any vote touching the slavery issue.

Southern Democrats such as Andrew Butler of South Carolina and Jefferson Davis of Mississippi demanded the untrammeled right to carry slavery into any and all territories won from Mexico, while a growing fac-tion of northern Democrats, including a rising young senator from Illinois, Stephen A. Douglas, favored the compromise doctrine (or so they consid-ered it) of "popular sovereignty," by which the question of slavery would be settled by a vote of territorial inhabitants upon application for statehood.

Whigs were similarly split. A substantial number of northern Whigs gravitated toward the Wilmot Proviso, which called for banning slavery altogether from territory won from Mexico and which had repeatedly been revived since it was first put forward in 1846. But with every reitera-tion of the Wilmot principle, southern Whigs moved closer to their Dem-ocratic counterparts and reacted with redoubled outrage. In October 1849, a bipartisan convention of slave states meeting in Mississippi issued a not-so-veiled threat that if the exclusion doctrine were adopted, they would leave the Union.

Divisions ran so deep that neither leading candidate for Speaker of the House, Robert Toombs of Georgia and Robert Winthrop of Massachu-setts, both Whigs, could muster a majority. Only after the rules were changed to allow election by plurality was the speakership finally filled. By the time the Georgia Democrat Howell Cobb, having won sufficient support from southern Whigs, was elected to the chair on December 22 the atmosphere had become poisonous. To read the mid-nineteenth-century congressional debates is to be relieved of the notion that govern-ment "gridlock" is a problem of recent origin.

Meanwhile, President Taylor was turning out to be better at deploying soldiers than dealing with politicians. Normally, once a territory reached the requisite population of sixty thousand free persons, it would apply to Congress for an enabling act granting permission to submit a constitution for congressional approval. Given what Jefferson Davis called the "con-glomerated mass of gold-hunters, foreign and native," pouring into Cali-fornia, most of whom were violently hostile to the prospect of competing with slave labor, it seemed all but certain that California would seek ad-mission as a free state.

The previous spring, Taylor had dispatched a slaveholding Georgia congressman, T. Butler King, on a mission to assess the situation. But even before receiving King's report, the president, advised by New York's senator William Seward, appeared to favor bypassing the usual territorial stage and allowing California to draw up a state constitution forthwith. To all intents and purposes, he was endorsing the doctrine of popular sovereignty and reducing Congress to a rubber stamp.

In the fall of 1849, a convention met at Monterey and, as expected, voted to organize as a free state. On the presumption that statehood was a done deal, it elected two senators, one of whom was the famed explorer, Mexican War veteran, son-in-law of Missouri senator Benton, and fervent slavery opponent John C. Frémont, who headed east to take his seat. As for the festering boundary dispute between Texas and New Mexico, Taylor expected New Mexico to follow California's lead into the Union as a free state and seemed oblivious to the fact that a stymied Texas and a free Southwest would further inflame the South.

By contrast to the explosive territorial issues, the question of what to do about fugitive slaves might seem to have been as minor as it was chronic. The census of 1850 was soon to count just over one thousand fugitives as having fled that year to the North, compared with some three million slaves remaining in the South. Yet decades of publicized incidents— vigilantism by pro- and antislavery mobs, rescues foiled and achieved, riots in the streets, disputes in the courts, and recriminations in the press, as well as the rising flood of writings by fugitives themselves—had "greatly magnified" (the historian Avery Craven's phrase) the issue. The optical metaphor is apt. Although fugitives from slavery never amounted to many by comparison with the millions still enslaved, they loomed large as symbols of what northerners regarded as justice prefigured and southerners regarded as proof of national dysfunction.

3.

Such were the circumstances when, on January 3, 1850, Virginia's senator James Mason stated his intention "to introduce a bill to provide for the more effectual execution" of the fugitive slave clause of the Constitution.

The following day the proposed bill was read aloud. No one could yet imagine what this piece of legislation, described by its sponsor as if it were a mere tweak or adjustment for carrying out a constitutional principle more effectively, would mean for the fate of the nation. Two weeks later it was approved by the Judiciary Committee and reported to the full Senate, with debate scheduled to begin on January 24.

Thus began a season of advocacy, attack, and amendment that was to last, through periods of inaction and intermittent bursts of debate, for more than eight months. Mason's bill asserted the right of slave owners or their agents to arrest a fugitive and take him "before any judge of the circuit or district courts of the United States" or any agent of the court such as a clerk, postmaster, customs collector, or commissioner in the state where the fugitive had been apprehended. The category of commissioner— an officer appointed by a circuit judge with no requirement for Senate confirmation—already existed, but the bill had the effect of enlarging their number and authority.

Upon receipt of a sworn affidavit that the person detained had in fact run from the signatory, commissioners were authorized to order and enforce a fugitive's return. They had the power to "call to their aid the bystanders, or *posse comitatus*, of the proper county" to assist "in the prompt and efficient execution of this law," and in a discrepancy that gave particular offense to enemies of slavery, they were to be paid five dollars if the decision went against the claimant and ten dollars if the judgment favored him. The stated rationale for this provision was that returning a runaway entailed more time and expense than letting him go, but some who opposed the new law exaggerated the allure of the five-dollar difference and called it "bribery" plain and simple. To them, commissioners were corrupt police answerable to no one except the slave owners who counted on them to do their dirty work.

Northerners cried foul at the incursion of federal agents into the free states. Southerners replied that the list of federal officers empowered in the North to return wayward slaves was comparable to the federal "forts, arsenals, and dockyards" located throughout the South. As for ordinary citizens, the bill imposed a fine of one thousand dollars on anyone harboring or attempting to rescue a fugitive. Even federal marshals who failed to cooperate with commissioners were subject to a monetary penalty. For the first time in the nation's history, the federal government would assume responsibility for recovering fugitive slaves, and anyone who interfered would be committing a federal crime.

Mason sunnily predicted that the bill would "meet with no resistance whatever." Whether he really believed that, or was feigning incredulity that any reasonable person could object, is hard to know. Either way, by the time debate opened on January 28, he was singing a different tune. "I have little hope," he now confessed, "that it will afford the remedy it is intended to afford" because "the disease is seated too deeply to be reached by ordinary legislation."

Andrew Butler, junior senator from South Carolina and chair of the Judiciary Committee who had proposed a fugitive slave bill of his own in the previous Congress, agreed:

> I have no very great confidence that this bill will subserve the ends which seem to be contemplated by it. The Federal Legislature . . . has too limited means to carry out the article of the Constitution to which this bill applies. . . . And I know that the cardinal articles of the Constitution are not to be preserved by statutory enactments upon parchment. They must be preserved in the willing minds and good faith of those who incurred the obligation to maintain them.

In this respect, proponents and opponents were of one mind. A decade later, in his first inaugural address, Lincoln was to say what everyone knew—that such a law could only be "as well enforced . . . as any law can ever be in a community where the moral sense of the people imperfectly supports the law itself."

4.

Enforceable or not, the proposed fugitive slave law was but a small piece in the larger structure that came to be known as the Compromise of 1850.

Its chief architect was Henry Clay, who, having led the efforts to settle the Missouri dispute in 1820 and the tariff crisis in 1832, had earned a storied reputation as a virtuoso at the art of compromise. After a seven-year absence from Washington, where for decades he had hoped to ascend to the presidency (Clay had first been elected to Congress in 1806), he now returned to discover that "the feeling of disunion [was] stronger than I supposed it could be." Still, he remained convinced that public sentiment could be rallied against it.

The Kentucky legislature had sent Clay back to the Senate by a vote of 95–42—a comfortable margin but far from unanimity. Almost seventy-three, he had spent the summer and the warm weeks of early fall hoping to cure a persistent cough in the springs at Saratoga and the sea breezes of Newport. Some of his fellow Kentuckians thought him superannuated. Others were sure that, whatever his age or the state of his health, in the matter of defending slavery he was weak.

They had cause to think so. For one thing, his reputation was not helped by his being the cousin of the rabble-rousing abolitionist Cassius M. Clay. For another, he had tried for no fewer than fifty years to push forward one plan or another in his home state for gradual emancipation. His latest idea was to schedule emancipation at age twenty-five and to deposit any wages slaves earned during their last years of servitude in a public fund reserved for financing their transportation to Liberia, the West African colony that had recently declared itself an independent nation founded on republican principles.

The idea of repatriating slaves to Africa seems to us today nothing more or less than "ethnic cleansing." And so it was, in the sense that antebellum colonizationists (black as well as white) could not conceive of a biracial nation in which blacks and whites could live together on anything like equal terms. The colonization movement had always been polluted—in some cases animated—by the idea that blacks were inferior creatures incapable of joining civilized society.

But there was also in the colonization program an element of ethnic nationalism—the idea that a true nation is the political expression of a racially distinct people whose destiny cannot be fulfilled in some alien land far from "home." In this sense, the movement partook, at least in the minds of some of its proponents, of the same spirit that drove the independence movements of Greece, Hungary, and, later, Italy and Germany—all of which sought to restore subjugated peoples to a nation of their own with which they had some ancestral connection.

Support for colonization existed even among black abolitionists, although most opposed emigration and regarded its primary advocate, the American Colonization Society, with suspicion. "What do I know of Africa?" one skeptic asked, "I am part Indian and part German," while another pointed out that "the best blood of Virginia courses through our veins." Despite such pointed caveats, Henry Highland Garnet expressed cautious support for African resettlement, writing to Frederick Douglass in 1848, "I would rather see a man free in Liberia than a slave in the United States." After the Fugitive Slave Act became law in 1850, Garnet's tentative interest (he would go on to found the African Civilization Society in 1858) became full-throated support. Martin Delany, in his 1852 treatise, *The Condition, Elevation, Emigration, and Destiny of the Colored People of the United States,* wrote that the situation of blacks in America had become so bad that "emigration is absolutely necessary to their political elevation."

Among white colonizationists, some thought that slavery had stunted the development of black culture, and that if slaves were returned to Africa, their interrupted progress could be resumed. Robert Goodloe Harper, the Maryland politician who invented the name Liberia, believed that once former slaves were restored to their homeland with the advantage of having been "Christianized" in America, they "would become proprietors of land, master mechanics, ship owners, navigators, and merchants, and by degrees schoolmasters, justices of the peace, militia officers, ministers of religion, judges, and legislators." Others made an economic argument akin to today's widespread opinion that immigrants, willing to work for menial wages, take jobs away from native American workers. "Reduce the supply of black labor, by colonizing the black laborer out of the country," President Lincoln told Congress as late as December 1862, "and, by precisely so much, you increase the demand for, and wages of, white labor."*

Well into the Civil War, Lincoln continued to speak—largely, one suspects, to placate the right wing of his white constituency, which feared the influx of blacks into northern society—of colonization as a means for achieving the "ultimate redemption of the African race and African continent." In short, advocates of colonization thought of themselves as centrists seeking a middle way between perpetuating slavery and emancipating slaves into a society unprepared to accept them as free persons.

On another heated issue of the day—the fate of slavery in the nation's capital—Henry Clay also sought middle ground by favoring an end to the slave trade while opposing outright abolition. Antebellum Washington might have been the capital city of a nation half-slave, half-free, but in reality it was a microcosm of the South—a marshy town in which, as Henry Adams (grandson of John Quincy Adams) described it, "the brooding indolence of a warm climate and a negro population hung in the atmosphere." Whites strolled in the shade of sweet-smelling catalpa trees, while blacks labored at forced roadwork under the baking sun. As they walked or rode to the Capitol, senators and representatives could hear the shouted bids at slave auctions and the cries of those being sold. Clay wished to put an end to this embarrassment.

When he returned to the city in late 1849, he was, as he had always been, an "ideologue of the center" for whom "compromise was itself a principle," and he was determined to put the principle once more into practice. "Today," as one historian remarks, "we are conscious that Clay's sectional compromises did not last and attempted to buy peace for whites

---

*Feeding the economic argument were such incidents as the 1849 strike by white carpenters and painters in Clay's hometown of Louisville, Kentucky. Employers broke the strike by hiring slaves in their place. See Fergus M. Bordewich, *America's Great Debate: Henry Clay, Stephen A. Douglas, and the Compromise That Preserved the Union* (New York: Simon & Schuster, 2012), 96. Whatever the motive or rationale, the colonization program never amounted to much. In the most active year, 1832, barely six hundred slaves left the United States (ibid., 95). Lincoln, though he remained nominally a colonizationist until late in the Civil War, had reached the conclusion by 1854 that "there are not surplus shipping and surplus money enough in the world to carry" America's slaves to Africa or anywhere else. "Speech at Peoria, Illinois," Oct. 16, 1854, in *The Collected Works of Abraham Lincoln*, ed. Roy P. Basler (New Brunswick, N.J.: Rutgers University Press, 1953), 2:255.

at the cost of indefinite postponement of freedom for blacks." But to look through the contending perspectives of his contemporaries is to get a different impression—of a man trying to steer between the pro- and antislavery passions that were threatening to destroy the nation.

Clay's reward was to catch hell from both sides. Here was another sense in which he adumbrated Lincoln, about whom Frederick Douglass was to write in memoriam that "reproaches came thick and fast upon him from . . . opposite quarters. He was assailed by Abolitionists; he was assailed by slave-holders."

So it was for Henry Clay, who, on the night of January 21, went out in a cold rain to visit his sometime ally and rival Daniel Webster. On January 29, 1850, apparently armed with a promise, or at least an intimation, of Webster's support, he stood in the Senate to present the outline of a compromise plan. Armed, too, with a shard of wood that he claimed to be a fragment of George Washington's coffin, Clay brandished it while he spoke as if it were a holy relic of the apostolic age of the Republic.

He ticked off eight points:

1. California would be admitted to the Union with no congressional stipulation regarding slavery—which meant that it would come in as a free state.

2. In the rest of the Mexican cession, territorial governments would be formed "without the adoption of any restriction or condition on the subject of slavery." This meant, in theory, that the local inhabitants could institute slavery upon application for statehood, but given the realities of climate and topography, as well as the precedent of slavery prohibition under Mexican law, in practice it meant that slavery would be excluded there too.

3. On the question of Texas, Clay proposed to keep its current boundaries roughly where they were despite a movement within and beyond Texas to expand its western border. Such an expansion would have meant that the already-enormous slave state would swallow up nearly half of what would eventually become the state of New Mexico.

4. Ever since the annexation of Texas in 1845, customs duties, which had once flowed through Galveston, Houston, and other gulf ports into the coffers of the Republic of Texas, had gone directly into the U.S. Treasury. Hoping to blunt a resurgent Texas independence movement and to make the status quo more palatable to expansionists, Clay proposed that the federal government assume the state's ballooning debt.

5. Amid rising calls to put an end to slavery in the District of Columbia, over which Congress had jurisdiction, Clay noted that the district had been formed out of land donated by Maryland and Virginia, where slavery remained legal. Knowing that any move to terminate slavery in Washington would threaten the larger compromise, he deemed it "inexpedient" to push for abolition now.

6. At the same time, he proposed to end the open buying and selling of slaves in the district. This was a cosmetic proposal. He would still permit "the sale by one neighbor to another . . . that a husband may be put along with his wife, or a wife with her husband." He also knew perfectly well that the slave-selling business would continue—indeed would be boosted—directly across the Potomac in Alexandria, Virginia, where business was already brisk.

7. Clay's seventh point, presented without reference to any of the specifics in Mason's bill, but acknowledging the issue of fugitive slaves, was "that more effectual provision ought to be made by law, according to the requirements of the constitution, for the restitution and delivery of persons bound to service or labor, in any State, who may escape into any other State or Territory of this Union."

8. Finally, he proposed to formalize the principle that "Congress has no power to prohibit or obstruct the trade in slaves between the slaveholding States."

A week later, on February 5, he rose again, this time to elaborate on his plan. The chamber was packed with spectators from the press and the public. "What a squeeze!" reported the *New-York Tribune*. "Benches, corners,

Henry Clay c. 1850

desks, avenues, doors, windows, passages, galleries, every spot, into, upon, under, behind, or before, from which man or woman could see or hear the lion of the day, were filled, used, or occupied." With a phrase that captured both his stature and his infirmity, Kate Chase, daughter of Ohio's antislavery senator Salmon P. Chase, described Clay as so tall that "he had to unwind himself to get up." In a voice somewhere between the drawl of a commoner and the languor of a patrician, he talked without break until late afternoon, when business was adjourned until the next morning.

5.

On the second day, Clay arrived at the issue of fugitive slaves. Pointing out that "of all the States in this Union, unless it be Virginia, the State of which I am a resident suffers most by the escape of their slaves to adjoining States," he noted the "seduction of family servants from their owners into free states." He lamented that "a man from a slave state cannot now, in any

degree of safety, travel with his servant to a free state, although he has no
purpose of stopping there any longer than a short time." He described a
Kentucky friend whose "little slave" had "escaped over to Cincinnati." Except for one phrase ("he was concealed") in which Clay identified the child
as a boy, he used the neuter pronoun as if the boy were a thing:

> He pursued it, recovered it—having found it in a house where he was
> concealed—took it out; but it was rescued by the violence and force of
> a negro mob from his possession—the police of the city standing by,
> and either unwilling or unable to afford assistance to him.

As for Mason's fugitive slave bill, which was still subject to revision,
Clay spoke in stern but cagey generalities, declaring that he would vote
"most cordially and willingly for the most stringent measures that can be
devised to secure the execution of the constitutional provision it alludes
to" and would "go with the furthest Senator from the South to impose the
heaviest sanctions on the recovery of fugitive slaves."

Looking back to the Supreme Court decision in *Prigg v. Pennsylvania*,
he conceded that citizens of free states could not be forced to aid in hunting down fugitives. But neither could they be allowed to impede the hunt.
"The Supreme Court of the United States," he said, has "decided that all
laws of impediment are unconstitutional." The personal liberty laws of the
North were therefore void:

> That whole class of Legislation . . . by which obstructions and im-
> pediments have been thrown in the way of the recovery of fugitive
> slaves, is unconstitutional, and has originated in a spirit which I trust
> will correct itself when those States come calmly to consider the na-
> ture and extent of their federal obligations.

This was wishful thinking. Clay was asking northerners to maintain a
patriotic neutrality on the fugitive question regardless of their personal
views on slavery itself. The federal government would perform the unpleasant business from which they were spared, but they were obliged to

get out of the way while the government performed it. It was time, as Mason put the matter with a grossly demeaning analogy, to recognize that without federal enforcement, "you may as well go down into the sea, and recover from his native element a fish which has escaped you."

Clay strained to make some fine distinctions among degrees of compliance:

> I do not say that a private individual is bound to make the tour of his State in order to assist an owner of a slave to recover his property; but I do say, if he is present when the owner of a slave is about to assert his rights and endeavor to obtain possession of his property, every man present, whether he be an officer of the General Government or the State Government, or a private individual, is bound to assist, if men are bound at all to assist in the execution of the laws of their country.

This was slippery language. What, exactly, was the force of the word "assist"? What did it mean to be "present"? Within sight or earshot of an arrest? In a neighborhood where a fugitive might be hiding? On the fringes of a crowd gathered at a jail or courthouse where his fate was being decided?

Evading such questions, he ended his long oration with a nervous platitude: the Union, he declared, was made for "posterity, undefined, unlimited, permanent and perpetual." There was something more plaintive than persuasive in his words, as future events would attest.

Ten

THE LAST TRUCE

1.

Some were nevertheless persuaded, or at least made an effort to persuade themselves. Alexander Stephens and Robert Toombs went to the president to tell him that Clay's proposals were the only alternative to disunion. Daniel Webster wrote to a worried friend that "there will be no disunion, or disruption. Things will cool off. California will come in. New Mexico will be postponed. No bones will be broken—& in a month, all this will be more apparent."

The senior senator from South Carolina, however, took a darker view. Too ill to attend Clay's two-day oration, Calhoun had doubtless read it, or at least heard it summarized. It did not dissuade him from his growing conviction that North and South could never be reconciled. One of Calhoun's close associates, referring to a recent essay by Henry Ward Beecher arguing that "there are two incompatible and mutually destructive principles wrought together in the government of this land," reported Calhoun's clipped response. "Mr. Clay," he said, "should read that article."

In the previous year, Herman Melville, following political developments from his home in western Massachusetts, had published an allegorical novel, *Mardi, and a Voyage Thither,* in which there appears a character modeled on Calhoun. Referring to the nullification dispute of twenty years earlier, Melville called this character Nulli—a "cadaverous, ghost-like man; with a low ridge of forehead; hair, steel-gray, and won-drous eyes" that burned with fierce intelligence despite his evident decline toward death. It was a timely portrait. When, a few minutes past noon on March 4, 1850, Calhoun entered the Senate chamber, everyone could see that he was dying.

Supported by South Carolinian James Hamilton, he walked slowly to his desk, from which he thanked the Senate for its courtesy in allowing a colleague to read his remarks. He had hoped that his fellow Carolinian Andrew Butler would be the one to read the speech, but Butler, pleading poor vision, asked the sponsor of the fugitive slave bill, James Mason (whom Calhoun's friend Joseph Scoville later described as a "small potato" unfit for the task), to do it. As Mason rose, Calhoun sank into his seat to listen to his own words.

As if tracking his descent, Melville undertook another portrait of Cal-houn that spring in a new novel, *Moby-Dick*, about a whale ship com-manded by a "monomaniac" captain who looks "like a man cut away from the stake, when the fire has overrunningly wasted all the limbs without consuming them."*

There was, indeed, little left of Calhoun, at least in body. Among those who saw him from the gallery on the Senate floor was the future Civil War general William T. Sherman, who judged that "he was evidently ap-proaching his end, for he was pale and feeble in the extreme." But, like Clay, Calhoun had not entirely lost his gift for political theater. As a young man, he had combed his hair straight up to make himself seem even taller than his six feet two inches. Now, in an attempt to hide his emaciation, he wrapped himself in a long bulky cloak.

Some who knew him reported that he had once shared Jefferson's view of slavery as a temporary evil that would someday pass away. "Mr. Cal-houn, in his earlier days," according to the legal scholar Francis Lieber, a contemporary who taught at the University of South Carolina before

---

*Alan Heimert, "*Moby-Dick* and American Political Symbolism," *American Quarterly* 15, no. 4 (Winter 1963): 498–534. Heimert reads *Moby-Dick* as a political allegory in which the fictional char-acters of the novel stand in for American political figures or ideologies of the 1840s—Ahab as Cal-houn; Bulkington as Benton; Flask "perched precariously" on the shoulders of the black harpooner Daggoo "like the southern economy itself" (502), among other correspondences.

John C. Calhoun c. 1849

moving to Columbia College in New York, "called slavery a scaffolding erected to rear the mansion of civilization, which must be taken down when the fabric is finished." But by mid-century, there was no one in the country more zealous for slavery than Calhoun.

Speaking to the Senate in 1837, he had called slavery a "positive good"—a phrase that became permanently attached to the burgeoning view among the slaveholding classes that the founding fathers had been wrong to proclaim human equality as a norm or aspiration. Calhoun was convinced that "there never has yet existed a wealthy and civilized society in which one portion of the community did not . . . live on the labor of the other." He believed that those in the bottom rank are better off assigned by law to dependency on their betters than set loose to fend for themselves. "There is, and always has been . . . a conflict between labor and capital," but the southern form of slavery "exempts us from the disorders and dangers resulting from this conflict." A stable society requires a docile underclass, and only slavery, if imperfectly, delivers it.

This was the view that became known as the "mud-sill" theory, so named by Calhoun's disciple James Hammond in an infamous speech delivered to the U.S. Senate not long before the Civil War:

> In all social systems there must be a class to do the menial duties, to perform the drudgery of life. That is, a class requiring but a low order of intellect and but little skill. Its requisites are vigor, docility, fidelity. Such a class you must have, or you would not have that other class which leads progress, civilization, and refinement. It constitutes the very mud-sill of society and of political government; and you might as well attempt to build a house in the air, as to build either the one or the other, except on this mud-sill. Fortunately for the South, she found a race adapted to that purpose to her hand.

Hammond was incalculably smug and vulgar by comparison to his mentor. He was a sexual predator whose abuse of young girls, despite his avid preference for the white race in all other matters, did not stop at the color line. Preying not only on his own teenage nieces but on at least one of his female slaves as well as her twelve-year-old daughter, he was shameless. When his wife asked him to sell his two slave mistresses, he declined on the grounds that "I am averse" to sending them away, because to do so would "involve injustice and cruelty to others."

In temperament, personal behavior, and force of intellect, there was a world of difference between Hammond and Calhoun. But Calhoun, too, extolled slavery as a boon not only for slave owners but for working whites, whether or not they owned slaves. Slavery, he believed, insulated them from the degradation suffered by wage laborers at the bottom rung of "free" society, who were treated as cogs in the industrial machine—to be thrown away and replaced when they wore out. The existence of a permanent black underclass—well cared for, in Calhoun's view, by slave masters for reasons of both benevolence and self-interest—made possible a stable, hierarchical society in which poor whites enjoyed what one historian calls "caste pride" by comparison to the dependent laborers below them.

There was nothing eccentric about these ideas. By the early 1850s, especially in the Deep South, it had become commonplace to assert that "no social state, without slavery as its basis, can permanently maintain a republican form of government." Nor was it a new idea. It had been identified years before by a perceptive Englishman, the diplomat Sir Augustus John Foster, as the key to understanding the American South, where white liberty was thought to depend on black slavery. "Virginians," Foster wrote in 1812, "can profess an unbounded love of liberty and of democracy in consequence of the mass of the people, who in other countries might become mobs, being there nearly altogether composed of their own Negro slaves." Calhoun concurred and approved.

But he also blended the slaveholder's argument from self-interest with a professed concern for the welfare of the slaves. In 1844, writing to the British foreign minister, Lord Pakenham, he reported that blacks in the North suffered from much higher rates of insanity (today it would be called depression) than did slaves in the South. Without the sheltering embrace of their masters, blacks were helpless when left to the mercy of white predators in the North, whether those preying on them were wage laborers who hated them for working for a pittance, or captains of industry who would enslave them in all but name.

Calhoun was no stranger to the North. Under the tutelage of Jonathan Edwards's grandson Timothy Dwight he had been educated at Yale, from which he went on to Tapping Reeve's renowned School of Law in Litchfield, Connecticut. In those New England years, he acquired—or perhaps had always possessed—an almost Calvinistic view of history. Human events were driven by ineluctable forces, while human beings were inclined by nature to despoil the rights of others and were constrained only by self-interest. Slavery, to his mind, mitigated these hard facts. It was a system by which the high and the low could live in harmony sustained by mutual dependency.

Calhoun thought like a theological casuist—the kind of philosopher who judges particular cases of behavior not by their practical consequences but by whether they accord with some grand theory or doctrine. He believed, for example, in the fundamental right of constituents to petition their representatives in Congress. Yet he supported the gag rule on the grounds that the refusal by Congress to debate the petitions did not

curtail the right of citizens to submit them. He was appalled by abolitionists, but he nevertheless refused to support legislation prohibiting the federal government from delivering abolitionist pamphlets through the U.S.
Postal Service. To give the federal government the power of censorship,
he believed, would be to give it "the most odious and dangerous" power
"that can be conceived." Yet he had no problem with alternative congressional legislation (never passed) that would have required the post office
to observe state laws against distributing abolitionist publications in states
where such laws were in force. He was nothing if not a resourceful thinker.

For Calhoun, a well-ordered society was one that encouraged willing
acquiescence from the ruled and responsible authority from the rulers—a
standard from which he seems rarely to have departed in his personal
conduct toward his own slaves. "I never heard of his using the lash," recalled one of his nieces, "even a slap or any species of violence," though she
seems to have forgotten at least one occasion when he ordered a runaway
lashed upon being caught away from his plantation. Still, seeing himself
"in the double capacity of master and guardian," he did not fit the mold of
the plantation master fanned by day on the veranda and prowling the slave
quarters by night. His chilly rectitude kept him aloof from the bons vi-
vants of his own caste even in the queen city of his own state, where "the
place of a Charleston gentleman was considered to be under the table"—
the last place where Calhoun was likely to be found.

Although he died more than ten years before the Confederacy was
born, he became, and remains, its most detested symbol. His social and
racial ideas are anathema today,* but in his own time his candor earned
him respect from some who reviled his views yet saw in them a reverse
reflection of their own conviction that slavery was a sin. Even John Quincy
Adams, in the 1820s, judged him a man "of fair and candid mind, of honorable principles, enlarged philosophical views," and "ardent patriotism."

---

*On February 11, 2017, Yale's president, Peter Salovey, announced that the Yale Corporation had
decided to remove Calhoun's name from the residential college that had been named in his honor in
1931. The decision was made because of "John C. Calhoun's legacy as a white supremacist and a national leader who passionately promoted slavery as a 'positive good.'" "Decision on the Name of
Calhoun College," Feb. 11, 2017, president.yale.edu/speeches-writings/statements/decision-name-
calhoun-college.

Few doubted his exceptional intellect, evident in his luminous "eyes, bright as coals, [which] move in jumps, as if he thought in electric leaps from one idea to another."

In its annual report for 1849, the Massachusetts Anti-slavery Society acknowledged Calhoun as "the very incarnation of the Slaveholding idea. He stands for an idea as no other statesman at Washington does. . . . He will leave his stamp upon his age as no other public man of his day will do. It will be a 'bad eminence,' indeed, that history will assign him, but it will be a conspicuous and enduring one." "Bad eminence" was a reference to the throne from which Milton's Satan—a figure both evil and charismatic—addressed his own parliament of fellow demons in *Paradise Lost*. At the 1849 meeting of the Anti-slavery Society Garrison himself introduced a resolution commending Calhoun as

incomparably to be preferred to those Northern time-servers and dough-faces, who professedly look upon Slavery with abhorrence, and yet are found ever ready to compromise the sacred principles of liberty, to betray the rights of the people of the North, and on bended knee to worship the Slave power of the South.

The resolution was unanimously approved.

The following year the society praised him again at the expense of "such men as Mr. Clay and Mr. Benton, at the South, and of their admirers at the North," who bobbed and ducked, unwilling to stand firm one way or the other on the slavery question—unlike the "marked, decided, understandable, unmistakeable . . . Mr. Calhoun," who does not shrink from defending "an actual, tangible Idea, however wicked it may be . . . an Idea that stands up by itself, in its own natural proportions, instead of being razeed down to regulation dimensions."*

By contrast to the weasel compromisers, Calhoun struck his adversaries

---

*"Razeed," derived from the French *vaisseau rasé,* referred to a ship from which one or more decks have been cut away in order to reduce its size and weight. In *Moby-Dick,* chapter 36, Captain Ahab, for whose portrait Melville likely had Calhoun in mind, tells his first mate, Mr. Starbuck, "Aye, aye! It was that accursed white whale that razed me." *Moby-Dick* (1850; Evanston, Ill.: Northwestern University Press, 1988), 163.

as a mirror image of themselves—someone who shared with them an uncompromising vision of human affairs in which ideas "absolutely right and absolutely wrong" were locked in epic struggle. "Even the sight of Satan himself," the American Anti-slavery Society report continued, "would be a welcome refreshment in the Limbo of Vanity, or Paradise of Fools," where most of his congressional colleagues could be found. "Even the Idea of the Absolute Excellence of Slavery though it may be much worse, is much less disgusting than the abortive monstrosities which try to unite theoretical abhorrence of Slavery with a daily practical support of it. It is for this reason that we like to see Mr. Calhoun stand up before the Nation, and boldly give utterance to the Idea with which he is possessed."

By early March, his health broken, Calhoun could not stand up for long, but the speech read by Mason did indeed give bold utterance to "the Idea with which he is possessed." Once again he defended slavery and all but said that due to the insufferable self-righteousness of the North the Republic was beyond saving. Northern animosity toward the "social organization" of the South had become fatal to the nation. Thinking of Clay's encomiums to the Union, and doubtless of his own dire condition, he told his colleagues that the Union "cannot . . . be saved by eulogies on the Union, however splendid or numerous. The cry of 'Union, Union, the glorious Union!' can no more prevent disunion than the cry of 'Health, health, glorious health!' on the part of the physician can save a patient lying dangerously ill."

Well before Emerson and other antislavery northerners reached the same conclusion, Calhoun was convinced that the United States had become two distinct nations. Lost was the "perfect equilibrium" of the early republic, when the total population (around four million in 1790) had been almost evenly divided between the sections, and ever since the free-state population had swelled until it now accounted for more than ten million of the nation's seventeen million persons. The proportionate consequence was "to give the northern section a predominance in every part of the Government."

Even worse, the government had "changed . . . from a Federal Republic into a great national consolidated Democracy," by which Calhoun meant a government controlled by a majority contemptuous of the rights of the minority. It had reached a state "as absolute as that of the Autocrat of Russia, and as despotic in its tendency as any absolute Government that ever existed." No major political figure before or since has come as close as Calhoun to saying that "what they call the Nation" is a sham. By restricting slavery, by subjecting "the great exporting portion of the Union" to onerous taxes, and by distributing the revenue disproportionately to the North, the national government was leaving one section to atrophy while the other prospered. The American experiment in federalism had failed.

This description of the United States in 1850 as two nations made a certain sense. Visitors from abroad were struck that North and South seemed to have almost nothing in common except a shared (more or less) language. Fewer than one in thirty southerners was foreign-born, while in the North the corresponding figure was one in seven. In Calhoun's South Carolina, the enslaved black population was approaching 400,000, more than the total population (around 300,000) of Webster's native New Hampshire, where free blacks numbered barely 500. In the North, New York, Boston, Philadelphia, and Albany, as well as newer settlements such as Buffalo, Milwaukee, and Chicago, had become true cities with populations in the scores or hundreds of thousands. In the South, with the exceptions of Baltimore, Richmond, and New Orleans, urban growth was negligible. On the eve of the Civil War, South Carolina had only three towns with more than 2,500 inhabitants.

Beyond such measurable differences, there were less quantifiable contrasts in the character of social life. Northern white women were beginning to venture out to engage public issues through "networks, bonds, voluntary associations, mothers' clubs"—entities that barely existed in the South, where women were still largely confined to private lives within the household. Among men, southern culture "honored violence as a sign of manhood," while men in the North—at least self-styled gentlemen—were expected to express "anger verbally instead of violently." Public education was developing rapidly in the North, only fitfully in the South. Rates of literacy and social mobility diverged sharply too.

So in one sense, Calhoun's view of the South under siege was confirmed by the facts. But in another sense, the facts made a farce of his indignant devotion to a society that not only crushed hope for blacks but curtailed the prospects of most whites. Writing a few years later, the North Carolinian Hinton Rowan Helper made the case that the real reason for stagnation in the South was the very institution Calhoun was hell-bent on defending. In his 1857 tract, *The Impending Crisis of the South,* Helper charged that slavery had

> depopulated and impoverished our cities by forcing the more industrious and enterprising natives of the soil to emigrate to the free states; brought our domain under a spare and inert population by preventing foreign immigration; made us tributary to the North, and reduced us to the humiliating condition of mere provincial subjects in fact if not in name.

Yet even if Helper was right, and even if one could somehow eject from Calhoun's thought the particulars of antebellum American life and politics—the tariff question, the problem of territorial jurisdiction, the fact and fate of slavery itself—there would still be something substantive left: his fear that majoritarian government, without curbs on its power, tends to devolve into tyranny. During the tariff crisis, he had written that "no government, based on the naked principle that the majority ought to govern, however true the maxim in its proper sense, and under proper restrictions, can preserve its liberty even for a single generation." To doubt this truth was to prove that the doubter "knows nothing of the human heart."

It may seem bewildering that this champion of slavery has been posthumously recognized as a cogent thinker ("the last American statesman," according to the historian Richard Hofstadter, "to do any primary political thinking") committed to the defense of minority rights. The minority Calhoun had in mind was, of course, his own slaveholding class, and he gave little thought—beyond asserting that slavery was good for slaves—to the rights of the racial minority on whom that class built its power and wealth. And yet his warning that majorities will always endanger the rights of minorities resonates today for anyone, on the left or right, wary of vesting unrestrained power in any government, popularly elected or not.

To Calhoun, American history had become a plot against the South— a plot so nefarious and so advanced that the South now faced an existential choice between submission and revolt. Goaded by abolitionists, the black and white races were being driven toward open warfare (a view shared by some northern conservatives) and the South toward desolation.

In this apocalyptic mood, Calhoun denounced President Taylor for issuing an "Executive Proviso" that was every bit as bad as the Wilmot Proviso. By tacitly approving the constitution adopted at Monterey, the president had usurped the authority of Congress to rule on what basis California would come into the Union. And because the Constitution assigned territorial governance to Congress, and—in Calhoun's view— guaranteed the right of all citizens to carry their property anywhere within the nation, it followed logically that slaves could no more be barred from California by executive fiat than by legislative action. Addressing the Senate on June 27, 1848, Calhoun had insisted that "we of the South have contributed our full share of funds, and shed our full share of blood for the acquisition of our territories. Can you, then, on any principle of equity or justice, deprive us of our full share in their benefit and advantage?" Now he reminded his colleagues that "it was the United States who conquered California," not some gang of volunteers or mercenaries from the North. The future of California must be "vested" in the whole United States. In short, the president, by accepting the proposition of a free California, had betrayed not only his native South but also the Constitution that he had sworn to defend.

Most of Calhoun's speech was in this vein—a catalog of injuries inflicted on the South. The closest thing to a remedial idea was a vague proposal, further developed in his posthumously published *Disquisition on Government,* that equilibrium between the sections could only be restored by a constitutional amendment dividing the office of the president into two co-equal halves, each with veto power. Thomas Hart Benton, who loathed him, later recalled that "Mr. Calhoun, intent upon extending slavery; and holding the Union to be lost except by a remedy of his own," proposed the idea, "which he ambiguously shadowed forth—a dual executive—two Presidents: one for the North, one for the South: which was itself disunion if accomplished." There is no reason to think that Calhoun thought such a scheme would actually work. He was shouting into the wind, and he knew it.

As for the fugitive slave question, two years earlier he had called it the "most vital of all questions" facing the Republic. Less than a year after that, addressing a group of slave-state representatives, he devoted several pages to the fugitive slave clause of the Constitution and to the "sophistry and subterfuges" by which it "had been evaded, and, in effect, annulled" by the northern states—an evasion amounting to "one of the most fatal blows ever received by the South and the Union."

Now, however, he wasted scarcely any breath on it. He remarked only in passing, as if in deference to the man reading his speech, that "the North must do her duty by causing the stipulations relative to fugitive slaves to be faithfully fulfilled." His expectations for Mason's proposed law were vanishingly low. The whole fugitive slave problem was no longer—if it ever had been—a problem for which there existed a solution in his mind, at least not within the current political structure. Instead, it had become a useful provocation for pushing reluctant southerners to make the right and only choice: disunion.

Calhoun's farewell speech was less a sermon than a funeral oration, explicitly for the nation, implicitly for himself. By the end of March, he was dead. "The cast-iron man who looked as if he had never been born and could never be extinguished" was gone. Tributes—some lavish, some grudging—poured in, including from many who regarded his ideas with opprobrium. One who declined to join the effusion of praise was Benton, who told Webster, "He is not dead. There may be no vitality in his body, but there is in his doctrines."

2.

Two days before Calhoun's speech, Webster had gone to see him in his sickroom. Like Clay, Webster had been surprised upon his return to

Washington by the "excitement & inflammation," but he continued to believe that "all this agitation . . . will subside without serious result." As winter settled in, his confidence flagged. On February 24, he wrote to his son, "I am nearly broken down with labor and anxiety. I know not how to meet the present emergency, or with what weapons to beat down the Northern and the Southern follies, now raging in equal extremes. . . . I have poor spirits, and little courage." No one knows what passed between Webster and Calhoun during their conference on March 2, but there is no reason to think that Calhoun was evasive about what he planned to say.

As for what Webster would say when his turn came to speak in the Senate, he probably did not know until just before he said it. Rumors flew that he would propose extending the Missouri Compromise line to the Pacific and breaking California into two states—one open to slavery, the other free. "I mean to make an honest, truth-telling speech; and a Union speech," he wrote to a friend on March 1, "but I have no hope of acquitting myself with more than merely tolerable ability."

Nearly twenty years earlier, in response to secessionist threats during the tariff crisis, Webster had made his name throughout the land with a ringing phrase: "Liberty and Union, Now and Forever, One and Inseparable!" As for slavery, he now wrote to the abolitionist William Henry Furness, "from my earliest youth, I have regarded slavery as a great moral & political evil. I think it unjust, repugnant to the natural equality of mankind, founded only in superior power, a standing & permanent conquest by the stronger over the weaker . . . [and] opposed to the whole spirit of the Gospel & to the teachings of Jesus Christ."

But how to reconcile the two—the evil of slavery and the good of union? In a letter of January 9, Furness had implored him to "give yourself utterly to the Right," by which he meant to beg Webster to condemn the fugitive slave bill and the whole accommodation to the Slave Power of which it formed an essential part. On February 15, Webster replied that he was "a good deal moved" by Furness's letter but could not "co-operate in breaking up social & political systems, on the warmth (rather than the strength) of a hope that in such convulsion, the hope of emancipation may be promoted."

Perhaps this was indifference cloaked in realism. Maybe it was sheer temporizing. Or it could have been genuine horror at the prospect of unleashing the dogs of war for uncertain ends. There was no such thing, Webster believed, as "peaceable secession." Moreover, "confusion, conflict, and embittered controversy, violence, bloodshed, & civil war would only rivet the chains of slavery more strongly."

This was not an implausible prediction in 1850. If the nascent secession movement had seized the popular will in the South, there was small reason to assume that there would have been sufficient will in the North to force seceded states back into the Union, much less to make war on slavery itself. "I am for the abolition of slavery," Garrison wrote on January 13 to the abolitionist Samuel J. May, "and therefore for the dissolution of the Union." Many shared his view that those two convictions were one.

Nor was it clear, if secession had come in 1850, that it would have been met by military force. Even if an attempt had been made to compel seceded states to return to the Union, it was doubtful before the North had "attained the preponderance of strength, or the technological sinews, or the conviction of national unity which enabled it to win the war that finally came in 1861," that such an attempt would have succeeded.

War in 1850 might just as well have released the Slave Power to pursue its dreams. It might have emboldened the expansionist faction in Texas, which was already threatening to take up arms to pursue its territorial ambitions in New Mexico. It might have encouraged slave owners, "dreaming of a new empire which would make the Gulf of Mexico a western Mediterranean," to drive into Cuba, the Caribbean, or farther into Mexico than Polk and Taylor had been willing to go. The whole unstable structure of the Union—which had served to constrain the Slave Power, if not as tightly as Calhoun believed—might have collapsed.

Such hypotheticals may sound fanciful, but perhaps less so if one bears in mind that when the "secession war" (Whitman's phrase) finally came a decade later, only very slowly did it become an antislavery war. For more than two years, its outcome was in grave doubt, a strong peace movement in the North arose with the objective of ending the bloodshed and returning to the status quo ante, and only the improbable combination of inspired leadership (Lincoln and, after many failed generals, Sherman and Grant), contingent battlefield events, the surging pace of slave escapes, and a grueling war of attrition that eventually wore down public resistance to the idea of black enlistment allowed the North to prevail and to destroy slavery at last.

This is a case where the historian's resistance to counterfactual speculation should be resisted. Only by imagining what might have happened if compromise had failed can we begin to understand those, like Webster, who acted in the present based on their best guess of what would happen in the future.

When, on March 7, Webster rose to speak, he was unaware of Calhoun's presence in the room. Referring to "an honorable member, whose health does not allow him to be here today," he was corrected by another senator who called out, "He is here!"—to which Webster responded with "may he long be here, and in the enjoyment of health to serve his country!" Then, having paid his respects, he proceeded to dispute Calhoun's claim that the federal government had pursued a systematic policy of choking the South. He pointed out that Congress had approved statehood for Alabama, Mississippi, Louisiana, Arkansas, Missouri, Florida, and most recently Texas—hardly the record of a government dominated by antislavery interests.

In Webster's alternative history lesson, the war against Mexico had been waged expressly in order to acquire new lands "south of the line of the United States, in warm climates and countries," which southerners expected to develop with slave labor. But because "events have not turned out as was expected," the South had experienced "disappointment and surprise."

After that remark—no doubt heard by Calhoun and his allies as a taunt in the guise of an understatement—Webster launched into a history of slavery from ancient Israel, Greece, Rome, and medieval Christendom, all the way up to the early American republic. He noted the regret with which the founders, southern as well as northern, viewed the presence of slavery in the new republic, and he traced the fateful growth of pro-slavery conviction as a result of "emergent and exigent interests"—namely, the astounding rise of the cotton industry to dominance in the world economy.

All this was to be lamented, but one must "view things as they are" rather than pine for how they once were or might have been.

The fulcrum of Webster's speech—the point at which he turned from scolding the South toward sympathizing with it—came when he arrived at the subject of the abolitionists, whom he decried for rejecting any "compromises or modifications . . . in consideration of difference of opinion or in deference to other men's judgment." They believe, he said, "that human duties may be ascertained with the exactness of mathematics," and they "do not see how too eager a pursuit of one duty may involve them in the violation of others." In preliminary notes for the speech, he had described them as "fault finders with the sun," people with a pathological hunger for perfection. Now, in the speech as delivered, he expanded the trope, condemning them as absolutists who, if they "detect a spot on the face of the sun, they think that a good reason why the sun should be struck down from heaven."*

All this was an overture to what everyone was waiting for—Webster's verdict on the fugitive slave bill.† With a long sentence that winds its way through six clauses while staying true to the dubious tradition of talking about slavery without calling it by name, he gave himself a drumroll:

> I will allude to other complaints of the South, and especially to one which has in my opinion just foundation; and that is, that there has been found at the North, among individuals and among legislators, a disinclination to perform fully their constitutional duties in regard to

---

*In *Moby-Dick*, when Ahab's first mate, Mr. Starbuck, condemns the captain's pursuit of "vengeance against a dumb brute" as blasphemy, Ahab replies, "Talk not to me of blasphemy, man; I'd strike the sun if it insulted me" (164). Melville had doubtless read Webster's speech. Webster's sunspot metaphor was a variant on Lyman Beecher's comparison, offered fifteen years earlier, of abolitionists to "he-goat men, who think they do God service by butting everything in the line of their march which does not fall in or get out of the way." Lyman Beecher to William Beecher, July 15, 1835, in *Autobiography, Correspondence, Etc. of Lyman Beecher, D.D.*, ed. Charles Beecher (New York: Harper and Brothers, 1866), 2:345.

† Webster had actually prepared a less draconian bill that included provision for jury trial for accused fugitives, and though he had shelved it, he remained uneasy with the summary nature of the judicial proceedings prescribed by Mason's bill. See Merrill D. Peterson, *The Great Triumvirate: Webster, Clay, and Calhoun* (New York: Oxford University Press, 1987), 470.

the return of persons bound to service who have escaped into the free states.

Then, at last, he came to the point:

> In that respect, the South, in my judgment, is right, and the North is wrong. Every member of every Northern legislature is bound by oath, like every other officer in the country, to support the Constitution of the United States; and the article of the Constitution which says to these States that they shall deliver up fugitives from service is as binding in honor and conscience as any other article.

The moment when Daniel Webster said "the South is right . . . and the North is wrong" might have been the moment that saved the nation from secession or, at least for a decade, staved it off.*

Others thought, and think, that Webster deserved not praise but re-crimination. His speech of March 7 made him the key figure in what has been ever since a fierce debate over the moral status of the emerging compromise and of the fugitive slave law at its center. Listening from the ladies' gallery that day, Frances Seward, the wife of New York's senator Seward, felt something close to nausea and declared that the sound of the word "compromise" had become "hateful" to her.

For anyone alert to slavery as an actuality rather than an abstraction, Webster's speech was, and is, hard to take—a speech filled with platitudes about the prudence of the new law but silent about its effect on those whose hopes for freedom it would crush. With that speech, he sealed his reputation as the spokesman—some would say the tool—of northern bankers and merchants alarmed by what might happen if the nation should fracture, by the prospect of disturbance of the textile industry, volatility in

---

*Stephen Lubet, *Fugitive Justice: Runaways, Rescuers, and Slavery on Trial* (Cambridge, Mass.: Harvard University Press, 2010), 132, suggests that Webster signaled his intent to support the fugitive slave bill at the very start of his speech by opening with these words: "I wish to speak to-day, not as a Massachusetts man, nor as a Northern man, but as an American." Lubet's point is that, in 1850, to call oneself "a Massachusetts man" was to announce one's opposition to the rendition of fugitive slaves.

Silhouette of Daniel Webster, 1844

commodity prices, disruption of credit markets for producers of cotton, rice, and sugar, and the attendant risk of financial panic. Still other commentators, then and since, have argued that the secession threat was a bluff and that Webster was making a big show of snuffing out a feeble flame that would have burned out on its own soon enough.

For anyone inclined to distrust him—and there were many—Webster did little to help himself. However much he might have been inwardly conflicted, his outward demeanor was one of cold certitude—haughty, confident, bombastic, and without Calhoun's intellectual ferocity or Clay's personal charm. The magnitude of his ego seemed equal to his girth. Seen in bulbous profile, belly thrust out, weight planted on disproportionately dainty feet, he was the very archetype of pomposity.

And yet some who heard his words sensed that he did not have his heart in them. General Sherman, who had been struck by Calhoun's deathly pallor, found Webster's speech "heavy in the extreme, and I confess

that I was disappointed and tired long before it was finished. No doubt
the speech was full of fact and argument, but it had none of the fire of
oratory, or intensity of feeling, that marked all of Mr. Clay's efforts."

Before committing the speech to print, Webster tinkered with it, trying to adjust the balance between conciliation and condemnation in his
remarks about the South. He added a protest against the widespread practice of jailing black sailors while northern ships were moored in southern
ports. As for his attacks on what he later called the "wandering and vagrant philanthropy" of the abolitionists, he deleted a passage in which he
had said that if all the funds raised for antislavery societies could be
pooled, the money would be enough to buy freedom for every slave in
Maryland.

In some respects, the speech was a triumph. It had a "tranquillizing
effect" on the markets, helping to reverse a decline in U.S. bond prices. In
the South, Webster was hailed as a man of prudence and moderation. In
Boston, a letter of commendation was published over the signatures of
eight hundred eminences, including Oliver Wendell Holmes Sr., the former president of Harvard Josiah Quincy, and its current president, Jared
Sparks. Personal benefits accrued too. A Washington banker canceled
Webster's debt. New York friends sent him a gold watch.

But appreciations were met with equally fervid bursts of contempt. In
antislavery circles, he was regarded as a feckless windbag. Speculation was
rife that southern Whigs had offered him their support to replace Taylor
as president in the next election. Having once been lionized for his paean
to "Liberty and Union, Now and Forever, One and Inseparable," he became the object of foaming mockery from none other than Ralph Waldo
Emerson, who wrote in his journal, "'Liberty! liberty!' Pho! Let Mr. Webster for decency's sake shut his lips once and forever on this word. The
word *liberty* in the mouth of Mr. Webster sounds like the word *love* in the
mouth of a courtezan." A year later, now speaking in public, Emerson
finished him off with a urinary metaphor. "All the arguments of Mr.
Webster," he said, "are the spray of a child's squirt against a granite wall."

Echoing Milton's account of Satan's fall in *Paradise Lost*, Whittier responded more decorously but to the same effect:

So fallen! so lost! the light withdrawn
Which once he wore!
    The glory from his gray hairs gone
    Forevermore!

Henry Ward Beecher, from his pulpit at Plymouth Church in Brooklyn, accused Webster of "fatal apostasy." A thousand miles away, the city council of Chicago declared him fit to keep company with Benedict Arnold and Judas Iscariot.

A particularly scorching attack came from Horace Mann, who, in the *Boston Atlas* of May 3, excoriated Webster for failing to support an amendment offered by Seward mandating a jury trial for fugitives in the state where they were apprehended. "Webster's intellectual life," Mann wrote privately to his wife, "has been one great epic, and now he has given a vile catastrophe to its closing pages."

On May 31, Webster counterattacked. In a letter to the *Boston Daily Advertiser,* he traced the history of the fugitive slave problem back through the 1793 law, to the Constitution, the Northwest Ordinance, and all the way to seventeenth-century extradition agreements between the British colonies of New England and their Dutch counterparts in New Netherland. He rattled off blue-blooded New England names—Cabot, Ames, Sedgwick, among others—who had supported through the centuries the principle of rendition for fugitives from service. He lamented that the case of *Prigg v. Pennsylvania* had been used by northern states as authority for establishing personal liberty laws that defied the Constitution.

As for Mann's insistence on jury trials for accused fugitives, he dismissed that demand on legalistic grounds, pointing out that rendition disputes were neither criminal cases nor civil lawsuits and therefore the constitutional right to trial by jury did not apply. Whatever the merits of this argument, the fact that Webster resorted to it revealed his failure to grasp that among his own constituents the fugitive slave question had become much more a matter of morality and conscience than of law.

So which side had him right? Was he a statesman or a sellout? Many writers, popular and scholarly, have debated this question for what is now approaching 175 years. One late nineteenth-century writer said of him that "enthusiasm for self killed his enthusiasm for humanity." In the twentieth century, he was grouped with such historical villains as the Nazi collaborator Quisling and the weak-willed Neville Chamberlain, who failed to see Nazism for what it was. Others, with equal conviction, defend him for standing his ground in the political storm. One of his successors in representing Massachusetts in the U.S. Senate, John F. Kennedy, portrayed him in a book called *Profiles in Courage* (1956) as a man of conscience who, by supporting a law unpopular among his constituents, accepted "political crucifixion" for the sake of saving his country.

The pendulum continues to swing. Some hear in the March 7 speech abject appeasement. On this view, if Webster were to appear again in a composite biography, he would be better served by the title *Profiles in Cowardice.* For others, he was an agonistic figure struggling within the limits of American constitutionalism to avert a catastrophe that would set back the slow advance of freedom. Still others hear in Webster's words "the calm and cruel confidence which belongs to those who are in step with time" because "time, he knew, had been, and would be, with the North."

In the end, there is no umpiring this dispute. He was sometimes bold, sometimes timorous. More often, as surely most people would have been, he was an unstable combination of the two.

3.

Four days later, the Senate was the scene of another long oration, delivered by New York's former governor and freshman senator, William H. Seward. The March 11 speech was Seward's first address to the Senate, expectations were low, and much of what he said amounted to the familiar (among antislavery Whigs) argument that the founders would not have tolerated slavery beyond the limits of where it existed at the time of the founding.

On the proposed fugitive slave bill, which he was later to characterize as a malicious attempt "to enforce upon the free States of this Union the domestic and social economy of the slave states," Seward remarked that with respect to fugitives, "the Constitution contains only a compact, which rests for its execution upon the states." By seeking to impose federal penalties for noncompliance, the proposed bill was doomed to fail. "Has any government ever succeeded in changing the moral convictions of its subjects by force?" In short, you may pass this law, but it won't work.

Seward also went out of his way to agree with Calhoun—who was still present in the chamber when Seward spoke on March 11—that indeed the North had developed faster and further than the South. Yes, year after year, the North grew more populous, while southern development stalled. But shall we therefore "alter the Constitution so as to convert the government from a national democracy, operating by a constitutional majority of voices, into a federal alliance, in which the minority shall have a veto against the majority"?

Toward the end of his speech, Seward uttered a phrase—already in circulation in antislavery circles—that caught the attention not only of his colleagues but of the press and the public: "There is a higher law than the Constitution." By these words, he did not mean to make an appeal above and beyond the Constitution, but rather to say that its authors had followed the law of God and nature in writing it. True, at the time of the founding, slavery still prevailed in some states, and through the "full faith and credit" clause the Constitution provided the slave states with a temporary reprieve pending the final triumph of freedom. But by design of the founders, the Constitution recognized no such concept as human property. There was therefore no constitutional basis for permitting slavery to expand onto a single acre of federal territory while time withered it away until it died.

Despite these unsurprising assertions from a northern antislavery man, Seward's speech caused consternation even among his friends, who feared—justifiably, it turned out—that the phrase "higher law" would make him sound like a raging abolitionist and could expose him to the charge of claiming personal communion with God. Nothing enraged southerners more than a sanctimonious northerner condemning their way of life as ungodly. Yet even though Seward denounced "all legislative compromises" as "radically wrong and essentially vicious," he had no impact on the prospects for a compromise deal. Within five months, the deal was sealed.

All through the spring, the select Committee of Thirteen—six Whigs and six Democrats, plus Clay as chair—worked and reworked a single "omnibus" bill containing essentially all of Clay's original proposals. Deliberations were in full swing when, on July 9, President Taylor, having consumed large quantities of iced milk and strawberries on a blistering Independence Day, died of what is generally called, for lack of a better diagnosis, acute gastroenteritis. His death was met with pro forma lamentation, but in fact it lifted the congressional mood and, by removing the threat of a presidential veto with the ascension of the pliable Millard Fillmore, seemed to clear the way toward agreement. In fact, when the omnibus bill finally came to the floor at the end of July, it was rudely received, amended to death, and, after half a year's effort, Clay's wizardry was suddenly spent.

In the meantime, Stephen Douglas, who had doubted all along that the votes were there for the omnibus, had been working a parallel track as chair of the Committee on Territories. His strategy was to break the compromise into separate bills, each of which had a better chance to attract coalitions of support. The three lions of the Senate—Clay, Calhoun, and Webster—were now gone. Calhoun had died in March, Clay retreated to Newport after his bill went down, and Webster, appointed by Fillmore, assumed the office of secretary of state just a week before the decisive vote. By mid-August, the irrepressible Douglas, wheeling and dealing with consummate skill, had garnered enough support for the separate provisions to pass by comfortable margins on separate votes, though it took him until mid-September to push through the abolition of the slave trade in the city where the senators lived and worked.

As for the fugitive slave bill, it had been buffeted all spring and summer by a barrage of conflicting amendments; some designed to toughen it, others to weaken it. From Mason himself, under pressure from colleagues in the Deep South, came an amendment applying the thousand-dollar fine not only to anyone actively colluding with a runaway slave but to anyone "obstructing" enforcement in any way. A second amendment ruled out testimony by the accused in any rendition hearing. These changes eventually became part of the final bill.

Another amendment, introduced by Jefferson Davis—who remained suspicious of the bill as a dangerous precedent for extending federal authority into state affairs—provided for civil suit by slave owners against anyone interfering with the rendition process. Another, proposed by the Maryland senator Thomas Pratt (opposed by Davis), would have granted slave owners the right to file suit against the U.S. government to recover monetary damages if a slave duly identified and located was not returned to him.* These amendments failed.

Northern and upper-South moderates offered amendments of their own, intended to soften the bill. From Clay's select committee came a proposal to require a tribunal in the runaway's home state to furnish a record "adjudicating the facts of elopement and slavery, with a general description of the fugitive." Another amendment would give fugitives the right to a jury trial in the state from which they had fled. In January, Seward moved an amendment guaranteeing jury trial and the right of habeas corpus to the accused. This was a nonstarter because southern senators regarded jury trial in a state where antislavery sentiment ran high as tantamount to gutting the bill.† As late as June, Webster—seeking to redeem himself in the eyes of his antislavery constituents, and perhaps to his own conscience—had offered a similar amendment but hedged it with admonitory language providing for trial by jury if "the fugitive shall deny that he owes service to the claimant under the laws of the State where he was held, and after being duly cautioned as to the solemnities and consequences of an oath, shall swear to the same." These amendments, too, went nowhere.

On August 24, Senate Bill No. 23 was approved, with support exceeding opposition by more than two to one. The final version of the fugitive slave bill was little changed from James Mason's original draft. It was

---

*Tennessee senator Hopkins Turney dismissed the idea, pointing out that if slave owners knew they could be paid by the government, they would have little incentive to seek return of the slave themselves. Stanley W. Campbell, *The Slave Catchers: Enforcement of the Fugitive Slave Law, 1850–1860* (New York: W. W. Norton, 1968), 22.

†New Jersey senator William Dayton tried to allay such fears by citing several cases where juries, even in fiercely abolitionist Burlington County, New Jersey, had remanded fugitives. See Campbell, *The Slave Catchers*, 18.

reported to the House and passed without alteration on September 12, thus joining the series of measures that came to be known collectively as the Compromise of 1850. On September 18, after consulting his attorney general on the question of its constitutionality, President Fillmore signed the fugitive slave bill into law.

How strong the so-called compromise really was may be judged by the fact that only four senators voted for all the bills that composed it. How durable it was may be judged by the fact that it lasted barely ten years.

From one point of view, it was a defensible armistice, a means of buying time as the antislavery movement gathered force for the great conflict to come. "Looked on merely as a truce between the two sections," one pro-Union historian wrote some fifty years after the fact, "what a victory for the North it turned out to be!" From another point of view, it was a cynical sacrifice by white politicians of black hopes in what was arguably the most corrupt bargain in American history.

Early in the process, three days after Webster's tide-turning speech and three weeks before he died, Calhoun wrote to his friend Thomas Clemson that if Webster "should be sustained by his constituents, and New England generally, it is not improbable . . . that the question may be adjusted or patched up, for the present, to break out again in a few years. Indeed, it is difficult to see how two peoples so different and hostile can exist together in one common Union." Of the many prognostications of what was to come, this was the most prescient.

Eleven

EXPLOSION

1.

At first, the compromise was greeted with bells and whistles. One New York recorded in his diary that the streets resounded with "howling and hurrahing and other demonstrations of patriotic furor, and a large quantity of vapid spouting." A cannon salute on Boston Common could be heard as far away as Cambridge and Charlestown. In Georgia, even some of the loudest advocates for secession now took a wait-and-see attitude ("upon a faithful execution of the *Fugitive Slave Law* . . . depends the preservation of our much beloved Union"), declaring their willingness to give it a chance. Secessionist sentiment seemed to slacken. In Washington, the crack and boom of fireworks were accompanied by the marine band parading around town playing patriotic tunes.

But not everyone showed up for the party. In an article enumerating all the senators who had found a way to avoid the vote, the *New York Herald* judged that "Mr. Clay was wide of the mark in supposing that the Fugitive bill would end the agitation—it only begins it." Under the title "Artful Dodgers," a New Hampshire paper reported that "between twenty and thirty Northern Whigs dodged the vote, by sneaking away from the post of duty." In fact, of the sixty senators, twenty-one never voted yea or nay on the bill. Among notable absentees was Missouri senator Benton, who considered it "injudicious" but was "willing for his friends to try it." According to the New Orleans *Daily Picayune*, Benton preferred "to stand neuter on the subject" and thereby put himself "in an excellent position to take a stand hereafter in favor of repeal if he shall find that course agreeable and profitable." In the case of Michigan senator Lewis Cass, perhaps it was defective hearing that kept him from responding amid the "noise and confusion" when his name came around in the roll call. Even the man who saved the compromise, Stephen Douglas, never cast a vote one way or the other on the bill. The fugitive slave bill, as the *Herald* put it, "has turned Whigs and Democrats into fugitives; and it is difficult to tell whether they or the runaway slaves run fastest from the law."

After it passed despite the missing votes, relief in some quarters was matched in others by anger, to which neutrality conferred no immunity. In November 1850, the president of Knox College in Galesburg, Illinois, Jonathan Blanchard, published an open letter to Douglas decrying Congress for its cruelty to fugitives but also for having inflicted an impossible choice on "law-abiding men, who wish to obey the laws and respect themselves." Blanchard, an evangelical minister, echoed Seward's "Higher Law" speech and invoked William Blackstone, whose classic *Commentaries on the Laws of England* declared that "the law of nature . . . dictated by God himself, is of course superior in obligation to any other. No human laws are of any validity if contrary to this." Douglas responded by saying that the evidentiary requirements of the new law would protect free blacks from kidnapping.

As for Daniel Webster, his alibi for missing the vote was watertight: by the time the final bill reached the Senate floor on August 24, he had left to assume office as secretary of state. Nevertheless, his speech of March 7 had established him so firmly in the public mind as the main sponsor of the bill that Henry David Thoreau, among others, referred to it simply as "Webster's fugitive-slave bill." In September, when a crowd assembled outside his Washington lodgings to cheer him for having saved the Union, Webster stepped out grandly to thank them. But back in Massachusetts, when he asked the management of Boston's leading hotel to lend him six cooks to prepare dinner for a foreign dignitary at his home in Marshfield, the cooks—all of them black—were reported to have said they would "see him in hell first."

Shortly after his speech to the Senate, Webster had written to a friend that "if we would avoid rebellion, out-breaks, and civil war, we must let Southern Slavery alone." Thanks to the new law, the constitutional provision for recovering fugitive slaves now had the full force of the federal government behind it. The people of the North were about to find out that southern slavery would not leave *them* alone.

2.

The first to be arrested under the terms of the new law was James Hamlet, a resident of Williamsburg, Brooklyn, who was seized at his workplace in lower Manhattan on September 26, eight days after it went into effect. Two years earlier, Hamlet had fled his owner in Baltimore, Mary Brown, who had inherited him from her late husband. When she learned that he was working as a porter in New York, she furnished an acquaintance with power of attorney and paid him to travel there (her son went along in order to confirm the fugitive's identity) to bring Hamlet back so she could sell him.

Taken before the clerk of the U.S. district court, who had been appointed a federal commissioner, Hamlet tried to dispute his status as a slave on the grounds that his mother was a free woman. But because the law blocked fugitives from testifying in their own defense, his statement was ruled inadmissible. After the summary hearing, he was handcuffed, taken off in a carriage guarded by "two men on the driver's seat and three inside," and driven to a pier where, in the custody of Mrs. Brown's agent, he was loaded onto a steamboat bound for Baltimore—there to be incarcerated in "the slave prison of the successor of Hope H. Slatter, a well-known hell upon earth," while awaiting "sale and shipment to a Southern market."

As it turned out, Mrs. Brown got her money, and Hamlet got his freedom back. With help from the African Methodist Episcopal Zion Church, to which he belonged, eight hundred dollars was raised to purchase his liberty, and by early October he was back in New York as a free man. On

THE FUGITIVE SLAVE LAW.....HAMLET IN CHAINS.

In this image from The National Anti-slavery Standard *(October 17, 1850),*
Hamlet, standing before New York City Hall, is rendered in a crucifixion pose
as a figure somewhere between a Roman slave and a diapered child.

October 5, several thousand people—black and white—gathered in the
park in front of city hall to welcome him. Invited onto the stage, he expressed his gratitude not with words but by waving a handkerchief with
which he wiped away his tears. One who had helped secure his freedom,
the black abolitionist Robert Hamilton, was reported to have said, "He is
a free man—that is a speech itself." Yet freedom was no longer something
to count on. Another fugitive living in New York City at the time, Harriet
Jacobs, later recalled that as soon as the new law went into effect, "every
colored person kept their eyes wide open, [and] examined the newspapers . . . to see what Southerners had put up at the hotels."

A few days before Hamlet's arrest, Theodore Parker had preached a
sermon in Boston titled "The Function and Place of Conscience in Relation to the Laws of Men." By the time he prepared his speaking notes for
publication, word had reached him of the New York incident, of which he
added an account to the printed text as a warning to the people of New
England that the long arm of the fugitive slave law would soon reach
them too. "A fugitive," he wrote,

has the same natural right to defend himself against the slave catcher, or his constitutional tool, that he has against a murderer or a wolf. The man who attacks me to reduce me to slavery, in the moment of attack has alienated his right to life, and if I were a fugitive, and could escape in no other way, I would kill him with as little compunction as I would drive a mosquito from my face.

With Christian ministers urging defiance by force—deadly, if necessary—anyone who thought the sectional crisis had been resolved was learning otherwise. Benjamin Curtis, the U.S. Supreme Court justice who, in keeping with contemporary practice, also presided over Boston's federal district court, published a statement that while he respected the belief of individual citizens that "fugitive slaves ought not to be restored to their masters," he urged "these Unitarian clergymen" to say whether they really believed "that the moral duty which we owe to the fugitive slave, when in conflict with the moral duty we owe to our country and its laws, is so plainly superior thereto, that we may and ought to engage in a revolution on account of it."

Most citizens—clergy and otherwise—accepted Curtis's implicit rebuke and made no call for revolution. As measured by the number of renditions completed versus those prevented, the fugitive slave law was actually a short-term success. One scholar counts sixty-seven runaways arrested in 1851—the highest number of any year before the Civil War— of whom thirty-nine were returned to slavery by a federal tribunal and another twenty returned without any judicial process. Of the remaining eight, three were released and five were rescued. But no enumeration can convey the law's divisive effect on the nation it was meant to unite. Opponents regarded compliant officials with disgust and treated them with derision. Supporters likened the requirement to send fugitives back to the South to the duty to "surrender . . . deserting seamen under our treaty stipulations with foreign powers," thereby inadvertently endorsing Calhoun's view that the so-called United States really was two nations.

In cities across the North, "Union safety" committees called upon citizens to obey the law as the "necessary fulfillment of the antecedent obligation imposed by the constitution." In the same cities, "vigilance" committees denounced the law as unconstitutional, provided legal aid to its victims, and sometimes helped to break them out of detention. Supporters ranked the fugitive slave law first among the "peace measures" passed by Congress. Opponents judged it *"null and void,* from the fact that it contravenes the Divine law." One Unitarian clergyman claimed he would rather see his own brother or son sent into slavery than defy the law and thereby destroy the Union. Another minister of the same denomination called it "the vilest law that tyranny ever devised" and swore never to obey it.

Meanwhile, Theodore Parker's prediction that the struggle would spread to New England had already come true. Nearly two years earlier, Ellen and William Craft's audacious escape from Georgia—with light-skinned Ellen disguised as a white man and William acting the part of her slave—had made them celebrities in their adopted city of Boston and rankling symbols of impudence and guile in the South. When the story of their escape became known, Wendell Phillips counted it among "the most thrilling in the nation's annals."

Ellen, the daughter of an enslaved mulatto mother and a white planter in Macon, Georgia, who owned them both, was a skilled seamstress. William, a dark-skinned carpenter who was frequently hired out, belonged to a bank to whom he had been turned over by his master in settlement of a debt. Sometime in the fall of 1848, he came up with an ingenious plan. "It occurred to me," he explained in their joint memoir published in 1860, that "as my wife was nearly white, I might get her to disguise herself as an invalid gentleman, and assume to be my master, while I could attend as his slave." At first the scheme seemed so improbable that Ellen balked, but recognizing that "it was not customary in the South for ladies to travel with male servants," she agreed to give it a try.

She cut her hair short, dressed in men's clothing complete with cravat, dress boots, and a foppish hat that William had purchased as if for himself, and the two of them, posing as master and slave, headed north. Because Ellen could not write, she feigned an injury, wrapped her right hand in a poultice, and kept her right arm in a sling. Reveling in the role of dutiful servant, William signed for her. As the Crafts later recalled with

Ellen Craft in disguise

wry satisfaction, they stayed audaciously in the best hotels, including the one in Charleston frequented by "John C. Calhoun and all the other great fire-eating statesmen." Ellen's disguise was so convincing that "two handsome young ladies" swooned at the sight of "him," one of them exclaiming to her father, "Oh! dear me, I never felt so much for a gentleman in my life!" As William notes, "they fell in love with the wrong chap."

By Christmas, the Crafts had reached Philadelphia. By early 1849, they were in Boston, where William opened a carpentry business, and they quickly became star attractions on the abolitionist speaking circuit. Their tale had particular appeal as proof not only of their own ingenuity but of the gullibility of the southerners whom they had fooled. They were living refutations of the idea—so dear to slave masters—that the differences between black and white in intelligence and demeanor were unmistakable. For abolitionists, they also became symbols of the heartlessness of New Englanders who refused to join the cause. "Probably not a church in this town," said the pioneer feminist and abolitionist Lucy Stone, "would open its doors to William and Ellen Craft, and suspend its services for a single half-day to allow them to tell the thrilling story of their escape from slavery, and its crucial wrongs." Then, in October 1850, the man who had once owned the Crafts, a Unionist Whig named Robert Collins, decided to test the new fugitive slave law by trying to get them back.

Undaunted—or perhaps encouraged—by the knowledge that they were not likely to be arrested in Boston as easily as Hamlet had been plucked from New York, Collins sent two bounty hunters, John Knight and Willis Hughes, after them. When word that hunters were on the way reached members of the Boston Vigilance Committee, they hid the Crafts in a series of safe houses and warned U.S. marshal Charles Devens that if he attempted to violate their rights, he would be sued.

The enraged Collins appealed to President Fillmore, who authorized the use of military force to aid in their recapture—a threat that friends of the Crafts met in kind. "I have had to arm myself," wrote Parker, who, on November 7, 1850, held a private ceremony sanctifying their unofficial marriage, and "have written my sermons with a pistol in my desk,— loaded, a cap on the nipple, and ready for action."

In the end, no federal troops were sent, and there was no firefight. After making their way overland through Maine to Nova Scotia—a refuge for fugitive slaves ever since the War of 1812—the Crafts embarked in December for Liverpool and a life in England, where they would spend the next eighteen years. "Weightier than the Constitution, stronger than laws, is one Ellen Craft," declared Wendell Phillips, "to open the hearts of Northern Freemen, that door which Daniel Webster wishes to shut." Phillips went on to proclaim that "the best way we know of to express our sympathy and respect" for the Crafts "is to labor for the overthrow of [the] Union."

Two of America's most famous fugitive slaves had thus escaped, but not the slave catchers. Knight and Hughes were arrested for slandering Ellen and damaging William's carpentry business. Upon posting bail, they were rearrested for attempted kidnapping and, for good measure, charged with violating a local ordinance against public smoking. After their arraignment, a mainly black crowd filled Court Square, hissing and chanting, "Bloodhounds," as they retreated to their hotel. According to Hughes's account, Parker showed up at his room to give him what he described as "a piece of friendly advice—that he had kept the mob off of me for two days, and was afraid he could not do it any longer." The Crafts not only had saved themselves but, by leaving the country, had thwarted Collins's plan to test the fugitive slave law in court.

3.

Before long, another opportunity arrived, in the person of a young male slave known as Shadrach—named for the righteous Hebrew youth enslaved by King Nebuchadnezzar (Daniel 1:6–7; 3:12–30) who passes unscathed through fire. In May 1850, Shadrach had escaped from his owner in Norfolk, Virginia. Once in Boston, he found work as a waiter in a coffeehouse. On the morning of February 15, 1851, having obtained a warrant the day before, slave catchers seized him while he was serving breakfast and took him "with his waiter's apron still on" to the nearby courthouse. News of the arrest spread quickly, and another mostly black and angry crowd gathered in Court Square.

Robert Morris, only the second black man in American history to be admitted to the bar, met with the prisoner and, after obtaining his verbal permission to submit a writ of habeas corpus, asked the well-connected young attorney Richard Henry Dana Jr. to take it to Chief Justice Lemuel Shaw of the Massachusetts Supreme Court, who brusquely denied it. "This won't do," Shaw said. "I can't do anything on this . . . the man is in legal custody, of a U.S. Marshal." Meanwhile, four more senior lawyers— Samuel Sewall (a descendant of the Puritan magistrate who had written against slavery in the previous century), Ellis Gray Loring (veteran of the *Aves* case), Charles List, and Charles Davis—constituted themselves as a pro bono legal team and sought a three-day postponement of the hearing date so they might prepare the prisoner's defense. When the younger brother of Justice Benjamin Curtis, U.S. commissioner George T. Curtis—whom Parker called the "kidnapper's jackal"—unexpectedly granted their request, Sewall, Loring, and List returned to their offices to work up the case. Davis, along with the abolitionist editor Elizur Wright, remained with Shadrach.

During the legal proceedings, some of the men milling outside had entered the building and mounted the stairs to the second floor, where the courtroom was located. When Davis and Wright walked out of the chamber, a rush of men stormed in, with Lewis Hayden, a fugitive from Kentucky and the "leading negro in Boston," at their head. They shoved and kicked the court officers, then hustled Shadrach down the stairs into the crowd outside, which, like a "black squall" (Dana's phrase), swirled around him. He was whisked from Boston to Cambridge, then to Concord, Leominster, and Fitchburg, from where he headed to Canada. After settling in Montreal, he opened a series of restaurants, one of which he named Uncle Tom's Cabin.

Back in Boston, the judicial process was not done. While abolitionists rejoiced that Shadrach's rescue had been authorized by a "writ of Deliverance issued under the Higher Law," federal marshals charged Davis with breaking the actual law by aiding Shadrach's escape. Representing himself with assistance from Dana, Davis was brought for a hearing before another Boston commissioner, Benjamin F. Hallett.

In mounting Davis's defense, Dana tried to raise doubts about what exactly had happened during the chaos of Shadrach's flight and who, if anyone, had instigated it. One witness claimed that Davis, while leaning against the courtroom door to prevent it from closing, had urged the crowd beyond the courtroom to "take him out, boys—take him out." Other witnesses attributed the incitement to Elizur Wright, whose trial as a co-conspirator would follow later. In order to avoid aggravating Commissioner Hallett—a staunch ally of Webster's—Dana and Davis concentrated on disputing such questions of fact rather than on the larger issue of the legitimacy of the law under which Shadrach had been arrested in the first place.

At one point, Dana even conceded that "this law was constitutionally passed" by Congress, and "though not constitutional, we think, in its provisions . . . it is the law until repealed or judicially abrogated." He further acknowledged that anyone who sets "higher law" above statutory law must be prepared either to accept punishment—"we are a republic . . . we obey the laws we make, and we make the laws we obey"—or to carry resistance to the point of revolutionary violence:

> We talk about a higher law on the subject of resistance to the law. And there is a higher law. But what is it? It is the right to passive submission to penalties, or, it is the active ultimate right of revolution. It is the right our fathers took to themselves, as an ultimate remedy for unsupportable evils. It means war and bloodshed.

For the moment, even the most zealous advocates of the "higher law" realized there was no hope of revolution, so they would have to content themselves with small, provisional victories. On February 26, they got such a victory when Hallett ruled the evidence against Davis insufficient to merit a trial. In the ensuing months, more "co-conspirators" were arrested, including Hayden, Morris, and Wright—all of whose cases ended in dismissal, acquittal, or a hung jury.

Throughout the winter, local and national newspapers published predictably contradictory accounts of what had happened. Some celebrated Shadrach's rescue as an act of noble resistance; others denounced it as a shocking outbreak of mob rule. "TE DEUM LAUDAMUS! Bless the Lord, Oh my soul," exulted the *Anti-slavery Bugle*, while the *Boston Daily Times*, incensed that Boston's blacks had taken the law into their own hands, bemoaned "the predominancy of Negrodom in the Athens of America." Speaking in the U.S. Senate on February 21, Henry Clay warned that the United States must decide "whether the government of white men is to be yielded to a government by blacks." Moncure Conway, who was in the Senate balcony, could "never forget the anger that shriveled up the already wrinkled face of Henry Clay" that day. Clay was incensed that the outrage in Boston had been committed "by negroes; by African descendants; by people who possess no part, as I contend, in our political system." From Alabama came warnings that "the day for dissolution of the Union had arrived."

On February 18, two or three days before Shadrach entered Canada (the exact date on which he crossed the border is uncertain), President

Fillmore issued a proclamation, jointly signed by Webster, "calling on all well-disposed citizens to rally to the support of the laws of their country." Because local authorities appeared unable or unwilling to suppress public disorder, the president instructed the secretary of war to order the commander of the small contingent of federal forces stationed at Boston Harbor to prepare for action at the request of any federal judge or marshal. Conservatives in Boston, in the words of the industrialist Abbott Lawrence, were "deeply mortified"—not by the actions of the president, but by the failure of Bostonians to obey the law.

Southerners and southern sympathizers in the North wanted more. The *Georgia Citizen* thought it past time to send "a naval and military force . . . sufficient to batter down the walls of Boston and lay it in utter ruin." From the other side of the slavery divide, congratulations poured in to the people of Boston for having proven that "the spirit which resisted the British Stamp Act and threw the tea into Boston harbor, still lingers in the bosom of the descendants of the Pilgrims." Never mind that most participants in the Shadrach rescue were descended not from Englishmen seeking refuge in America but from Africans forced to America as slaves. As for the descendants of the Pilgrims (not a few white antislavery leaders were just that), they did not have to wait long to be tested again.

4.

On February 21, 1851, a young slave named Thomas Sims who had been hired out as a bricklayer in Savannah stowed away on a vessel bound for Boston. As the ship approached port, fearing that the captain would put him in irons and have him shipped back to Georgia, Sims managed to escape by jumping into a dinghy carried by the ship as a lifeboat. Once ashore, he made the mistake of writing to his wife, a free woman in Savannah. His owner, a rice planter named James Potter who endorsed the so-called Georgia Platform demanding full execution of the fugitive slave law as a condition for preserving the Union, became aware of their correspondence, obtained a certificate signed by a Georgia judge confirming that Sims was his property, and sent two men to Boston to reclaim him.

PRACTICAL ILLUSTRATION OF THE FUGITIVE SLAVE LAW.

On the left, William Lloyd Garrison supports a slave woman while brandishing his gun at a slave catcher, equipped with noose and shackles, mounted on the back of Daniel Webster. Behind Garrison stands an armed black man; another holds a slave owner by the hair and is about to whip him. Amid the chaos, Webster, holding the Constitution, offers a crashing understatement: "This, though Constitutional, is extremely disagreeable."

Potter's agents—whom Dana, again an attorney for the defense, described with withering irony as "low-bred, dissolute, degraded beings" in whose hands "no man's property would be safe a moment"—secured a warrant from Commissioner Curtis for Sims's arrest. "In the name of the President of the United States of America," the document stated, "you are hereby commanded forthwith to apprehend Thomas Sims now alleged to be in your District, a colored person, charged with being a fugitive from service in the State of Georgia."

That same night, three policemen found Sims walking on the street with several companions. When he resisted arrest, they charged him with disorderly conduct and with stealing a watch they discovered on his person. Before being subdued and taken in handcuffs to the Boston courthouse, he briefly broke loose and slashed one of the officers with a pocketknife, which Theodore Parker later called "a most unlucky knife, which knocked at a kidnapper's bosom, but could not open the door." In order to comply with the 1843 Massachusetts "Latimer law" forbidding use of state facilities in a fugitive slave case, Marshal Devens declared the courthouse a federal jail.

News of these events was met in antislavery circles with a mixture of horror and welcome. William Lloyd Garrison, hosting an emergency meeting of the Vigilance Committee at the offices of the *Liberator*, was in an I-told-you-so mood, as if this latest case only proved his long-held conviction that North and South must cut all connection. Other members, hoping to find an orderly path out of the crisis, pondered their legal options. Some were pacifists. Others urged another round of action in the streets. Lewis Hayden, as if to embarrass the dithering whites, huffed and puffed that black Bostonians would take matters into their own hands just as they had done in the Shadrach case.

In fact, the prosecutions of those who had assisted in Shadrach's rescue had persuaded scores of black Bostonians to leave the city, and Hayden—under indictment himself—admitted privately to one committee member that he was bluffing in the hope that his white friends would not realize "how really weak we are." Although most black people in Boston—roughly 2,000 in a city of 140,000—had more reason to worry about losing their jobs to Irish immigrants than about their personal vulnerability to the fugitive slave law, many were enraged. Even before the Shadrach rescue, Henry Weeden, a tailor active in the effort to integrate Boston's public schools, had given his rage pointed expression upon receiving an overcoat belonging to the U.S. marshal Watson Freeman:

Boston Dec 4, 1850

Mr Watson Freeman
Sir

Your Coat came to me this morning for repairs. I take this method of returning it. Without complying with Your request. With me Principle first. Money afterwards.

> Though a poor man I crave the patronage of no Being that
> would volunteer his services to arrest a Fugitive Slave or that *would
> hang 100 Niggers for 25 cents each*—
> Henry Weeden
> 10 Franklin Avenue

Across the nation, enabled by the telegraph, newspapers recounted the Boston events at a pace remarkably close to what we would call "real time." "The authorities of the City and the Federal Government," wrote the Washington *Daily National Intelligencer* on April 7, 1851, "cannot again be taken by surprise" and "are already on the *qui vive,* so that no suddenly-conceived and unopposed rescue, as in the case of Shadrach, can be accomplished in this case." All sides agreed that the Sims case would be "a critical test for the fate of the nation," but they disagreed bitterly about what it would take to pass the test.

Working behind the scenes was Webster, who, in one scholar's assessment, had a "singular devotion to enhancing his presidential prospects by demonstrating to the South that Boston would enforce the Fugitive Slave Act." In late November, while the Crafts were still in the country but before the Shadrach fiasco, Webster had organized a rally in Faneuil Hall, where, seventy-five years earlier, such firebrands as Sam Adams and James Otis had urged rebellion against Britain but which now rang with voices demanding deference to the law. After Shadrach's escape, in a letter to President Fillmore, Webster called the Boston resisters "insane," pushed for the prosecution of Shadrach's accomplices, helped to draft Fillmore's proclamation, and might have threatened to resign as secretary of state if the president did not bring Boston into line.

Local authorities had learned some lessons from the Shadrach case. Within hours of Sims's arrest, another crowd gathered, but this time hundreds of armed police, supplemented by militia and civilian volunteers, encircled the courthouse and secured its doors with heavy chains. With its lone inmate, the fortified courthouse loomed over Boston, as Charles Sumner described it, like the "Bastille of the Slavocracy."

In his capacity as an ordained pastor, Parker, now known as "Minister-at-Large for Fugitive Slaves," was permitted to see the prisoner. A pack of "ruffians," he wrote—by which he meant Irish—"mounted guard at the entrance, armed with swords, fire-arms, and bludgeons. . . . Inside the watch was kept by a horrid looking fellow . . . a naked cutlass in his hand and some twenty others, their mouths nauseous with tobacco and reeking also with half-digested rum paid for by the city." Wendell Phillips "counseled every colored man who had ever felt the chains of Southern oppression, to fill his pockets with pistols." Horace Mann presided over a packed meeting where Thomas Wentworth Higginson, later to command a black regiment in the Civil War, gave a speech so "vehement" by his own account that it brought "the community to the verge of revolution." "O city without a soul!" wrote Longfellow. "When and where will this end?" Bronson Alcott, writing in his diary, broadened the question to encompass the whole nation: "What is a republic taking sides against itself?"

Sims's defense team included Charles Loring and Samuel Sewall, who was a veteran of the Shadrach case, joined by Robert Rantoul, a distinguished attorney and member of Congress. Opposing counsel was Seth J. Thomas, reviled as "the legal pimp of the slave catchers." Trying to forestall a hearing before Commissioner George T. Curtis, Sewall prepared an affidavit declaring that Sims "never knew such a person as James Potter." When he presented it to Justice Shaw, who had been forced to stoop under the chains to enter the courthouse, Shaw ignored it. Parker later took satisfaction in recalling the indignity visited upon the chief justice: "Think of old stiff-necked Lemuel visibly going under the chains! That was a spectacle!"

Spectacle or not, Shaw was unyielding. When Sims's lawyers filed a motion for habeas corpus, he relented only to the extent of allowing a hearing before the three judges of the Massachusetts Supreme Court. Fearing that delay would allow time for resistance to organize, the court took barely two hours to issue a unanimous opinion, much of it probably prepared in advance. The writ was denied, and the state court refused to intercede in the federal proceedings.

Yet in a long comment appended to the text of the decision itself—a strikingly personal note from a jurist known for his cool rationality—Shaw allied himself with Lord Mansfield's famous dictum in the *Somerset*

*Massachusetts chief
justice Lemuel Shaw
in 1850*

case that slavery is "so odious, that nothing can be suffered to support it, but positive law." He then reviewed the creation of the U.S. Constitution, whose prohibition of "states . . . from harboring fugitive slaves, was an essential element in formation" of the Union—a compromise, he believed, without which the nation could never have been formed. "It seems, therefore, to be conclusively settled that although other powers may denounce [slavery], and declare it founded in force and violence, injustice and wrong, yet they cannot disregard the rights flowing from it, when legalized by another power." In this respect, the Constitution guaranteed to the states of the American Union the same rights as those conferred on sovereign states by international law. The only alternatives were disunion or, sooner or later, civil war.

Throughout his opinion, as if to confirm his bona fides as a despiser of slavery, Shaw reverted again and again to the theme that only positive law can uphold such an odious institution. But there was no denying that such positive laws were on the books—namely the statutes of Georgia and the federal fugitive slave law—and had to be enforced. Thus, positive law must be "acted upon . . . whether conformable to the dictates of natural justice or otherwise." By authority of the Constitution, this meant that those states in which slavery is prohibited must return fugitives to those where it is permitted.

By authority of Congress, the power to decide whether the accused must return to the state of Georgia belonged to the federal commissioner, who would base his decision solely on evidence provided by the claimant. Because almost none of Shaw's private papers—letters, diaries, or the like—survive, the extent to which his heart and mind were at odds over this disjunction between justice and law is something that cannot be known. Yet the defensive tone of his opinion suggests that he felt it keenly.

However much it did or did not pain him, Shaw's decision ensured that Sims's fate would remain in Curtis's hands. Ever since the Shadrach case, Dana had been affronted by the sight of a commissioner "actually occupying the judge's seat," but now he and the rest of Sims's legal team had no choice but to deal with him. On Monday, April 7, Sewall presented Curtis with a request that the hearing be postponed so the defendant's attorneys could prepare their case. Having granted such a request in the Shadrach case, the commissioner was in a déjà vu state of mind and refused.

When the hearing resumed the next day, Tuesday, April 8, Sims's lawyers attempted a defense that was both broad and narrow. On constitutional grounds, they claimed that any suit involving "a right of personal liberty" required trial by jury. They challenged the validity of the certificate issued by the Georgia court because Sims had not had legal counsel to assist him in contesting it. They argued that the difference between the five dollars a commissioner would earn for acquittal and the ten dollars he would get for rendition made him an interested party and thus denied the defendant due process as guaranteed by the Fifth Amendment. On the grounds that Article 3 restricts federal judicial power to duly appointed judges, they argued that the law was unconstitutional in vesting such authority in a mere commissioner. None of these arguments was likely to prevail with the man occupying that office. At the end of the Tuesday session, Curtis ordered a recess so he could consider his decision.

Fearing the worst, Vigilance Committee members were simultaneously working other avenues. They had Potter's agents arrested on a charge of kidnapping, which forced the two men to pay a hefty bail. They unsuccessfully petitioned the Massachusetts State Senate to demand again that the state judiciary—in other words, Shaw—issue a writ of habeas corpus so that Sims "not be surrendered, exiled, or returned to bondage, until proven to be a slave by due course of law." In another futile effort to free Sims from federal custody, they filed a writ of personal replevin, ordinarily used as an instrument for initiating a claim on stolen property, but when the sheriff served the writ on Marshal Devens, he denied its pertinence to the case.

Rebuffed at every level of the legal hierarchy, Sims's lawyers were getting desperate. They cooked up a criminal complaint against their own client for having assaulted one of the arresting policemen, contending that Marshal Devens must hand him over to state authorities because a criminal charge took precedence over the civil claim under the fugitive slave law. Southern newspapers described this maneuver as "an impudence unparalleled even in this age of audacity." On Thursday, April 10, Sims's legal team filed two more writs of habeas corpus, both of which were rejected.

Anticipating that Curtis was about to order Sims's rendition, "revolutionists" (Higginson's word) on the Vigilance Committee used the recess to prepare a radical rescue plan, including "a physical assault on the courthouse." When that idea was rejected, Higginson, having determined that the prisoner was free to walk about the third-floor room in which he was confined, floated the idea that Sims should go to the window at a prearranged time as if for fresh air, leap onto a pile of mattresses below, and jump into a waiting carriage. But the authorities got wind of the plan and had iron bars installed on the window before it could be carried out. From his office, Dana could see Sims gazing out from behind the bars and wrote in his journal, "Our Temple of justice is a slave pen!"

On Friday morning, April 11, with more resignation than relish, Curtis announced his ruling. Nine armed guards surrounded the defendant—five behind him, two on either side—while he listened as the commissioner determined his fate. Curtis rejected the claim that Sims had a right to trial by jury in Massachusetts, on the grounds that "the liberty of the party is not in contestation here, for final adjudication," by which he meant that jurisdiction was reserved to courts in the state from which Sims had fled. Most ominously not only for Sims but for all future fugitives, he ruled that the purpose of Article 4, Section 2, Clause 3 of the Constitution "was to prevent State legislation from interfering with or impairing the right of the master to the service or labor of his slave." In short, personal liberty laws such as the 1836 Massachusetts "Act to Restore the Trial by Jury on Questions of Personal Freedom" were moot. The only contestable question was whether the prisoner was in fact the property of James Potter, and on this point the commissioner accepted the Georgia certificate.

As Curtis recited his damning findings, Sims was heard to call out, "I will not go back to Slavery. Give me a knife, and when the Commissioner declares me a slave, I will stab myself in the heart, and die before his eyes!" At a meeting later that day, the former Harvard president Josiah Quincy, shaken out of the accommodating mood in which he had signed the public letter praising Webster, lamented that "the Boston of 1851 is not the Boston of 1775." What had been a "City on a Hill" for its Puritan founders had "become a mere shop—a place for buying and selling goods; and I suppose, also of *buying and selling men*." That night Theodore Parker led a vigil in Court Square, where, before dawn, a phalanx of armed guards formed a human passageway through which Sims was led, "his sable cheeks . . . bathed in tears" as protesters shouted, "Shame! shame!"

When Sims's armed escort reached the end of Long Wharf to deliver him to the vessel—owned by a cooperative Boston shipping magnate, John H. Pearson—that would take him back to Georgia, a witness was heard to cry out, "Sims! preach liberty to the slaves!" Sims was reported to have answered, "And is this Massachusetts liberty?" Forty years later, in his great short novel *Billy Budd*, Lemuel Shaw's son-in-law, Herman Melville, recounted the impressment of a young sailor—tantamount to a legal kidnapping—from a merchant vessel, the *Rights-of-Man*, and his forced transfer to a British warship. As Billy crosses by boat under guard from relative freedom to military incarceration, his shipmates bid him farewell, to which he cries out, "Goodbye to you too, old Rights-of-Man."

Shortly after returning to Savannah, Thomas Sims was subjected to a public whipping. "I congratulate you and the country upon a triumph of law in Boston," President Fillmore wrote to Secretary of State Webster. "She has done nobly. She has wiped out the stain of the former [Shadrach] rescue and freed herself from the reproach of *nullification*." James Pennington, keeping up with events from New York, took a different view. "The whole land," he wrote, "is full of blood."

Not long after his rendition to Georgia, Sims was auctioned to a Virginia buyer, from whom he escaped in 1863 during the siege of Vicksburg. After serving as a recruiter for the Union army in Nashville, he closed out his life in Washington, D.C., where, in 1877, the former U.S. marshal in Boston, Charles Devens—the same man who had executed the order to send him back to slavery a quarter century earlier—was appointed by President Rutherford B. Hayes to the office of attorney general. Sometime in the early 1880s, Devens, who previously had tried without success to buy Sims's freedom after depriving him of it, hired him as a messenger for the U.S. Department of Justice.

5.

The successful enforcement of the fugitive slave law in Boston was a momentous event not only because it took place at the nerve center of abolitionism but because it was the first recorded instance of a fugitive slave legally returned from New England into slavery. But if supporters thought they had broken the back of the resistance, they were soon proved wrong.

The Sims case only stiffened the opposition. Calls for violent resistance became increasingly common, including from gentlemen with venerable Yankee names. Henry Ingersoll Bowditch, a prominent Harvard professor of medicine who considered Shadrach's rescue "the most noble deed done in Boston since the destruction of the tea in 1773," founded the "Anti-man-hunting League," which armed itself with billy clubs and conducted drills on how to beat slave hunters into submission. Throughout what might be called the New England diaspora, other sons of pedigreed families went further. From his post in Syracuse, New York, the attorney Charles B. Sedgwick wrote that "no sacrifice of blood is too great to establish the principle that Slaves cannot be hunted & chained & driven off from Massachusetts—if these kidnappers were to be killed it would teach a useful lesson & I hope they wont go away alive."

Until now, though he referred to the fugitive slave law in his private journal as a "filthy" thing, New England's best-known intellectual, Ralph Waldo Emerson, had kept his distance from the public uproar. Years later, Ann Bigelow, founder of the Concord Women's Anti-slavery Society, remembered her famous neighbor in less than glowing terms while asserting the role of women in the abolitionist movement. "Mr. Nathan Brooks," she wrote—Brooks was a Concord lawyer whose wife, Mary Merrick Brooks, was an active abolitionist—"and Mr. Ralph Waldo Emerson were always afraid of committal, we women, never." But spurred on by the Sims rendition, Emerson delivered a speech on May 3, 1851, to the citizens of Concord in which he decried the law as "a statute which enacts the crime of kidnapping" and announced that "the Union is no longer desirable." Charles Sumner, gratified by the news that Emerson had spoken out, begged him to do so more often "since you have access to many, whom other Anti-Slavery speakers cannot reach."

By summer, the conflict between law and conscience was spreading far beyond Boston. On August 15, 1851, in Buffalo, New York, a fugitive was seized by agents dispatched by his owner in Kentucky. Accompanied by the slave catchers, a U.S. marshal and two police officers tracked a cook named Daniel to the below-decks kitchen of a steamship at anchor in Lake Erie. There they served him with an arrest warrant issued by a local commissioner. Trying to back out through the hatchway, Daniel threatened to "walk over corpses" if the officers attempted to take him, but he stumbled in the cramped space and "fell upon the stove and was badly burned." Taken before the commissioner "with blood oozing out of his mouth and nostrils," he was remanded to his former owner's agents.

Like the Shadrach and Sims cases, the Buffalo case was fought out not only in court but in the press. The *Buffalo Morning Express* decried "the bludgeon process of executing the laws in Buffalo." The *Commercial Advertiser,* the preferred newspaper of what abolitionists called "compromise politicians" and "lower-law co-laborers," described Daniel as "a fine, athletic negro, of great value, doubtless, to his owner," and commended law-enforcement officials for their professionalism in the face of a restive black crowd. The mayor, who quieted the crowd by walking alongside the carriage while it carried the prisoner from the commissioner's office to the courthouse, was singled out for special praise. But then, to the dismay of law-and-order enthusiasts, the federal judge Alfred Conkling of the Northern District of New York did what Lemuel Shaw had not done: he issued a writ of habeas corpus releasing Daniel pending a challenge to the legality of his detention. Daniel promptly escaped to Canada, but not before a letter was published over his name expressing remorse for having run from his master and his pleasure at the prospect of returning to Kentucky. The letter was exposed as a fraud in the antislavery press in an article titled "Daniel in the Den and Out."

6.

Even before the Buffalo incident, Secretary of State Webster, speaking in Syracuse in May 1851, had responded to the spreading acts of defiance by raising the cry of treason. With venomous accuracy (he would be dead the next year), the local Liberty Party newspaper described him as a "decrepit old man . . . lank with age, whose sluggish legs were somewhat concealed by an overshadowing abdomen" and whose "large and lustrousless eye . . . had more of the meaningless glare of a dead man's . . . than of life." But Webster was still able to rouse himself to righteous indignation leavened, in his view, by sweet reason:

> I do not say the law is perfect. I proposed some amendments to it, but was called from the Senate before it was adjusted.* The law passed, and I have not yet heard the man whose opinion is worth a sixpence, who has said that that law is not perfectly constitutional. . . . What then? Is it not to be obeyed? . . . Is it not a matter of conscience? But what do we hear? We hear of persons assembling in Massachusetts

---

*Webster was referring back to his belated proposal, in June 1850, of an amendment providing for a jury trial for accused fugitives.

and New York, who set themselves over the Constitution, above the law . . . and who say this law shall not be carried into effect. . . . And have they not pledged their lives, their fortunes, and their sacred honor to defeat its execution?

After this satiric invocation of the Declaration of Independence on behalf of men whom he regarded as criminals, Webster made what he considered the irrefutable point:

For what? For the violation of the law, for the committal of treason to the country; for it is treason, and nothing else. (Great applause.) I am a lawyer, and I value my reputation as a lawyer, and I tell you, if men get together and declare a law of Congress shall not be executed in any case, and assemble in numbers and force to prevent the execution of such law, they are *traitors*, and are guilty of treason, and bring upon themselves the penalties of that crime. No! no! It is time to put an end to this imposition upon good citizens, good men and good women. It is treason, *treason*, TREASON, and nothing else, (cheers,) and if they do not incur the penalties of treason, it is owing to the clemency of the law's administration, and to no merit of their own.

Garrison responded by addressing himself to Fillmore, who was widely suspected to be a place holder for Webster:

Down with the Traitors, Mr. President. . . . Drag the editor from his desk, the preacher from the pulpit, the merchant from his counting-house. Giving information is treason; denunciation is treason; refusing to aid kidnappers is treason; freedom of the press, freedom of speech, is treason.

This was the toxic atmosphere in which the fugitive slave law was about to be tested again—this time in Lancaster County, Pennsylvania, where the response would be the most explosive yet.

Twelve

TRIALS OF CONSCIENCE

1.

In November 1849, almost a year before the fugitive slave law went into effect, four young black men fled Baltimore County, Maryland, where they were kept as slaves by a wheat farmer named Edward Gorsuch. Gorsuch, who prided himself on being a lenient master, had been coming around slowly to an antislavery view and had even promised to emancipate his slaves. He was not prepared, however, to free them until they reached the age of twenty-eight, and when they chose not to wait, he was offended. The offense was compounded in his mind when he discovered that before they left, they had been pilfering his wheat.

Time did nothing to temper Gorsuch's anger. In August 1851, he learned that two of his former slaves were living with a black farmer, William Parker, in a free black community in Lancaster County, Pennsylvania, near the town of Christiana. That region of central Pennsylvania had a history of conflict between its substantial black population (more than three thousand persons by 1850) and white kidnappers who ran a thriving business of abduction and sale to buyers in the South. Some of these human traffickers grabbed any black man, woman, or child off the road or from the fields who seemed likely to fetch a good price. Others, pretending to observe the legal niceties, surveilled their prey before sending a physical description to southern collaborators, who would then obtain a certificate (often fraudulent) authorizing capture. Under these conditions, the black community was on high alert, which rose higher with the passage of the fugitive slave law. William Parker, who had escaped from slavery in Kentucky twelve years earlier, was among the leaders of what has been called a "secret black militia" tasked with the job of community protection.

Into this patrolled zone, on September 11, 1851, Edward Gorsuch arrived with several men including his own son and a deputy U.S. marshal, Henry Kline, who carried a warrant for the arrest of Gorsuch's former slaves. They were greeted by a crowd of black men wielding shovels, clubs, and a number of guns. Also in the greeting party was an unarmed white neighbor of Parker's, Castner Hanway, a man of Quaker sympathies who warned the slave catchers to leave before things got ugly.

Three months later, at Hanway's trial, Kline recalled their encounter. Mr. Hanway, he said, was "sitting on a sorrel horse, and [I] went up to him and said, 'Good morning, sir,' and he made no reply. I then asked him his name, and he allowed it was none of my business." Kline then handed him the warrant, which Hanway read "not only once, but twice" while "some fifteen or twenty . . . colored people" watched.

U.S. district attorney John W. Ashmead asked Kline to tell the court exactly what Mr. Hanway "said at the time":

> After I got through telling him . . . who I was, and he had refused to assist me, I told him what the Act of Congress was, and urged him to assist me. After I had told him my warrants, he read them and handed them back, and he said the colored people had a right to defend themselves, and he was not going to help me, and I asked if he would keep them away, and he said No,—he would not have anything to do with them.

Ashmead then asked Kline to tell the court and jury what happened next. "After he refused," said Kline,

> I told him what the act of Congress was as near as I could tell him. That any person aiding or abetting a fugitive slave, and resisting an

officer, the punishment was $1000 damages for the slave, and I think to the best of my knowledge imprisonment for five years. I told him that. He said he did not care for any act of Congress or any other law. That is what he said.

The standoff continued. Gorsuch refused to leave, his former slaves refused to surrender, gunfire broke out, and he was mortally wounded. The younger Gorsuch, too, was shot, though not fatally. The hunters retreated in panic, and Parker, along with several others—presumably including the targeted fugitives—fled north through New York. At Rochester, they were aided by Frederick Douglass, who helped them get passage to Canada.

2.

Three weeks after the events at Christiana and three hundred miles almost due north, another uprising took place against another attempt to execute the fugitive slave law. On October 1, 1851, while the Liberty Party was holding its convention in Syracuse, New York, a red-haired, light-skinned black man (he had probably been fathered by his mother's master) who had fled from slavery in 1844 was seized as a fugitive in the barrel-making shop where he worked. Known as Jerry, he was arrested for what seems to have been a trumped-up misdemeanor charge designed to convince him that he should submit quietly, which he did. Upon arriving at the office of U.S. commissioner Joseph F. Sabine, he was confronted by an agent of his most recent owner in Missouri and told that he was under detention as a runaway.

For reasons of conscience or prudence or some combination of both, Sabine was queasy about the fugitive slave law and nervous about trying to enforce it. Leading white and black abolitionists, including Gerrit Smith, Samuel J. May, and Samuel Ringgold Ward, were either residents or regular visitors in Syracuse, each with a popular following. "It is cowardly to resign before my first case comes to trial," the commissioner confided to his wife, "but what else can I do?" Trying to encourage him, she advised, "Hold on to your commission," and "let no other man have your place."

Sabine held on long enough to see an angry crowd invade his office while he tried to conduct Jerry's hearing. A few minutes into the proceedings, Jerry broke free and dashed out an open doorway while the crowd got between him and his pursuers. His arms still in shackles, he ran through the streets until two officers caught, beat, and threw him into a cart to take him back. One witness recalled that the scene "made me ashamed of the land of my native country; a country of which I had been taught to be proud. I saw this fugitive from, not *justice,* but *injustice,* dragged through the streets like a dog, every rag of clothes stripped from his back; hauled upon a cart like a dead carcass and driven away to the police office for a mock trial."

Barricaded now in a more secure room at the police station, Jerry kept up a wild screaming until, at the request of the police chief, May and Ward came to pacify him. The clerical visitors succeeded in calming him down—not by persuading him to accept his fate, but by assuring him that he would be rescued soon.

By the time the hearing resumed late that afternoon, it seemed likely that the prisoner would be acquitted. But Smith, who was thinking beyond Jerry and Syracuse, had concluded that "the moral effect of such an acquittal will be as nothing to a bold and forcible rescue." Estimated by another resistance leader, the former slave Jermain Loguen, at more than twenty-five hundred people, the crowd started throwing rocks and bricks through the police station windows. When one stone barely missed the commissioner's head, he stopped the hearing without any plan to resume it.

Shortly after nightfall, the full-fledged attack began. Armed with clubs, axes, and a battering ram, a group of black and white men smashed into the building, broke into the room where Jerry was being held, and overwhelmed the guards. Jerry was spirited away and hidden by sympathizers for several days at several locations throughout the city while arrangements were made to get him to Canada.

While these events were taking place in Syracuse, back in Pennsylvania the Christiana conflict had moved from William Parker's farmhouse to a Philadelphia courtroom. On October 6, a grand jury issued a first slate of indictments of twenty-eight black men and four whites on multiple counts of treason (more indictments would follow), including the

Quaker Castner Hanway, who was accused of leading the mob and was the first to stand trial. The Hanway trial, which ran from the last week of November until mid-December 1851, captured the nation's attention like no other until the prosecution of John Brown in 1859.

Conservative newspapers demanded that the Christiana rioters suffer "the penalty of Treason—hanging by the neck," while, like Shadrach's rescuers in Boston, the defenders at Christiana were celebrated in the antislavery press as heirs to the heroes of the American Revolution. In the *Voice of the Fugitive*, Henry Bibb's paper published at his refuge in Windsor, Ontario, Bibb wrote a tribute to William Parker:

> This man deserves the admiration of a Hannibal, a Toussaint L'Ouverture, or a George Washington. A nobler defense was never made in behalf of liberty on the plains of Lexington, Concord, or Bunker Hill than was put forth by William Parker at Christiana.

Hanway's legal team included Pennsylvania congressman Thaddeus Stevens, who had once represented a slave owner seeking return of his runaway but was now a fierce antislavery man. Presiding was Justice Robert Grier of the U.S. Supreme Court (it was still customary for Supreme Court justices to travel the circuit hearing cases in the federal courts), who is mainly remembered today for voting with the majority in the notorious *Dred Scott* case of 1857. Grier was assisted by district judge John Kane, a unionist Democrat who had presided over several fugitive slave cases in his Philadelphia courtroom located in, of all places, Liberty Hall—some of which resulted in rendition, some in acquittal.

Perhaps because of the glare of publicity, the complexity of the questions at issue, or simply the dread of a long trial, a stream of prospective jurors during voir dire asked to be excused—a request to which Judge Grier reacted with a mixture of exasperation and sympathy:

> MR. MASSEY (a prospective juror). "My disease is *angina pectoris*, I have to walk very slowly, and then frequently have to stop. . . . Any violent exertion will bring on the disease."

JUDGE GRIER. "But sitting still would not bring it on."

MR. MASSEY. "Any agitation will bring it on."

JUDGE GRIER. "I am in nearly the same situation myself."

Another prospective juror feared he would be unable to follow the testimony:

MR. TAYLOR. "I am hard of hearing at the best of times, and at
present I labor under a very severe cold in the head, and it affects
my hearing; and I should be unwilling to sit upon a case of so great
importance, unless I could hear all the evidence presented."

JUDGE GRIER. "Your disease has become epidemic to-day. Mark
him excused."

With a jury finally impaneled, the trial got under way on November 24. It soon became evident that the real issue at stake would be not the behavior of the defendant—against whom the charge of inciting violence grew more implausible with each witness—but whether breaking the fugitive slave law constituted treason. In this sense, Webster, who had insisted ever since the Shadrach rescue that defying the fugitive slave law was a treasonable act because it threatened the Republic, was present in the courtroom in principle if not in person.

After the concluding arguments, Judge Grier made clear in his charge to the jury that he had no patience with challenges to the fugitive slave law itself:

It may not be said of this law, or perhaps of any other, that it is perfect, or the best that could possibly be enacted; or that it is incapable of amendment. But this may truly be said, that while there are so many discordant opinions on the subject, it is not possible that a better compromise will be made; and, most probably, none of us will live to see an Act on this subject made to please everyone.

But when it came to Webster's assertion that breaking the law amounted to treason, the judge was having none of it. "The resistance of the execution of a law of the United States accompanied with any degree of force, if for a private purpose, is not treason," he said. "To constitute that offence the object of the resistance must be of a public and general nature."

Perhaps surprisingly, given his failure six years later to dissent in the *Dred Scott* case from Chief Justice Taney's opinion that the black man had "no rights which the white man was bound to respect," Grier expressed sympathy for the resisters, especially those who were black:

> Individuals without any authority, but incited by cupidity, and the hope of obtaining the reward offered for the return of a fugitive, had heretofore undertaken to seize them by force and violence, to invade the sanctity of private dwellings at night, and insult the feelings and prejudices of the people. It is not to be wondered at that a people subject to such inroads, should consider odious the perpetrators of such deeds and denominate them kidnappers—and that the subjects of this treatment should have been encouraged in resisting such aggressions.

When the jury took barely ten minutes to return a verdict of not guilty, the prosecutor dropped all remaining indictments against all others charged in the Christiana incident.

3.

The foregoing events—the Hamlet case; the escapes by the Crafts and by Shadrach; the Sims rendition; the rescue of Jerry; the armed defense (or attack, depending on one's point of view) at Christiana, whose name, like "Stonewall" in the next century, became a byword for a nascent resistance movement—all did their part to inflame the nation. Yet if one could draw a map of mid-century America showing the variable intensity of public opinion, the places where most people remained cool would have outnumbered those where many had caught the fever.

In the North, a quiet if not silent majority still wanted to believe that fugitive slaves were somebody else's problem. In the South, the publicized rescues sparked outrage, even though, as one scholar remarks, "compared with the number of slaves returned, the number of rescues was small"—not to mention that the total number of fugitives, recaptured or not, was incomparably smaller in relation to the enslaved millions. It is also true that some features of the fugitive slave law that seem outrageous now in retrospect—the prohibition of testimony by the accused, for example—were less controversial at the time, even among opponents of the law. Most defendants in civil and criminal cases in antebellum America, on the premise that they were interested parties whose testimony could not be trusted, were not permitted to testify on their own behalf. Cross-examination was not yet an accepted courtroom practice, and the first state to permit defendants to testify in civil disputes was Connecticut, in 1848. Massachusetts did not allow testimony by criminal defendants until 1866. In this context, the exclusion of testimony from accused fugitives was neither extreme nor unusual.

At the same time, in the disapproving words of one federal judge, more and more Americans seemed to be embracing a "new discovery in ethics; that there are obligations and duties depending upon the dictates of conscience of a higher nature than the laws of our country." This discovery had once belonged to intellectuals like Thoreau, who used the phrase "higher law" in his 1849 essay "Resistance to Civil Government" (better known as "Civil Disobedience"), in which he wrote that "the only obligation I have a right to assume is to do at any time what I think right." It was Emerson's principle of self-reliance put into practice.

First delivered as a speech in the immediate aftermath of the Mexican War, Thoreau's essay was written before the idea of individual immunity to the rule of law was given new impetus by the fugitive slave bill. Early in 1850, while the bill was still under debate in Congress, Henry Ward Beecher declared that "if the compromises of the Constitution include requisites that violate Humanity, I shall not be bound by them." Once the bill was passed and enacted, Charles Beecher summed up his brother's point in the title of one of his own sermons: *The Duty of Disobedience to Wicked Laws* (1851).

Given the gulf of time, the voices that carry through now tend to be those of the famous (Douglass or Emerson) exalting those who defied the law as heroes, or the infamous (Webster or Shaw) condemning the same people as traitors. Meanwhile, lesser-known men of troubled conscience—people in conflict with themselves who struggled to know what to think and how to act when law came into conflict with conscience—are barely audible through private journals or reminiscences by relatives or friends. Yet in some respects these people bring us closer to the heart of America's moral crisis in the pre–Civil War years than those who committed themselves without compunction to one side or the other.

They included Charles Devens, who, as U.S. marshal in Boston during the Sims case, had stood by a law in which he did not believe because he considered it his civic duty to do so. In a prefatory memoir to a posthumous selection of Devens's writings, the Civil War historian John Codman Ropes described his friend's torment at "participating, even in an official capacity, in the wretched task of surrendering a fugitive slave." That Devens continued to feel the burden of the task after Sims's rendition was made manifest by his efforts to purchase freedom for Sims and, in later years, to find him employment.

There are hints of similar self-division in Judge John Kane, who assisted Justice Grier in the Christiana case and believed firmly in enforcing the fugitive slave law. In an empathetic memoir, Kane's daughter-in-law Elizabeth, wife of his son Thomas, wrote that the judge "thought the Law the noblest profession a man could follow [while] Tom thought it a school for perverting a man's conscience"—so much so that the younger Kane resigned his position as a commissioner rather than send fugitives back to the South. He believed in "the right of a member of society to break any law of which his conscience disapproved, if he did so openly and without attempting to escape outlawry." When he renounced his appointment as a commissioner rather than carry out the law, his father, who had employed him as a law clerk, "calmly and sadly" found him in contempt of court and even sentenced him to a year in prison, though it is not clear that any part of the sentence was served.

Tom continued to live, with Elizabeth, in his father's house, which the young couple converted into a station of the Underground Railroad, while the judge, whose "naturally tender heart longed for the freedom of Tom's," turned a blind eye to their activities. "The family," Elizabeth recalled, "had their secret jests over the 'black beggars'" (here she seems to be quoting the judge) "over whom he sometimes stumbled without seeing them" when he came downstairs before dawn. In his robes, Judge Kane was a law-and-order man. In his nightclothes, he was the lawbreakers' accomplice.

The same conflict divided the family—and evidently the mind—of Joseph Sabine, commissioner in the Syracuse case, who was saved from having to choose between conscience and duty by the disruption of Jerry's rendition hearing and whose brother William was active in the Syracuse branch of the Underground Railroad. Even in the case of Judge Shaw, one suspects that his angry impatience at Dana manifested a certain anger at himself. It was Lincoln who best articulated the inner conflict such men felt when he wrote in 1855 to his friend Joshua Speed that "the great body of the Northern people," among whom he included himself, "do crucify their feelings, in order to maintain their loyalty to the constitution and the Union."

Looking back from the late nineteenth century, the writer John Jay Chapman, who would later publish a laudatory biography of Garrison, came to the defense of those who submitted to the law not out of sympathy for slavery but because of what he called a "committed conscience":

> I do not know what more awful subject for a poem could have been found than that of the New England judge enforcing the fugitive slave law. For lack of such a poem the heroism of these men has been forgotten, the losing heroism of conservatism. It was this spiritual power of a committed conscience which met the new forces as they arose, and it deserves a better name than these new forces afterward gave it.

For most readers and writers today, the type whom Chapman had in mind—men like Kane, Grier, Sabine, Devens, even the stiff-necked Webster and Shaw—are well forgotten. They have been consigned, like the "neutrals" in Dante's *Inferno,* to spend eternity in the anteroom of hell.

The sentence is harsh. These were people caught up in what has been called an "inner civil war"—of which it is hasty to think that all the courage was on one side and all the cowardice on the other. While Devens was

*Richard Henry Dana Jr.
in 1849*

acting "in face of the unpopularity and misconstruction of motives and personal abuse in which his action was sure to involve him," Dana was crowing in his journal that he had received "a handsome congratulatory letter from the [Massachusetts] Attorney General upon my defense of Davis, & a gratifying testimonial in the shape of a box of beautiful fresh flowers" from a lady in Plymouth, along with an admiring note from her husband. Whether Dana was acknowledging the irony that doing right meant doing well, or was reveling in sheer self-satisfaction, his pleasure fairly leaps off the page as he writes about his work for the Shadrach defendants: "I believe I have never done anything professionally that has gained me so much credit." During the fugitive slave crisis, acquiescence could bring shame, and resistance could buy social cachet.

A particularly compelling case of committed conscience was to be found far from Boston, in a slave state, in the person of William Greenleaf Eliot, mainly remembered today as the founder of Washington University in St. Louis and for the genealogical fact that he was the grandfather of T. S. Eliot. In his own time, Eliot's reputation for probity and generosity was such that Dickens paid him his respects on his American tour and Emerson called him the "Saint of the West."

A self-exiled New Englander, Eliot had been groomed to join Boston's ministerial elite before he decided, in 1834, to answer a call to fill the pulpit of the First Unitarian Church in Missouri. He hated slavery. He hated it at least as much as did his Boston peers—Fuller, Thoreau, Emerson, or Eliot's close friend James Freeman Clarke, who also went west, to Louisville, Kentucky, but lasted only three years before retreating back to Boston. Eliot stayed in St. Louis, but with no illusions. "Over the best and most pampered slave," he wrote after the Civil War, "the sword of uncertainty always hung, suspended by an invisible hair, from which it came to pass, that, under the best of circumstances, the best condition of slavery was worse than the worst condition of freedom." The journal he kept from the 1840s through the Civil War reveals the mind of a morally resolute New Englander coming to grips with the sins of a slave society from within rather than decrying them from without.

Eliot's journal is filled with self-interrogation. "Upon no other" subject, he wrote in one entry in 1848, "have I been more anxious to do what is right.

> I never pass by the slave jails on Olive Street without saying almost, sometimes quite loud: "May the curse of God abide on this vile traffic." Yet I have spoken of it in public comparatively seldom, only once or twice each year. . . . In conversation I have always spoken freely. Has it been through want of moral courage?

Haunted by this question, and thinking of his friend Clarke's self-liberating return to Boston, he reflects that

> ten or five years ago, I had only to come out as an "Abolitionist" & altho' I wd have been required to leave my place here, I could have returned to friends & kindred, with the honors of a martyr, without his losses: "covered with glory" & with the certainty of good settlement. But *my* gain would have been the only gain.

William Greenleaf Eliot in 1850

St. Louis, where Eliot remained until his death in 1887, was a city where most black people—those nominally free as well as those legally enslaved—lived under ghastly circumstances, psychological as well as material. In a state where manumitted slaves could remain only by obtaining a license at a price few could afford, Eliot put up his own money to aid them and asked his parishioners to do the same. After Eliot's death, one of his eulogists, Joseph Shippen, recalled that "he himself once bought a slave woman to save her from ruin, and owned her until he could set her free; and to my involuntary expression of astonishment at the example, he said he cared little for the opinion of the world, he only thought to save the poor woman."

Eliot organized a school (known around town as Nigritia) for black children. He worked to persuade the legislature to initiate a gradual emancipation. After the outbreak of the Civil War, when President Lincoln countermanded an emancipation order issued by the commander of Union forces in the West, John C. Frémont, for fear of pushing Missouri into the Confederacy, Eliot sided with the general against the president. During the war, when pro-slavery mobs operated freely in the city, he sheltered in his own home, at risk to his and his family's safety, a hunted fugitive slave named Archer Alexander, who had been accused of giving information about Confederate positions to Union troops.*

And yet, before the war, Eliot never took a public stand against the fugitive slave law. Convinced that the higher law doctrine "is the more dangerous because it can always bring to its aid the conscientious feelings of those . . . whose wishes & interests & prejudices & enmities & sectional jealousies are all made to assume the sacredness of duty," he believed that "the Country which makes this appeal must do so with sword in hand, in open revolt & struggle." Like the Websterites, he hoped until the last moment to forestall disunion and war, which to some of his counterparts in Boston might have been a titillating prospect but to him seemed likely to tighten the grip of slavery, brutalize even more the lives of black people, and set back what hopes there were of gradual emancipation. This was the context in which he regarded the higher law doctrine as "the most dangerous of popular delusions."

It is easy to scorn him, in the words of the prophet (Revelation 3:15–16), as "neither cold nor hot," an overcautious man unwilling to take risks, looking for some middle way that did not exist. Some did so scorn him in his own time. Another of his eulogists, the English-born Robert Collyer, who filled a Unitarian pulpit in Chicago, remarked that Eliot's opposition to abolitionism before the war "had set me rather against him because I was a strong abolitionist, but only," he confessed in light of Eliot's example, "as the man's ox was 'strong at light work.'" Collyer acknowledged that Eliot, living in a slave state, carried the heavier burden. Paraphrasing Isaiah 53:3, he eulogized him as "a man of sorrows and acquainted with grief" who "knew how the land lay and the light." Joseph Shippen, also a resident of Illinois, tried to grasp the moral complexities of living in Missouri before the war and came to see that being in a slave state "in the days of slavery," Eliot "was a friend and sympathizer with the oppressed and

---

*After the Civil War, Eliot provided to the sculptor Thomas Ball a photograph of Alexander, upon which Ball based the figure of the slave in what became the Freedman's Memorial in Washington, D.C. See Eliot, *The Story of Archer Alexander* (Boston, 1885), and Kirk Savage, *Standing Soldiers, Kneeling Slaves: Race, War, and Monument in Nineteenth-Century America* (Princeton, N.J.: Princeton University Press, 1997), 116–17.

down-trodden, doing much to alleviate their condition and to inspire a fellow-feeling in their behalf. But he withheld from, and even disapproved of the abolition agitation which for twenty-five years preceded the war of the Rebellion . . . a non-interference with the subject that was nevertheless hard to reconcile and comprehend."

In order to come to terms with such a man, one must try to grasp what it meant to live with a hatred of slavery but without knowledge of the imponderable future. No one in Eliot's circumstance could have known that despite all the compromise efforts—of which the fugitive slave law was the most painful and exigent—disunion and war would come all the same and that the fugitive slave problem would disappear with the disappearance of slavery itself. If the dreaded war came, no one could know whether it would end with slavery weakened or strengthened, perpetuated or destroyed. No one before the Civil War knew any of these things—a fact to which Eliot, after the war, gave eloquent expression:

> A true history of that fierce struggle will probably never be written. There were no impartial judges, no unprejudiced witnesses, to observe or record the facts. Right-minded men could hardly tell where the lines of right and wrong crossed each other. Living in St. Louis the whole time and long before, and knowing many of those engaged in the strife on either side, I thought I saw both sides as they really were, but, in truth I saw neither. The complications of actions and motive, both right and wrong, were past finding out. One thing, however, is sure: that the right prevailed at last. Thank God for that.

4.

Whether in New York, Massachusetts, Pennsylvania, Missouri, or anywhere else where the grip of slavery was less than complete, the public and private struggles triggered by the fugitive slave law had the effect, in the words of one of Castner Hanway's defense attorneys, of putting "the law . . . on trial itself in this country." He might have added that the trial was conducted not only in the minds of lawyers, judges, and ministers, or in the streets and courts, but also in newspapers, periodicals, and books.

Time has obscured this fact because most of the writers whom we now count as literary classics touched on the issue only glancingly. In all his correspondence from the year 1851, Emerson expended more words asking newspaper editors to refrain from printing summaries of his paid lectures on philosophical subjects (he worried that such reports would suppress turnout for his next talk) than on the fugitive slave law. In *Moby-Dick*—written from the spring of 1850 to the fall of 1851—Melville seems to wink at his father-in-law, Judge Shaw, with a sentence that must have startled the judge when (or if) he read it: "Delight is to him, who gives no quarter in the truth, and kills, burns, and destroys all sin though he pluck it out from under the robes of Senators and Judges." Later in the book, Melville gestures again in Shaw's direction with the story of the black cabin boy Pip abandoned at sea after he becomes an impediment to the mission of the ship.

In his next book, *Pierre; or, The Ambiguities* (1852), Melville returned to the theme, this time more directly. Late one night, the young protagonist comes knocking at the door of a clergyman whom he accuses of complicity in expelling a young woman (she is suspected of being the illegitimate child of Pierre's father and his mistress) from the neighborhood. The confrontation between the hot young man and the cold minister, to whom Melville gave the mocking name "Falsgrave," reads like a synopsis of the confrontation between Dana, who was a friend of Melville's, and Judge Shaw. "In heaven's name, what is the matter, young gentleman?" the minister wants to know, to which the young man replies, "Everything is the matter; the whole world is the matter. . . . Heaven and earth is the matter, sir! . . . How is she to depart? Who is to take her? Art thou to take her? Where is she to go?" Mr. Falsgrave also bore a likeness to a real-life minister, Moses Stuart, whose opinion of the fugitive slave law ran like this: "We pity the restored fugitive . . . when he is sent back to be delivered into the hands of enraged cruelty. But when he is sent back to a lenient and Christian master, the matter is less grievous. The responsibility, however, of bad treatment for the slave, rests not in the least degree on us of the North."

Melville's portrait of the gutless minister was, to say the least, unflattering. More than thirty years later, he made amends. In his valedictory masterpiece, *Billy Budd,* about a young sailor who strikes a fatal blow against an officer who has falsely accused him of fomenting mutiny (a capital crime), he constructed the whole narrative around the problem of duty versus conscience. The choice is personified in Captain Vere, another figure bearing resemblance to Shaw, who agonizes over whether to follow the naval code in sentencing Billy to death or to acquit him in accordance with justice. As the literary scholar Brook Thomas has written, "Shaw faced the same conflict between higher law and positive law as Vere does in *Billy Budd.*" We will never know if Shaw himself was closer in reality, or in Melville's mind, to Falsgrave or to Vere, but the trajectory of the writer's emotion suggests that the later portrait is the better likeness.

Nathaniel Hawthorne, whose relationship to Melville mirrored that of the phlegmatic minister to the badgering young man in *Pierre,* wrote to Longfellow in the summer of 1851 that "this Fugitive Law is the only thing that could have blown me into any respectable degree of warmth on this great subject of the day." In fact, Hawthorne's "warmth" was barely tepid. According to the Virginia-born abolitionist Moncure Conway, who greatly admired his writing, he was afflicted when it came to slavery "by a blindness which seems the very counterpart of his clear vision."

Having lived in Concord, where his neighbors the Alcotts sheltered fugitives with help from Thoreau in getting them aboard northbound trains, Hawthorne took a certain pride in being contrarian. "I have not, as you suggest," he wrote to a friend after the Shadrach and Sims events, "the slightest sympathy for the slaves; or, at least, not half so much as for the laboring whites, who, I believe, as a general thing, are ten times worse off than the Southern negroes. Still, whenever I am absolutely cornered, I shall go for New England rather than the South; and this Fugitive Law cornered me." He did not stay in his corner for long. A leading theme of

Hawthorne's published works from *The Scarlet Letter* (1850) to *The Marble Faun* (1860) is the folly of wishing too soon for too much freedom.

By far the most consequential literary intervention came not from any of the established figures but from an unheralded writer, Harriet Beecher Stowe, sixth child of the thundering preacher Lyman Beecher. When Stowe's father was elected to the presidency of Lane Theological Seminary in Cincinnati in 1832, he moved the family—including the future ministers Edward, Charles, and Henry and his twenty-year-old-daughter, Harriet—from Connecticut to Ohio. There, in 1836, she married a widowed faculty member, Calvin Stowe. As Henry Clay complained in his long compromise speech to the Senate in February 1850, Cincinnati was a busy entry point for runaways from and through Kentucky. For Harriet Beecher Stowe, it became the incubator of her antislavery passion.

Just as the fugitive bill was coming under debate in Congress that spring, Calvin Stowe accepted a teaching offer from Bowdoin College in Brunswick, Maine. Upon returning east with her husband and children, Harriet approached Gamaliel Bailey, editor of the antislavery paper *National Era,* with a proposal for a series of sketches about slavery. On March 9, 1851, she wrote to him that "the time is come when even a woman or a child who can speak a word for freedom and humanity is bound to speak."

Bailey, who had already published several of Stowe's sketches about rural life, gave her a contract. The result, published in installments from June 1851 to April 1852, was a series of fictional sketches of slaves under physical and psychological assault—among them, the beautiful Eliza, who escapes from bounty hunters by leaping across the frozen Ohio River with her baby in her arms; the mysterious and brooding Cassy, who belongs to the brutal Simon Legree; and Tom, whose gentleness and generosity grow apace as he is sold farther and farther south, eventually to Legree, who has him tortured before ordering his overseers to beat him to death.

The magazine pieces were gathered and published on March 20, 1852, as a book titled *Uncle Tom's Cabin; or, Life Among the Lowly,* with a first print run of 5,000. Within a year, it had sold 300,000 copies in America and over a million in Britain, making it the second-bestselling book of the

Harriet Beecher Stowe in 1852, the year Uncle Tom's Cabin *was published*

nineteenth century after the Bible. Because it appeared at a time when reading aloud was common and books were shared by family and friends, the number of people who heard or read it might have been ten times the number who bought it. Stowe's novel made the name of Simon Legree synonymous with cruelty, Uncle Tom the symbol of stoic faith (his reputation for obsequiousness came later), and Eliza the quintessential image of the fugitive slave. *Putnam's Monthly* magazine declared that "the history of literature contains nothing parallel to it, nor approaching it."

In the North, Frederick Douglass rejoiced that Stowe had "baptized with holy fire myriads who before cared nothing for the bleeding slave."* In

---

*Other black activists were less favorable toward Stowe's novel, objecting in particular to the characterization of George Harris, Eliza's husband, who, having escaped with his family to Canada and then to France, concludes the novel by moving with his family to Liberia. Even though blacks ought to be allowed to stay and "mingle" in the United States, Harris feels he must have "a country, a nation, of my own" (Harriet Beecher Stowe, *Uncle Tom's Cabin; or, Life Among the Lowly* [1852], ed. Kenneth S. Lynn [Cambridge, Mass.: Harvard University Press, 1962], 446). One black journalist wrote that Stowe's choice to send the novel's most spirited and daring black man to Africa meant that she believed that blacks, slave or free, cannot "live on the American continent. Death or banishment is our doom, say the Slaveocrats, the Colonizationists, and . . . Mrs. Stowe!!" The Connecticut minister the South, her portrait of Legree was likened to a "malignant" attack on the institution of marriage, as if she had chosen an abusive husband to represent "the normal condition of the relation" between loving spouses. In the presence of Mark Twain, who became a friend of Stowe's in later life, she recounted how, soon after *Uncle Tom's Cabin* was published, she received in the mail a severed human ear as a token of contempt—cut, presumably, from a would-be runaway. It does not seem to have occurred to the sender that the contents of the package confirmed the truth of what she said.

In the figure of Captain Ahab, Melville had portrayed Calhoun in a book that almost no one read. Stowe now gave a portrait of Webster in a book that everyone read. He appears in *Uncle Tom's Cabin* as the fictional "Senator Bird" of Ohio, "whose idea of a fugitive was . . . the image of a little newspaper picture of a man with a stick and bundle." When his wife laments the plight of runaway slaves, he tut-tuts at her for failing to recognize the priority of "great public interests" over mere feelings. "Your feelings are all quite right, dear, and interesting, and I love you for them; but, then, dear, we mustn't suffer our feelings to run away with our judgment." And yet Stowe endowed Senator Bird with a good heart. When confronted in his own kitchen with a "cut and bleeding" runaway in the person of Eliza, he loses his scruples in a flash and swings into action to save her and her child from the slave hunters.

Wife, daughter, and sister of Protestant clergymen, Stowe had composed a brilliantly visual presentation of love and martyrdom that was closer in spirit to the Catholic liturgy than to what Emerson called the "corpse-cold" Protestantism of New England. In her initial proposal to Bailey, she had said that "my vocation is simply that of *painter*" because "there is no arguing with *pictures,* and everybody is impressed by them, whether they mean to be or not." Henry James was later to describe *Uncle Tom's Cabin* as "less a book than a state of vision." In the figure of Eliza and her baby, she placed before her readers a vividly rendered image of Madonna and Child. Further on in the book, she organizes the story

---

Leonard Bacon claimed that he had heard Stowe say that if she were to write the novel again, "she would not send George Harris to Liberia." See Benjamin Quarles, *Black Abolitionists* (New York: Oxford University Press, 1969), 220–21.

around the image of the suffering Christ in the person of Tom. She knew exactly what she was doing. When she describes Eliza in the kitchen melting the heart of Senator Bird, she uses the phrase "the real presence of distress"—a theological reference to the Catholic doctrine of transubstantiation, which teaches that the wine and wafer are miraculously transformed into the blood and body of Christ. The elemental Catholic images—pietà and crucifix—are deployed in *Uncle Tom's Cabin* as a means to overcome the obstruction of sympathy by reason.

Part of Douglass's appreciation of Stowe's novel may be attributed to the fact that he, too, understood the power of the "picture passion" to touch the heart. Among "all our religious denominations," he wrote about the new medium of photography (which, like Lincoln, he used to present himself to the public in different moods and roles), "the Roman Catholic understands this picture passion best. It wisely addresses the religious consciousness in its own language—the child language of the soul. Pictures, images, and other symbolical representations speak to the imagination. The mighty fortress of the human heart silently withstands the assaults by the rifled cannons of reason, but readily falls before the magic power of mystery." There could be no better account of the power of *Uncle Tom's Cabin* in evoking through word-pictures the pathos of a hunted mother and the pity of a god-man crucified.

After her book was denounced by southern critics as lies and slander, Stowe published a defense titled *A Key to "Uncle Tom's Cabin,"* in which she assembled documentary evidence to substantiate her claims while accusing unrepentant slave owners of failing to live by Christ's teaching in Matthew 25:40:

> In the last judgment will He not say to you, "I have been in the slave-prison,—in the slave-coffle. I have been sold in your markets; I have toiled for naught in your fields; I have been smitten on the mouth in your courts of justice; I have been denied a hearing in my own church,—and ye cared not for it. Ye went, one to his farm, and another to his merchandise." And if ye shall answer, "When, Lord?" He

shall say unto you, "Inasmuch as ye have done it to the least of these, my brethren, ye have done it unto me."

Like her brothers and her father, Stowe wanted to believe that slave owners could be shamed by sin and moved by love. Yet *Uncle Tom's Cabin* was ultimately an argument against itself. From the opening chapters, in which Tom's owner, a decent man who feels real affection for his faithful slave but nevertheless sells him under financial duress, she shows again and again that conscience is no match for the coercive force of the market. If she was a crypto-Catholic, she was also a proto-Marxist in the sense that she recognized that in the war between conscience and material interest the latter is most likely to prevail. The whole structure of racial ideology (the natural dependency of blacks, the superiority of whites, the dignity of slavery, and all the rest) was nothing but a veneer of rationalization pasted onto an economic foundation. If the foundation were to be shaken—by, say, a collapse in cotton prices—the edifice would come tumbling down. Stowe attributes this view to a clear-sighted slave owner, but she clearly believed it herself:

> Now, when any one speaks up, like a man, and says slavery is necessary to us, we can't get along without it, we should be beggared if we give it up, and, of course, we mean to hold on to it,—this is strong, clear, well-defined language; it has the respectability of truth to it. . . . But when he begins to put on a long face, and snuffle, and quote Scripture . . . well, suppose that something should bring down the price of cotton once and forever, and make the whole slave property a drug in the market, don't you think we should soon have another version of the Scripture doctrine? What a flood of light would pour into the church, all at once, and how immediately it would be discovered that everything in the Bible and reason went the other way!

In spite of herself, Harriet Beecher Stowe saw no way out of the slavery impasse short of the violent destruction of the slave economy and forcing southern society to reorganize itself. She was not ready to concede this truth explicitly, but it was implicit in every word of her devastating book.

5.

While the initial furor over *Uncle Tom's Cabin* was dying down, Boston had become a battlefield again. Even though the Sims case had ended in rendition, many Bostonians had lulled themselves into thinking that slave hunters were not likely henceforth to use their city as a testing ground. That illusion evaporated on May 24, 1854, when a young slave named Anthony Burns, who had escaped to Massachusetts from eastern Virginia, was arrested on Court Street. Two days after the arrest, a multiracial crowd including Higginson and other veterans of the Sims case stormed the courthouse in a failed attempt to free him. In the chaos, a deputy U.S. marshal, James Batchelder, was stabbed to death.

As the crowd faced off with police and militia, federal troops and antislavery activists converged on the scene. The new president, Franklin Pierce (a college classmate of Hawthorne, who had written a campaign biography for him in 1852), was no less determined than Fillmore to put down disorder. Burns's rendition hearing before Commissioner Edward G. Loring (not to be confused with the Lorings who had argued in the *Aves* and Sims cases) moved swiftly, with Dana and Morris leading the defense. On June 2, Loring remanded Burns to his owner in a decision that included a flailing attempt to explain himself as a reluctant executioner rather than a "merciless judge." Many good people, he acknowledged, regarded as "wicked and cruel" the statute that his constitutional duty compelled him to enforce.

Unlike Sims, who was a tough character given to drinking and brawling, Burns at his sentencing was tentative and meek. For fear of worsening the retribution he would suffer when sent back to Virginia, he did not wish at first to contest the case, and he had to be coaxed into accepting legal counsel. Throughout the hearing, he was surrounded by "a numerous body-guard" of over a hundred men, deputized by the U.S. marshal Watson Freeman and "taken chiefly," in the estimate of Samuel May Jr.

(who shared the anti-Irish sentiment common among abolitionists), "from the vilest sinks of scoundrelism, corruption and crime in the city." Burns, who looked to Dana like "a piteous object, rather weak in mind and body . . . completely cowed and dispirited," remained quiet throughout the proceedings, having told Parker that "if I must go back, I want to go back as easy as I can."

When, after delivery of the negative verdict, Wendell Phillips came to say farewell, Burns asked him, "Mr. Phillips, . . . Must I go back?" Phillips later recalled, "I went over in my own mind the history of Massachusetts. I thought of her schools, her colleges of learning, her churches, her courts, her benevolent and philanthropic institutions, her great names, her Puritans, her Pilgrims, and I was obliged to say, 'Burns, there isn't humanity, there isn't Christianity, there isn't justice enough here to save you; you must go back.'" In an eerie repetition of the Sims spectacle, crowds massed along the route as the prisoner, under armed escort numbering some fifteen hundred troops, was marched to the ship that would return him to Alexandria, Virginia. In a letter to Horace Mann, the physician, reformer, and abolitionist Samuel Gridley Howe recalled seeing in the crowd "a comely coloured girl of eighteen, who stood with clenched teeth and fists, and with tears streaming down her cheeks." Howe tried to console her: "Do not cry, poor girl—he won't be hurt." "'Hurt!' said she, 'I cry for shame that he will not kill himself!—oh! Why is he not man enough to kill himself!'" Upon arrival in Richmond, Burns was imprisoned for four months until his master sold him to a North Carolina slave owner for nine hundred dollars.

The Burns case echoed the Sims affair, but its consequences were larger. In conjunction with events in Washington—where, on May 30, led again by Stephen Douglas, Congress approved the Kansas-Nebraska Act extending the principle of popular sovereignty to territories from which slavery had been previously excluded under the Missouri Compromise—the case galvanized the antislavery movement and attracted new converts. Men who had once stood with Webster—who had died in the fall of 1852—now switched sides. Amos Lawrence, among the leading "Cotton Whigs" who had been in Webster's orbit and who had volunteered to help

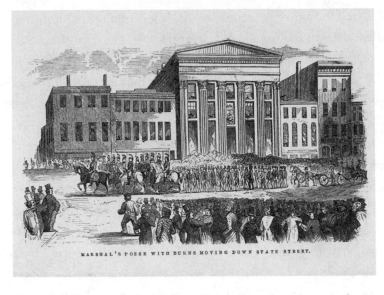

MARSHAL'S POSSE WITH BURNS MOVING DOWN STATE STREET.

The marshal's posse moving Anthony Burns down State Street to the pier

arrest Shadrach's rescuers in 1851, visited Dana before Burns's trial to say that the "solid men of Boston" had been shaken out of their moral lethargy by the Kansas-Nebraska bill and wanted now to pay for the fugitive's defense. John H. Pearson, the shipowner who had furnished the vessel that carried Sims back to Georgia three years earlier and who still controlled landing rights at Boston's Long Wharf, refused to allow a government steamer to drop anchor there to receive Burns. The Boston police captain Joseph Hayes sent a resignation letter to the mayor, declaring his refusal to participate "in the execution of that infamous 'Fugitive Slave Law.'" Amos Lawrence summed up how much had changed: "We went to bed one night old-fashioned, conservative, Compromise Union Whigs & waked up stark mad Abolitionists."

Others, unable to wake themselves, thrashed in the nightmare. Ezra Stiles Gannett, minister of the Federal Street Church, where the eminent William Ellery Channing had preached against slavery in the 1830s and 1840s, had urged compliance with the fugitive slave law but now burst into tears when John Parkman, a member of his congregation as well as of the Boston Vigilance Committee, informed him that Burns had been sent back to Virginia. Parkman later said of Gannett that "no one during that week," including those like himself who had participated in the rescue attempt, "seemed to take so much to heart the event which made it so sad and memorable."

A week after Burns's rendition, Gannett preached a sermon on Matthew 6:23 ("if therefore the light that is in thee be darkness, how great is that darkness") in which he put on public display his private conflict between conscience and "Loyalty to the Law." The "struggle between opposing tendencies in [his] intellect and temperament" had reached the point of what one historian calls "psychic violence." Years later, in a memorial account, Gannett's son could not decide between blaming his father for lacking the abolitionists' resolve or crediting him with seeing what "the Abolitionists could not, and others would not, see; that disunion almost certainly meant war"—an outcome that his father believed would not bring "relief to the slaves" but was "certain to bring worse enslavement."

History has been hard on Gannett and others like him because we know that the events of the ensuing decade proved them wrong. They have become examples of the proverbial bystander—constrained by fear or, worse, indifference, "contemptible moderates," in the words of the political philosopher Isaiah Berlin (who was thinking of his own reputation during the Cold War), "miserable centrists" whose caution made them useless in a soul-trying time. This is a distorted judgment. It rests on the retrospective knowledge that the war they feared did indeed come, that what began as a war for the Union became a war against slavery, and that, as Eliot wrote after all the killing and dying were done, "the right prevailed at last." To dismiss these men "as mediocre, timid, and weak" and to credit their more radical opponents with "flair and foresight" is to subject them all to what has been aptly called "outcome bias." It is to wrench them out of the context of their times.

The historian David Potter offers a better way to see them:

> The problem for Americans . . . who wanted slaves to be free was not
> simply that southerners wanted the opposite, but that they themselves
> cherished a conflicting value: they wanted the Constitution, which

protected slavery, to be honored, and the Union, which was a fellow-
ship with slaveholders, to be preserved. Thus they were committed to
values that could not be logically reconciled.

What the Burns rendition did in combination with the Kansas-Nebraska
Act—not only for Boston, but for the whole nation—was to show that the
values of emancipation and union could never be reconciled short of war.

As with any historical event, it is of course impossible to draw a direct
line of cause and effect from the Burns case to events that followed. But
one thing is sure: it expanded the membership of the antislavery movement and raised the temperature of those who were already part of it.
Whittier felt his blood boil:

> And, as I thought of Liberty
> Marched handcuffed down that sworded street,
> The solid earth beneath my feet
> Reeled fluid as the sea.

Thoreau, disgusted by the sniveling lassitude of his fellow citizens,
declared that there were now "perhaps a million slaves in Massachusetts"—
by which he meant everyone who had held themselves aloof during the
Burns affair. Two days after the rendition, Theodore Parker preached a
scorching sermon, "The New Crime Against Humanity," in which he
reviled Judge Shaw, who played no role in the Burns case, though Loring
had quoted a passage from Shaw's decision in the Sims case. Parker quoted
it now too, but with a caustic substitution: where Shaw had said that because slavery "was not created, established, or perpetuated by the Constitution . . . the framers of the Constitution could not abrogate Slavery, or
the rights claimed under it," Parker reworked the words as if they had
been spoken by a Roman consul defending the killing of heretics: "The
framers of the constitution could not abrogate the custom of persecuting,
torturing, and murdering Christians, or the rights claimed under it."

Southern voices replied in kind. The *Norfolk Herald* quoted Burns
flaying the abolitionists for the selectivity of their sympathy. Even if there

was a touch of truth in some of what he was said to have said, the article in which he was quoted was the nineteenth-century equivalent of a hostage video:

> None of his abolition friends cared for him until they found out that he was a "runaway nigger," and then they were ready enough to help him. A common nigger there (he said) was of no account with them— he might starve and rot; but if he was only a "runaway," they were almost ready to fall down and worship him. "Look at these clothes," said he, pointing to the elegant dress suit he had on—"do you think they would have given them to any common nigger? Shugh!"

Unknown to his captors, Burns found a way to make his real feelings known. Despite the chains on his wrists, he managed to cut through the floorboards of his cell with a spoon, obtained ink from a slave in the room below, and scratched out a letter to Dana that he threw down to a black man walking past his barred window. Beseeching Dana and his friends to liberate him by buying him—"I am for sale"—he wrote with a poignancy deepened by his struggle to express himself:

> *Richmond August 23th 1854*
>
> I am yet Bound in Jail and are waring my chings Night and day But is Waitinge for Som kinededliver to Come that I May Bee DeLivered & the Man or Men that Brought me here sad that they was going to By Me But I dont heir No More a Boute it and I think that it is the Last that I shall heir thay tole My oner to Not Let you all have Me But I am for Sale And if you all my friends will please to healp your friend this Much I will Bee to you all A friend all My days And if you will get Sum of your friends to come to Alexandra and not to say that he come from Boston and inquier where Mr Suttle keep Store And Ask him if hath Sole his man and what he will take for him that he wood

Like to By Me and you can get Low he wood take $800
dollars for me Now & I pray in the name of the Lord that
you will Bee to healp me out suffereinge one time please
Anthony Burns dont rite to me until I tel you

6.

In his speech to the citizens of Concord following the Shadrach rescue
and the Sims rendition, Emerson had called the fugitive slave law a "university to the people." With every new incident, its enrollment grew. But
what exactly did it teach?

It taught that compromise with the South was no longer conceivable.
On March 2, 1850, after Clay's oration in the Senate, but before Webster's
reply, Whitman published a poem in the New York *Evening Post* called
"Song for Certain Congressmen":

> *Beyond all such we know a term,*
> *Charming to ears and eyes,*
> *With it we'll stab young Freedom,*
> *And do it in disguise;*
>
> . . .
>
> *That term is "compromise."*

Higginson, dripping with contempt for those who clung to the so-called
peace measures while fugitives were dragged through the streets, lamented
that "there are always compromisers. There are always men . . . who if anyone claims that two and two make six, will find it absolutely necessary to
go half way, and that two and two make five." Charles Sumner, now representing Massachusetts in the U.S. Senate, was even more direct about the
poisonous effect of compromise on American morals. "From the beginning
of our history," he wrote, "the country has been afflicted with compromise.
It is by compromise that human rights have been abandoned." No northern
senator was more reviled by his southern counterparts than Sumner, but in

this case they cordially agreed with him—except that the abandoned rights they had in mind were those not of slaves but of slave owners.

There were more lessons. The fugitive slave law taught that anyone who believed it still possible to live outside the web of slavery was deluded. For decades, antislavery activists had tried to make this clear. "I am just as much a murderer," one writer (probably Whittier) wrote in an anti-slavery paper in 1845, "if I turn a crank which through five hundred con-necting links cuts off a man's head, as though I had done it directly by taking the sword into my own hand." Soon after the publication of *Uncle Tom's Cabin*, Harriet Beecher Stowe made the same point in a letter to a British admirer. America, she wrote, was finally learning "by what an infinite complexity of ties, nerves, and ligaments this terrible evil is bound in one body politic; how the slightest touch upon it causes even the free States to thrill and shiver. . . . Nobody can tell the thousand ways in which by trade, by family affinity, or by political expediency, the free part of our country is constantly tempted to complicity with the slaveholding part."

For some, this lesson had been a long time coming. In the late 1830s, just when he burst into public notice, Emerson, in the privacy of his jour-nal, had expressed icy irritation at his wife for bemoaning the plight of "obtuse and barbarous" Africans shipped to America:

> Lidian grieves aloud about the wretched negro in the horrors of the middle-passage; and they are bad enough. But to such as she, these crucifixions do not come. They come to the obtuse & barbarous to whom they are not horrid but only a little worse than the old suffer-ings. They exchange a cannibal war for a stinking hold. They have gratifications that would be none to Lidian.

But by the 1850s, after Shadrach, Sims, Christiana, Syracuse, and Burns, Emerson was chastising himself for having waited so long to grieve with her:

You have just dined, and however scrupulously the slaughter-house is concealed in the graceful distance of miles, there is complicity . . . race living at the expense of race.

The fugitive slave law was indeed an education. For those who had thought that slavery was not their problem, it forced them to think again. The words of Commissioner Curtis after the Sims affair—"we have no responsibility, not even of a moral kind, in the act that is done"—were no longer credible. The better argument now belonged to those who retorted, "So long as slavery exists, and the Union continues, we are in fact abettors of that crime."

Thirteen

THE END OF COMPROMISE

1.

Long after the fugitive slave crisis had receded into the textbooks, the twentieth-century writer Dwight Macdonald remarked (without reference to any particular historical event) that "it is a terrible fact, but it is a fact, that few people have the imagination or the moral sensitivity to get very excited about actions which they don't participate in themselves . . . and hence about which they feel no personal responsibility." It was this recalcitrant fact that Harriet Beecher Stowe had in mind when she brought Senator Bird face-to-face with Eliza in his kitchen.

For the crusade against slavery, the fugitive slave law was a godsend. In the free states, it expanded the citizenry's sense of responsibility by turning slavery from an abstraction into an actuality. When a runaway was sent back to his owner, as in the cases of Sims and Burns, anger ignited in the North. When a runaway was rescued, as in the cases of Jerry and Shadrach, outrage surged in the South. For anyone looking to push the sectional conflict toward a final confrontation, every publicized case was a no-lose proposition.

Knowing this was so, abolitionists worked hard to keep the human effects of the law in the public eye. In 1855, Benjamin Drew published *A North-Side View of Slavery*, a compilation of portraits of refugees from slavery who found sanctuary in Canada. The next year saw the first edition of *The Fugitive Slave Law and Its Victims* by Samuel May Jr., a comprehensive list of the law's casualties, beginning with James Hamlet.

May included in his book cases where slave catchers succeeded, as well as cases where they were thwarted, such as the 1853 attack in Wilkes-Barre, Pennsylvania, on an escaped slave who held federal marshals at bay with a carving knife until his neighbors drove them off. The book ranged widely—from Boston, New York, and Pennsylvania, all the way to Wisconsin, where Joshua Glover, escaped from St. Louis, was held in 1854 in a Milwaukee jail until, as one of his rescuers later remembered, "twenty strong and resolute men seized a large timber some eight or ten inches square and twenty feet long and went for the jail door; bumb, bumb, bumb, and down came the jail door and out came Glover."

May also called attention to kidnappers, who, emboldened by the latitude of the law and by the "mercenary, lustful, and diabolical spirit it nurtures," seized people who had never been enslaved and tried to sell them. Noting more than fifty kidnapping cases in which the victims were free blacks, May portrayed southerners as willing customers, though he acknowledged at least one who indignantly declined. "I am a Kentuckian and a slaveholder," he quotes a prospective buyer, "but I would as soon poison my mother as to purchase a negro I knew to be free."

Some of the cases May described had legal repercussions, such as the Glover case, which led to an 1855 ruling by the Wisconsin Supreme Court that the Fugitive Slave Act was unconstitutional—a judgment overturned four years later by the U.S. Supreme Court in the case of *Ableman v. Booth* (Ableman was the U.S. marshal who had attempted Glover's rendition; Booth was the man who had led the rescue). Another incident of legal consequence, on which May commented only briefly because it was not strictly a fugitive slave case, was the 1852 release by the New York Superior Court of eight slaves brought to New York City by their Virginia owner, Jonathan Lemmon, who planned to transport them to Texas. In ordering Lemmon's slaves released by virtue of their having been brought onto free soil, the court invoked Justice Mansfield's ruling in the historic *Somerset* case of 1772 as precedent for the claim that slavery can exist only in a locality where positive law supports it—which, eighty years later, the laws of New York State did not do.*

Of all the incidents May described, the one that struck most deeply into the national psyche was that of Margaret Garner, an enslaved woman from Boone County, Kentucky, whose name, by the time she appeared in the second edition of his book (published in 1861), was already famous. Pregnant—possibly by her master, who may have used her for sexual satisfaction when his wife bored or refused him—she fled in January 1856 with her husband and four of her children across the frozen Ohio River near Covington, Kentucky, by means of stolen horses and a sleigh. The story of Garner was so close to that of Eliza in *Uncle Tom's Cabin* that she seemed a case of life imitating art—except that in Garner's case her flight ended not in deliverance but in catastrophe. The runaways hoped to find refuge in the home of a relative, also an escaped slave, living just south of Cincinnati. Tracked there by slave catchers in the company of U.S. marshals, Garner, overwhelmed by terror and despair, took a kitchen knife and cut the throat of her two-year-old daughter, then slashed at her three surviving children, trying to kill them too rather than leave them to the life of degradation she had known. "If in her deep maternal love," said the abolitionist Lucy Stone, who counseled Garner during the subsequent hearing, "she felt the impulse to send her child back to God, to save it from coming woe, who shall say she had no right to do so?"

In the aftermath of the horror, Garner became caught up in a tug-of-war between state and federal authorities. Those who were horrified *by* her wanted her returned to her owner in Kentucky under the federal fugitive slave law. Those who were horrified *for* her wanted her tried in the Ohio courts, from which they hoped for mercy. The presiding judge sided with the owner and ordered her rendition by ferry across a thawed stretch of the Ohio River back to Kentucky. But even after her return, the dispute over jurisdiction continued, and her owner moved her about, trying to stay a step ahead of Ohio agents seeking her extradition for trial on a manslaughter charge. When the trail got too hot, he sent her off to Arkansas,

---

*The same judge, Elijah Paine Jr., who ordered the slaves freed in the Lemmon case helped to raise funds for compensating their owner for his financial loss.

then Louisiana, and finally to Mississippi, where, sometime in 1858 (no one bothered to record the exact date or place), she died, probably of typhoid, having lost another child by drowning during one of the forced journeys.

Like Dorcas Allen, who committed infanticide in 1837, and the suicidal Anna who tried to jump to her death in 1817, Margaret Garner became a symbol of the desperation to which slavery drove mothers who knew what the future held for their children, especially their daughters. Her story was a gruesome reminder of the unresolved conflict between state and federal authority. It encouraged the adoption of new personal liberty laws, which several northern states instituted over the course of the 1850s. And it attested to the stupefying fact that an enslaved woman had no claim to her own children, who could be sold as if they were animals, furniture, or any other marketable asset.*

Beginning with conflicting coverage in the *Cincinnati Enquirer* (edited by the same man who, as U.S. marshal, worked for her return to Kentucky) and the antislavery *Gazette,* which published sympathetic accounts of her torment, Margaret Garner became a familiar figure not only in newspapers but also in novels, the first of which, Hattia M'Keehan's *Liberty or Death; or, Heaven's Infraction of the Fugitive Slave Law,* appeared in 1858. Frances Harper's poem "The Slave Mother: A Tale of Ohio," published the previous year, focused on one of Margaret's surviving sons:

> She is a mother pale with fear,
> Her boy clings to her side,
> And in her kirtle vainly tries
> His trembling form to hide.

> He is not hers, although she bore
> For him a mother's pains;
> He is not hers, although her blood
> Is coursing through his veins!

---

*In chapter 12 of *Uncle Tom's Cabin,* Stowe describes an "incident of lawful trade" in which the sale of a child drives his mother to suicide.

He is not hers, for cruel hands
May rudely tear apart
The only wreath of household love
That binds her breaking heart.
. . .

No marvel, then, these bitter shrieks
Disturb the listening air:
She is a mother, and her heart
Is breaking in despair.

Garner became a subject, too, for artists—notably Thomas Satterwhite Noble, whose painting *The Modern Medea* was first exhibited after the Civil War, in 1867—and later in opera, film, and most famously in Toni Morrison's 1987 novel *Beloved.**

As the train of fugitive slave cases rolled on, the antislavery movement moved too—toward greater militancy. Men who had once denounced the law but stopped short of defying it felt their compunction dissolving. During an 1857 fugitive slave hearing in Indianapolis, the defendant's attorney made no secret of the fact that if he failed in court to win his client's release, he would urge his friends to organize a post-trial rescue and would join the rescue himself. Orators spoke only and always of the "Fugitive Slave *Bill,*" refusing to dignify the hated legislation with the word "Law." Abolitionist meetings, once solemn, became raucous—even buoyant. Speaking after the Burns and Garner cases at New York's Broadway Tabernacle, Theodore Parker, as reported in the *New-York Tribune,* dropped his ministerial tone and delighted the crowd with plain talk: "It is an old saying that if two will ride on the same horse one must ride behind. [Laughter]. Ladies and Gentlemen, these two parties have been on one horse ever since the adoption of the Federal Constitution, and all the time Slavery has sat in the saddle, and Freedom has been glad to sit on the

---

*An opera, *Margaret Garner,* composed by Richard Danielpour to a libretto by Toni Morrison, premiered in Detroit in 2005. A film version of *Beloved* starring Oprah Winfrey was released in 1998.

The Modern Medea—the Story of Margaret Garner.
*Print after the painting by Thomas Satterwhite Noble,
published in* Harper's Weekly, *May 18, 1867*

crapper. [*Renewed* laughter]." Whether Parker meant it was time to switch places or to get off the horse, he did not say.

By the mid-1850s, even for writers who had previously shown little interest, runaway slaves had become a compulsory subject. In "Song of Myself" (1855), Whitman celebrated himself as a conductor on the Underground Railroad with rifle at the ready, prepared to defend a fugitive's life with his own:

> *The runaway slave came to my house and stopt outside,*
> *I heard his motions crackling the twigs of the woodpile,*
> *Through the swung half-door of the kitchen I saw him limpsy and weak,*
> *And went where he sat on a log and led him in and assured him,*
> *And brought water and fill'd a tub for his sweated body and bruis'd feet,*
> *And gave him a room that enter'd from my own, and gave him some coarse*
> *   clean clothes,*
> *And remember perfectly well his revolving eyes and his awkwardness,*
> *And remember putting plasters on the galls of his neck and ankles;*

He staid with me a week before he was recuperated and pass'd north,
I had him sit next me at table, my fire-lock lean'd in the corner.*

The steady flow of writings—poems, stories, speeches, newspaper accounts, judicial rulings, sermons—registered the fact that every effort,
successful or not, to enforce the fugitive slave law was making the state of
the Union more dire.

2.

No one can say exactly where the law ranked among the forces that pushed
the nation toward secession and civil war. Between the so-called Compromise of 1850 and the election of Lincoln in 1860, the list of provoca-
tions driving apart North and South grew ever longer, with diminishing
intervals between them, each enlarging the impact of the last.

On May 30, 1854, just days before news reached him of Anthony
Burns's rendition, President Pierce signed into law the Kansas-Nebraska
Act. This was an attempt—led by Stephen Douglas, the same man of
pummeling energy who had pushed through the grand bargain of 1850—
to settle the question of whether slavery would be permitted in the vast
territories acquired fifty years earlier through the Louisiana Purchase.
The area in question stretched from the strip of Indian Territory just
above Texas (later part of Oklahoma) all the way north to the Canadian
border and west to the Rocky Mountains. But rather than clarifying the
future of this huge expanse—comparable in size to the whole Mexican
cession—the Kansas-Nebraska Act pushed pro- and antislavery forces
into what turned out to be a violent rehearsal of civil war.

Three years later, in a posthumous endorsement of Calhoun's doctrine,
the Supreme Court ruled in the *Dred Scott* case in 1857 that Congress had

---

*While some writers were pulled into the churn of events, others kept themselves out. During the
Burns case, Harriet Beecher Stowe (now living thirty miles from Boston, in Andover, Massachusetts)
remained reticent, as if bewildered by the whirlwind she had helped to sow. "It would have looked
better," remarked Anne Warren Weston of the Boston Female Anti-slavery Society, "if she had shewn
her face to the people in Boston. But she did not." *Proceedings of the Massachusetts Historical Society*
(Boston, 1911), 44:334.

no authority to restrict slavery in the federal territories—a decision by which northern Whigs and even some northern Democrats became convinced that Court, Congress, and President James Buchanan (the Pennsylvania Democrat who succeeded Pierce that same year) had been conspiring to release slavery from all constraint. Two years after that, in 1859, John Brown, an abolitionist with a record of committing murder for the cause, led a raid into northern Virginia with the aim of fomenting a slave uprising throughout the South. All these events seemed designed by some warrior god bent on inflaming hatred on both sides.

The first in this sequence of shocks, the Kansas-Nebraska Act, was an attempt to defuse the slavery problem by submitting it to what Stephen Douglas called the "great principle of self-government," by which he meant that the fate of slavery should be left to local voters. In their famous debates four years later, Lincoln was to accuse Douglas of enabling the repeal of the Missouri Compromise, which had excluded slavery above the 36°30′ parallel, by professing "indifference" toward slavery while harboring "a covert real zeal" to see it spread.

In fact, Douglas was a pragmatist without much conviction about slavery one way or the other. To his mind, the chronic conflict was not a deep moral struggle but a hindrance to the nation's business, and he thought he saw a way to remove the issue altogether from the sphere of national politics. Hoping to placate southern Whigs as well as the southern wing of his own Democratic party, he proposed to extend to Kansas-Nebraska the same principle—"popular sovereignty," or, as it was sometimes called, "squatter sovereignty"—that the Compromise of 1850 had applied to Utah and New Mexico. His credo boiled down to this: leave it to the locals! If Congress simply recused itself, southerners would be mollified, and northerners would come to see that Kansas-Nebraska, because of its (mostly) northerly climate and the character of its settlers, would never become "slave-holding country."

On the last point, there is no reason to doubt Douglas's sincerity. He envisioned the West, from Illinois to California, not as slave country but as a magnet for industrious migrants from the East and from abroad. He saw it, too, as the future site of a great railroad that would carry agricul-

*Stephen A. Douglas
in 1859*

tural and industrial products from coast to coast. The best evidence that
he believed in his vision is that with a group of venture capitalists he
bought thousands of acres at the western tip of Lake Superior near what is
now the border of Minnesota and Wisconsin—land whose value he expected to soar as development of "the greatest railroad in the world" pro-
gressed.

But, quite apart from the risk of tampering with the fragile sectional
balance achieved by the Missouri Compromise of 1820 and sustained,
however provisionally, by the "peace measures" of 1850, Douglas, like
many others whose vision was clouded by hope, greed, or both, failed to
see the fatal flaw in popular sovereignty as a practical matter. Leaving the
decision about slavery to local voters was an invitation for opposing forces
to pour into the contested territory in a rush to outnumber and outvote
each other. By the summer of 1854, they were doing just that. The
Kansas-Nebraska Act—or the "Nebraska swindle," as the black abolitionist William J. Watkins preferred to call it—set off a stampede of enraged
adversaries, each side well financed and well armed, converging on disputed territory formerly closed to slavery and spoiling for a fight.

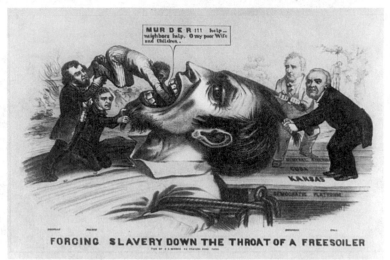

"Forcing slavery down the throat of a freesoiler."
Published in Philadelphia by J. L. Magee, 1856

The first phase of the contest was relatively peaceful. Supporters of slavery, in Lincoln's words, were "within a stone's throw of the contested ground" and could simply step across the Missouri border, cast their votes in a drunken blur, then go home again to dry out until the next round. Emigrants from free states, on the other hand, for whom "the battle-field [was] too far from *their* base of operations," were still relatively sparse. The immediate result was that pro-slavery candidates won the first "elections" (given the extent of the fraud and corruption, quotation marks are warranted) for the territorial legislature.

Upon appeal to the federally appointed governor, a revote was ordered in some districts, and antislavery candidates did a little better. Meeting in the summer of 1855 at the town of Lecompton in eastern Kansas, the legislature ignored the new results and seated an overwhelmingly pro-slavery majority, which passed a raft of slave codes, including one prescribing the death penalty for anyone aiding a fugitive slave. In October, Free-Soilers, committed to the principle that slavery should not be permitted to expand, and whose numbers were starting to catch up to those of their adversaries, convened a countergovernment in Topeka and demanded new elections.

RUINS OF THE FREE STATE HOTEL, LAWRENCE.
From the Daguerreotype taken for Mrs Robinson.

Ruins of the Free State Hotel

By now, men on both sides were "walking arsenals." The New England Emigrant Aid Company—financed in part by Amos Lawrence, who had been converted to antislavery activism by the Burns case—sent funds and guns to Free-Soil farmers looking to pick up stakes and move to the fresh fields of Kansas. After Henry Ward Beecher, whose brother Edward had been an early advocate of "moral suasion," declared that trying to teach slave owners the error of their ways was like reading "the Bible to Buffaloes," the carbines carried by antislavery men in Kansas became known as "Beecher's Bibles."

Thomas Wentworth Higginson, who traveled to the scene in the spring of 1856, reported in the *New-York Tribune* that "ever since the rendition of Anthony Burns, in Boston, I have been looking for *men*. I have found them in Kansas." Years later, he noted proudly that "certain rifles which we had brought" to Kansas ultimately made their way into the hands of John Brown for use at Harpers Ferry. Both sides had concluded that the time for talking was over and the time for shooting had arrived.

The first wave of organized violence broke out in May 1856, when a mostly Missourian "posse" attacked the Free-Soil town of Lawrence (named in honor of Amos Lawrence), plundering homes, destroying the two newspaper offices, and burning down the hotel.

Remarkably, despite the use of artillery as an instrument of demolition, and the promise by pro-slavery leaders to litter the whole territory with "the carcasses of the Abolitionists," the only casualty was a pro-slavery man killed by falling masonry. But in the minds of antislavery men, the attack demanded reprisal, and as the blow-for-blow logic took hold, the conflict entered a cycle of escalation.

Among those itching to fight was John Brown, a peripatetic abolitionist who had been radicalized some twenty years earlier by the murder of Elijah Lovejoy and swore thereafter to devote his life to the cause. On the night of May 24, 1856, Brown led a small party of avengers on a rampage along Pottawatomie Creek in eastern Kansas, where pro-slavery sentiment was strong. Brown's "army" dragged five men out of their homes in front of their wives and children, hacked four of them to death with long knives sharpened for the purpose, and shot the fifth. The victims might have been chosen for their connection to a local district court that had issued warrants for the arrest of men accused of violating territorial laws against antislavery agitation. One was a bailiff, another a grand juror, a third the brother of the man who owned the tavern where the court met, and the fourth a district attorney pro tem. The fifth fatality was a young man whose only connection to the court was that he was the son of the juror.

Part of what enraged Brown was news that pro-slavery violence had broken out, too, in Washington, D.C. Harangues, insults, threats, and even fistfights were nothing new in Congress, but on May 22, 1856, things rose—or fell—to a new level. Beginning on May 19 and continuing through the next day, Charles Sumner—who regularly demanded repeal of the Fugitive Slave Act, which he called "a machine of torture"—delivered a speech in which he described the Missouri settlers as "murderous robbers" and "drunken spew and vomit." He was particularly vitriolic about one of their supporters, South Carolina's senator Andrew Butler, whom he accused of taking "the harlot, slavery," for his mistress. These words were received by southerners as a spray of venom that made the fulminations of the late John Quincy Adams seem friendly. While Sumner was speaking,

John Brown, *by John Steuart
Curry, oil on canvas, 1939*

Stephen Douglas was heard to mutter, "That damn fool will get himself
killed by some other damn fool."

This time Douglas showed foresight. Two days after Sumner finished
speaking, Congressman Preston Brooks of South Carolina, a cousin of
Butler's, entered the chamber and strode up to the seated senator waving
his walking stick made of gutta-percha, which gave it a flexible strength
somewhere between that of a cane and a whip. Before Sumner could
scramble to his feet, Brooks swung it again and again at his head until he
crumpled to the floor, his face a bloody pulp. He was not quite killed, as
Douglas had expected, but it took him years to recover. Satisfaction in the
South was matched by outrage in the North even among those who
thought he had been asking for it.

A year later, the Supreme Court did its part to fan the flames. Two decades earlier, in 1834, an enslaved man named Dred Scott had been taken
by his owner, an army physician named Emerson, into Illinois during a

two-year stint of military service, and then for another year after the doctor was transferred to Fort Snelling, into Wisconsin Territory. Upon Dr. Emerson's death in 1843, his estate—including Scott, his wife, and their two daughters—was inherited by the doctor's widow, who, having taken the Scotts with her to St. Louis, hired out Dred but refused his request that he use his portion of the wages to buy his and his family's freedom.

In 1846, Dred Scott attempted to sue for his freedom on the grounds that his original owner had taken him for extended periods first to the free state of Illinois and then to Wisconsin Territory, from which slavery was excluded by the Missouri Compromise. For more than a decade, the case crawled along, with Scott represented by a series of antislavery lawyers who took it through the Missouri courts in a cycle of wins, losses, and appeals. At first, the defendant was Mrs. Emerson (whom Scott also accused of abuse), then her brother-in-law, John Sanford, to whom she turned over management of her interests.* In 1853, Scott's St. Louis attorney, noting that Sanford was a resident of New York City while his client claimed to be a free citizen of Missouri, took the case to the U.S. Circuit Court on the grounds that a dispute between citizens of different states must be adjudicated by the federal judiciary.

By the time the case reached the U.S. Supreme Court, Scott was represented by the antislavery (or at least anti-expansion-of-slavery) Montgomery Blair of Maryland, who had abandoned the Democratic Party over the Kansas-Nebraska Act. Blair was assisted by none other than George T. Curtis, the former Boston commissioner who had returned Thomas Sims to slavery in Georgia but who now acted on behalf of an enslaved man.

Blair and Curtis faced a discouraging panel of judges. Five were southerners, including the eighty-year-old chief justice, Roger Taney of Maryland; two were northern Democrats, Samuel Nelson of New York and the Pennsylvanian Robert Grier, who had presided over the Christiana case. Rounding out the nine-man bench were John McLean of Ohio and

---

*When the case reached the Supreme Court, it was entered in the docket as *Scott v. Sandford*. The defendant's name was misspelled in the first filing and never corrected.

Benjamin R. Curtis of Massachusetts—George T. Curtis's older brother—who, before his Senate confirmation to the high court, had presided over the Massachusetts First Circuit, where participants in the Shadrach rescue were tried. Although those cases ended in acquittal or dismissal, Richard Henry Dana Jr. sneered that Curtis's rulings were "small & second rate."

Despite the odds, Scott's counsel pressed on. Much of the argument went back and forth over whether Scott had been merely a sojourner in Illinois and Wisconsin and therefore remained legally enslaved under the laws of Missouri or whether his residency in a free state and territory rendered him free. If those had remained the key questions, the *Dred Scott* case would be a footnote in history. But in the course of argument, counsel for Sanford made the fateful decision to claim that the exclusion of slavery from the Wisconsin Territory was invalid because congressional exclusion of slavery from federal territory, as prescribed by the Missouri Compromise, was unconstitutional. The case was thereby transformed from a private suit into a public dispute of huge consequence. At stake now was the question of whether Congress had authority to exclude slavery from any federal territory at all.

The Court might still have ducked that question by confining its ruling to the sojourn versus residency issue. But when, on March 6, 1857, Chief Justice Taney read the majority opinion—from which Curtis and McLean dissented—it was broad and sweeping. Not only did the Court rule that Scott was not a citizen of Missouri and therefore had no standing to file suit, but Taney wrote for the majority that members of the "negro African race" could not claim U.S. citizenship, though he conceded that individual states could grant them state citizenship. In a phrase that became instantly notorious, he declared that no slave or descendant of a slave had any "rights which the white man was bound to respect."* In this obiter dictum (an opinion that went beyond the contested issue, in

---

*Ironically, one of the most comprehensive surveys of antebellum laws restricting the rights of blacks in the north was written by Taney in his opinion in the *Dred Scott* case, arguing that neither slaves nor descendants of slaves had ever been accorded citizenship rights.

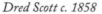

Dred Scott c. 1858   *Roger B. Taney c. 1858*

this case the question of Dred Scott's status as slave or free), the chief justice further denied not only to Congress but also to any territorial government the power to exclude slavery, on the grounds that such exclusion would violate the slave owner's right to due process under the Fifth Amendment.

.Whatever its force as legal precedent, Taney's opinion had an incendiary effect on the tinderbox nation. By vindicating southerners, it drove antislavery northerners to new heights of outrage at what seemed the wholesale takeover of the federal government by the Slave Power. It aligned the Supreme Court with Congress in effectively repudiating the Missouri Compromise as an overreach of congressional power, and it went even further in disallowing the prohibition of slavery by any territorial legislature, popularly elected or not.

Not a few northerners saw the decision as the capstone of a plot that had begun with Pierce and Douglas colluding to open the Kansas-Nebraska territory to slavery and now culminated with Taney and Buchanan scheming to destroy the power of Congress to restrict its spread at all.* The following year, in his first debate with Stephen Douglas, Lincoln described the *Dred Scott* decision as a first step toward the *"perpetuity and nationalization of slavery,"* opening the way "for the Supreme Court to decide that no *State* under the Constitution can exclude it, just as they have already decided that under the Constitution neither Congress nor the Territorial Legislature can do it."

3.

Each of these rapid-fire victories by the slavery interest provoked an equal and opposite reaction, of which the most politically significant was the emergence of an aggressive new antislavery party. Formally organized in the summer of 1854, the Republican Party was a coalition of northern Whigs peeled off from the disintegrating party of Clay and Webster, northern Democrats fed up with the intransigence of their southern counterparts, border-state Democrats committed to stopping the spread of slavery, and outright abolitionists willing to work with the new party, even though for most Republicans immediate emancipation remained a fringe idea. By 1856, the party was coherent enough to nominate the charismatic John C. Frémont for president, who, though he lost to the Democrat Buchanan, polled more than a million votes and carried eleven states in the Northeast and the upper Midwest and whose victory seemed sufficiently possible to Governor Henry Wise of Virginia that he was reputed to have made contingency plans to send in the militia to stop Frémont's inauguration.

Over the next four years, Republicans gained majorities in northern state legislatures, collected governorships and mayoralties, achieved a plurality in the House, and substantially reduced the Democratic majority in the Senate. Their leaders included the former Whig governor and senator

---

*The most famous articulation of this conspiracy theory came from Abraham Lincoln in his "House Divided" speech delivered at Springfield on June 16, 1858: "We cannot absolutely know that all these exact adaptations are the results of a preconcert. But when we see a lot of framed timbers, different portions of which we know have been gotten out at different times and places by different workmen— Stephen [Douglas], Franklin [Pierce], Roger [Taney], and James [Buchanan], for instance—and when we see these timbers joined together . . . we find it impossible to not believe that Stephen and Franklin and Roger and James all understood one another from the beginning, and all worked upon a common plan or draft." *Collected Works of Lincoln*, 2:465–66.

Abraham Lincoln in 1858

from New York William H. Seward, the former Whig and Free-Soil governor Salmon P. Chase of Ohio, and the former Illinois Whig Abraham
Lincoln, who had left Congress in 1849 after only one term but was
"aroused" by the Kansas-Nebraska Act to reenter politics.

Soon after passage of the Kansas-Nebraska Act, in a speech delivered
in that proverbial bellwether city, Peoria, Illinois, Lincoln declared that
"the whole nation is interested that the best use shall be made of these
territories. We want them for the homes of free white people." Here was
the basic Republican agenda: to prevent enslaved black laborers from
blocking the economic advancement of free whites. But if Republicans
were in large measure a white man's party devoted to white men's interests, they were also a jumble of disparate elements that, in the words of the
historian Eric Foner, "dissolve into one another":

> resentment of southern political power, devotion to the Union, anti-
> slavery based upon the free-labor argument, moral revulsion to the
> peculiar institution, racial prejudice, a commitment to the northern
> social order and its development and expansion.

Lincoln himself was a living anthology of all these elements. In the same speech in which he called for a white West, he spoke passionately against the idea that any man of any color could justly own another man. Three years later, in the summer of 1857 after outrage over the Kansas-Nebraska Act had been compounded by the *Dred Scott* decision, he told an audience in Springfield, Illinois, that whenever the slightest hope flickered in the heart of a black man, government, bankers, intellectuals, and even churches would mobilize together to snuff it out:

> All the powers of earth seem rapidly combining against him. Mammon is after him; ambition follows, and philosophy follows, and the Theology of the day is fast joining the cry. They have him in his prison house; they have searched his person, and left no prying instrument with him. One after another they have closed the heavy iron doors upon him, and now they have him, as it were, bolted in with a lock of a hundred keys, which can never be unlocked without the concurrence of every key; the keys in the hands of a hundred different men, and they scattered to a hundred different and distant places; and they stand musing as to what invention, in all the dominions of mind and matter, can be produced to make the impossibility of his escape more complete than it is.

The empathetic rage conveyed by this deadly accurate metaphor went far beyond self-interest. No one who heard him could possibly doubt that Lincoln was appalled by the injustice of slavery not only or mainly on behalf of white people disadvantaged by it but because black people were condemned by it to living without hope.

Through the rest of the decade, the intensity of invective between North and South continued to grow. In 1856, southerners had been shocked by the success of antislavery candidates in the slave-owning state of Missouri. Montgomery Blair's brother Francis P. Blair Jr., who campaigned as a Free-Soil Democrat but supported the Republican Frémont, won election to Congress on a platform favoring compensated emancipation and a free Kansas. Shortly thereafter, an ally of Blair's was elected

mayor of St. Louis. Even if antislavery opinion took overtly racist form—
"What will be done with the niggers" once they are set free? asked the
Missouri Democrat, then answered its own question by declaring, "We are
only interested in whites"—slave owners were alarmed to the point of
panic. When, as Lincoln was soon to say, they spoke of Republicans, they
did "so only to denounce us as reptiles." They would "grant a hearing to
pirates or murderers, but nothing like it to 'Black Republicans,'" whose
sheer evil became a unifying cry throughout the South.

As the North moved left, the South moved right. Some southerners
even talked of reversing the ban on the Atlantic slave trade that had been
one of the constitutional compromises. The rabidly pro-slavery editor
James D. B. DeBow, whose New Orleans–based magazine, *DeBow's Review,* was published in Washington during his term as director of the U.S.
Census (1853–1857), insisted that Africans abducted as slaves to the
United States had no cause to complain but should be grateful for their
introduction to Christian civilization. The South Carolinian William
Grayson believed that to pull them out of Africa would be doing them a
favor by rescuing them from the "sloth and error" in which they had been
"sunk for countless years." Late in 1856, South Carolina's governor, James
H. Adams, called openly for reviving the Atlantic slave trade, and two
years later the sloop *Wanderer,* renowned for its speed and maneuverabil-
ity, outran British patrols on the west coast of Africa and brought a cargo
of four hundred African boys to Jekyll Island, off the coast of Georgia.
The following year, Stephen Douglas estimated that in recent times some
fifteen thousand persons had been carried illegally from Africa into the
slave states.

All this came as no surprise to Lincoln, who had predicted that sooner
or later the principle of popular sovereignty (he liked to mock Douglas for
crooning the prefix "gur-reat pur-rinciple" whenever he spoke of it) would
be invoked as justification for reviving the Atlantic slave trade. "If it is a
sacred right for the people of Nebraska to take and hold slaves there,"
Lincoln warned, "it is equally their sacred right to buy them where they
can buy them cheapest; and that undoubtedly will be on the coast of

Africa."* As North and South traded charges and taunts, their estrangement continued to accelerate.

Then, on October 16, 1859, John Brown dealt a mortal blow to whatever hopes remained of preventing an irreparable break. Ever since his exploits in Kansas, Brown had been looking for new ways to carry the fight to the enemy. With financial and logistical help from veterans of the fugitive slave struggle, including Higginson, Parker, and Gerrit Smith, he recruited a raiding party that attacked the federal arsenal at Harpers Ferry, Virginia. Prominent among those who helped him solicit funds and recruit men was the fugitive slave Harriet Tubman, renowned in abolitionist circles as a fearless Underground Railroad conductor, whom Brown called "one of the best and bravest persons on this continent—*General Tubman*, as we call her."

Brown's wild idea was to distribute munitions to local slaves and raise a black liberation army starting in Virginia, which would swell with enlistees as it marched through the South. Among those whom he approached for help was Frederick Douglass, who, at least by Douglass's own account, tried to convince Brown not only that his plan would fail but that it would "rivet the fetters more firmly than ever on the limbs of the enslaved."

In the short run, Douglass was right. There was no uprising. The only casualty of the raid was a baggage handler for the railroad, a black man shot and killed when Brown tried to commandeer a train for transporting the first cache of arms. Within forty-eight hours, Brown was captured by a company of U.S. marines commanded by Colonel Robert E. Lee. Two of Brown's sons and several civilians died in the action. Charged with treason and murder, he was tried and convicted, and on December 2, 1859, he was hanged.

In the longer run, Brown probably hastened the coming of the Civil War

---

*The last ship known to have discharged a cargo of enslaved Africans in the United States dropped anchor at Mobile, Alabama, sometime between the fall of 1859 and the summer of 1860. The last survivor of that voyage, who was given the name Cudjoe Lewis, lived until 1935. In 1931, the novelist Zora Neale Hurston interviewed Lewis for a book, posthumously published in May 2018 as *Barracoon: The Story of the Last 'Black Cargo,'* edited by Deborah G. Plant.

and thereby the emancipation he had sought. Among southerners, he turned Calhoun's valedictory warning that their way of life was under siege into a mainstream opinion. Among northerners, he deepened the divisions over how to resist the Slave Power. Some exalted him as a martyr whose death, in Emerson's words, "will make the gallows as glorious as the cross"—to which Hawthorne responded that "nobody was ever more justly hanged."

Others tried to split the difference. In February 1860, in the speech by which Lincoln advanced his ultimately successful pursuit of the Republican nomination by introducing himself to the political elite of New York City, he did not exactly repudiate Brown's ideals, but he denounced his methods. "John Brown was no Republican," he said, but rather an "enthusiast" (a nineteenth-century synonym for "fanatic") who "broods over the oppression of a people till he fancies himself commissioned by Heaven to liberate them." Seward, too—presumptive head of the Republican Party and still widely regarded as its likely presidential candidate in the next election—tried to dissociate himself from Brown. But fewer and fewer southerners believed the disavowals. They believed, instead, that Brown was a portent of things to come.*

Amid the uproar, Seward and Lincoln's party, which Douglas described as "an Abolition party under the name and disguise of a Republican party," was increasingly seen as the political wing of a militant—thanks to Brown, even a military—movement, which included a disquieting number of blacks. From enemies of the party, the moniker "Black Republicans" became a routine term of abuse. Linked by shared racial fear, both northern conservatives and southern slave owners were appalled by a party they saw as committed to destroying the age-old hierarchy of white over black. While many Republicans focused solely on keeping slavery out of the territories (a policy perfectly compatible with racial animus), some black and white veterans of the fugitive slave struggle such as Samuel Ringgold Ward and Charles Sumner attacked not only the expansionist

---

*Melville wrote a poem about Brown titled "The Portent," published in his 1866 collection, *Battle-Pieces,* in which he describes Brown's body swinging from the gallows as foreshadowing doom for the South: "Hanging from the beam, / Slowly swaying (such the law), / Gaunt the shadow on your green, / Shenandoah!" *Battle-Pieces and Aspects of the War,* ed. Sidney Kaplan (Boston: University of Massachusetts Press, 1972), 11.

ambitions of the South but racial inequality in the North. Black militants pushed, too, for eligibility to serve in the militia of northern states, while others claimed the right to kill slave catchers if the legal system failed to protect fugitives. And they all celebrated the fact—which the Republican Party did a great deal to *make* a fact—that the "question of American slavery is no longer a question between the black man and the slave-owner, but a question between the people of the North and South."

Meanwhile, the Democratic Party was breaking up into northern and southern factions almost as hostile to each other as they were to Republicans and their fellow travelers. Unable to agree on a candidate at their Charleston convention, Democrats ended up holding rival conventions in Baltimore, where the North-South fissure only deepened. In the end, one group nominated Stephen Douglas, the other John C. Breckinridge of Kentucky, who, as Buchanan's vice president, had endorsed the so-called Lecompton Constitution drawn up by the pro-slavery faction in Kansas. Southern support for Douglas had always been equivocal, and by rejecting the Lecompton Constitution as a power grab by pro-slavery Kansans, he had lost most of his southern allies while failing to win back northerners who had abandoned him over popular sovereignty. A fourth candidate, John Bell, was nominated by the hastily assembled Constitutional Union Party, made up of a residue of conservative northern Whigs and southern Democrats who opposed secession, in some cases because they believed—presciently, as it turned out—that "slavery was safer in than out of the Union."

4.

On November 6, 1860, Abraham Lincoln was elected president of the United States with a plurality of the vote in the four-candidate election. Breckinridge, Bell, and Douglas split the southern vote, while Lincoln carried eighteen states in the North and the West, polling nearly two million votes (about 40 percent of the total), almost twice as many as Frémont had won four years earlier. Of the four candidates, in an era when it was unusual for presidential candidates to campaign at all, only Douglas had dared to make appearances in both North and South—a decision that required considerable personal courage. Offering himself as the last hope by which the Union could be saved, he managed to carry only one state, Missouri. The search for compromise was over.

The Republicans' sweep to power had been—so far—a peaceful political revolution. But over the winter of 1860–1861, as it prepared for the transition, the party remained an unstable coalition of competing elements with divergent views on whether slavery could be destroyed without outright war. Twenty-three-year-old Henry Adams, serving as private secretary to his father, Charles Francis Adams, who had been elected to Congress as a Republican from Massachusetts, described the division:

> The policy of the one wing led to a violent destruction of the slave power; perhaps by war, perhaps by slave insurrection. The policy of the other wing was to prevent a separation in order to keep the slave power more effectually under control, until its power for harm should be gradually exhausted, and its whole fabric gently and peacefully sapped away.

Many historians have followed Adams in sorting Republicans into two categories: radicals (led by Sumner in the Senate and Pennsylvania representative Thaddeus Stevens in the House) and moderates (including Lincoln, Seward, and the elder Adams). But in the eyes of southerners, there was no such thing as a moderate Republican. The president-elect had repeatedly stated his personal revulsion at the institution of slavery, and no matter how often he paired that assertion with assurance that he would respect the constitutional bar to federal interference, southerners took small comfort. This was the same man, after all, who had said in 1854 that "those who deny . . . the humanity of the slave . . . and make mere merchandise of him, deserve kickings, contempt, and death."

From the southern point of view, Lincoln's rise to power meant that something worse than the Wilmot Proviso was about to become the policy of the U.S. government. Since the birth of the Republican Party, it had been its policy to exclude slavery not only from the Mexican cession but from any and all federal territories, and now, having achieved control of the executive and legislative branches, it had the means to do so. As for the *Dred Scott* decision, which theoretically blocked implementation of such a policy, Lincoln tiptoed around the question of whether he would obey it. "We offer no *resistance* to it," he had said soon after the ruling, but "we think the Dred Scott decision is erroneous," and "we know the court that made it, has often over-ruled its own decisions, and we shall do what we can to have it over-rule this."

In short, southerners expected Republicans to attack slavery with every weapon on every front. They expected them to press for abolition in the District of Columbia, whereby freedom would be brought to their door-step.* They expected them to disrupt the domestic slave trade by claiming jurisdiction over coastal waterways. And the main Republican policy of excluding slavery from the territories, which would starve the South of fertile land, was received as a frontal assault.

As for the fugitive slave law, slave owners expected that it would be disregarded under a Republican administration even more completely than it already had been. As the northward flight of slaves from the upper South accelerated, the value of human property would decline, and slave owners in the border states would start selling it off. With western territories entering the Union under the slavery prohibition (Kansas came in as a free state on January 29, 1861), Republican control not only of the presidency and Congress but eventually of the Supreme Court would be assured—with cataclysmic consequences. The denouement of the Republican plan was nothing less than the self-destruction of the South. Slavery would be contained and cornered until, "like a scorpion girt by fire" (a metaphor commonly invoked at the time), it would go into its final frenzy and sting itself to death.

The North had installed a president who quoted scripture in predicting that "a house divided against itself cannot stand" and who promised that the Union "will become *all* one thing, or *all* the other." Southerners took him at his word. Six weeks after the election, led by South Carolina, the process of secession began. Within three months, seven states had

---

*Abolition in the capital was indeed achieved by the Republican Congress, but not until April 1862, when the war had been going on for a year.

announced their intention to leave the Union. In February 1861, with a month to go before Inauguration Day, the Confederacy declared itself a new nation.

Faced with what looked very much like the end of the Union, Lincoln—whose devotion to the Union, as Georgia representative Alexander Stephens later remarked, "rose to the sublimity of a religious mysticism"—still believed, and would continue to believe well into the Civil War, that latent Union sentiment in the South could be tapped as a counterforce to the extremists and that secession could be reversed.* He did not stop trying to tamp down southern anxiety about his intentions. A month after the election, he wrote to the *New York Times* editor Henry J. Raymond to assure him that he did "not hold the black man to be the equal of the white" and "was never in a meeting with negroes in my life." Again and again, he repeated that he would respect the constitutional barrier to federal interference wherever slavery existed by state law. On December 22, 1860, he wrote to Stephens, with whom he had served in Congress and who had joined him in opposing the Mexican War, "Do the people of the South really entertain fears that a Republican administration would, *directly*, or *indirectly*, interfere with their slaves, or with them, about their slaves? If they do, I wish to assure you, as once a friend, and still, I hope, not an enemy, that there is no cause for such fears."

Some in Lincoln's own party feared that he was pandering to the traitors, but they need not have worried. All his assurances were for naught. Three months after receiving Lincoln's letter, Stephens, speaking in Savannah, announced the credo of the new Confederacy. In proclaiming human equality, he said, the founding fathers had been "fundamentally wrong." Their "assumption of the equality of races . . . was an error" that the new Confederacy was born to correct. Our "cornerstone rests upon the great truth that the negro is not equal to the white man; that slavery—subordination to the superior race—is his natural and moral condition."

---

*Even in the depths of the Civil War, Lincoln never stopped trying to build what one historian calls "off-ramps" by which southerners could walk back their commitment to secession. See Elizabeth Brown Pryor, *Six Encounters with Lincoln: A President Confronts Democracy and Its Demons* (New York: Viking, 2017), 325.

As for the new president's promises (Stephens delivered his speech less than three weeks after Inauguration Day) that slavery would remain safe from federal interference, Mr. Lincoln had said repeatedly as well that he would place slavery "in the path of ultimate extinction." On that point, southerners had no trouble believing him.

ſ.

What they did not believe was Lincoln's pledge to respect constitutional constraints on his power to hasten the day of extinction. And so, once again, the fugitive slave problem moved to the center of contention as a symptom, symbol, and substantive instance of what Lincoln's erstwhile rival Seward—soon to be his secretary of state—had called the "irrepressible conflict."

Whatever his private scruples, Lincoln had always been consistent in his public statements about the fugitive slave issue. "Stand WITH the abolitionist in restoring the Missouri Compromise," he had urged at the start of the Kansas-Nebraska turmoil, "and stand AGAINST him when he attempts to repeal the fugitive slave law." When Douglas charged him with supporting repeal of the law, he vigorously denied it. He even suggested that he was open to toughening the existing law, as long as any revision included provisions for protecting free persons against kidnapping. "I would give them [the South] any legislation for the reclaiming of their fugitives, which should not, in its stringency, be more likely to carry a free man into slavery, than our ordinary criminal laws are to hang an innocent one." These were among the statements that led Frederick Douglass, after the Civil War, to say of Lincoln that "he was willing to pursue, recapture, and send back the fugitive slave to his master, and to suppress a slave rising for liberty" if that is what it took to preserve the Union.

But—as had been the case since the adoption of the Constitution— acknowledging the legitimacy of laws concerning fugitive slaves was one thing and enforcing them was another. Besides, Lincoln had made those assurances earlier while scoffing at southerners for expecting northerners to "arrest and return their fugitive slaves with greedy pleasure." Now, in his inaugural address, he spoke in clotted, self-qualifying language that sounded to the South (as well as to conservatives in the North) like a long-winded deflection. With flat understatement, he conceded that "there is much controversy about the delivering up of fugitives from service or labor." Describing the fugitive slave clause of the Constitution "as plainly written . . . as any other of its provisions," he read aloud the entire clause, concluding with the self-evident comment that "the intention of the lawgiver is the law." Then he took up the fugitive slave law of 1850, which he seemed to endorse halfheartedly, as if quibbling with himself:

> There is some difference of opinion whether this clause [the fugitive slave clause of the Constitution] should be enforced by national or by State authority, but surely that difference is not a very material one. If the slave is to be surrendered, it can be of but little consequence to him or to others by which authority it is done. And should anyone in any case be content that his oath shall go unkept on a merely unsubstantial controversy as to how it shall be kept?

The new president concluded his discussion of the fugitive slave problem with an uncharacteristically wordy sentence, as if to avoid getting to the point:

> I take the official oath to-day with no mental reservations and with no purpose to construe the Constitution or laws by any hypercritical rules; and while I do not choose now to specify particular acts of Congress as proper to be enforced, I do suggest that it will be much safer for all, both in official and private stations, to conform to and abide by all those acts which stand unrepealed than to violate any of them trusting to find impunity in having them held to be unconstitutional.

In the days of Webster and Fillmore, it had been hard enough to enforce the fugitive slave law. Southerners already missed President Buchanan, who, in his last message to Congress, had denounced "palpable violations of constitutional duty . . . in the acts of different State legislatures to defeat the execution of the fugitive slave law." Now, after decades of evidence to the contrary, the new president pretended that it made no difference whether responsibility for applying the law rested with the states or with the federal government. With this double-speaking prevaricator in office, enforcement would be hopeless.

In fact, over the years and months preceding Lincoln's election, the number of violent confrontations over fugitives had declined. Incidents were still reported in the national press, but none reached the notoriety of the earlier cases at Christiana, Syracuse, or Boston. In May 1857, near Mechanicsburg, Ohio, violence had broken out between U.S. marshals trying to capture a fugitive slave and local men protecting him. State and federal courts issued conflicting orders for the arrest and release of the combatants—a cycle broken when Ohio's governor, Chase, negotiated a deal to pay the slave owner a thousand dollars in return for giving up claim to his slave. For his part, President Buchanan ordered federal charges dropped against those accused of impeding the arrest.

In December 1858, a federal grand jury in Cleveland issued indictments of thirty-seven men—including theology students and faculty, as well as five former slaves living near Oberlin College—for forcibly removing a fugitive from the custody of a federal marshal and helping him escape to Canada. In response, an Ohio grand jury indicted several men on the other side of the confrontation, including a federal marshal, for kidnapping a Negro. This standoff, too, ended in a deal between state and federal authorities to drop the conflicting charges.

Of greater concern to the South than these incidents was the surge of new personal liberty laws adopted during the 1850s in northern states from Michigan to Maine. These were the laws to which Buchanan had referred in his last message to Congress. They prohibited state officers from assisting, and state facilities from being used, in the capture of fugitives under federal law. They included provisions intended to protect free blacks from kidnapping and, in direct conflict with the law of 1850, to prevent the return of runaways without due process (by which was meant jury trial) in the state of capture. They were greeted in the South with something between exasperation and outrage.

In January 1860, the Virginia legislature had added to its report "Harpers Ferry Outrages" a sixty-page appendix detailing the personal liberty laws, which it described as "enactments conceived in a spirit of hostility to the institutions of the south, at war with the true intent and meaning of the federal compact, and adopted for the avowed purpose of rendering nugatory some of the express covenants of the Constitution of the United States." The language might have been officious, but the rage was raw.

Almost a year later, the fugitive slave issue remained an open sore. With secession now evidently imminent, the *New York Times* editor Raymond proposed that the free states should compensate owners of fugitive slaves rather than sending them back. Even among Republicans, there was some movement to repeal or soften the personal liberty laws. On December 18, 1860, the U.S. Senate convened the Committee of Thirteen, which included such major figures as Douglas of Illinois, Davis of Mississippi, Toombs of Georgia, and Seward of New York trying to find a way to defuse the crisis. That effort, too, went nowhere. Seward tried to revive the old proposal to grant accused runaways jury trial in the sanctuary state. Toombs answered by calling for an explicit ban on jury trial as well as on the use of habeas corpus to obstruct enforcement. Davis proposed an amendment to the U.S. Constitution protecting slave property in all respects, never "to be divested or impaired by the local law of any other State, either in escape thereto or of transit or sojourn of the owner therein." On December 30, 1860, the committee reported to the Senate that it was unable to reach agreement on a "plan of adjustment."

Ever since, historians have disputed which of the many contentions between North and South deserves pride of place in the story of the coming of secession and the Civil War. Which was the proverbial straw that broke the camel's back? Which was the spark that lit the conflagration? These questions are, of course, unanswerable, and in hindsight each precipitating event of the 1850s—the passage and aftermath of the fugitive slave law, the Kansas-Nebraska struggle, the *Dred Scott* decision, the insurrection attempt of John Brown—seems to lead inevitably to the next.

But if it is too much to say that the dispute over fugitive slaves was *the* cause of the Civil War, it makes sense to say that it launched the final acceleration of sectional estrangement. It converted erstwhile conserva-tives in the North from Websterism to abolitionism. It proved that under sufficient provocation blacks and whites would fight together in common cause. It helped to push the South toward a final break and "prepared the way for Northern acceptance of Civil War." As a key element in the so-called Compromise of 1850, it discredited the very idea of compromise until the word itself became toxic.

The word "compromise" derives from the Latin verb *compromittere*: to make a mutual promise. By the Middle Ages, it had acquired a technical meaning: to resolve some contested issue (most likely a dispute over prop-erty or debt) by submitting it to a third party (the *compromissarius*) whose only interest in the outcome is to persuade the parties, as one would say today, to "get over it" and "move on." Over time the technical meaning—something like what is now called binding arbitration—dropped away, and the word assumed the meaning it has had ever since: an agreement between disputants who concede something to each other in order to terminate their dispute. One way to understand what happened in the United States in the 1850s is to watch the word "compromise" lose its positive connotation and acquire "the primarily pejorative meaning" it carries today—as in such phrases as "compromised position" or "to compromise one's principles."

By the 1850s, to credit someone with the will to compromise was to condemn him. At the beginning of the decade, while the fugitive slave bill was being debated in Congress, Samuel Ringgold Ward told a Boston audience that "there is no term which I detest more than this, it is always the term which makes right yield to wrong; it has always been accursed since Eve made the first *compromise* with the devil." When Webster, speaking in the Senate in the midst of that debate, tried to repudiate the "ultras" on both sides of the slavery divide for thinking "that nothing is good but what is perfect," he might have hoped that his speech would be received as a monument to compromise, but it turned out to be his politi-cal tombstone. After the Civil War, Jacob Green, a fugitive from Ken-tucky, declared with satisfaction that "every compromise which the moderation of former times had erected to stem the course of this monster evil [slavery] has been swept away."

In the South, the same exhaustion with chasing the phantom of compromise took hold. After years of deferral, "the crusade for Southern independence" was poised to deliver what one historian calls a "cathartic" release. And all along the spectrum from enthusiasm to fatalism on the question of secession, southerners identified the failure of the North to abide by the fugitive slave law as a primary casus belli. In December 1860, the authors of the *Declaration of the Immediate Causes Which Induce and Justify the Secession of South Carolina from the Federal Union* counted it high among their grievances: "Fourteen of the States have deliberately refused for years past to fulfill their constitutional obligations"—by which was meant the flouting of the fugitive slave clause and the adoption of laws intended to obstruct its enforcement—for which "we refer to their own statutes for the proof." Among the proofs they had in mind was the *Lemmon* case, in which the Superior Court of New York had freed the slaves of a traveling Virginian, a ruling upheld by the New York Court of Appeals in March 1860. As the authors of the South Carolina *Declaration* reported with furious incredulity, "In the State of New York, even the right of transit for a slave has been denied by its tribunals."

After the Civil War, Alexander Stephens, who had served as vice president of the Confederacy, wrote in his journal to much the same effect: "slavery was without doubt the occasion of secession," and "out of it arose the breach of compact, for instance, on the part of several Northern States in refusing to comply with Constitutional obligations as to rendition of fugitives from service, a course betraying total disregard for all constitutional barriers and guarantees."

For both sides in the conflict, the fugitive slave clause of the Constitution and the notorious law by which the compromisers of 1850 had tried to enforce it only proved the futility of trying to meet the other side halfway. The final breakdown of comity—of a society in which "contending interests have a basic minimal regard for each other"—was at hand. In December 1860, a last vain attempt at compromise was proposed by Kentucky senator John J. Crittenden, a protégé of Henry Clay. Crittenden's plan included a constitutional amendment barring Congress from abolishing slavery in the states or interfering with the interstate slave trade; it provided compensation to slave owners for unreturned runaways, repealed the personal liberty laws, and extended the Missouri Compromise line all the way to the Pacific. That last element proved to be an insuperable problem for Lincoln and most Republicans because it opened the way for the expansion of slavery into territories both current and "hereafter acquired." Because it violated the cardinal Republican principle that the spread of slavery must be stopped, Lincoln rejected it.

By 1861, the only song that North and South could sing together was a little ditty that appeared in *Vanity Fair* magazine shortly after the outbreak of war but before the great bloodletting began:

> *The veriest spawn of the "Father of Lies"*
> *Is that creeping creature called Compromise.*
> . . .
> *Come to your senses! Up! Arise!*
> *Ere ye strike on the rock of Compromise!*

Everyone, North and South, who came upon these lines would have recognized the allusion to John 8:44:

> You are of your father the devil, and your will is to do your father's desires. He was a murderer from the beginning, and does not stand in the truth, because there is no truth in him. When he lies, he speaks out of his own character, for he is a liar and the father of lies.

Here was the last point on which North and South agreed: anyone who still believed in compromise—exemplified by the doomed bargain of 1850, of which the fugitive slave law was the crumbling keystone—was at best a foolish child, at worst the devil's spawn.

Fourteen

"AND THE WAR CAME"

1.

All prior experience was poor preparation. Every previous conflict—with the exception of the centuries-long war against the slaves themselves—was, by comparison, a playground tussle. At the outset of the Civil War, the U.S. Army numbered some fourteen thousand men. Its senior officer was seventy-four-year-old Winfield Scott, who had been a brigadier general in the War of 1812, in which perhaps forty thousand U.S. soldiers served under arms. Scott had also fought in the Mexican War, in which U.S. combatants numbered around a hundred thousand. In the war that was about to begin, some three million men would serve on both sides of the conflict, fighting would stretch from the Atlantic to the Mississippi and the Gulf of Mexico, and at least three-quarters of a million lives would be extinguished, with millions more mutilated before it was done.*

---

*Historians continue to revise upward estimates of Civil War casualties. In a recent study, "A Census-Based Count of the Civil War Dead" (*Civil War History* 57, no. 4 [Dec. 2011]), J. David Hacker suggests that casualties were previously undercounted by as much as 20 percent, in part because earlier estimates failed to include deaths from wounds or disease that proved fatal months or years after combat ceased. Hacker suggests that the true death toll was at least 750,000, possibly as high as 850,000. Even these numbers may be too low. Jim Downs, in *Sick from Freedom: African-American Illness and Suffering During the Civil War and Reconstruction* (New York: Oxford University Press, 2012), points out that emancipated slaves who died from illness or starvation tended not to be counted among the war dead. See also Margaret Humphreys, *Marrow of Tragedy: The Health Crisis of the American Civil War* (Baltimore: Johns Hopkins University Press, 2013), who asserts that "the Civil War . . . killed more than a million Americans" (311).

It started in the predawn darkness of April 12, 1861, when South Carolina militia batteries opened fire on the federal installation at Fort Sumter in Charleston Harbor. People within earshot, as well as many who heard of the bombardment from afar, believed it was a tantrum that would soon subside into the usual hum of verbal animosity. Charleston ladies went out at morning light to watch under their parasols, accompanied by slaves carrying picnic baskets. Commanded by the Kentucky-born major Robert Anderson, the federal garrison within the fort surrendered not quite thirty-six hours later, having withstood some four thousand shells without casualties.* Mary Chesnut, wife of South Carolina senator James Chesnut Jr., who had left the Senate within a week of Lincoln's election and signed the note of ultimatum delivered to Major Anderson at 3:20 a.m. on April 12, wrote in her diary, "After all that noise and our tears and prayers, nobody has been hurt." It is hard to say whether she was relieved or wanted a refund for a ticket to a disappointing show.

Within hours, President Lincoln called up seventy-five thousand volunteers to put down what he called a domestic insurrection. On April 19, he ordered a blockade of southern ports. In response, four more states (Virginia, Arkansas, Tennessee, and North Carolina) followed the original seven and seceded from the Union, yet many people still expected the conflict to be limited and brief. Years later, General William T. Sherman recalled that "orators of the South used, openly and constantly, the expressions that there would be no war, and that a lady's thimble would hold all the blood to be shed." Given the doubt on both sides that the North had a will to resist, it was not an implausible boast.

Frederick Douglass, agreeing with the southern scoffers, was sure that "all talk about putting down rebellion and treason by force are as impotent and worthless as the words of a drunken woman in a ditch." Fainthearted ness was evident even among some of the most passionate leaders of the antislavery movement. On April 9, Wendell Phillips was addressing an abolitionist meeting in New Bedford, Massachusetts, when he received telegraph dispatches—premature, it turned out, but not by much—that the

---

* Two Union soldiers died when a shell exploded in preparation for a ceremonial gun salute after the fort had already been surrendered.

artillery assault on Fort Sumter had begun. From these reports, Phillips could not tell whether "the guns are firing . . . out of Fort Sumter, or into it." Either way, he proclaimed that the southern states "who think that their peculiar institutions require a separate government . . . have a right to decide that question, without appealing to you or me." Phillips added that "on the principles of '76, Abraham Lincoln has no right to a soldier in Fort Sumter" and that, in any event, resistance to the secessionists would be futile.

But after the real assault three days later, the North found an unexpected appetite to fight. Herman Melville described the sight of boys strutting down the main street of Pittsfield, Massachusetts, toward the killing fields:

> *One noonday, at my window in the town,*
>   *I saw a sight—saddest that eyes can see—*
> *Young soldiers marching lustily*
>   *Unto the wars,*
> *With fifes, and flags in mottoed pageantry;*
>   *While all the porches, walks, and doors*
> *Were rich with ladies cheering royally.*

In New York, news of the Sumter attack was greeted as if a bully had issued a dare for a street fight. Volunteers marched down Broadway with bits of knotted rope dangling from their guns to symbolize their intent to bring back rebel prisoners like trussed hogs.

Blood was up, too, in the South. Northern troops passing through Baltimore en route to defend the national capital were attacked by pro-secession mobs. Southern-born officers resigned their U.S. commissions and returned to their native states. In a capital city rife with Confederate partisans and spies, Lincoln's bodyguards scanned the rooftops for snipers while the president, looking through the White House windows with the aid of a telescope, could see a Confederate flag taunting him from Alexandria just across the Potomac.

For the next three months, both sides worked to turn state militia into coordinated armies. As late as July 19, Congressman Justin Morrill of Vermont, speaking in the House of Representatives, opposed a bill to increase appropriations for the U.S. Military Academy at West Point. Like most of his colleagues, he doubted that the so-called war would amount to much, and he took the view that "we have manufactured more officers than we have use for." There would be a scuffle or two; then both sides would come to their senses. "All the States which are now in a state of rebellion," he predicted, "will soon be back."

A few days later, with Washington in a mood of what one congressman described as "jocund levity," the first major action was imminent. Under the command of General Edwin McDowell, a federal army of some thirty thousand men massed at Centreville, Virginia, planning to drive Confederate troops under General P. G. T. Beauregard from the railroad junction at Manassas, about twenty-five miles southwest of Washington. A few miles away in Silver Spring, Maryland, Elizabeth Blair Lee, sister of Lincoln's friend and ally Montgomery Blair, was on "tiptoe of expectation" for a Union triumph. Six weeks earlier she had written to her husband that the blockade would bring the rebels to their knees, Congress would appropriate funds for large-scale "Negro *Deportation*," there would be an "up rising of poor *white folks*" against the plantation "aristocrats," and Britain, however friendly it might feel toward the planters who supplied it with cotton, would never come to the aid of the South because "she knows that the power of this nation is north."

Early on the morning of July 21, Mrs. Lee could hear "the belchings of the Cannon" as the first Battle of Bull Run (named for a stream that flowed from the Bull Run Mountains in Loudoun County, Virginia) got under way. Initial bulletins were encouraging, but by mid-afternoon federal forces were in retreat from a Confederate counterattack, and by evening they had disintegrated into what the *Times* of London correspondent called the "*debris*" of an army. Overnight and all the next day they ran, then trudged, toward Washington, where civilians, having expected a heroes' parade, gaped at thousands of dazed boys stumbling through the streets until they dropped from wounds or exhaustion. By Walt Whitman's account, "half" the "lookers-on" were "secesh of the most venomous kind—they say nothing; but the devil snickers in their faces" at the sight of the "*baffled, humiliated, panic-struck*" dregs of McDowell's army.

"The vaunted Union," Whitman exclaimed, which "we thought so strong, so impregnable—lo! It seems already smash'd like a china plate."

Two days after the debacle, Pennsylvania's representative Thaddeus Stevens rose in the House to support the proposed increase in appropriations for West Point that Morrill had opposed. He predicted that "the battles which are to be fought are to be desperate and bloody" and that "many thousand valuable lives will be lost." At the time, Stevens had a reputation as a hothead, but given what we know in retrospect, his words now sound Churchillian.

2.

But what was this war—already more prolonged than most had expected—all about? A few weeks before the assault on Fort Sumter, Whitman had encountered the mayor of Brooklyn in a saber-rattling mood aboard the Fulton ferry, who told him that if only the southern "fire-eaters would commit some overt act of resistance . . . they would then be so effectively squelch'd" that "we would never hear of secession again." The mayor said nothing about slavery, at least as far as is known. Looking back a decade later, Whitman would write that the nation had been "insolently attack'd by the secession-slave-power"—a compound phrase that conveyed his indecision over whether the Civil War was a war for union or a war against slavery, or some mixture of the two. For him and for many—probably most—white northerners, slavery remained a secondary issue. Secession was the provoking sin.

Others, however, regarded the attack on Fort Sumter as the provocation they had been waiting for to launch a frontal attack on the Slave Power at last. Thomas Wentworth Higginson exulted that "war has flung the door wide open, and four million slaves stand ready to file through."

To conservative unionists, the prospect was so alarming that they jumped to shut the door. On July 13, the Democratic representative William Holman of Indiana spoke in the House to insist that "the sole object of the government, in the present and future military operations, ought to be, to maintain the integrity of the Union . . . and the protection of the constitutional rights of the loyal citizens of every state"—by which he meant the right to own slaves. On July 25, Congress passed a resolution, sponsored by Kentucky's representative John Crittenden in the House and Andrew Johnson of Tennessee in the Senate, which declared in language close to Holman's that the North was waging war solely to restore the Union and with no "purpose of overthrowing or interfering with the rights or established institutions" of the rebellious states.

To follow the public and private debates about war aims over the first year of the conflict is to watch the flow of antislavery sentiment rise and fall in a recurring rhythm. Sometimes the rising tide seemed to eat away at slavery, only to recede and reveal that its foundation was still in place. But abolitionists sensed that time was on their side. Hoping to persuade state legislatures to allow black enlistment in the militia, African Americans from Ohio to New York held rallies and even organized military drills. Massachusetts's governor, John Andrew, a veteran of the Boston Vigilance Committee who had been active on behalf of Anthony Burns, led the push to open the ranks to black volunteers, only to be told by Lincoln's friend Montgomery Blair to "drop the nigger." Sometimes this kind of rebuke was meant to quash the idea that the Civil War had any bearing on the future of slavery; sometimes it was meant as a bide-your-time form of strategic advice.

The back-and-forth between abolitionists on the left and conservative unionists on the right became almost metronomic, with Lincoln in the middle, taking hits from both sides. In the fall of 1861, a few weeks after the humiliation at Bull Run, Charles Sumner believed that the president and his generals would see that the quick "overthrow of slavery will make an end of the war." But Lincoln, in his December message to Congress (the equivalent of today's State of the Union address), warned that open action against slavery could cause the war to "degenerate into a violent and remorseless revolutionary struggle" by driving the border states into the Confederacy and provoking the solid South to fight more fiercely.*

---

*In his message from the executive department to Congress, Lincoln declined to include a report from his secretary of war, Simon Cameron, in which Cameron proposed that "those who make war against the Government justly forfeit all rights of property" and added that "it is as clearly a right of the Government to arm slaves, when it may become necessary, as it is to use gun-powder taken from

Uncertainty over war aims was evident, too, in the South. Almost a year later, in September 1862, after a savage engagement in Maryland near Antietam Creek barely twenty miles from the Pennsylvania border—the battle that stopped Robert E. Lee's advance by which he had hoped to stir secessionist sentiment in Maryland and antiwar panic throughout the North—Oliver Wendell Holmes Sr. traveled south from Boston in search of his wounded son (the future Supreme Court justice). Along the way, Dr. Holmes quizzed a young Confederate prisoner of war about why he was fighting and got this laconic answer: "For our homes." Other captured Confederates told him that "they did not know, and manifested great indifference to the whole matter, at which another of their number, a sturdy fellow, took offence, and muttered opinions strongly derogatory to those who would not stand up for the cause they had been fighting for"—whatever, exactly, that was.

3.

In their postwar chronicle of Lincoln's life, the president's private secretaries, John Nicolay and John Hay, remarked that "the first movement of armed forces proved that the slavery question was destined to be as omnipresent in war as it had been in national politics." The initial form the question took was a familiar one: What should be done with slaves who fled their masters?

It first presented itself barely a month after the shelling of Fort Sumter, at Fort Monroe, a heavily fortified federal installation just east of Newport News, Virginia, on the coast above the inlet formed by the confluence of the James and York rivers. The officer in charge was Benjamin Butler, a portly and by some accounts pompous New England lawyer whose first military assignment had been to lead a company of Massachusetts militia to secure the city of Baltimore, where he ordered cannon placed on Federal Hill to intimidate secessionist sympathizers. Butler considered his

---

the enemy." Quoted in James M. McPherson, *Battle Cry of Freedom: The Civil War Era* (New York: Oxford University Press, 1988), 357.

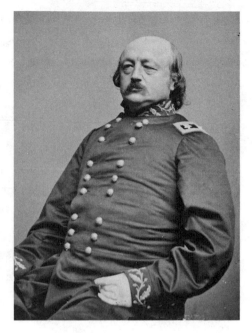

Maj. Gen. Benjamin Butler c. 1860–1865. Butler's biographer James Parton referred to such photographs as "annihilating caricatures," which failed to capture the general's "imposing presence." Parton, General Butler in New Orleans *(New York, 1864), p. 291*

reassignment to Fort Monroe a demotion but was mollified by assurances that he would find excellent hogfish and soft-shell crab at his new posting.

Fort Monroe, where the cause of ending slavery was about to be advanced, overlooked the shoreline where the first shipment to North America of enslaved Africans had been deposited by a Dutch vessel nearly 250 years before. On May 22, 1861, Butler arrived there to take command. The next day, three slaves—Frank Baker, Shepard Mallory, and James Townsend—came to him seeking asylum. They had been compelled to work constructing fortifications for the 115th Virginia Militia under General John Magruder, and when they learned that their master intended to sell or rent them to perform the same kind of work in North Carolina, they fled and were admitted to the fort by Union sentries. On that same day, May 23, the voters of Virginia ratified the ordinance of secession that had been passed by a state convention shortly after Lincoln's militant response to the attack on Fort Sumter.

Confederate troops were building defenses around their batteries with the help not only of local slaves like the three runaways but by a "rigorous military impressment" of slaves "from the well-stocked plantations of lower Virginia." Butler was thus confronted with a dilemma: theoretically, the fugitive slave law remained in force, and because his government did not recognize the validity of secession, the law would seem to apply in Virginia as much as anywhere else. But to return runaway slaves would be to put them back to work protecting the very armaments that threatened the men under his command.

On May 24, Butler was informed that a Confederate officer was approaching the fort under a flag of truce. Concerned that the visitor could gain valuable intelligence by seeing "us piling up sandbags to protect the weak points there," Butler rode out to the picket line to meet him. The emissary turned out to be someone he knew, Major John Carey, who reminded the general that they had last encountered each other under congenial circumstances at the Democratic Party convention at Charleston, where both had voted repeatedly for Jefferson Davis. What followed was an exchange of more consequence than either man imagined at the time—"one of the most sudden and important revolutions in popular thought," according to Nicolay and Hay, "which took place during the whole war."

Here, by Butler's account, is what Carey told him and what he said in reply:

> "I am informed," said Major Carey, "that three negroes belonging to Colonel Mallory have escaped within your lines. I am Colonel Mallory's agent and have charge of his property. What do you mean to do with those negroes?"
>
> "I intend to hold them," said I.
>
> "Do you mean, then, to set aside your constitutional obligation to return them?"
>
> "I mean to take Virginia at her word, as declared in the ordinance of secession passed yesterday. I am under no constitutional obligations to a foreign country, which Virginia now claims to be."

After Carey absorbed this rebuke, the exchange resumed with testy politeness:

"But you say we cannot secede," [Carey] answered, "and so you cannot consistently detain the negroes."

"But you have seceded, so you cannot consistently claim them. I shall hold those negroes as contraband of war, since they are engaged in the construction of your battery and are claimed as your property. The question is simply whether they shall be used for or against the Government of the United States."

Then Butler made an offer he knew Carey would refuse:

"Yet, though I greatly need the labor which has providentially come to my hands, if Colonel Mallory will come into the fort and take the oath of allegiance to the United States, he shall have his negroes, and I will endeavor to hire them from him."

"Colonel Mallory is absent," was Major Carey's answer.

We courteously parted.

Benjamin Butler was no abolitionist. Far from it. Not only had he supported Davis at the Charleston convention, but just the month before he had offered federal troops to Maryland's governor, Thomas Hicks, to put down any slave insurrection that might break out in Baltimore. When, a year later, he became Union commander of occupied New Orleans, he was accused of turning away hundreds of black men, women, and children desperate for sanctuary at Union headquarters in the New Orleans Custom House.* Yet having improvised the contraband policy at Fort Monroe in

---

*On July 3, 1862, an anonymous letter, most likely written by a Union army chaplain from Connecticut, appeared in the New York Times under the title, "Equivocal Conduct of the General—Slaves Turned Out to Their Owners." The letter describes the aftermath of Butler's order that only fugitives who had found employment with Union officers could remain: "The day before the order was carried into effect, boys and girls, men and women, went from room to room with solicitations for work. Said a mother, 'take my children, if I must go back to suffer.' Well nigh one hundred were kept as cooks, waiters, Company laundresses, hospital nurses and laborers about the Custom-house. Those for whom no place could be found, plead with us to rescue them—depicting the revenge they must suffer for confiding in the Yankees, and telling us that we ought not to have taken them at first, and then to send them back. At the fixed time all the negroes were collected in the open area of the Custom-house. Dread, sorrow, despair could be seen on many faces. Women who had fled miles from a hated despotism, mothers with their infants, families of children, the old and decrepit, were there. One by one, such as had not tickets of employment, moved away, attended by guards. Tearful entreaties were

1861, Butler remained proud of himself as a pioneer of emancipation. After the war, he would accuse John Hay of denying him full credit for his impromptu invention of the concept of human contraband, which he regarded, correctly, as a major contribution to the Union war effort. "Fort Monroe," Nicolay and Hay recalled, "became to the discontented blacks . . . the center of a vague hope, both of escape from removal to the dreaded far South, and of possible liberation from bondage."

With fresh Union troops arriving by naval transport almost daily, Butler pushed beyond the fort itself. Local slave owners retreated into the interior, abandoning their homes as well as their slaves, and soon the Stars and Stripes flew from the cupola of Colonel Mallory's mansion. By July 1861, some nine hundred fugitives, including five hundred women and children, had found refuge within Butler's perimeter. Among those who tended to them was Harriet Tubman, who worked as a volunteer cook and nurse.

His soldiers, some of whom had never seen a black person, much less a slave, were impressed by the courage and resolve of the "contrabands," by their desire to give information about Confederate troop movements, by their eagerness to learn to read and write, and most of all by their determination to taste freedom—a wish and hope shared by young and old alike, "even old men and women, with crooked backs, who could hardly walk or see."

On May 27, Butler reported the situation to General Winfield Scott and asked for guidance. Three days later Butler got his answer, not from Scott, but from Secretary of War Simon Cameron, who told him that regardless of federal obligations before the secession crisis no peacetime law should hamper him in wartime. In view of the fact that fugitive slaves, if returned, would be put back to work aiding the enemy, he must under no circumstances return them.

Today there is a phrase—"mission creep"—to describe what happens

---

in vain. Children often preferred to stay, even if their parents must go. Bitterly disappointed and hopeless they lingered in the basement, still imagining that their friends, the Yankees, would help them." John Fabian Witt, *Lincoln's Code: The Laws of War in American History* (New York: Free Press, 2012), 202–3, suggests that Butler's action in New Orleans helped to prompt Congress to include in the Second Confiscation Act (July 17, 1862) the prohibition against returning fugitive slaves to their masters.

Slaves seeking admittance to Fortress Monroe, woodcut from
Frank Leslie's Illustrated Newspaper, *June 8, 1861*

when a defensive war becomes an offensive war, or a war with limited objectives becomes a campaign for "regime change." What began at Fort Monroe has been aptly described as a case of "good mission creep."* Under the pressure of military necessity, the means if not the stated aims of the Civil War were changing, and the institution of slavery was becoming a case of collateral damage. News of what was happening spread throughout the nation—received with dismay or horror by some, with positive excitement by others. "*Where* we are drifting, I cannot see," wrote Lydia Maria Child, "but we are drifting *some*where; and our fate, whatever it may be, is bound up with these . . . 'contrabands.'"

As the illusion of a short war fell away, every incursion of Union forces into the slave states raised anew the question of what to do with the surging flood of fugitives. They were an asset to the Union army ("I have no doubt," Montgomery Blair told Butler, that "you will get your best spies

---

*Ta-Nehisi Coates introduced this phrase into the discussion at a conference on the Civil War at Yale University, March 29, 2012.

from among them"), but they were also a burden. Some who hoped for a broad emancipation suggested that slaves separated from their masters be shipped to Haiti; others envisioned their transfer to the North as servants or industrial workers. Butler's successor at Fort Monroe, General John Wool, believed that "Black People should have the same rights as white people" and established a policy of paying them wages. This was another step toward the formal termination of their status as slaves, but because their meager wages barely covered the cost of food and clothing, their condition while working for the Union army was often not materially different from what it had been under slavery.

Two months after Butler half wittingly set in motion the process of military emancipation, Congress passed a series of measures that, in their "patently contradictory" nature, revealed the unsettled state of federal policy. In the chaotic aftermath of Bull Run, with reports circulating that rebel troops had used slaves on the battlefield to handle ammunition if not to bear arms, the House took up a resolution—sponsored by the Illinois Republican Owen Lovejoy, brother of the murdered Elijah Lovejoy—stating that "it is no part of the duty of the soldiers of the United States to capture and return fugitive slaves." Lincoln's postmaster general Montgomery Blair agreed that "secession niggers," especially the able-bodied, should not be sent back to their masters. After a part of Lovejoy's resolution calling for repeal of the fugitive slave law was dropped, it passed the House, but it had no force of law, and the administration—determined to keep border states in the Union, and still harboring hope that secessionists would see the folly of what they had done—continued to proceed cautiously. On July 22, the House, followed by the Senate on July 25, approved another resolution, this one reaffirming that it was no part of the government's intent to interfere with slavery in the seceded states. Some members believed that reassuring southerners of their property rights would keep peace hopes alive; others believed that any intimation that the rebels could ever get their slaves back would prolong the war. As the fighting dragged on, the fissure in northern opinion deepened.

In early August, Congress took another step by passing the First Confiscation Act, by which all property "used for insurrectionary purposes" became subject to seizure by Union forces. Signed by Lincoln on August

6, the act essentially codified Butler's decision as federal law, though Butler had already gone further by admitting fugitives to Fort Monroe, among them women and children, who had no direct role in the Confederate war effort. The Confiscation Act included a section, authored by Illinois senator Lyman Trumbull, whose language echoed the fugitive slave clause of the Constitution in stipulating that the labor of "persons held in service" would be forfeited by "the person to whom such labor or service is claimed." Speaking for conservatives in the North as well as in the border states, Crittenden of Kentucky warned that Congress was "giving an anti-slavery character and application to the war."

Lincoln, too, remained concerned that moving too aggressively against slavery could alienate an essential part of the northern public and drive wavering border states into the Confederacy. Yet as both a practical and a moral matter, it was inconceivable that slaves, once separated from their owners and having given aid in one form or another to the Union cause, would ever be returned to servitude. The idea of obtaining the labor of runaways with a promise or intimation of freedom and then returning them to their former masters (an idea that Alexander Hamilton had decried as "cruelly perfidious" after the Revolution, when some of his fellow revolutionaries pressed Britain to return fugitive slaves) was anathema even to people for whom abolition had never been a compelling cause. De facto emancipation was under way, and it was the slaves themselves, by taking flight and joining the Union fight as workers if not yet soldiers, who had launched it.

For those who wanted Lincoln's government to push for full and final freedom, the pace of events was much too slow. But it was fast enough to frighten conservatives, who feared that the war for union was turning into a crusade against slavery. As the war itself drove the causes of union and emancipation toward convergence, field commanders found themselves at odds with politicians, including President Lincoln, who continued trying to hold them apart.

Nowhere were the contradictions of federal policy more evident than in the border state of Missouri, which had remained in the Union but where tensions ran high between pro-slavery farmers and antislavery Missourians concentrated in and around the strategically vital city of St. Louis. After

John C. Frémont c. 1861

Union troops seized the arsenal there from a pro-secessionist militia in July 1861, Confederate sympathizers went so far as to establish a government in exile, and Missouri became the scene of a civil war within the Civil War.

On August 30, John C. Frémont—Republican presidential candidate five years earlier, now military commander of the Western Department— issued a proclamation declaring martial law throughout the state and expanding his confiscatory power to include not only slaves used directly in the Confederate war effort but slaves owned by any disloyal master. Frémont enjoyed support among people of strong antislavery conviction, from William Greenleaf Eliot in St. Louis to Richard Henry Dana in Boston, who hailed him as "a hero, every inch of him, so quiet and yet so full of will and courage and conduct!" Others were not so sure, such as Missouri's pro-Union governor, Hamilton Gamble, who was trying to hold together a coalition of loyalists, including slave owners—a task made much more difficult by Frémont's unilateral directives.

On September 2, Lincoln wrote to Frémont forbidding him to carry out executions under martial law "without first having my approbation or consent" and asking him, "in a spirit of caution and not of censure," to modify his order lest it "alarm our Southern Union friends, and then turn them against us—perhaps ruin our rather fair prospect in Kentucky." With southern forces poised to enter Kentucky (Lincoln could not have known it, but the invasion began on the same day he wrote his letter), the full-scale defection of Missouri slaveholders from the Union cause could have been disastrous. "If any of the Border States fell into the Confederacy," writes the historian James Oakes, "the rest might topple out of the Union like dominoes, and the war would be lost." Yet Frémont balked. With frank insolence, he replied to Lincoln on September 8 demanding that the president "openly direct me to make the correction" concerning which slaves he had authority to seize from which masters. He even dispatched his wife, daughter of the late Missouri senator Thomas Hart Benton, to Washington to lobby the president on his behalf. On September 10, Lincoln received Jessie Benton Frémont in a mood that struck her—a vivacious woman unaccustomed to rejection—as cold and noncommittal. Mrs. Frémont had read him right. The next day Lincoln "very cheerfully" complied with her husband's request for a direct order and commanded him to modify his emancipation decree to conform to the narrower provisions of the Confiscation Act lately passed by Congress. Abolitionists were furious. Writing after the war, Thomas Wentworth Higginson—never a Lincoln admirer—denounced the "vacillating policy of the Government" by which "they were but defending liberty with one hand and crushing it with the other."

Throughout the first year of fighting, the thrust and parry continued between government and generals. President and Congress, too, traded directives and counter-directives that were at least as much political statements intended for consumption by the public as they were efforts to manage the war. Yet day-to-day decisions about the fate of fugitive slaves were being increasingly dictated by conditions on the ground rather than by calculations in Washington. Whatever fine distinctions government tried to make, the war was sure to blur them.

Missouri remained the exemplary case. In November 1861, General Henry W. Halleck, who succeeded to the western command after Lincoln dismissed Frémont, issued an order that fugitive slaves were not to be permitted within military encampments. But what, then, should be done with those at Fulton or Columbia who had given "much valuable information that could not be obtained from white men"—thereby aiding Union troops in finding hidden stores of the enemy? "To drive them from camp" and leave them exposed to retaliation from their former masters was hardly consistent with what Halleck himself called the "proper offices of humanity." Rumors abounded that some runaway slaves turned away by Union troops were being apprehended and killed by their enraged masters. In one documented case from December 1861 (no doubt most such events were never recorded), a Maryland slave owner whipped to death a slave who had been sent back to him after running to Union lines—a crime for which the perpetrator was never arrested, much less punished. Even Charles Colcock Jones, the Georgia minister who preached that slaves should be treated with Christian charity, regarded those who fled as "traitors," while Jones's son, impatient with his father's scruples, urged him to see that "terror must be made to operate upon their minds, and fear prevent what curiosity and desire for utopian pleasures induce them to attempt" to flee.

If humanitarian arguments were not enough to dissuade Union officials from sending runaways back, there were also military considerations. Within days of the Maryland murder, a Union soldier serving in Missouri wrote to Secretary Cameron that because "every negro returned to these traitors, adds strength to their cause in this state, it is not a legitimate business for the army to be engaged in catching the niggers of traitors." Besides, runaway slaves who entered Union camps were willing to perform menial tasks from cooking and mending to emptying the slop buckets. Officers as well as enlisted men were loath to lose them.

As the war dragged on, it was combatants more than politicians who made up the rules—motivated by a combination of personal conviction, obedience to local commanders, conditions on the battlefield, and sometimes whim or happenstance. With the advance of Union forces, "every excursion and raid into the interior produced more fugitives," and while the First Confiscation Act technically applied only to those "coming within [Union] lines" and contained an explicit ban on enticing them to do so, such distinctions meant less and less as the fog of war rolled in.

On March 6, 1862, Lincoln, well aware that the slave system was beginning to crumble but still looking to calm slave owners especially in the border states, sent a message to Congress recommending a program of compensated emancipation—a plan that he had already proposed, without success, to the slaveholders of Delaware four months earlier. Thaddeus Stevens derided the idea as "the most diluted, milk and water gruel proposition . . . ever given to the American nation" at the same time that Frederick Douglass, even as he pressed Lincoln to authorize enlistment of black troops to aid the war effort, described him as "a brave man trying against great odds, to do right."

On March 13, 1862, Lincoln signed an article of war that had been introduced in Congress by his friend Francis P. Blair Jr. prescribing the penalty of court-martial for any military officer who sent fugitive slaves back to their masters. On April 3, General David Hunter, commander of Union troops operating in coastal Georgia, ordered the emancipation of "all persons of color lately held to involuntary service by enemies of the United States." And in an intimation of things to come, Hunter sought permission from the War Department to arm them. To an inquiry from the new secretary of war, Edwin Stanton, about whether reports were true that he was conscripting fugitive slaves, Hunter replied in the negative, explaining that he had organized "a fine regiment of persons whose late masters are 'Fugitive Rebels.'" When that piece of friendly irony elicited no response, Hunter resumed his recruiting, but when the War Department refused to pay, he was forced to suspend it.

Despite manifest inconsistencies in government policy, the institution of slavery was plainly breaking down. Wherever the Union army penetrated Confederate territory, it became, according to one incensed Kentucky slaveholder, a "negro freeing machine." On March 21, General Ambrose Burnside, Union commander on the eastern shore of North Carolina, reported to Secretary Stanton that local "negroes [were] wild with excitement and delight" at the arrival of his troops and that the town of New Bern, occupied by his forces, was "being overrun with fugitives from surrounding towns and plantations." At the same time, Congress continued to seek nonmilitary means to hasten the failure of the failing institution. On April 10, Congress pledged federal financial aid to any state that would undertake a program of compensated emancipation. On April 16, it took the long-deferred step of abolishing slavery in the District of Columbia and provided funds for compensating slave owners and for financing a voluntary colonization program. The number of slaves directly affected by this limited abolition act was small (around three thousand), but its political and symbolic importance was large. For the first time in American history, the federal government had banned slavery from a jurisdiction where it had previously held legal standing. As the news spread, fugitives from Maryland and Virginia poured into the capital, where they were defended by federal troops from vigilantes seeking to re-enslave them.

Meanwhile, General Hunter was not done. On May 9, he declared all slaves in South Carolina, Georgia, and Florida free—an order that Lincoln nullified ten days later. Within weeks, Congress banned slavery from all federal territories. This action, which finally implemented the founding platform of the Republican Party, affected even fewer slaves than had been liberated in the District of Columbia, but in this case, too, the political and moral implications exceeded the practical effects.

Lincoln was now speeding up and slowing down the emancipation process simultaneously. On July 12, he appealed again to the border states to support a program of gradual, compensated emancipation and predicted, on the basis of rapidly accumulating evidence, that otherwise slavery "will be extinguished by . . . the mere incidents of war." On that same day, with the passage of the Second Confiscation Act, Congress declared that slaves belonging to any person supporting the rebellion were free whether or not they were utilized directly in war-related activity. Five days later, Lincoln signed both the Confiscation Act and the Militia Act, authorizing employment of "persons of African descent" in "any military or naval service for which they may be found competent." Both bills significantly enlarged the scope of emancipation: in the first case, by declaring runaways from disloyal slave owners "forever free"; in the second case, by granting freedom not only to slaves who took up arms but also to their wives, mothers, and children.

Amid the fast-moving events, the Army of the Potomac, under George McClellan, had been preparing since May to advance on the Confederate capital at Richmond. It is one of the deep ironies of the Civil War that an early conclusion in favor of the Union would likely have been more favorable to slave owners than the long war of attrition that stretched on for almost three more bloody years. In the summer of 1861, after the Union defeat at Bull Run, Charles Sumner had told Lincoln that it was "both the worst event & best event in our history; the worst, as it was the greatest present calamity & shame,—the best, as it made the extinction of Slavery inevitable." Now the Union missed another opportunity to bring the war to an early end, or at least to shorten it. If McClellan had moved decisively in that spring of 1862, "the war might have ended then and there, with slavery weakened, but intact." But he overestimated the enemy's troop strength, expended weeks in protracted probing actions, and, after successfully resisting sustained attacks by Lee's Army of Northern Virginia (the "Seven Days Battles") in the last week of June, pulled the bulk of his force back to Washington.

4.

The conflict that had been expected to last a few weeks had now persisted for more than fifteen months. Despite hopes on both sides that a major battlefield victory, or the demoralizing effect of hostile troops operating in enemy territory, or sheer war weariness, would persuade the other side to capitulate or come to the negotiating table, the fighting showed no sign of slackening, much less coming to an end.

One of the astonishing facts of American history is that the murderous ferocity of the Civil War was matched on both sides by determination to carry it on. This fact is all the more remarkable because neither side was remotely prepared for the new technologies of killing—land mines, incendiary shells, and repeating rifles (ancestors of today's automatic weapons) that replaced the old smoothbore rifles, which had been accurate only up to around seventy-five yards. The new firearms, some of them effective to five hundred yards, helped to make the Civil War the first modern war—a war, that is, in which combatants often had little sense of the human face of the enemy. Facilitated by the new weapons, the killing became almost "spreelike."

The capacity for killing also far outstripped the science of healing. Anesthesia (chloroform or ether or, when neither was available, whiskey)

Undated photograph of amputated limbs

was primitive, and antisepsis almost unknown. Between amputations it was standard practice to wipe off the surgical saw with any handy rag, or if a surgeon took time to try to save an arm or leg by extracting shrapnel or bone splinters, the result was likely to be a withered limb as useless as if it were gone.

When Ulysses S. Grant came to write his memoir twenty years after the end of the war, the matter-of-factness of his prose could not conceal his lasting shock at what he had witnessed. Of the Battle of Shiloh, fought in southwestern Tennessee in April 1862, he recalled that the battlefield "over which the Confederates had made repeated charges the day before [was] so covered with dead that it would have been possible to walk across the clearing, in any direction, stepping on dead bodies, without a foot touching the ground." In the September 1862 battle between the Army of Northern Virginia under Robert E. Lee and the Army of the Potomac under McClellan, near Antietam Creek in northern Maryland, some four thousand men died in one day—a pace of about four hundred per daylight hour—with twenty thousand wounded.

The dead remained unburied for days. A full week after the fighting ended, one Union surgeon described "blackened bloated corpses with blood and gas protruding from every orifice, and maggots holding high carnival over their heads." It has been estimated that after the Battle of Gettysburg in July 1863—where combined casualties reached fifty thousand, including at least eight thousand dead—some "six million pounds of human and animal carcasses lay" rotting in the heat. During the siege of Petersburg, conducted by Grant from the summer of 1864 until the spring of 1865, starving Confederate soldiers picked through the dung of their horses searching for kernels of undigested corn.*

The Civil War was a machine of unprecedented efficiency for consuming young lives. It required the continual resupply of willing or conscripted fighters, and so, despite widespread fear that blacks in the army would pose a public menace, the longer the war dragged on, the more pressure mounted in the North to recruit black soldiers.

It is always hard to assess "public opinion"—a phrase too static to capture the fluctuations of what people actually think—but it may be safely said that almost everywhere in Civil War America the idea of arming blacks remained politically explosive. Racism in the North, where the word "nigger" appeared even in official communiqués, was given fresh impetus by a war that seemed to many northern whites an unwarranted fight on behalf of unworthy southern blacks. One grisly manifestation of this attitude was the rioting that engulfed New York City in the summer of 1863 after Lincoln imposed the nation's first military draft, when white mobs roamed through what is now midtown Manhattan, beating, raping, and murdering black people and burning the Colored Orphan Asylum to the ground.

Yet the war also made the reality of slavery painfully visible to Union soldiers who had previously known it as a remote abstraction. White farm

---

*Death on a massive scale was only the war's most visible effect. Among survivors, untold thousands suffered invisible wounds. Physically sound but traumatized by what they had done or seen, many found themselves regarded on the home front as spineless or weak-minded, bearing the stigma of cowardice. Stephen Crane, who was born six years after the war and learned about it by reading military memoirs in which he found little mention of such inglorious facts, took up the theme in what became the most famous of Civil War novels, *The Red Badge of Courage* (1895). And of course the psychological damage extended, as it does in every war, far beyond those who actually came under fire—to mothers, fathers, siblings, and wives so distressed by seeing their sons or brothers or husbands go off to war that symptoms of morbid anxiety and suicidal depression became common on the home front. See Jeffrey W. McClurken, *Take Care of the Living: Reconstructing Confederate Veteran Families in Virginia* (Charlottesville: University of Virginia Press, 2009), 139–40.

Soldiers' graves near
General Hospital, City
Point, Virginia, c. 1864

boys from Iowa or New Hampshire encountered blacks of their own age, or the age of their parents—male and female, proud or cowering, imploring them for food, water, work, and most of all safety from their former masters. Some soldiers were moved by what they saw; others, for reasons having little to do with sympathy or solidarity, welcomed the service of blacks desperate to avoid being turned away. Whether by conviction or for the sake of convenience, one Wisconsin volunteer thought the war was "abolitionizing the whole army."

By the summer of 1862, a marked change had taken hold in Washington on the question of permitting blacks to bear arms. At first, recruitment proceeded quietly, almost surreptitiously, for fear of public disfavor. On August 25, Secretary of War Stanton authorized General Rufus Saxton in South Carolina to recruit five thousand blacks from the ranks of fugitive slaves. "This must never see daylight," Stanton warned, "because it is so much in advance of public opinion." Taking a different view, Illinois congressman Elihu Washburne predicted that the "General who takes the most decided step in this respect will be held in the highest estimation by the loyal and true men of the country." Writing to Grant at his headquarters in Tennessee, Washburne declared that "the negroes must now be made our auxiliaries in every possible way they can be, whether by working or fighting."

Before the war was over, nearly 200,000 black soldiers, accounting for roughly 10 percent of the federal army—more than half of them former slaves—would fight for the Union. They were compensated at a fraction of what was paid to their white counterparts, and those who fell into Confederate hands were treated with vicious brutality.* After the war, Thomas Wentworth Higginson, who commanded a South Carolina regiment composed of former slaves, expressed his conviction that "their demeanor under arms . . . shamed the nation into recognizing them as men."

Higginson's judgment that "the nation" had been chastened by the bravery of black soldiers might have been inflated by hope, but their recruitment had certainly been a major step in transforming the war for union into an abolition war. By the summer of 1862, fearing that military stalemate would lead to renewed calls in the North for negotiation, Lincoln had concluded that "we had about played our last card, and must change our tactics, or lose the game." On July 22, he showed his cabinet a preliminary draft of what would become the Emancipation Proclamation, warning that at the start of the New Year, "all persons held as slaves within any state or states, wherein the constitutional authority of the United States shall not then be practically recognized, submitted to, and maintained shall then, thenceforward, and forever, be free." At first, the plan was met with nervous caution. Montgomery Blair worried that it would "cost the Administration the fall elections." Seward, once an antislavery firebrand, suggested that public announcement should be postponed until success on the battlefield might make it more palatable to the northern public.

---

*On July 31, 1863, responding to Confederate threats to enslave or execute black Union soldiers, President Lincoln issued General Order 252, stating that for "every one enslaved by the enemy or sold into slavery, a rebel soldier shall be placed at hard labor on the public works, and continued at such labor until the other shall be released and receive the treatment due to a prisoner of war," and "for every soldier killed in violation of the laws of war, a rebel soldier shall be executed." Despite this promise of reciprocity, in April 1864 at Fort Pillow, north of Memphis, Tennessee, Confederate troops under Nathan Bedford Forrest executed hundreds of black Union soldiers after they had surrendered. Consulting with his cabinet on how to respond, Lincoln concluded that "blood can not restore blood, and government should not act for revenge," but he warned the Confederate government that southern prisoners of war would be treated as hostages if such an atrocity were to happen again. McPherson, *Battle Cry of Freedom*, 794.

Meanwhile, Lincoln's critics on the left were running out of patience. On August 19, Horace Greeley published a furious letter in the *New-York Tribune*, accusing the president of heeding "the councils, the representations, the menaces, of certain fossil politicians hailing from the Border Slave States" and of failing to enforce the congressional confiscation acts, with the result "that the Union cause . . . is now suffering immensely, from the mistaken deference to rebel Slavery." Three days later, in a letter released to the *National Intelligencer*, Lincoln replied with words that have been cited as evidence that his professed opposition to slavery was somehow incidental or insincere:

> *Hon. Horace Greeley:*
>
> *Dear Sir*
> I have just read yours of the 19th, addressed to myself through the New-York Tribune. . . . As to the policy I "seem to be pursuing" as you say, I have not meant to leave any one in doubt. . . .
> My paramount object in this struggle *is* to save the Union, and is *not* either to save or to destroy slavery. If I could save the Union without freeing *any* slave I would do it, and if I could save it by freeing *all* the slaves I would do it; and if I could save it by freeing some and leaving others alone I would also do that. What I do about slavery, and the colored race, I do because I believe it helps to save the Union; and what I forbear, I forbear because I do *not* believe it would help to save the Union. . . . I have here stated my purpose according to my view of *official* duty; and I intend no modification of my oft-expressed *personal* wish that all men every where could be free.

Always a meticulous verbal craftsman, Lincoln did not write "what I decline to do," or "what I prefer not to do." Instead, he gave repetitive emphasis to the word "forbear," by which he conveyed his decision to refrain from an action by which he was strongly drawn.

Unaware that Lincoln had already decided to announce emancipation once a battlefield victory improved his political position, Greeley was not assuaged. On September 17, less than one month after their exchange of letters, that victory came. After a series of minor engagements with Confederate units, federal forces repulsed Lee's invasion of Union territory in savage fighting in the vicinity of Antietam Creek. Five days later, Lincoln released the preliminary version of the proclamation. Despite its exemption of slave states remaining in or returning to the Union, its effect was immediate and widespread. From Kentucky, which had remained in the Union, one federal officer wrote to a friend that "under the Presidents proclamation of Sept 22d 62, I cannot conscientiously force my boys to become the slavehounds of Kentuckians." The preliminary Emancipation Proclamation was preliminary only in name.

On December 1, in his annual message to Congress, the president reviewed the year's events and looked forward to the emancipation scheduled to commence one month hence. "The dogmas of the quiet past," he wrote, "are inadequate to the stormy present." Then he spoke specifically to those who still distinguished between the cause of union and the cause of emancipation. "In *giving* freedom to the *slave*," he said, "we *assure* freedom to the *free*—honorable alike in what we give and what we preserve. We shall nobly save or meanly lose the last best hope of earth. Other means may succeed; this could not fail."

At a White House ceremony on January 1, 1863, Lincoln kept his promise—or, as some would have said, made good on his threat. The Emancipation Proclamation declared that all persons held to involuntary service in parts of the nation still in rebellion against the federal government "henceforth shall be free." Witnesses reported that as he reached for the pen, his hand trembled. Some suggested that the tremor was a sign of hesitation—a claim he later took pains to refute. More likely it was a consequence of long bouts of hand shaking on the White House receiving line. Perhaps it was a symptom of exhaustion. Or perhaps he trembled because he knew he was signing the most significant document in American history since the Declaration of Independence and the Constitution.

Some writers have disputed the gravity and consequence of the proclamation on the grounds that because the great majority of America's slaves lived in areas where the federal government as yet had no power to enforce it, it had little immediate effect. Frederick Douglass thought otherwise. "The proclamation," he wrote after the war, "changed everything." It changed the character of the war from "a mere strife for territory and dominion" into a "contest of civilization against barbarism." It put the moral authority of the president behind what had begun as a series of ad hoc military decisions. The causes of union and emancipation were formally conjoined at last.

Three months later, General Halleck wrote to Grant in a tutorial tone, as if the new policy still needed a rationale:

> It is the policy of the Government to withdraw from the enemy as much productive labor as possible. So long as the rebels retain and employ their slaves in producing grains, &c., they can employ all the whites in the [battle] field. Every slave withdrawn from the enemy is equivalent to a white man put hors de combat.

Although few if any black soldiers were to fight in the ferocious battle at Gettysburg in July (most were serving in units engaged in the West and the South), by that time black recruitment and emancipation had been settled Union policies for more than six months. Lincoln's reticence in the great commemorative address he delivered at the battlefield in November is therefore telling. He never uttered the word "slavery." His allusion to it—"this nation, under God, shall have a new birth of freedom"—was elliptical, a kind of shorthand from which the public could infer (or not) what he meant, namely the deliverance of four million people hitherto enslaved. He placed much more emphasis on defending "government of the people, by the people, for the people" from the slave owners' insurrection. As for the war on slavery, he spoke obliquely, as if in code.

5.

Among stalwart believers in slavery, many continued to deceive themselves about what was happening. Mary Chesnut, for one, wondered

Lincoln in 1863

"why," if slavery was really so cruel and malign, "don't they all march over the border where they would be received with open arms"?

In fact, they were doing just that. In northeast Virginia, almost half the male slaves of prime working age fled in the first two years of the war. By the late summer of 1862, one Confederate officer estimated that a million dollars' worth of slaves was fleeing every week. A Presbyterian missionary serving in 1863 with Union troops in Louisiana reported that if you "go out in any direction,"

> you meet negroes on horses, negroes on mules, negroes with oxen, negroes by the wagon, cart and buggy load, negroes on foot, men, women and children; negroes in uniform, negroes in rags, negroes in frame houses, negroes living in tents, negroes living in rail pens covered with brush, and negroes living under brush piles without any rails, negroes living on the bare ground with the sky for their covering; all hopeful, almost all cheerful, every one pleading to be taught, willing to do anything for learning.

Until the second half of the twentieth century, it was customary to tell the story of the Civil War as a tale of gallant white warriors bestowing freedom upon grateful black people. That story has belatedly been revised to take account of the persistent virulence of northern as well as southern racism, the manifold suffering of former slaves, and, most of all, their role in their own liberation by mounting what the historian Steven Hahn calls "the greatest slave revolt in modern history." The old narrative was partially true: the Civil War was indeed a war of deliverance. But it also released a surge of fugitives whose first encounters with "freedom" were often traumatic and cruel.

Those who tried to enlist in the Union army ran the risk of being beaten or killed before reaching the recruiting station. In an affidavit dictated in 1864, one Missouri slave recounted how he found a fellow runaway "lying in a little ice house" belonging to his owner, with a group of white men looking down at him in the at-ease stance of satisfied hunters standing over their kill. "He was dead. He had been Shot through the heart, the ball coming to the Skin on his back." It was not an uncommon occurrence.

Wives and parents of runaways were shackled, whipped, and locked up at night in order to prevent them from following their husbands or children. In the shifting no-man's-land between Union and rebel control, gangs of armed whites beat, raped, and shot unattended slaves in frenzies of preemptive retribution before the "damned Yankees" showed up. In Maryland, even after slavery was officially abolished in November 1864, former slaves found themselves at the mercy of "Organized Bands Prowling apon Horse Back around the Country armed with Revolvers and Horse Whips threatning to Shoot every Negroe that gives Back the first word after they Lacerate his flesh with the Whip."

During the retreat of Lee's army from Gettysburg in July 1863, panicked former slaves as well as free blacks living in Pennsylvania poured through neighboring villages and towns, filling the "roads Northward for hours, loaded with house hold effects, sable babies, &C," liable to be seized by rebel soldiers heading south. Mounted soldiers snatched up terrified children to take them "home"—a sight that, from a distance, might have looked like sons or daughters tethered to protective fathers. Adult captives were executed, sometimes by hanging, sometimes dragged by mule and rope until they expired, or, if they lasted inconveniently long, their skulls were smashed by rifle butts. In the last weeks of 1864, many who tried to join Sherman's troops on the famous (infamous in the South) march from Atlanta to Savannah were seized by local whites. Some were decapitated, their heads impaled on stakes as signposts to dissuade others.

Despite the barbarism and chaos, by the end of the war roughly 400,000 former slaves were living as nominally free persons under the protection of Union troops. "Nominally" is the operative word. Most lived in makeshift refugee camps where conditions were harsh. Maria Mann, Horace Mann's niece, who worked in 1863 as a teacher in an Arkansas contraband camp, reported that newly emancipated slaves "arrived to the Union camp with swelling, open sores, and eaten up with vermin." Because slave owners tried whenever possible to move male slaves farther south, hoping to keep "workers who carried the most capital value and the Yankees away from each other," the camp population was disproportionately made up of women and children.

As for able-bodied males, once the Emancipation Proclamation declared that "such persons of suitable condition will be received into the armed service of the United States," the camps functioned as what has been called "instant recruiting stations." But the line between enlistment and conscription was thin. Sites of charity, the camps were also dens of corruption. Supplies intended for the relief of dislocated blacks were stolen and sold at inflated prices to local whites. In exchange for food and shelter, women and girls often had no choice but to prostitute themselves.

In the eastern theater of war, contraband camps, as they continued to be known, were typically set up in fixed locations—such as those at Fort Monroe, or in the city jail of Frederick, Maryland, or on Robert E. Lee's confiscated property overlooking the Potomac, where former slaves were put to work burying the Union dead in what became Arlington National Cemetery. In the West, the camps were more likely to be temporary and mobile as federal and Confederate forces seized and lost control of contested ground. Whether fixed or on the move, they were perilous places

where runaways remained vulnerable to recapture by agents of their former masters or by freelance slave catchers looking to profit from the continually replenished supply of human merchandise.

The process of emancipation is thus both a stirring and a sordid story.
Wounded or idle Union soldiers volunteered to teach children and adults
how to read. Former slaves built relationships with Union troops that
could be described as friendships. But betrayals, too, were common. At
the contraband camp on Craney Island, near Newport News, Union soldiers were known to sell fugitive slaves in return for reward money. Slaves
putatively under Union protection remained at risk of kidnapping, especially those held in camps where Confederate troops were stationed
nearby. As federal policy shifted toward encouraging black enlistment,
scores of thousands of male fugitives, from Georgia and Mississippi to
Kentucky and Missouri, were subject to "enlistment practices so coercive"
that they were barely distinguishable from kidnapping.

6.

In hindsight, it all seems predestined, as if a great chain of necessity led
from General Butler's decision of May 1861 to hold fugitives as contraband at Fort Monroe, to General Hunter's emancipation orders of April
and May 1862, to the Emancipation Proclamation of 1863, and finally to
the Thirteenth Amendment, passed by Congress in January 1865 and
ratified by the states almost a year later, eight months after Lincoln's as-
sassination. At long last, "except as a punishment for crime whereof the
party shall have been duly convicted,"* slavery was impermissible everywhere in the United States according to the Constitution that had once
permitted it. Yet to imagine this outcome as somehow preordained is to be
misguided by hindsight, whereby "everything unexpected in its own time

---

*In her influential book *The New Jim Crow: Mass Incarceration in the Age of Colorblindness* (New
York: New Press, 2010), Michelle Alexander gives a scathing account of mass incarceration as a new
form of racial subjugation.

is chronicled on the page as inevitable." Lincoln got it right when, shortly before his death, he called the result of the war "astounding."

So it felt to everyone who experienced it. The current of astonishment flows through Civil War diaries, memoirs, speeches, and memoranda, in close company with what one historian calls the sense of *"contingency*—the recognition that at numerous critical points during the war things might have gone altogether differently." Every day of the war was a lesson in human impotence. What inscrutable force determined who lived and who died, which side failed and which prevailed? There were many names for this force—some called it chance or luck, others called it fate, God, or providence. By whatever name, it seemed impervious to human will. The theme is everywhere, from Lincoln's famous remark "I have never claimed to have controlled events, but confess plainly that events controlled me," to the writings of ordinary soldiers marveling at the arbitrary apportionment of life and death. Thirty years after fighting at the Battle of Perryville in October 1862, one Tennessee soldier remembered the inexplicable divergence between the fates of two comrades:

> We helped bring off a man by the name of Hodge, with his under jaw
> shot off, and his tongue lolling out. We brought off Captain Lute B.
> Irvine. Lute was shot through the lungs and was vomiting blood all
> the while, and begging us to lay him down and let him die. But Lute
> is living yet.

As for what the war would mean for the fate of the enslaved population, historians rightly caution against "the fallacy of imagining emancipation as an inevitable result of the conflict." As one scholar writes, "with different battlefield accidents," the war "might have further entrenched and expanded human bondage."

What kinds of "accidents"? Consider the tide-turning battle at Gettysburg. Over two days, in preparation for an infantry assault on enemy positions atop Cemetery Ridge, Confederate artillery fired on Union ordnance. Almost all the shells overshot their targets. No one knows why.

Reports of troop locations might have been faulty. Fuses might have burned more slowly than the gunners calculated, or perhaps the recoil from the first discharges scarred the ground, sinking the wheels of the caissons and thereby raising the shooting trajectory too high.

What if the shells had hit home? Would Union troops have abandoned their positions? Would Lee's army have broken through and threatened Washington? Would Lincoln's government have fled north, prompting Britain to recognize the Confederacy and to dispatch its navy to break the Union blockade? Would McClellan, as Lincoln expected long after the battle was won, have carried the 1864 election on a platform promising to end the war and to restore the Union with the right to own slaves preserved in the former Confederacy?

And then there is the question of what happened—or did not happen— immediately following the Battle of Gettysburg. The Union commander George G. Meade—his troops exhausted, supply lines strained, the Potomac swollen by rain—failed, in Lincoln's words, to "pressingly pursue" Lee's retreating army through Maryland across the river into Virginia. In a letter of July 14, Lincoln wrote to Meade in a tone somewhere between fury and lamentation. "You stood," he said, "and let the flood run down, bridges be built, and the enemy move away at his leisure, without attacking him." He went on: "Again, my dear general, I do not believe you appreciate the magnitude of the misfortune involved in Lee's escape—He was within your easy grasp, and to have closed upon him would, in connection with our other late successes, have ended the war—As it is, the war will be prolonged indefinitely." Lincoln never sent that letter. Perhaps he withheld it because on second thought he felt he had been unfair to the commander of an exhausted army, or perhaps his anger subsided once he had poured it onto the page.

Many stories and novels have since been written imagining what might have happened had this or that Civil War battle gone differently—a what- if literature whose "counterfactual" plots may seem outlandish now but were perfectly plausible then. One twentieth-century novelist conjures up a defeated North where vigilante violence against blacks is rampant and white people are convinced that "we might have won that war if it hadn't been for the Abolitionists." In this alternate universe, Mexico City has been occupied by the victorious "Confederate Legion" and renamed Leesburg—the new capital of a slave-based empire.

As late as the summer of 1864, Lincoln himself was pessimistic—worried not so much that the war would be lost outright as that it would stall into stalemate, or that even if the North emerged victorious in some provisional sense, it would lose the peace. In the late summer of 1864, convinced that he would lose the upcoming election to the "peace candidate," General George McClellan, he invited Frederick Douglass to the White House. Almost two decades later, Douglass gave this account of their meeting, which took place on August 19:

> [Mr. Lincoln] saw the danger of premature peace, and, like a thoughtful and sagacious man as he was, he wished to provide means of rendering such consummation as harmless as possible. I was the more impressed by his benevolent consideration because he before said, in answer to the peace clamor, that his object was to save the Union, and to do so with or without slavery. What he said on this day showed a deeper moral conviction against slavery than I had ever seen before in anything spoken or written by him. I listened with the deepest interest and profoundest satisfaction, and, at his suggestion, agreed to undertake the organizing of a band of scouts, composed of colored men, whose business should be somewhat after the original plan of John Brown, to go into the rebel states, beyond the lines of our armies, and carry the news of emancipation, and urge the slaves to come within our boundaries.

Even after he was reelected in November, Lincoln remained worried that the Emancipation Proclamation—equivalent to what today would be called an executive order—was vulnerable to revision or reversal by some future president.

In recounting the struggle over slavery, we tend to celebrate those who seem bold and prophetic and to denigrate those who seem tentative and timid. Thus, men such as Clay and Webster, who tried to prevent civil war, fall into disrepute, and men such as William Greenleaf Eliot, who hated slavery with every fiber of his being but feared that the war would only serve the interests of the slave owners, disappear from the story almost completely. Discouraged by early Union defeats, and concerned that public opinion in the North would not support a prolonged conflict, Eliot railed in December 1862 at "the abolition Pharisees" for "having set the house on fire" and standing back to "rub their hands and chuckle to see how splendidly it burns." Eventually, the war proved him wrong. But before dismissing such men as "mediocre, timid, and weak," one might ask oneself how many of us would welcome such a war, especially without the knowledge of hindsight? As Lincoln's anguish—not fully dispelled until Sherman took Atlanta on September 2, 1864—attests, not before the last months of fighting was it clear that the South could be compelled to abandon slavery by force of arms.

By the time he delivered his second inaugural address on March 4, 1865—a month before the surrender at Appomattox and six weeks before his death—Lincoln had come to see the "mighty scourge of war" as a divine punishment visited not only upon the South but upon all America. He was speaking now in the accents of Jeremiah. America's unexpiated sin was the original sin of slavery, for which God "gives to both North and South, this terrible war, as the woe due to those by the offence came." And if it should "continue until all the wealth piled by the bond-man's two hundred and fifty years of unrequited toil shall be sunk, and until every drop of blood drawn with the lash, shall be paid by another drawn with the sword," there would be no cause to doubt God's justice or to presume the blessing of his mercy.

Lincoln's sublime words echoed—no doubt unwittingly—words published nearly forty years earlier when emancipation had been but a dim dream. In the June 29, 1827, issue of one of America's first black newspapers, *Freedom's Journal*, its editors had written, "Americans, let us remember the dealings of God, to other nations," for which "national sins have always been followed by national calamities." The Civil War was a calamity—not only as measured by the scale of the suffering it inflicted on black and white alike, but because the freedom it brought was belated, partial, and sudden, so sudden that it consigned black Americans to a new kind of limbo between legal recognition that they were no longer slaves and moral recognition that they were persons fully equal to those who had enslaved them.

"Poor dusky children of slavery, men and women of my own race," wrote Elizabeth Keckley, herself a former slave, in 1868, "the transition from slavery to freedom was too sudden for you!" She implied no second thoughts—no wish to rewrite history with the war deleted, or shortened, or postponed yet again. But she expressed a prescient awareness of how long the road to full and true emancipation would be.

There is no calculating the unsettled debts of slavery. Since the Civil War, black Americans have been subjected to more than a century and a half of ingenious variations—if not quite replications—of the lethal assault to which they had been subjected by slavery itself. There is no enumerating them. But any inventory would have to include the forced labor system that took hold after Reconstruction in the South, by which numberless African Americans were found guilty of "crimes" such as "vagrancy" and sentenced to chain gangs or delivered as uncompensated workers "into mines, lumber camps, quarries, farms, and factories." It would include the millions of black Americans systematically excluded from the social welfare programs made available after the Great Depression to white Americans by the New Deal. It would include the injuries not only of de jure segregation but of de facto segregation, which persist to this day. It would include the gross disproportion of the number of young black men languishing in America's prisons—many of them serving sentences out of all proportion to the severity of their crimes, or locked up for lack of competent counsel. It would include the daily insults to self-respect delivered to black Americans for no other reason than the fact of their blackness.

7.

In early 1862, on a side trip from a journey to Washington, Nathaniel Hawthorne ventured a few miles into northern Virginia. There he and his party encountered a small band of fugitive slaves trudging north. One of his traveling companions, an English journalist, remarked that "anything more helpless or wretched than their aspect, I never saw." Passersby tossed them coins and scraps of food as "they crouched in the hot sunlight" seemingly with "no idea, no plan, and no distinct purpose." In a pseudonymous essay published that July, Hawthorne described the scene, referring to the fugitives with the terminology of the day:

> One very pregnant token of a social system thoroughly disturbed was presented by a party of contrabands, escaping out of the mysterious depths of Secessia. . . . I felt most kindly towards these poor fugitives, but knew not precisely what to wish in their behalf, nor in the least how to help them. For the sake of the manhood which is latent in them, I would not have turned them back; but I should have felt almost as reluctant, on their own account, to hasten them forward to the stranger's land; and I think my prevalent idea was, that, whoever may be benefited by the results of this war, it will not be the present generation of negroes, the childhood of whose race is now gone forever, and who must henceforth fight a hard battle with the world, on very unequal terms.

Three years after Hawthorne's essay appeared, and six weeks after President Lincoln was assassinated, Frederick Douglass looked back at the carnage of the Civil War and reflected that "many thoughtful and patriotic men . . . doubted and trembled while contemplating the possibility of just such a conflict." Unlike Hawthorne, Douglass had welcomed it. "Let the conflict come, and God speed the Right," he had written in the tense weeks before the outbreak of hostilities at Fort Sumter. Now he eulogized Lincoln, echoing the late president's second inaugural address. "The cost of the experiment in blood and treasure has been vast," Douglass said, "but the results attained and made attainable by it will fully compensate for all loss."

There could hardly have been two men more different in experience and temperament than Nathaniel Hawthorne and Frederick Douglass—each, in his way, a representative American. Hawthorne was a dispassionate white observer of lives that, in this case, he could scarcely imagine. Douglass was an impassioned advocate for black people, to whose struggle his own life gave witness. Yet both foresaw with ruthless clarity that while at long last freedom, in Douglass's notably conditional phrase, had been "made attainable," millions of former slaves and their posterity would face a "hard battle with the world, on very unequal terms," for generations to come.

In a belated act of formal recognition of what the war had already accomplished, Congress repealed the fugitive slave law on June 28, 1864. On April 9, 1865, the guns fell silent. The rebellion was over, the Union restored, and after more than two centuries there was no more slavery from which to run. The vast work of repairing its human devastation had barely begun.

ACKNOWLEDGMENTS

To try to enumerate all the people to whom I owe thanks for their tolerance during the writing of this book would be folly. It would require a very long list of family, friends, and colleagues who put up with my moods and refusals to do this or that because of a book whose completion date I kept deferring. I hope they will understand my casting my gratitude here in the form of a general thank-you.

I must, however, thank by name several friends whose kindness and generosity went far beyond all reasonable expectation. Kenneth Abraham showed me how to think more clearly about legal and historical questions. Eric Himmel, a steadfast friend for over fifty years, read the whole manuscript and made invaluable suggestions, as did another old friend, the eminent historian Dan Carter. My colleague of more than thirty years, Eric Foner, took time from his own work to provide detailed commentary whose value I cannot overstate. Martha Hodes did the same with comparable generosity and effect.

While immersed in the historiography of antebellum America, I came to understand in a way I had not fully done before that writing about history is an act of collaboration with countless authors both living and dead. My debt to generations of superb scholars who have illuminated the dark and complex American experience with slavery and emancipation is registered as best I can in the notes.

While working on this book I was often reclusive, but I did accept a handful of invitations to speak at academic gatherings, where I was provoked to deeper reflection. At the Shelby Cullom Davis Center at Princeton, Matthew Karp, Philip and Deborah Nord, and Sean Wilentz made especially helpful suggestions. I benefited, too, from an invitation to speak with graduate students at Harvard, where John Bell's insights were particularly helpful. My fellow panelists at a Civil War conference at Yale—Ta-Nehisi Coates, Gary Gallagher, Stephanie McCurry, and John Fabian Witt—helped to sharpen my thinking. In her work and in person, Manisha Sinha has been a stimulating interlocutor. William McFeely and the late Robert Silvers responded to early versions of portions of the book with comments that encouraged me to press on. Often, I found myself thinking of my late friend and colleague Nathan Huggins, whose writing, teaching, and conversation first set me on the path that eventually led me to attempt this work.

I am grateful to archivists and librarians at the Boston Atheneum, American Antiquarian Society, Missouri Historical Museum, New York Public Library, Library of Congress, and the libraries of Washington University, Columbia University, Harvard University, and Syracuse University.

At different stages of the research I was assisted by Rachel Serlen, Julien Hawthorne, Michael Abraham, and Elena Abbott. When the manuscript was at last ready to move into production, I turned to an exceptionally talented graduate student—now faculty colleague—Zachary Roberts. Before we began to work together, I already had some sense of Zach's gifts, but I was not prepared for his manifold sensitivity, range of knowledge and curiosity—as well as his stamina, professionalism, and steady good humor whenever I needed a boost, which was often.

I owe deep thanks to my incomparable agent, Jennifer Rudolph Walsh, whose loyalty has meant a great deal to me over many years. At Penguin Press, I'm afraid I compelled the formidable Ann Godoff and my incisive editor, Ginny Smith—whose acute responses to the work-in-progress made it much better—to draw deep from their reserves of patience. Ginny's assistant, Caroline Sydney, was invariably and graciously helpful, as were Amanda Dewey, who designed the book in harmony with its tone and themes, and Kate Griggs, who oversaw the whole production process with great sensitivity and care.

Finally, I must thank my beloved wife, Dawn, whose capacity for forbearance was sometimes pushed to the brink during the years required for writing this book. As always, she subjected my prose to her peerless close reading, resulting in many improvements in structure, analysis, and expression. She also spent hundreds of hours finding, reading, and helping me understand court transcripts, newspapers and periodicals, biographical records, and other texts essential to the narrative. The word gratitude does not begin to express what I feel at every moment of our partnership in work and life.

ILLUSTRATIONS

325 Julian Vannerson, "Stephen A. Douglas, Senator from Illinois, Thirty-fifth Congress," in *McClees' Gallery of Photographic Portraits of the Senators, Representatives & Delegates of the Thirty-fifth Congress* (Washington, D.C.: McClees & Beck, 1859), 252. (Prints and Photographs Division, Library of Congress, Washington, D.C.)

326 "Forcing slavery down the throat of a freesoiler" (Philadelphia: J. L. Magee, 1856). Lithograph on wove paper. (Stern Collection, Rare Book and Special Collections Division, Library of Congress, Washington, D.C.)

327 Sara T. L. Robinson, *Ruins of the Free State Hotel, Kansas Territory*, 1856. (Courtesy of Kansas State Historical Society)

329 John Steuart Curry, *John Brown*, 1939. Oil on canvas. (Arthur Hoppock Hearn Fund, 1950, Metropolitan Museum of Art, New York)

332 Dred Scott, c. 1858. Albumen photograph after daguerreotype. (MHS Photographs and Prints Collection, Courtesy of Missouri History Museum, St. Louis)

332 Roger B. Taney, c. 1855–1865. Negative, glass, wet condition. (Brady-Handy Photograph Collection, Prints and Photographs Division, Library of Congress, Washington, D.C.)

334 Calvin Jackson, "Abraham Lincoln, Taken in Pittsfield, Illinois, Two Weeks Before the Final Lincoln-Douglas Debate in Lincoln's Unsuccessful Bid for the Senate, October 1, 1858." (Prints and Photographs Division, Library of Congress, Washington, D.C.)

357 Mathew Brady, "Portrait of Maj. Gen. Benjamin F. Butler, Officer of the Federal Army," c. 1860–1865. (Civil War Glass Negatives and Related Prints Collection, Prints and Photographs Division, Library of Congress, Washington, D.C.)

361 *Stampede Among the Negroes in Virginia—Their Arrival at Fortress Monroe, from Sketches by Our Special Artist in Fortress Monroe.* Wood engraved illustration in *Frank Leslie's Illustrated Newspaper*, June 8, 1861, 56–57. (Prints and Photographs Division, Library of Congress, Washington, D.C.)

364 John Chester Buttre, John C. Frémont, c. 1861. Engraving. (Robert B. Honeyman Jr. Collection of Early Californian and Western American Pictorial Material [Graphic], BANC PIC 1963.002:0488-A. Courtesy of the Bancroft Library, University of California, Berkeley)

370 "Field Day" (CP1043). OHA75 (Contributed Photographs Collection, Otis Historical Archives, National Museum of Health and Medicine, Silver Spring, Maryland)

372 City Point, Virginia. "Soldiers' Graves near General Hospital," c. 1861–1869. (Civil War Glass Negative Collection, Prints and Photographs Division, Library of Congress, Washington, D.C.)

377 Alexander Gardner, Abraham Lincoln, Nov. 8, 1863 [printed c. 1900]. (Prints and Photographs Division, Library of Congress, Washington, D.C.)

NOTES

Introduction

1 **"we had slavery"**: Abraham Lincoln, "Speech at Chicago, Illinois," July 10, 1858, in *The Collected Works of Abraham Lincoln*, ed. Roy P. Basler (New Brunswick, N.J.: Rutgers University Press, 1953), 2:501.

2 **"sad satire to call"**: Moncure Conway, *The Rejected Stone; or, Insurrection vs. Resurrection in America* (Boston: Walker, Wise, 1862), 8.

2 **The founding fathers tried**: Recent scholars have mounted a challenge to the view of the United States as two societies—one slave, one free—by arguing that in many respects the border between slavery and freedom was "illusory and indistinct." See Steven Hahn, *The Political Worlds of Slavery and Freedom* (Cambridge, Mass.: Harvard University Press, 2009), 3. There is much merit to this view, as reflected in economic interdependence and political alliance between North and South, and in the experience of fugitive slaves who found nothing like genuine freedom in the so-called free North. The present book takes this challenge seriously, but nevertheless presents the story of fugitive slaves as part of the larger story of two linked but ultimately incompatible societies.

4 **"One section of our country"**: Abraham Lincoln, "First Inaugural Address," March 4, 1861, in *Collected Works of Lincoln*, 4:268–69.

6 **"most disgraceful, atrocious"**: Rodney French, quoted in Gordon S. Barker, *Fugitive Slaves and the Unfinished American Revolution: Eight Cases, 1848–1856* (Jefferson, N.C.: McFarland, 2013), 38.

6 **"the only tub thrown"**: *DeBow's Review* (1860), quoted in Stanley Campbell, *The Slave Catchers: Enforcement of the Fugitive Slave Law, 1850–1860* (New York: W. W. Norton, 1972), 5.

6 **"faithful execution depends"**: *Debates and Proceedings of the Georgia Convention* (1850), quoted in David M. Potter, *The Impending Crisis, 1848–1861*, ed. Don E. Fehrenbacher (New York: Harper & Row, 1976), 128.

6 **"might be palsied"**: The New York minister was C. B. Ray. *Boston Daily Atlas*, Oct. 9, 1850.

6 **"rent out hell"**: The Ohio minister was William P. Newman, a Baptist preacher who had escaped from slavery in the 1830s. See Newman to Frederick Douglass, Oct. 1, 1850, in *The Black Abolitionist Papers, Vol. 4, The United States, 1847–1858*, ed. C. Peter Ripley (Chapel Hill: University of North Carolina Press, 1991), 63.

6 **When Massachusetts representative**: Mann, in Glenn M. Linden, *Voices from the Gathering Storm: The Coming of the American Civil War* (Wilmington, Del.: Scholarly Resources, 2001), 69.

6 **"none that was not ready"**: Ralph Waldo Emerson, "Address to the Citizens of Concord on the Fugitive Slave Law," May 3, 1851, in *Emerson's Antislavery Writings*, ed. Len Gougeon and Joel Myerson (New Haven, Conn.: Yale University Press, 1995), 56.

6 **"I hate to see"**: Lincoln to Joshua F. Speed, Aug. 24, 1855, in *Collected Works of Lincoln*, 2:320.

7 **"craven willingness to bargain"**: Ta-Nehisi Coates, *We Were Eight Years in Power* (New York: One World, 2017), 82.

8 **"We went to bed"**: Quoted in James M. McPherson, *Battle Cry of Freedom: The Civil War Era* (New York: Oxford University Press, 1988), 120.

8 **"Respect and Enforce"**: North Carolina *Standard*, May 3, 1851, quoted in Avery Craven, *The Coming of the Civil War* (Chicago: University of Chicago Press, 1957), 265.

8 **demanded federal intervention**: Years later, Henry Adams remarked that "between the slave power and states' rights there was no necessary connection. Whenever a question arose of extending or protecting slavery, the slave-holders became friends of centralized power." Henry Adams, *John Randolph* (1882; repr., New York: Fawcett, 1961), 178–79.

8 **"emigration is absolutely necessary"**: Quoted in Benjamin Quarles, *Black Abolitionists* (New York: Oxford University Press, 1969), 215.

8 **"If the Union be"**: Charles Sumner, quoted in Roy B. Morris, *The Long Pursuit: Abraham Lincoln's Thirty-Year Struggle with Stephen Douglas for the Heart and Soul of America* (New York: Harper Collins, 2008), 73.

9 **"the fugitive slave bill"**: Frederick Douglass, "The Anti-slavery Movement: Extracts from a Lecture Before Various Anti-slavery Bodies, in the Winter of 1855," in *My Bondage and My Freedom*, ed. Philip A. Foner (New York: Dover, 1969), 463.

9 **"the law will be"**: Quoted in Larry Gara, "The Fugitive Slave Law: A Double Paradox," *Civil War History* 10, no. 3 (Sept. 1964): 234.

9 **"to assume control"**: *Cong. Globe*, 31st Cong., 1st Sess., Aug. 21, 1850, app., 1614.

9 **an "illusive triumph"**: *Charleston Mercury*, quoted in Gara, "Fugitive Slave Law," 233.

9 **empowering the federal government**: Eric Foner, *Gateway to Freedom: The Hidden History of the Underground Railroad* (New York: W. W. Norton, 2015), 224.

10 **"Humanity cries out"**: Herman Melville, *Mardi and A Voyage Thither* (1849; repr., Evanston, Ill.: Northwestern University Press, 1970), 534.

10 **an outraged South**: See Matthew Karp, *This Vast Southern Empire: Slaveholders at the Helm of American Foreign Policy* (Cambridge, Mass.: Harvard University Press, 2016).

10 **"right may be distinguished"**: Daniel Webster, "The Constitution and the Union, March 7, 1850," in *The Papers of Daniel Webster: Speeches and Formal Writings, vol. 2, 1834–1852*, ed. Charles M. Wiltse (Hanover, N.H.: University Press of New England, 1988), 521.

10 **"right-minded men could"**: William Greenleaf Eliot, *The Story of Archer Alexander, from Slavery to Freedom* (Boston: Cupples, Upham, 1885), 44.

10 **Thoreau called "spectatordom"**: Henry David Thoreau, *Walden*, in *Walden, Civil Disobedience, and Other Writings*, ed. William Rossi (New York: W. W. Norton, 2008), 33.

11 **"Were I about"**: "A Lecture Delivered Before the Female Anti-slavery Society of Salem," in *William Wells Brown: A Reader*, ed. Ezra Greenspan (Athens: University of Georgia Press, 2008), 108.

12 **"to obey the law"**: Jonathan Blanchard, *Western Citizen*, Nov. 18, 1850, 2.

12 **"first to throw himself"**: Nathaniel Hawthorne, *Life of Franklin Pierce*, in *Tales, Sketches, and Other Papers* (Boston: Houghton, Mifflin, 1883), 422.

12 **"we must arrest"**: Abraham Lincoln, "Address at Cooper Institute, New York City," Feb. 27, 1860, in *Collected Works of Lincoln*, 3:548. Lincoln repeated the same phrase in a speech at Manchester, New Hampshire, three days later. "Speech at Manchester, NH," March 1, 1860, in *Collected Works of Lincoln*, 3:551.

13 **"Comity exists in"**: Richard Hofstadter, *The Progressive Historians: Turner, Beard, Parrington* (Chicago: University of Chicago Press, 1968), 454.

14 **"the maneuverings of two armies"**: *Charleston Mercury*, Nov. 21, 1850, 2, gleefully quoting the *New York Herald* of a few days earlier.

14 **"pursuit of one duty"**: Webster, "Constitution and the Union, March 7, 1850," 521.

Chapter 1: The Problem

17 **"more effectual execution"**: Mason gave notice of his intention to introduce the legislation under that name on January 3, 1850. *Cong. Globe*, 31st Cong., 1st Sess., 99. A similar bill had been proposed in the spring of 1848 by South Carolina senator Andrew Butler, chair of the Judiciary Committee, but it had failed to advance.

17 **"Tories and Refugees"**: Washington to Daniel Parker, April 28, 1783, in *The Writings of George Washington from the Original Manuscript Sources, 1745–1799*, ed. John C. Fitzpatrick (Washington, D.C.: Government Printing Office, 1931–44), 26:364.

18 **"spirit of the master"**: Thomas Jefferson, "Query XVIII," *Notes on the State of Virginia* (1785), in *Thomas Jefferson: Writings* (New York: Library of America, 1984), 214, 289.

18 **"uncharitable to one another"**: Madison, quoted in Paul Finkelman, *An Imperfect Union: Slavery, Federalism, and Comity* (Chapel Hill: University of North Carolina Press, 1981), 27.

19 **"concession[s] to reconcile"**: *History of the Trial of Castner Hanway and Others for Treason* (Philadelphia, 1852), 10.

19 **a weak directive**: As the historian Thomas Morris writes with pointed understatement, "because the clause was phrased in the passive voice, considerable uncertainty resulted." *Free Men All: The Personal Liberty Laws of the North, 1780–1861* (Baltimore: Johns Hopkins University Press, 1974), 18.

19 **Phrased in the passive voice**: The language of the fugitive slave clause followed closely that of the Northwest Ordinance, which, while banning slavery from the new federal territory, stipulated that "any person escaping into the same, from whom labor or service is lawfully claimed in any one of the original States, such fugitive may be lawfully reclaimed, and conveyed to the person claiming his or her labor or service as aforesaid."

20 **"We have obtained a right":** Charles Cotesworth Pinckney, "Speech in the South Carolina House of Representatives over the Calling of a State Ratifying Convention (January 17, 1788)," in *The American Debate over Slavery, 1760–1865: An Anthology of Sources,* ed. Howard L. Lubert, Kevin R. Hardwick, and Scott J. Hammond (Indianapolis: Hackett, 2016), 40.

20 **Amid claims and counterclaims:** Don E. Fehrenbacher, *The Slaveholding Republic: An Account of the United States Government's Relations to Slavery,* ed. Ward M. McAfee (New York: Oxford University Press, 2001), 210.

20 **"allows the recovery of fugitive slaves":** Thomas Hart Benton, *Thirty Years' View; or, A History of the Workings of the American Government for Thirty Years from 1820 to 1850* (New York: D. Appleton, 1883), 2:733.

21 **"inadequate to the object":** Virginia congressman Thomas L. Moore, quoted in Stanley Harrold, *Border War: Fighting over Slavery Before the Civil War* (Chapel Hill: University of North Carolina Press, 2010), 25.

21 **What obligations, exactly:** The historian Don E. Fehrenbacher asks this pointed question in *The Slaveholding Republic,* 208.

21 **It had neither clear jurisdiction:** Fehrenbacher, *Slaveholding Republic,* 211, 214.

21 **By the 1830s:** These cases are conveniently assembled in an invaluable anthology edited by Paul Finkelman, *Slavery, Race, and the American Legal System, 1700–1872,* 16 vols. (Clark, N.J.: Lawbook Exchange, 2012). The four volumes of series 2 address fugitive slaves in American courts.

21 **Another common term:** James Madison, quoted in Finkelman, *Imperfect Union,* 27.

22 **Some slaves who escaped:** Simon Schama, *Rough Crossings: Britain, the Slaves, and the American Revolution* (New York: Harper Perennial, 2007), 5.

22 **"God knows, no man":** *Report of the Case of Charles Brown, a Fugitive Slave, Owing Labour and Service to Wm. C. Drury, of Washington County, Maryland. Decided by the Recorder of Pittsburgh, February 7th, 1835,* quoted in Paul Finkelman, *Fugitive Slaves and American Courts,* series 2 (Clark, N.J.: Lawbook Exchange, 2012), 1:61–62.

22 **In explaining his verdict:** Finkelman, *Fugitive Slaves and American Courts,* 95.

22 **"If a horse wandered away":** David G. Smith, *On the Edge of Freedom: The Fugitive Slave Issue in South Central Pennsylvania, 1820–1870* (New York: Fordham University Press, 2013), 19.

22–23 **Farther south, on the frontier:** There was traffic, too, in the other direction, when runaways who had been re-enslaved by Indians sometimes fled their new captors and begged for protection among slave-owning whites. See Adam Rothman, *Slave Country* (Cambridge, Mass.: Harvard University Press, 2007), 60.

23 **"tweets of the master class":** Baptist, quoted in DeNeen L. Brown, "Hunting Down Runaway Slaves: The Cruel Ads of Andrew Jackson and 'the Master Class,'" *Washington Post,* May 1, 2017.

23 **"coolly read in families":** Charles Dickens, *American Notes for General Circulation* (1842; repr., Oxford: Oxford University Press, 1997), 233–35. Richard Hofstadter notes that Dickens, without acknowledgment, based much of his commentary on Theodore Weld's *American Slavery as It Is* (1839). See Richard Hofstadter, ed., *Great Issues in American History, vol. 2, From the Revolution to the Civil War, 1765–1865* (New York: Vintage Books, 1958), 323.

24 **In Maryland, which led:** Campbell, *Slave Catchers,* 6; John Hope Franklin and Loren Schweninger, *Runaway Slaves: Rebels on the Plantation* (New York: Oxford University Press, 1999), 282; Barbara Jeanne Fields, *Slavery and Freedom on the Middle Ground: Maryland During the 19th Century* (New Haven, Conn.: Yale University Press, 1985), 16.

24 **Census data suggest:** Larry Gara, *The Liberty Line: The Legend of the Underground Railroad* (Lexington: University of Kentucky Press, 1996), 30.

24 **For one thing:** Fields, *Slavery and Freedom on the Middle Ground,* 16.

25 **It is hardly surprising:** Smith, *On the Edge of Freedom,* 6.

25 **"on an average":** Webster to Edward Sprague Rand et al., May 15, 1850, published in *Boston Daily Advertiser,* May 31, 1850, in *The Papers of Daniel Webster: Correspondence,* vol. 7, *1850–1852,* ed. Charles M. Wiltse and Michael J. Birkner (Hanover, N.H.: University Press of New England, 1986), 92. Webster was quoting Representative William H. Bissell of Illinois.

25 **"the sheer volume":** Harriet Frazier, *Runaway and Freed Missouri Slaves and Those Who Helped Them, 1763–1865* (Jefferson, N.C.: McFarland, 2004), 89.

25 **"upon whom this new fugitive slave law":** Jonathan Blanchard, "The Fugitive Law—Judge Douglas Reviewed," *Western Citizen,* Nov. 19, 1850, 2.

25 **as one authority puts it:** Foner, *Gateway to Freedom,* 4. For a discussion of the range of estimates, see David Blight, ed., *Passages to Freedom: The Underground Railroad in History and Memory* (Washington, D.C.: Smithsonian Books, 2004), 243; Franklin and Schweninger, *Runaway Slaves,* 282.

25 **a "carceral" world:** See Walter Johnson, "The Carceral Landscape," in *River of Dark Dreams: Slavery and Empire in the Cotton Kingdom* (Cambridge, Mass.: Harvard University Press, 2013), 209–43.

26 **Sanctions against slave owners:** Robert H. Gudmestad, *A Troublesome Commerce: The Transformation of the Interstate Slave Trade* (Baton Rouge: Louisiana State University Press, 2003), 124–25.

26　**antislavery agitation in the South:** William Freehling, *The Road to Disunion, vol. 1, Secessionists at Bay, 1776–1854* (Oxford: Oxford University Press, 1990), 464*ff*, stresses the variety of antislavery sentiment in the South and argues that as late as the late 1840s emancipationist politics were alive and well in Kentucky.

26　**Slavery became the "flywheel":** Greg Grandin, *The Empire of Necessity: Slavery, Freedom, and Deception in the New World* (New York: Metropolitan, 2013), 24.

26　**world's largest cotton producer:** Daniel Walker Howe, *What Hath God Wrought: The Transformation of America, 1815–1848* (New York: Oxford University Press, 2007), 128.

26　**"twelve hundred million dollars":** *Middlesex Standard,* Oct. 3, 1844. The author of the article might have been J. G. Whittier.

27　**"men, women, and children":** Eric Foner, *The Fiery Trial: Abraham Lincoln and American Slavery* (New York: W. W. Norton, 2010), 17.

27　**"gangs of Negroes":** Charles Mackenzie, *Facts, Relative to the Present State of the British Cotton Colonies and to the Connection of Their Interests* (1811), quoted in Sven Beckert, *Empire of Cotton: A Global History* (New York: Vintage Books, 2014), 109.

27　**"by the voice of a stammering boy":** Jesse Torrey, *A Portraiture of Domestic Slavery* (Philadelphia, 1817), 32–34.

28　**"slaves bred rather than died":** Lawrence Goldstone, "Constitutionally, Slavery Is Indeed a National Institution," *New Republic,* Sept. 17, 2015.

28　**the "staple states":** John C. Calhoun, "On the Revenue Collection Bill (Commonly Called the Force Bill), in Reference to the Ordinance of the South Carolina Convention, Delivered in the Senate, February 15th and 16th, 1833," in *The Works of John C. Calhoun,* ed. Richard K. Crallé (New York: Appleton, 1856), 2:197*ff*.

28　**It was a terrible symmetry:** James Oakes, *The Scorpion's Sting: Antislavery and the Coming of the Civil War* (New York: W. W. Norton, 2014), 34; Fields, *Slavery and Freedom on the Middle Ground,* 15.

28　**Clay promoted this policy:** Freehling, *Secessionists at Bay,* 465, 471–72. Freehling describes Clay as "more whitener than abolitionist" (472).

28　**"sentenced to solitary confinement":** William Lloyd Garrison, "My Second Baltimore Trial," *Liberator,* Jan. 1, 1831, 2.

29　**"always purchasing for":** *Baltimore Sun,* July 18, 1838, 3. The same advertisement ran repeatedly.

29　**The enslaved population in Georgia:** Jeffrey Robert Young, "Slavery in Antebellum Georgia," in *New Georgia Encyclopedia,* Oct. 20, 2003, georgiaencyclopedia.org. See also Eugene R. Dattel, "Cotton in a Global Economy: Mississippi, 1800–1860," *Mississippi History Now,* Oct. 2006, mshistorynow.mdah.state.ms.us.

30　**"the larger the body of negroes":** Frederick Law Olmsted, *The Cotton Kingdom: A Traveller's Observations on Cotton and Slavery in the American Slave States* (1856), ed. Arthur M. Schlesinger Sr. (New York: Modern Library, 1984), 444.

30　**"planters systematically sealed":** Ira Berlin, *Many Thousands Gone: The First Two Centuries of Slavery in North America* (Cambridge, Mass.: Harvard University Press, 1998), 360. The preceding paragraph draws on Stanley L. Engerman, Richard Sutch, and Gavin Wright, "Slavery," in *Historical Statistics of the United States* (Cambridge, U.K.: Cambridge University Press, 2000).

30　**"no slave dare leave":** Charles Ball, *Fifty Years in Chains* (1836; repr., Mineola, N.Y.: Dover, 1970), 98.

30　**"out of the house or plantation":** South Carolina code, quoted in Andrew Frede, *People Without Rights: An Interpretation of the Fundamentals of the Law of Slavery in the U.S. South* (New York: Garland, 1992), 65.

30　**"flakes of flesh":** Ball, *Fifty Years in Chains,* 238.

31　**"a field lately ploughed":** William Grimes, *Life of William Grimes, the Runaway Slave* (1825; 1855), ed. William L. Andrews and Regina E. Mason (Oxford: Oxford University Press, 2008), 65, 103.

32　**"offering to hunt down slaves":** Frederick Douglass, "Speech at Finsbury Chapel, Moorfields, England, May 2, 1846," in *My Bondage and My Freedom,* ed. David W. Blight (New Haven, Conn.: Yale University Press, 2014), 332.

32　**"made a business":** Olmsted, *Cotton Kingdom,* 387.

32　**fled into woods or swamps:** Sylviane A. Diouf, *Slavery's Exiles: The Story of the American Maroons* (New York: New York University Press, 2014), 38.

33　**"The old doctrine":** Douglass, *My Bondage and My Freedom,* ed. Blight, 77.

33　**"iron collar [was] riveted":** Henry Bibb, *Narrative of the Life and Adventures of Henry Bibb* (1849), in *Slave Narratives,* ed. William L. Andrews and Henry Louis Gates Jr. (New York: Library of America, 2000), 497–98; William J. Switala, *Underground Railroad in Pennsylvania* (Mechanicsburg, Pa.: Stackpole Books, 2008), 22–23.

33　**In order to prepare himself:** Grimes, *Life of William Grimes,* 40, 56.

33 **To witness this world:** See the description of Rosedown plantation in the Feliciana Parish of Louisiana, in *The Garden Diary of Martha Turnbull, Mistress of Rosedown Plantation,* ed. Suzanne Turner (Baton Rouge: Louisiana State University Press, 2012), xi, 229.

34 **"run down and attacked":** Johnson, *River of Dark Dreams,* 242.

34 **"would rather be shot":** Olmsted, *Cotton Kingdom,* 121.

34 **"owners don't mind":** Olmsted, *Cotton Kingdom,* 388.

34 **In the Great Dismal Swamp:** Olmsted, *Cotton Kingdom,* 160*ff.*

34 **better prospects for escape:** William J. Switala, *Underground Railroad in Delaware, Maryland, and West Virginia* (Mechanicsburg, Pa.: Stackpole Books, 2004), 74.

34 **"We could see no spot":** Frederick Douglass, *Narrative of the Life of Frederick Douglass, an American Slave, Written by Himself,* ed. Benjamin Quarles (Cambridge, Mass.: Harvard University Press, 1960), 118.

35 **"under the pretext":** Bibb, *Narrative,* 474.

35 **Slave owners sometimes sent:** Hank Trent, introduction to *Narrative of James Williams, an American Slave* (1838), ed. Hank Trent (Baton Rouge: Louisiana State University Press, 2013), xiii.

35 **"liable to be sold into slavery":** Oakes, *Scorpion's Sting,* 64.

35 **"very small business":** Quoted in John Barnwell, *Love of Order: South Carolina's First Secession Crisis* (Chapel Hill: University of North Carolina Press, 1982), 18.

36 **"Africa's poor sons and daughters":** Henrietta Lee to General David Hunter, July 20, 1864, in *The Women of the South in War Times,* ed. Matthew Page Andrews (Baltimore: Norman, Remington, 1920), 203.

36 **"setting at defiance all laws":** Charles Colcott Jones to Charles Colcott Jones Jr., June 12, 1854, in *The Children of Pride, vol. 1, Many Mansions,* ed. Robert Manson Myers (New York: Popular Library, 1972), 42.

36 **students who called themselves:** Smith, *On the Edge of Freedom,* 34.

37 **"yearning to bask":** Blight, *Passages to Freedom,* 240–41.

37 **They encountered hostility:** Smith, *On the Edge of Freedom,* 27.

37 **"It would be some consolation":** E. B. Dudley to Webster, May 4, 1850, in *Papers of Webster: Correspondence,* 7:82.

38 **"any person using language":** William Goodell, *The American Slave Code in Theory and Practice* (New York: American and Foreign Anti-slavery Society, 1853), 322–23.

38 **"a blot on the record":** These words were published retrospectively in 1862 by William Hemphill, minister of the Associate Reformed Presbyterian Church of Due West, South Carolina. Quoted in Robert McCluer Calhoon, *Political Moderation in America's First Two Centuries* (New York: Cambridge University Press, 2009), 229.

38 **Memoirs by former slaves:** Stanley Harrold, *The Abolitionists in the South, 1831–1861* (Lexington: University Press of Kentucky, 1995), 94–96.

39 **"Too lazy to scratch":** Bibb, *Narrative,* 443.

39 **how much fugitives were costing:** Campbell, *Slave Catchers,* 6.

39 **Some slave owners feared:** Oakes, in *Scorpion's Sting,* 33–34, describes an antislavery strategy whereby "the annual flight of slaves into the North, from Delaware to Missouri, would become a flood tide that southern masters would be unable to stop. The only way for Border State slaveholders to prevent a mass exodus of fugitives would be to sell off their slaves to the cotton states, or pack up and leave. But masters hoping to avoid the unprecedented insecurity of slavery in the Border States would be denied the option of carrying their slaves into the territories. Instead, each new territory would enter the Union as a free state. Meanwhile, the Border States—depleted of slaves and therefore slaveholders—would begin abolishing slavery on their own."

39 **"my own negroes are as happy":** *A Plantation Mistress on the Eve of the Civil War: The Diary of Keziah Goodwyn Hopkins Brevard, 1860–1861,* ed. John Hammond Moore (Columbia: University of South Carolina Press, 1993), 49.

39 **"Sweet is repose":** William J. Grayson, *Selected Poems by William J. Grayson* (New York: Neale, 1907), 135.

39 **"in spite of their defense":** Kenneth M. Stampp, *The Imperiled Union: Essays on the Background of the Civil War* (Oxford: Oxford University Press, 1980), 260.

40 **"strikingly peculiar" kind:** Abraham Lincoln, "Fragment on Pro-slavery Theology," Oct. 1, 1858, in *Collected Works of Lincoln,* 3:205.

40 **a prominent Louisiana physician:** Samuel A. Cartwright, *Diseases and Peculiarities of the Negro Race* in *The Cause of the South: Selections from "De Bow's Review," 1846–1867,* ed. Paul F. Paskoff and Daniel J. Wilson (Baton Rouge: Louisiana State University Press, 1982), 35, 34.

41 **"Many of the free":** "Speech of William Wells Brown," *National Anti-slavery Standard* (New York), May 26, 1860, 4. Brown delivered versions of this speech throughout the 1850s. See Ezra Greenspan, *William Wells Brown: An African-American Life* (New York: W. W. Norton, 2014), 168.

42 **"the gravest and most vital":** *Cong. Globe,* 30th Cong., 1st Sess., April 20, 1848, app., 501–4.

42   **For a growing number:** Oakes, *Scorpion's Sting*, 71.
42   **"People of any color":** Abraham Lincoln, "Annual Message to Congress," Dec. 1, 1862, in *Collected Works of Lincoln*, 5:535.

Chapter 2: Slavery and the Founders

43   **"resembled a slaughter house":** Grandin, *Empire of Necessity*, 39.
43   **one ship sailed:** Bernard Bailyn, "Considering the Slave Trade: History and Memory," *William and Mary Quarterly* 58, no. 1 (Jan. 2001): 246.
44   **vessels were equipped:** Marcus Rediker, *The Slave Ship: A Human History* (New York: Viking, 2007), 70.
44   **Almost all failed:** Historian Marcus Rediker notes two revolts, one off the Gold Coast in 1729, another off the Windward Coast in 1749, that resulted in destruction of the crew and escape of the slaves. Rediker, *Slave Ship*, 298.
44   **more than 90 percent:** Bailyn, "Considering the Slave Trade," 246, who cites David Eltis et al., *The Trans-Atlantic Slave Trade: A Database on CD-ROM* (Cambridge, U.K.: Cambridge University Press, 1999). The Eltis database has been updated and is available online: slavevoyages.org.
44   **The same witness spoke:** Rediker, *Slave Ship*, 16–18.
44   **at least a million human beings:** James Walvin, *Crossings: Africa, the Americas, and the Atlantic Slave Trade* (London: Reaktion Books, 2013), 9, 69, 82.
45   **came through such ports:** Fergus M. Bordewich, *Bound for Canaan: The Underground Railroad and the War for the Soul of America* (New York: HarperCollins, 2005), 20.
45   **majority were sent inland:** See Walvin, *Crossings*, 61–62.
45   **"replacement was cheaper":** Barnwell, *Love of Order*, 4.
45   **"unlike an imported slave":** George Fredrickson, *White Supremacy: A Comparative Study in American and South African History* (New York: Oxford University Press, 1981), 58.
46   **fitted with spiked collars:** See Museum of London Docklands 2014 exhibit as cited by Akhil Sharma, "London's Legacy in the Slave Trade," *New York Times*, June 13, 2014.
46   **"to raise a convenient party":** Christopher Tomlins, *Freedom Bound: Law, Labor, and Civic Identity in Colonizing English America* (Cambridge, U.K.: Cambridge University Press, 2010), 437.
46   **eligible for compensation:** Diouf, *Slavery's Exiles*, 29–30.
46   **nightly slave patrol:** See Grimes, *Life of William Grimes*, 71n52.
46   **"deserting slaves and wild beasts":** Lieutenant Governor William Bull, quoted in Diouf, *Slavery's Exile*, 9.
46   **"loudest yelps for liberty":** Samuel Johnson, *Taxation No Tyranny* (London: T. Cadell, 1775), 89.
47   **"no Christian can keep":** Quoted in Garry Wills, *Head and Heart: American Christianities* (New York: Penguin Press, 2007), 151.
47   **"to fight for ourselves":** Quoted in Ron Chernow, *Alexander Hamilton* (New York: Penguin, 2004), 122–23.
47   **"zealous for their own liberties":** Jefferson to Chastellux, Sept. 2, 1785, in *Papers of Thomas Jefferson*, 8:468, quoted in Annette Gordon-Reed and Peter S. Onuf, *"Most Blessed of the Patriarchs": Thomas Jefferson and the Empire of the Imagination* (New York: Liveright, 2016), 4.
48   **"*the Receiver is as bad*":** Benjamin Franklin, "A Conversation on Slavery, 26 January 1770," *Public Advertiser*, Jan. 30, 1770, founders.archives.gov/documents/Franklin/01-17-02-0019. In 1776, Jefferson was thirty-three, and Franklin was seventy.
48   **"in complaisance to Georgia":** Jefferson, quoted in Fehrenbacher, *Slaveholding Republic*, 17.
49   **"the southern states":** James Madison, June 17, 1788, in David Robertson, *Debates and Other Proceedings of the Convention of Virginia* (Richmond, 1805), 321–22.
49   **"Those who are taxed":** Dickinson, quoted in Bernard Bailyn, *The Ideological Origins of the American Revolution* (Cambridge, Mass.: Harvard University Press, 1967), 232–33.
49   **"they who have no property":** Hopkins, quoted in Oakes, *Scorpion's Sting*, 53.
49   **that "to hesitate":** Witherspoon, quoted in Charles Augustus Briggs, *American Presbyterianism* (New York: Charles Scribner's Sons, 1885), 351. Princeton in the 1760s was still known as the College of New Jersey. For Sawney, see Jeff Broadwater, *James Madison: A Son of Virginia and a Founder of the Nation* (Chapel Hill: University of North Carolina Press, 2012), 188.
49   **became shorthand for:** A scan of their surviving papers—both public and private—recently made possible by the Founders Online project of the National Archives, reveals hundreds of similar statements. See founders.archives.gov/.
49   **"is a human Creature":** Franklin, "Conversation on Slavery, 26 January 1770."
50   **"as well as I can expect":** Quoted in Edmund S. Morgan, *Benjamin Franklin* (New Haven, Conn.: Yale University Press, 2002), 105–6. See David Waldstreicher, *Runaway America: Benjamin Franklin, Slavery, and the American Revolution* (New York: Hill and Wang, 2004), 251n43. Peter apparently did not outlive

Franklin and thus was never freed. Waldstreicher writes that "[Franklin] owned a series of slaves between about 1735 and 1781 and never systematically divested himself of them" (xii–xiii).

50 **"a breeding Negro woman":** Carl van Doren, *Benjamin Franklin* (New York: Viking, 1952), 129. Franklin's last public act, in February 1790, was to sign a petition to Congress on behalf of the Pennsylvania Society for Promoting the Abolition of Slavery. See Walter Isaacson, *Benjamin Franklin: An American Life* (New York: Simon & Schuster, 2003), 465.

50 **inherited ten slaves:** Ron Chernow, *Washington: A Life* (New York: Penguin Press, 2010), 10.

50 **endowed with funds:** See Craig Wilder, *Ebony and Ivy: Race, Slavery, and the Troubled History of America's Universities* (New York: Bloomsbury, 2013).

50 **were slave owners:** On Mason, see Jeff Broadwater, *George Mason: Forgotten Founder* (Chapel Hill: University of North Carolina Press, 2006), 193–94. Broadwater writes that Mason "consistently voiced his disapproval of slavery" but did little if anything to address that disapproval, failing even to free his slaves upon his death (194). On Wilson, see Nicholas Pedersen, "Lost Founder: James Wilson in American Memory," *Yale Journal of Law and the Humanities* (Summer 2010): 273.

50 **fathered children by:** For a summary of current knowledge on the question of Jefferson's children and a bibliography of relevant sources, see "Thomas Jefferson and Sally Hemings: A Brief Account," monticello.org/site/plantation-and-slavery/thomas-jefferson-and-sally-hemings-brief-account. See also Annette Gordon-Reed, *Thomas Jefferson and Sally Hemings: An American Controversy* (Charlottesville: University Press of Virginia, 1997).

50 **"imperious necessity compels":** Washington to Tobias Lear, May 6, 1794, quoted in Chernow, *Washington,* 709.

50 **a commercial distillery:** For Washington's whiskey business, see mountvernon.org/the-estate-gardens /distillery/.

51 **confidential legal advice:** See Paul Finkelman, "The Kidnapping of John Davis and the Adoption of the Fugitive Slave Law of 1793," *Journal of Southern History* 56, no 3 (Aug. 1990): 397–422.

51 **the exact meaning:** Finkelman, *Imperfect Union,* 52–55.

51 **"before the expiration":** Lear to Washington, April 24, 1791, *Founders Online,* National Archives, last modified June 29, 2017, founders.archives.gov/documents/Washington/05-08-02-0099. Original source: *The Papers of George Washington, Presidential Series, Vol. 8, 22 March 1791–22 September 1791,* ed. Mark A. Mastromarino (Charlottesville: University Press of Virginia, 1999), 129–34. For the ambiguous language of the law, see Smith, *On the Edge of Freedom,* 42. For Stevens's role in *Butler v. Delaplaine,* see Hans L. Trefousse, *Thaddeus Stevens: Nineteenth-Century Egalitarian* (Chapel Hill: University of North Carolina Press, 1997), 14.

51 **"yourself and Mrs. Washington":** Erica Armstrong Dunbar, "George Washington, Slave Catcher," *New York Times,* Feb. 16, 2015.

51 **"fat and lusty":** Quoted in Chernow, *Washington,* 110.

52 **"mulatto girl, much freckled":** Erica Armstrong Dunbar, *Never Caught: The Washingtons' Relentless Pursuit of Their Runaway Slave, Ona Judge* (New York: Atria, 2017), 111.

52 **"by nature slaves":** Aristotle, *Politics,* bk. 1, chaps. 3–7, *The Politics of Aristotle,* ed. Ernest Barker (Oxford: Oxford University Press, 1958), 8–18.

53 *"If a man strikes":* New American Standard translation.

53 **the Pauline Mandate:** Larry R. Morrison, "The Religious Defense of American Slavery Before 1830," *Journal of Religious Thought* 37, no. 2 (Fall 1980/Winter 1981): 19–20. See also Mark A. Noll, *The Civil War as a Theological Crisis* (Chapel Hill: University of North Carolina Press, 2006), 34–35.

53 **"If domestic slavery":** *National Intelligencer,* as quoted in the *Richmond Enquirer,* Dec. 3, 1819, in Morrison, "Religious Defense of American Slavery Before 1830," 23.

53 **"the whole divine revelation":** Quoted in Noll, *Civil War as a Theological Crisis,* 40.

53 **"the lord of that slave":** New American Standard translation.

54 **Jesuit priests sold:** For Georgetown's involvement in the slave trade, see the recently established Georgetown Slavery Archive, led by historian Adam Rothman: adamrothman.georgetown.domains/gsa/.

54 **early American Protestants:** Winthrop D. Jordan, *White over Black: American Attitudes Towards the Negro, 1550–1812* (Chapel Hill: University of North Carolina Press, 1968), 300.

54 **"one of the crying sins":** Danbury Town Meeting, 1774, cited in Jordan, *White over Black,* 299.

54 **"we hear no more":** Phillis Wheatley, "On the Death of the Rev. Mr. George Whitefield," *Poems on Various Subjects* (1773), in *Early American Writings,* ed. Carla Mulford (Oxford: Oxford University Press, 2002), 891. Jefferson was impressed by Wheatley's piety but judged her poetry to be "below the dignity of criticism." Jefferson, "Query XIV," *Notes on the State of Virginia,* 267.

54 **Whitefield had decided:** See Carla Gardina Pestana, "Whitefield and Empire," in *George Whitefield: Life, Context, and Legacy,* ed. Geordan Hammond and David Ceri Jones (Oxford: Oxford University Press,

2016). Pestana writes, "[Whitefield's] efforts to improve the slave's plight while leaving them as chattel located him in the Anglican mainstream, but unlike many other clergymen who also accepted slavery while demanding amelioration, Whitefield personally held numerous slaves. Bethesda, the orphanage he started and owned (and for which he raised large sums), eventually invested heavily in slave labour, which Whitefield saw as the only way to make it solvent. He advocated for the legalization of slavery in the colony" (94).

54 **"cared less about slaves":** Wills, *Head and Heart*, 107. For a nuanced discussion of Edwards's views on slavery (like Jefferson, he opposed the African slave trade), see Kenneth S. Minkema, "Jonathan Edwards's Defense of Slavery," *Massachusetts Historical Review* 4 (2002): 23–59.

55 **"some form of unfreedom":** Grandin, *Empire of Necessity*, 7. See also Richard Beeman, *Plain, Honest Men: The Making of the American Constitution* (New York: Random House, 2010), 311, who writes that "slavery was part of the normal fabric not only of American life, but of life as most humans on the earth had known it."

55 **"My wife caused Prue":** William Byrd, *The Great American Gentleman, William Byrd of Westover in Virginia: His Secret Diary for the Years 1709–1712*, ed. Louis B. Wright and Marion Tinling (New York: G. P. Putnam's Sons, 1963), 229.

55 **"a living tool":** Aristotle, *Nicomachean Ethics*, bk. 8, chap. 11, *Nicomachean Ethics*, ed. David Ross (London: Oxford University Press, 1971), 212.

56 **"degenerating sense of 'nobodiness'":** Martin Luther King Jr., "Letter from Birmingham Jail," in *Why We Can't Wait* (New York: Signet Classic, 2000), 70.

56 **"I was reconciled":** Byrd, *Great American Gentleman*, 230.

56 **"those who labour":** Jefferson, "Query XIX," *Notes on the State of Virginia*, 290.

57 **"hunger, thirst, frost":** Gottlieb Mittelberger, quoted in Richard Hofstadter, *America at 1750: A Social Portrait* (New York: Vintage, 1973), 38.

57 **"lure children with sweets":** Hofstadter, *America at 1750*, 36.

57 **"groan beneath a worse":** Hofstadter, *America at 1750*, 46.

58 **experience of a servant:** John Van Der Zee, *Bound Over: Indentured Servitude and American Conscience* (New York: Simon & Schuster, 1985), 33.

58 **"neither read a letter":** Henry Melchior Muhlenberg, *Notebook of a Colonial Clergyman*, ed. Theodore G. Tappert and John W. Doberstein (Philadelphia: Fortress Press, 1959), 117.

58 **scale of exploitation:** Society for the Reformation of Juvenile Delinquents in the City of New-York, *Tenth Annual Report* (1835), 16, quoted in Austin Reed, *The Life and the Adventures of a Haunted Convict*, ed. Caleb Smith (New York: Random House, 2016), xxvi. Reed's narrative of his incarceration was written in the late 1850s and rediscovered at an estate sale in Rochester, New York, in 2009. See Reed, *Life and Adventures of a Haunted Convict*, 219.

58 **"be treated as":** Quoted in Caleb Smith, "Editors' Introduction," in Reed, *Life and Adventures of a Haunted Convict*, xxvi.

58 **to risk punishment:** Hofstadter, *America at 1750*, 55.

59 **"third best hat":** Nathaniel Hawthorne, "My Kinsman, Major Molineux" (1831), in *Hawthorne: Tales and Sketches* (New York: Library of America, 1982), 73.

59 **"Ran away from":** Quoted in Van Der Zee, *Bound Over*, 354.

59 **longer terms of servitude:** See Hofstadter, *America at 1750*, 54.

60 **"practices of unfreedom":** David Waldstreicher, *Slavery's Constitution: From Revolution to Ratification* (New York: Hill and Wang, 2009), 28. For the prevalence of flogging as a household norm, see Philip Greven, *The Protestant Temperament: Patterns of Child-Rearing, Religious Experience, and the Self in Early America* (New York: Knopf, 1977), esp. 278–80. For the shower bath, see Reed, *Life and Adventures of a Haunted Convict*, 201–3.

60 **"hierarchy of dependencies":** Gordon S. Wood, *The Radicalism of the American Revolution* (New York: Knopf, 2009), 186.

60 **"Who aint a slave?":** Herman Melville, *Moby-Dick* (1850; repr., Evanston, Ill.: Northwestern University Press, 1988), 6.

60 **"It is common":** Douglass, "Speech at Finsbury Chapel, Moorfields, England, May 2, 1846," 330.

61 **Whether racist ideas:** See Oscar Handlin and Mary F. Handlin, "The Origin of the Southern Labor System," *William and Mary Quarterly* 7, no. 2 (April 1950): 199–222.

61 **"Cursed be Canaan":** Ancient as well as modern commentators have disputed whether Ham's transgression might have been more than looking upon his father's genitals. Some believe he might have mocked Noah publicly, or had sexual contact with him, or even castrated him. See, for example, Frederick W. Bassett, "Noah's Nakedness and the Curse of Canaan : A Case of Incest?," *Vetus Testamentum* 21, no. 2 (1971): 232–37.

62 **"criterion for categorizing":** David M. Goldenberg, *The Curse of Ham: Race and Slavery in Early Judaism, Christianity, and Islam* (Princeton, N.J.: Princeton University Press, 2005), 200.

62 **"intermediate species between":** Thomas F. Gossett, *Race: The History of an Idea in America* (New York: Oxford University Press, 1997), 48. For a contemporary example of racist physiology, see also Cartwright, *Diseases and Peculiarities of the Negro Race in the Cause of the South.*

62 **"Negro barely outranking":** W. E. B. Du Bois, "The Concept of Race (1940)," in *The Oxford W. E. B. Du Bois Reader,* ed. Eric J. Sundquist (New York: Oxford University Press, 1996), 77.

63 **"monstrosities between man":** Hitler, *Mein Kampf,* quoted in William L. Shirer, *The Rise and Fall of the Third Reich* (New York: Simon & Schuster, 1960), 118. See David Levering Lewis, *W. E. B. Du Bois: Biography of a Race, 1868–1919* (New York: Henry Holt, 1993), who writes that Du Bois understood that "in the final analysis, anti-Semitism was the German analogue of American color prejudice" (600).

63 **"black women over":** Jefferson, "Query XIV," *Notes on the State of Virginia,* 265.

63 **two distinct lines:** Jefferson admired the work of the Scottish philosopher Lord Kames, who tried to reconcile the biblical story of Adam and Eve as progenitors of all mankind with the putative evidence that blacks were a separate species. See Bruce Dain, *A Hideous Monster of the Mind: American Race Theory in the Early Republic* (Cambridge, Mass.: Harvard University Press, 2002), 35–36.

63 **"slaves had no souls":** *Life of James Mars, a Slave Born and Sold in Connecticut. Written by Himself* (Hartford, 1864), repr. in *I Was Born a Slave: An Anthology of Classic Slave Narratives,* ed. Yuval Taylor (Chicago: Lawrence Hill Books, 1999), 726.

63 **"Their natural faculties":** Hamilton to Jay, Middlebrook, N.J., March 14, 1779, in *The Papers of Alexander Hamilton,* ed. Harold C. Syrett and Jacob E. Cooke (New York: Columbia University Press, 1961), 2:17–18.

64 **"nature of slavery":** Benjamin Franklin, "Observations Concerning the Increase of Mankind," in *The Papers of Benjamin Franklin,* ed. Leonard W. Labaree (New Haven, Conn.: Yale University Press, 1959–), 4:225–34. See also Waldstreicher, *Runaway America,* 271n40.

64 **"so convenient a thing":** Benjamin Franklin, *The Autobiography of Benjamin Franklin* (New Haven, Conn.: Yale University Press, 1964), 88.

64 **"Give me Liberty":** It is not known whether Henry ever actually uttered those words, attributed to him by William Wirt, *Sketches of the Life and Character of Patrick Henry* (Philadelphia, 1817), 123.

64 **"Inconveniency of living":** Henry to Robert Pleasants, Jan. 18, 1773, quoted in Waldstreicher, *Slavery's Constitution,* 42.

Chapter 3: A Compromised Constitution

65 **"States were divided":** Max Farrand, ed., *The Records of the Federal Convention of 1787* (New Haven, Conn.: Yale University Press, 1937), 1:486, quoted in Finkelman, *Imperfect Union,* 23.

65 **By the 1780s, the number of slaves:** For an account of black population distribution in the North, see Berlin, *Many Thousands Gone,* 47–63.

65 **slaves had declined since the 1760s:** Eric Foner, *Tom Paine and Revolutionary America* (New York: Oxford University Press, 1976), 44.

66 **If a northern gentleman:** For a thorough study of New England's long involvement with slavery, see Wendy Warren, *New England Bound: Slavery and Colonization in Early America* (New York: Liveright, 2016).

66 **"S is the sugar":** Hannah Townsend and Mary Townsend, *The Anti-slavery Alphabet,* quoted in *American Antislavery Writings: Colonial Beginnings to Emancipation* (New York: Library of America, 2012), 486.

66 **twenty-five owned slaves:** Beeman, *Plain, Honest Men,* 67, 309.

66 **Franklin denounced slavery:** See Waldstreicher, *Runaway America,* 251n43.

66 **Hamilton had married:** See Chernow, *Alexander Hamilton,* 210.

66 **"web of slavery":** James McBride, *The Good Lord Bird* (New York: Riverhead Books, 2013), 172.

67 **"the intermediate state":** Aristotle, *Nicomachean Ethics,* bk. 2, chap. 9, p. 47. Aristotle defined courage, for instance, as a quality that lies between the excess of rashness and the deficiency of cowardice (bk. 2, chap. 9, p. 44).

67 **"better instructed themselves":** John Locke, *An Essay Concerning Human Understanding,* bk. 4, chap. 16, sec. 4. (London: Dent, 1961), 2:255.

67 **called "temperate liberty":** The phrase is from "Query VIII," *Notes on the State of Virginia,* 211. Jefferson opposes the middle state of "temperate liberty" to the extremes of "absolute monarchy" and "unbounded licentiousness."

67 **"stoop" in humility:** Franklin to Samuel Mather (Cotton Mather's son), May 12, 1784, in *Benjamin Franklin: Representative Selections,* ed. Chester E. Jorgenson and Frank Luther Mott (New York: Hill and Wang, 1962), 472.

67–68 **"founded on compromise":** Quoted in Avishai Margalit, *On Compromise and Rotten Compromises* (Princeton, N.J.: Princeton University Press, 2010), 12.

68 **the "prudent mean":** Hamilton used the phrase "prudent mean" in several contexts. In Federalist No. 65, for example, he described the impeachment procedure as prescribed by the Constitution, whereby judicial power is located in the Senate presided over by the chief justice. Hamilton described this arrangement as a "prudent mean" between the court itself sitting in judgment of the accused or combining the court with the Senate as a sort of super-tribunal. The "prudent mean" was to vest judicial power in the Senate presided over by the chief justice, thereby combining court and legislature in cases where the executive is charged with overstepping the bounds of his office. See *The Federalist,* ed. Jacob E. Cooke (Middletown, Conn.: Wesleyan University Press, 1961), 443.

68   **would be bicameral:** For a lucid account of how electing congressional representatives from districts rather than by statewide vote has undermined proportional representation, see Elizabeth Kolbert, "Drawing the Line," *New Yorker,* June 27, 2016, 68–71.

68   **"curse of heaven":** Aug. 8, 1787, in Farrand, *Records of the Federal Convention of 1787,* 2:221.

68   **"half of mankind":** Aug. 22, 1787, in Farrand, *Records of the Federal Convention of 1787,* 2:371. This is Charles Pinckney (1757–1824), who introduced the fugitive slave clause along with Pierce Butler and who would later become governor of South Carolina, not to be confused with his older cousin Charles Cotesworth Pinckney (1746–1825), also known as General Pinckney, who was also in attendance at the convention.

68   **"I wish from my soul":** Quoted in Fehrenbacher, *Slaveholding Republic,* 206.

69   **"tremble for my country":** Jefferson, "Query XVIII," *Notes on the State of Virginia,* 289.

69   **"stopping the importations":** Aug. 22, 1787, in Farrand, *Records of the Federal Convention of 1787,* 2:371. Curtailing the slave trade was as likely to be prompted by concern to slow the growth of the black population and to "protect the home market" as by any moral considerations. See William Lee Miller, *Arguing About Slavery* (New York: Knopf, 1996), 181. Miller is writing specifically about the exclusion of the foreign slave trade from Louisiana in 1804 under President Jefferson.

69   **"curious silence to explain":** Waldstreicher, *Slavery's Constitution,* 9.

69   **"hid slavery away":** Abraham Lincoln, "Speech at Peoria, Illinois," Oct. 16, 1854, in *Collected Works of Lincoln,* 2:274.

70   **"covenant with death":** Manisha Sinha, *The Slave's Cause: A History of Abolition* (New Haven, Conn.: Yale University Press, 2016), 471.

70   **"If in its origin":** Frederick Douglass, "Should the Negro Enlist in the Union Army?," July 6, 1863, quoted in *Frederick Douglass: Selected Speeches and Writings,* ed. Philip S. Foner and Yuval Taylor (Chicago: Lawrence Hill Books, 1999), 536.

70   **Constitution certainly protected it:** Some scholars have discerned the presence and pressure of slavery in several other articles and clauses of the Constitution as well (David Waldstreicher, in *Slavery's Constitution,* enumerates eleven)—in, for example, the prohibition of federal taxation on exports, which would protect the slave states; and in the "full faith and credit" clause of Article 4, which protected the slave states from federal intervention. The Tenth Amendment of the Bill of Rights—"the powers not delegated to the United States by the Constitution, nor prohibited by it to the States, are reserved to the States respectively, or to the people"—also implied that there could be no interference by the federal government in the institution of slavery short of constitutional amendment. For a subtle account of how the Constitution both tolerated and undermined slavery, see Sean Wilentz, *No Property in Men: Slavery and Antislavery at the Nation's Founding* (Cambridge, Mass.: Harvard University Press, 2018).

70   **"never receive the plan":** Charles Pinckney, quoted in W. E. B. Du Bois, *The Suppression of the African Slave Trade* (1896; repr., Baton Rouge: Louisiana State University Press, 1969), 55.

70   **"a desert waste":** Pinckney, quoted in David O. Stewart, *The Summer of 1787: The Men Who Invented the Constitution* (New York: Simon & Schuster, 2007), 195. For the moratorium on importing slaves, see ibid.

70   **"Negroes were our wealth":** Rawlins Lowndes, quoted in Du Bois, *Suppression of the African Slave Trade,* 67–68.

71   **"laying the foundation":** Wilson, quoted in Finkelman, *Imperfect Union,* 25.

71   **"great was the disgust":** *Supplement to the New-York Legal Observer, Containing the Report of the Case of George Kirk, a Fugitive Slave, Heard Before the Hon. J. W. Edmonds, Circuit Judge. Also the Argument of John Jay, of Counsel for the Slave* (New York: Legal Observer Office, 1847), 17, reprinted in Finkelman, *Fugitive Slaves and American Courts: The Pamphlet Literature,* series 2, 1:334–35.

72   **It was achieved:** For the representation vs. taxation compromise, see Beeman, *Plain, Honest Men,* 154; Waldstreicher, *Slavery's Constitution,* 79.

72   **called "log-rolling":** Du Bois, *Suppression of the African Slave Trade,* 58.

72   **"assembly of demi-gods":** Jefferson to John Adams, Paris, Aug. 30, 1787, in *Thomas Jefferson: Writings* (New York: Library of America, 1984), 909.

73   **"We need not seek":** John André, "Suggestions for Regaining Dominion over the American Colonies," quoted in Benjamin Quarles, *The Negro in the American Revolution* (Chapel Hill: University of North Carolina Press, 1961), 112.

73   **matter of military strategy:** See David Brion Davis, *Inhuman Bondage: The Rise and Fall of Slavery in the New World* (New York: Oxford University Press, 2006), 150; and Christopher Leslie Brown, *Arming Slaves* (New Haven, Conn.: Yale University Press, 2006), 190.

73   **"slaves had been running away":** Quarles, *Negro in the American Revolution*, 115.

73   **"whatever loyalty there was":** Robert Middlekauff, *The Glorious Cause: The American Revolution, 1763–1789* (New York: Oxford University Press, 1982), 316.

73   **"impress the minds":** Quoted in Robert G. Parkinson, *The Common Cause: Creating Race and Nation in the American Revolution* (Chapel Hill: University of North Carolina Press, 2016), 400–401. Parkinson documents how colonial newspapers were filled with reports of "traitorous" slaves fighting for the British, while scarcely reporting the fact that "there were hundreds of African Americans and Indian soldiers serving under Washington's command" (528).

74   **Some modern historians:** Eric Foner, *The Story of American Freedom* (New York: W. W. Norton, 1998), 34.

74   **"largest unknown slave rebellion":** Sinha, *Slave's Cause*, 51; the phrasing is Sinha's, but she attributes the idea to Gary B. Nash, *The Unknown American Revolution: The Unruly Birth of Democracy and the Struggle to Create America* (New York: Penguin Press, 2005), 339, 435. For discussion of the estimate, see Cassandra Pybus, "Jefferson's Faulty Math: The Question of Slave Defections in the American Revolution," *William and Mary Quarterly* 62, no. 2 (April 2005): 243–64.

74   **"haven for fugitive slaves":** Foner, *Gateway to Freedom*, 34.

74   **"flocked to the Enemy":** Robert Honyman (May 11, 1781), quoted in Parkinson, *Common Cause*, 509.

74   **"vast Concourse of runaway":** Josiah Parker to Marquis de Lafayette, Aug. 19, 1781, quoted in Parkinson, *Common Cause*, 517.

75   **a bloody and brutal war:** For an extended account of violence and brutality on both sides of the Revolution, see Holger Hoock, *Scars of Independence: America's Violent Birth* (New York: Crown, 2017).

75   **"Slaves which have absconded":** Washington to Harrison, May 6, 1783, quoted in Schama, *Rough Crossings*, 149.

75   **"piece of injustice":** Letter of Thomas Walke, May 3, 1783, National Archives, research.archives.gov /id/2441090.

75   **condemned his inaction as "scandalous":** Madison to Jefferson, May 13, 1783, founders.archives.gov /documents/Jefferson/01-06-02-0247.

76   **Hamilton had seen:** Chernow, *Alexander Hamilton*, 11, 19–20.

76   **"In the interpretation of treaties":** Alexander Hamilton, "The Defence No. III," July 29, 1795, in *Papers of Alexander Hamilton*, 18:519, quoted in Chernow, *Alexander Hamilton*, 213. Hamilton was a member of the New York Manumission Society, but there is no record of his having spoken on the slavery issue at the Constitutional Convention.

76   **Congress tried nevertheless:** Fehrenbacher, *Slaveholding Republic*, 25.

76   **failure to resolve:** Fehrenbacher, *Slaveholding Republic*, 25.

76   **would be "cruelly perfidious":** John Jay, "Report to Congress," Oct. 13, 1786, quoted in Fehrenbacher, *Slaveholding Republic*, 26.

77   **"No price can compensate":** Jay, "Report to Congress," Oct. 13, 1786, quoted in Fehrenbacher, *Slaveholding Republic*, 26.

77   **these future states:** There were several recent precedents for the prohibition, which Jefferson had favored in an earlier (1784) ordinance for territorial government that he had proposed but was never enacted. See Peter S. Onuf, *Statehood and Union: A History of the Northwest Ordinance* (Bloomington: Indiana University Press, 1987), 110.

78   **"asylums for the oppressed":** Timothy Pickering to Rufus King (1785), quoted in Stewart, *Summer of 1787*, 146.

78   **"New England settlers":** Dane to Daniel Webster, March 26, 1830, quoted in Stewart, *Summer of 1787*, 146.

78   **while permitting them:** Stewart, *Summer of 1787*, 145–49.

79   **"property in slaves":** Aug. 8, 1787, in Farrand, *Records of the Federal Convention of 1787*, 2:443.

79   **moved to add a phrase:** Aug. 8, 1787, in Farrand, *Records of the Federal Convention of 1787*, 2:443.

79   **"If any Person":** Beeman, *Plain, Honest Men*, 330.

80   **southern delegates gave up:** See Stewart, *Summer of 1787*, 173.

80   **"most successful horse-trades":** William M. Wiecek, *The Sources of Antislavery Constitutionalism in America, 1760–1848* (Ithaca, N.Y.: Cornell University Press, 1977), 79.

81   **"virtually no discussion":** Fehrenbacher, *Slaveholding Republic*, 36. For the process by which the final language was arrived at, see also Gordon Lloyd, *Day-by-Day Summary of the Convention*, teachingamericanhistory.org/convention/summary/.

81   **"speedy, even collegial":** Beeman, *Plain, Honest Men*, 332.

81   **"if any servant":** Quoted in Wiecek, *Sources of Antislavery Constitutionalism in America*, 78.

82 **"Were they not restrained"**: John Adams to John Quincy Adams, Jan. 8, 1805, *National Archives Online*, founders.archives.gov/documents/Adams/99-03-02-1374.

82 **"Whatever may be"**: William Tilghman, *Wright v. Deacon* (Pennsylvania Superior Court, 1819), quoted in Steven Lubet, *Fugitive Justice: Runaways, Rescuers, and Slavery on Trial* (Cambridge, Mass.: Harvard University Press, 2010), 24–25.

82 **"The distracting question"**: Edward Coles, *History of the Ordinance of 1787* (Historical Society of Pennsylvania, 1856), 28–29.

83 **"The first clause"**: Benton, *Thirty Years' View*, 2:773.

83 **latter logically required**: See Onuf, *Statehood and Union*, 110–11.

83 **a few grumbles**: Fehrenbacher writes that "the subject did not even arise in the Constitutional Convention until two weeks before adjournment." *Slaveholding Republic*, 207.

83 **language of command**: Fehrenbacher, *Slaveholding Republic*, 208.

83 **"The right to recover"**: Benton, *Thirty Years' View*, 2:773.

84 **he doubted it**: Thomas Hart Benton, "Speech at St. Louis," Nov. 9, 1850, reported in the *Brattleboro (Vt.) Semi-weekly Eagle*, Nov. 21, 1850.

84 **"really willing to take the risk"**: Beeman, *Plain, Honest Men*, 332.

Chapter 4: The First Test

85 **"we would have made"**: "Speech in South Carolina House of Representatives, January 1788," in Farrand, ed., *Records of the Federal Convention of 1787*, 3:254–55.

85 **"the federal consensus"**: See Wiecek, *Sources of Antislavery Constitutionalism in America*, 15–16.

86 **"The biggest problem"**: James Oakes, *Freedom National: The Destruction of Slavery in the United States, 1861–1865* (New York: W. W. Norton, 2013), xi.

86 **"no power is given"**: Quoted in Wiecek, *Sources of Antislavery Constitutionalism in America*, 82.

86 **"interfere in the emancipation"**: Quoted in Fehrenbacher, *Slaveholding Republic*, 139. See also James G. Basker, ed., *Early American Abolitionists: A Collection of Anti-slavery Writings, 1760–1820* (New York: Gilder Lehrman Institute, 2005), 217–20.

86 **"deny[ing] the fact"**: "Federalist No. 54," in *Federalist*, 367–68.

87 **"dispersing unlawful Assemblies"**: The quoted phrase is from a 1741 North Carolina law, cited in Andrew Fede, *People Without Rights: An Interpretation of the Fundamentals of the Law of Slavery in the U.S. South* (New York: Garland, 1992), 64. For a succinct summary of eighteenth-century criminal law concerning slaves, see Mark V. Tushnet, *Slave Law in the American South: State v. Mann in History and Literature* (Lawrence: University Press of Kansas, 2003), esp. chap. 1. See also Fede, *People Without Rights*, 161.

87 **mobs were free**: Martha Hodes, *White Women, Black Men: Illicit Sex in the 19th-Century South* (New Haven, Conn.: Yale University Press, 1997), 60; Eugene Genovese, *Roll, Jordan, Roll: The World the Slaves Made* (New York: Vintage, 1972), 33–34.

88 **In one much-publicized case**: Genovese, *Roll, Jordan, Roll*, 34; Fede, *People Without Rights*, 66–67.

88 **no records exist**: Melton A. McLaurin, *Celia, a Slave: A True Story* (Athens: University of Georgia Press, 1991), 113.

88 **a female slave in Missouri**: McLaurin, *Celia, a Slave*, 107–9.

88 **"force, menace, or duress"**: Section 29, Article 2, of the Missouri Statutes for 1845, quoted in McLaurin, *Celia, a Slave*, 107.

88 **"will-less and always willing"**: Saidiya Hartman, *Scenes of Subjection: Terror, Slavery, and Self-Making in Nineteenth-Century America* (New York: Oxford University Press, 1997), 80–81.

89 **"It would be wrong"**: Aug. 25, 1787, in Farrand, *Records of the Federal Convention of 1787*, 2:417. See also Noah Feldman, *The Three Lives of James Madison: Genius, Partisan, President* (New York: Random House, 2017), 164.

89 **"the positive enactments"**: Ronald M. Dworkin, "The Law of the Slave-Catchers" (1975), quoted in Christopher L. M. Eisgruber, "Justice Story, Slavery, and the Natural Law Foundations of American Constitutionalism," *University of Chicago Law Review* 55, no. 1 (Winter 1988): 289.

89 ***"municipal laws of countries"***: John Locke, *Second Treatise of Government* (1689), chap. 2, sec. 12, ed. C. B. Macpherson (Indianapolis: Hackett, 1980), 12.

89 **"repugnant to reason"**: Quoted in Robert M. Cover, *Justice Accused: Antislavery and the Judicial Process* (New Haven, Conn.: Yale University Press, 1975), 15.

90 **"compel the slave"**: Quoted in Wiecek, *Sources of Antislavery Constitutionalism*, 34.

90 **"The state of slavery"**: William M. Wiecek, "Somerset: Lord Mansfield and the Legitimacy of Slavery in the Anglo-American World," *University of Chicago Law Review* 42 (1975): 86–87. Wiecek notes that the text of the decision was recorded by a young English lawyer named Capel Lofft and that several variants

exist. According to Wiecek, the Lofft report is the most reliable and legitimate and is thus "more acceptable to the historian than its competitors" (145). For a comprehensive discussion of the controversy surrounding the reported decision, see ibid., 141–46.

90   **"there had been no determination":** Mansfield to Thomas Hutchinson, quoted in Wiecek, *Sources of Antislavery Constitutionalism*, 34.

91   **"generally felt as putting":** Arthur Lee to Joseph Reed, Feb. 18, 1773, in William B. Reed, ed., *Life and Correspondence of Joseph Reed*, 2 vols. (Philadelphia, 1847), 1:48, quoted in Christopher Leslie Brown, *Moral Capital: Foundations of British Abolitionism* (Chapel Hill: University of North Carolina Press, 2006), 117–18.

91   **"Slaves cannot breathe":** William Cowper, "The Task," bk. 2 (1785), in *Cowper: Poetical Works*, ed. H. S. Milford (London: Oxford University Press, 1967), 147.

91   **ebullience was premature:** See Wiecek, *Sources of Antislavery Constitutionalism*, 32. For the ambiguous condition of British blacks in the late eighteenth century, see Brown, *Moral Capital*, 284–85.

91   **"Hypocrisy" of Great Britain:** Quoted in Brown, *Moral Capital*, 118.

91   **"I am a citizen":** Quoted in Bordewich, *Bound for Canaan*, 51. Also in Lydia Maria Child, *Isaac T. Hopper: A True Life* (Boston, 1853), 100.

91   **loosely linked group:** Bordewich, *Bound for Canaan*, 30.

92   **"residence on free soil":** Thomas D. Morris, *Free Men All: The Personal Liberty Laws of the North, 1780–1861* (Baltimore: Johns Hopkins University Press, 1974), 13.

93   **"we have an oracle":** John Cotton, *A Practicall Commentary, or an Exposition with Observations, Reasons and Uses upon the First Epistle General of John* (London: 1654), 167.

93   **"New England Conscience":** See Austin Warren, *The New England Conscience* (Ann Arbor: University of Michigan Press, 1966).

93   **drenched in moralistic self-delight:** Foner, *Gateway to Freedom*, 37.

93   **"tinge of crimson":** *Witness to Sorrow: The Antebellum Autobiography of William J. Grayson*, ed. Richard J. Calhoun (Columbia: University of South Carolina Press, 1990), 154.

94   **"hyena in human shape":** C. R. Fontaine, quoted in Matthew Karp, *This Vast Southern Empire*, p. 8.

94   **"intolerant and turbulent spirit":** J. Henly Smith to Alexander H. Stephens, Washington, April 3, 1860, Alexander H. Stephens Papers, Library of Congress.

94   **"Emerson and Beecher":** Diary of Daniel Robinson Hundley, Aug. 1864, in *Prison Echoes of the Great Rebellion* (New York: S. W. Green, 1874), 109. I owe this reference to Matthew Fernandez.

94   **"the property which every man has":** Quoted in Oakes, *Scorpion's Sting*, 60.

94   **"warm halls of the heart":** Herman Melville, *Pierre; or, The Ambiguities* (1852), ed. Harrison Hayford, Hershel Parker, and G. Thomas Tanselle (Evanston, Ill.: Northwestern University Press, 1971), 71.

94   **"what law should be":** Cover, *Justice Accused*, 17.

94   **"slavery in time":** Ellsworth, quoted in Beeman, *Plain, Honest Men*, 325.

95   **"There were probably few members":** Du Bois, *Suppression of the African Slave Trade*, 62.

95   **"a Negro not younger":** Jones to Madison, Nov. 18, 1780, *Founders Online*, National Archives, last modified June 29, 2017, founders.archives.gov/documents/Madison/01-02-02-0108. Original source: *The Papers of James Madison*, ed. William T. Hutchinson and William M. E. Rachal, 17 vols. (Chicago: University of Chicago Press, 1962–1991), 2:182–85.

95   **"Would it not be as well":** Madison to Jones, Nov. 28, 1780, *Founders Online*, National Archives, last modified June 29, 2017, founders.archives.gov/documents/Madison/01-02-02-0120. Original source: *Papers of Madison*, 2:209–11.

96   **"proclaim instant freedom":** "Letter to John Adams, from Fredericksburg, VA, June 9, 1775," quoted in Parkinson, *Common Cause*, 100.

96   **"engage in the marine service":** Quoted in Fehrenbacher, *Slaveholding Republic*, 19.

96   **greeted by "contemptuous huzzas":** Jordan, *White over Black*, 302.

96   **"We are much disgusted":** Christopher Gadsden to Samuel Adams, July 6, 1779, quoted in Fehrenbacher, *Slaveholding Republic*, 20.

96   **"The policy of our arming":** Washington to Laurens, March 20, 1779, in *Writings of George Washington from the Original Manuscript Sources*, 14:267.

97   **"at least subconsciously aware":** Charles Grier Sellers Jr., "The Travail of Slavery," in *The Southerner as American*, ed. Charles Grier Sellers (New York: E. P. Dutton, 1966), 44.

97   **the euphemistic language:** See Alan Taylor, *The Internal Enemy: Slavery and War in Virginia, 1772–1832* (New York: Norton, 2013), 225–26.

98   **"that the black color":** "Observations Intended to Favour a Supposition That the Black Color (as It Is Called) of the Negroes Is Derived from the Leprosy. Read at a Special Meeting July 14, 1797," *Transactions of the American Philosophical Society* 4 (1799): 289–97. In a letter to Jefferson of February 4, 1797, Rush called

his friend's attention to the hypothesis. See Rush to Jefferson, Feb. 4, 1797, in *The Papers of Thomas Jefferson, Vol. 29, 1 March 1796–31 December 1797,* ed. Barbara B. Oberg (Princeton, N.J.: Princeton University Press, 2002), 284.

98   **"A slaveholding nation":** David Brion Davis, *The Problem of Slavery in the Age of Revolution, 1770–1823* (Ithaca, N.Y.: Cornell University Press, 1975), 326.

98   **"I hate it":** Lincoln, "Speech at Peoria, Illinois," Oct. 16, 1854, in *Collected Works of Lincoln,* 2:255.

98   **"to extirpate this abomination":** Gudmestad, *Troublesome Commerce,* 124–25.

99   **After completing his term:** See Broadwater, *James Madison,* 188. See also Feldman, *Three Lives of James Madison,* 49–52.

100   **"I have judged":** James Madison to James Madison Sr., Sept. 8, 1783, *Founders Online,* National Archives, last modified June 29, 2017, founders.archives.gov/documents/Madison/01-07-02-0170. Original source: *Papers of Madison,* 7:304–5.

100   **"the ability to hold":** F. Scott Fitzgerald, *The Crack-Up* (New York: New Directions, 1956), 69.

100   **she was amazed:** See Harriet Martineau, *Retrospect of Western Travel* (London: William Clowes and Sons, 1838), 2:3–8.

101   **slave owner named Davis:** Finkelman, "Kidnapping of John Davis," 402.

102   **hired him out:** My account of the Davis case is heavily indebted to Finkelman, "Kidnapping of John Davis," 397–422. See also Harrold, *Border War,* 21–23.

102   **hired a team:** Finkelman, "Kidnapping of John Davis," 402.

102   **"assaulted, seized, imprisoned":** Harrold, *Border War,* 22.

102   **grand jury indicted:** An amendment and supplement to the law was passed March 29, 1788, that specifically outlawed transporting or otherwise "tak[ing] or carry[ing] . . . by force or violence . . . any negro or mulatto . . . with the design and intention of selling and disposing, or of causing to be sold, or of keeping and detaining, or of causing so to be, as a slave, or servant for term of years."

102   **"first interstate conflict":** Finkelman, "Kidnapping of John Davis," 402.

102   **"an authenticated copy":** Finkelman, "Kidnaping of John Davis," 405.

104   **Senate sent a bill:** Finkelman, "Kidnapping of John Davis," 411.

105   **"obstruct or hinder":** See Finkelman, "Kidnapping of John Davis," 417.

105   **"blessing" for slave owners:** Finkelman, "Kidnapping of John Davis," 416.

106   **signed the bill:** See Fehrenbacher, *Slaveholding Republic,* 213.

106   **required to advertise:** See Fehrenbacher, *Slaveholding Republic,* 213–14.

106   **"an intimate union":** Ralph Waldo Emerson, *Emerson in His Journals,* ed. Joel Porte (Cambridge, Mass.: Harvard University Press, 1982), 423.

Chapter 5: Caught

107   **told their stories to witnesses:** Charles Ball dictated his narrative, originally published as *Slavery in the United States: A Narrative of the Life and Adventures of Charles Ball, a Black Man,* to Isaac Fisher, a Pennsylvania attorney. Fisher writes in his preface to the 1837 edition that the printed narrative "does not retain the identical words of the original" but "faithfully preserve[s] . . . the sense and import" and attempts to present the story "as simple, and . . . as plain, as the laws of language would permit." *Fifty Years in Chains,* xix. On the identity of Isaac Fisher, see the introduction to that edition (iii).

107   **80 percent of fugitives:** John Hope Franklin and Loren Schweninger, *Runaway Slaves: Rebels on the Plantation* (New York: Oxford University Press, 1999), 212–24. Franklin and Schweninger base their estimate on runaway slave advertisements in Virginia, North Carolina, Tennessee, South Carolina, and Louisiana from the 1830s through the 1850s.

108   **some 10 percent:** David W. Blight, *A Slave No More: Two Men Who Escaped to Freedom, Including Their Own Narratives of Emancipation* (Boston: Mariner Books, 2007), 33.

108   **Probably he lived:** Gary Collison, *Shadrach Minkins: From Fugitive Slave to Citizen* (Cambridge, Mass.: Harvard University Press, 1997), 41–42.

108   **reward for returning:** Olivia Carlisle, "Trends in the Runaway Slave Advertisements," *N.C. Runaway Slave Advertisements, 1750–1840,* libcdm1.uncg.edu/cdm/trends/collection/RAS.

108   **"yellow complexion, has a scar":** *Carolina Federal Republican,* April 16, 1810, 4, libcdm1.uncg.edu/cdm/ref/collection/RAS/id/1869.

108   **"Slavery is not":** Ta-Nehisi Coates, *Between the World and Me* (New York: Spiegel & Grau, 2015), 69–70.

108   **She might have:** See Stephanie Cole, "Servants and Slaves: Domestic Service in the Border Cities, 1800–1850" (Ph.D. diss., University of Florida, 1994), 93. See also Josephine F. Pacheco, *The Pearl: A Failed Slave Escape on the Potomac* (Chapel Hill: University of North Carolina Press, 2005), 3.

109   **community of "maroons":** Diouf, *Slavery's Exiles,* 8–9, and throughout.

109 **had gone underground:** Gara, *Liberty Line, 30,* gives an example of an enslaved woman who had been hired out in Frankfort, Kentucky, and who, living with a free black barber, wrote to her master to say she had achieved freedom in Canada.

109 **"If we disappear":** John Bartlow Martin, "Butcher's Dozen & Other Murders," in *True Crime: An American Anthology,* ed. Harold Schechter (New York: Library of America, 2008), 464.

109 **population of free blacks:** In Washington, where runaways hid from the census takers, the population count was known to be especially unreliable. See Damani Davis, "Slavery and Emancipation in the Nation's Capital," *Prologue Magazine* 42, no. 1 (Spring 2010), archives.gov/publications/prologue/2010/spring /dcslavery.html. See also Mary Kay Ricks, *Escape on the Pearl: The Heroic Bid for Freedom on the Underground Railroad* (New York: HarperCollins, 2007), 259.

110 **Adopting a phrase:** The phrase "Era of Good Feelings" has been traced to Benjamin Russell, *Columbian Centinel,* July 12, 1817.

110 **a border war:** See Harrold, *Border War.*

110 **armed black men:** See Harrold, *Border War,* 25–27.

110 **assembled special battalions:** Taylor, *Internal Enemy,* 5.

110 **"all those who may be":** Quoted in Taylor, *Internal Enemy,* 211.

111 **"on no account":** Henry, Earl Bathurst (secretary of state for war and the colonies) to Thomas S. Beckwith (assistant quartermaster general to British forces in North America), March 20, 1813; Alexander Cochrane, "Proclamation," April 2, 1814; George R. Gleig, "Campaigns of the British Army at Washington and New Orleans, 1814–15," in *The War of 1812: Writings from America's Second War of Independence,* ed. Donald R. Hickey (New York: Library of America, 2013), 211–13, 424–25, 531.

111 **"the bare sight":** Lincoln to Andrew Johnson, March 26, 1863, in *Collected Works of Lincoln,* 6:149–50.

111 **"To the old folks":** Isabel Wilkerson, *The Warmth of Other Suns* (New York: Vintage Books, 2010), 57.

112 **motivation to flee:** Taylor, *Internal Enemy,* 6. For the inclusion of slaves along with land as property subject to primogeniture before the Revolution, see C. Ray Keim, "Primogeniture and Entail in Colonial Virginia," *William and Mary Quarterly* 25, no. 4 (Oct. 1968): 546.

112 **runaways were taken:** Bordewich, *Bound for Canaan,* 70*ff.*

113 **"an opportunistic peddler":** Jeffrey Ruggles, *The Unboxing of Henry Brown* (Richmond: Library of Virginia, 2003), 19.

113 **"of ruffians, moved by":** Levi Coffin, quoted in Bordewich, *Bound for Canaan,* 79.

113 **"The people of the north":** Douglass, *My Bondage and Freedom,* ed. Blight, 143.

114 **"a media scandal":** Edward E. Baptist, *The Half Has Never Been Told: Slavery and the Making of American Capitalism* (New York: Basic Books, 2014), 27.

115 **to "ferret out":** Quoted in Gudmestad, *Troublesome Commerce,* 36.

115 **"Madam, the Greeks":** William C. Bruce, *John Randolph of Roanoke, 1773–1833* (New York: Putnam's, 1922), 2:203. Decades later, in *Uncle Tom's Cabin,* Harriet Beecher Stowe used the contrast between a fugitive slave and a Hungarian freedom fighter to make the same point: "If it had been only a Hungarian youth, now bravely defending in some mountain fastness the retreat of fugitives escaping from Austria into America, this would have been sublime heroism; but as it was a youth of African descent, defending the retreat of fugitives through America into Canada, of course we are too well instructed and patriotic to see any heroism in it." Harriet Beecher Stowe, *Uncle Tom's Cabin; or, Life Among the Lowly* (1852), ed. Kenneth S. Lynn (Cambridge, Mass.: Harvard University Press, 1962), 203. Emerson, in his essay "Self-Reliance," stated the matter more briefly: "Thy love afar is spite at home." *The Collected Works of Ralph Waldo Emerson, vol. 2, Essays: First Series,* ed. Joseph Slater, Alfred R. Ferguson, and Jean Ferguson Carr (Cambridge, Mass.: Harvard University Press, 1979), 30.

115 **Whenever he spoke:** Milton Cantor, introduction to Henry Adams, *John Randolph* (Greenwich, Conn.: Fawcett, 1961), x.

115 **"misfortune to be":** "Speech on Internal Improvements," *Debates and Proceedings in the Congress of the United States* (Washington, D.C., 1856), 18th Cong., 1st Sess., Jan. 1824, 1308.

115 **emancipation would be forced:** "Speech on Internal Improvements," 1308.

115 **"pronounce all slaves":** Henry, quoted in Finkelman, *Imperfect Union,* 28.

116 **"his reluctant bride":** Mark Twain, *Following the Equator,* in *Mark Twain: A Tramp Abroad, Following the Equator, Other Travels,* ed. Roy Blount Jr. (New York: Library of America, 2010), 550.

117 **"attempt at elopement":** James Barbour to Henry Clay, Oct. 2, 1828, in *The American Diplomatic Code, Embracing a Collection of Treaties and Conventions Between the United States and Foreign Powers: From 1778– 1834,* ed. Jonathan Elliot (Washington, D.C.: 1834), 2:678.

117 **"depart from the principle":** Gallatin to Clay, Sept. 26, 1827, in *The Writings of Albert Gallatin,* ed. Henry Adams (Philadelphia: J. B. Lippincott, 1879), 2:389.

118 **"rendezvous for runaway slaves":** William Jay, *A View of the Action of the Federal Government, in Behalf of Slavery, 2nd ed.* (New York: American Anti-slavery Society, 1839), 64–65.

118   **"think themselves justified":** Harrold, *Border War*, 23.

118   **"with power and authority":** Ruggles, *Unboxing of Henry Brown*, 17.

118   **Free black sailors:** Adam Arenson, *The Great Heart of the Republic: St. Louis and the Cultural Civil War* (Cambridge, Mass.: Harvard University Press, 2011), 86. See also Lois E. Horton, "Kidnapping and Resistance: Antislavery Direct Action in the 1850s," in Blight, *Passages to Freedom*, 152.

118   **Slave patrols were fortified:** Harrold, *Border War*, 25, 27.

118   **Shoes, issued to reduce:** Grimes, *Life of William Grimes*, 38.

118   **statute in Missouri:** Frazier, *Runaway and Freed Missouri Slaves and Those Who Helped Them*, 90.

119   **white Methodist elder:** Paul Finkelman, *Slavery in the Courtroom: An Annotated Bibliography of American Cases* (Union, N.J.: Lawbook Exchange, 1998), 158–59. Ironically, the defendant's lead defense lawyer was Roger Taney, who, as chief justice of the United States, delivered the devastating pro-slavery decision in the 1857 case of Dred Scott.

119   **hub of abolitionism:** Sandra Harbert Petrulionis, *To Set This World Right: The Antislavery Movement in Thoreau's Concord* (Ithaca, N.Y.: Cornell University Press, 2006), 11.

119   **William Lloyd Garrison:** See Garrison, "My Second Baltimore Trial," 2, and the expanded version, *A Brief Sketch of the Trial of William Lloyd Garrison for an Alleged Libel on Francis Todd, of Newburyport, Mass.* (1834), 7. The first edition of Garrison's "brief sketch" was written while he was in prison, and it was the publication of this pamphlet that caught the attention of Tappan, who secured his release. See V. Tchertkoff and F. Holah, *A Short Biography of William Lloyd Garrison* (London: Free Age Press, 1904), 32.

120   **He regarded abolitionists:** Marc Leepson, *What So Proudly We Hailed: Francis Scott Key, a Life* (New York: Macmillan, 2014), 182–84.

120   **Key was sufficiently moved:** John Quincy Adams, *Diaries, vol. 2, 1821–1848*, ed. David Waldstreicher (New York: Library of America, 2017), 415.

120   **Outside the courts:** See Harrold, *Border War*, esp. chap. 1.

120   **a destitute black boy:** Carol Wilson, *Freedom at Risk: The Kidnapping of Free Blacks in America, 1780–1865* (Lexington: University Press of Kentucky, 1994), 10–14.

120   **surge in kidnapping:** Horton, "Kidnapping and Resistance," 151–52. See also Wilson, *Freedom at Risk*, which details the many ways in which kidnapping of free blacks occurred throughout the border states.

121   **"separated from the white race":** Cyprian Clamorgan, *The Colored Aristocracy of St. Louis* (1858), quoted in Margo Jefferson, *Negroland* (New York: Pantheon, 2015), 19. In the national census of 1850, slaves were marked with an *M* for mulatto or *B* for black.

121   **Ohio legislature threatened:** Harrold, *Border Wars*, 10.

121   **three Ohioans accused:** Harrold, *Border Wars*, 60.

121   **"slaves as white":** Harrold, *Border Wars*, 59.

121   **"Without legal security":** Harrold, *Border Wars*, 59.

121   **Her lawyers claimed:** Thomas C. Holt, "Understanding the Problematic of Race Through the Problem of Race-Mixture" (paper presented to the American Anthropological Association, Sept. 2004), 5–8, available online: understandingrace.org/resources/pdf/myth_reality/holt.pdf. See also Walter Johnson, "The White Slave, the Slave Trader, and the Politics of Racial Determination in the 1850s," *Journal of American History* 87, no. 1 (June 2000): 13–38.

122   **"the question now":** Quoted in Angela Murphy, *The Jerry Rescue: The Fugitive Slave Law, Northern Rights, and the American Sectional Crisis* (New York: Oxford University Press, 2016), 43.

122   **"an abolitionist pamphlet":** Quoted in Richard Hildreth, *Archy Moore, the White Slave; or, Memoirs of a Fugitive. With a New Introduction* (New York: Miller, Orton & Mulligan, 1856), x.

122   **"trace of African blood":** Hildreth, *Archy Moore, the White Slave*, 8.

123   **"Every lady," wrote one:** Quoted in Hodes, *White Women, Black Men*, 3. Mary Boykin Chesnut's celebrated diaries enjoyed a revival of appreciation following their republication in 1981. C. Vann Woodward in his Pulitzer Prize–winning 1981 edition of the diaries cites the literary critic Edmund Wilson's high appraisal of the diaries, which he called "a masterpiece" and "a work of art" whose attention "to establishing . . . an atmosphere, an emotional tone," recalls more the work of a novelist than a diarist. Edmund Wilson, quoted in C. Vann Woodward, "Introduction: Diary in Fact—Diary in Form," in *Mary Chesnut's Civil War*, ed. C. Vann Woodward (New Haven, Conn.: Yale University Press, 1981), xv. Indeed, Chesnut later wrote three novels, though they were not published in her lifetime.

123   **"the female slave":** Quoted in Charles H. Nichols, *Many Thousand Gone: The Ex-slaves' Account of Their Bondage and Freedom* (Bloomington: Indiana University Press, 1963), 37. The tragic mulatto tale was later to be taken up by black writers, as in William Wells Brown's novel *Clotel; or, The President's Daughter* (1853), which followed the lives of two daughters of Thomas Jefferson by his enslaved mistress. Long after the end of slavery, the psychological cost of crossing the racial divide persisted as a literary theme in works by black and white writers alike—Charles Chesnutt's *Wife of His Youth, and Other Stories of the Color Line* (1899), Nella Larsen's *Passing* (1929), Fannie Hurst's *Imitation of Life* (1933), and Philip Roth's *The Human Stain*

(2000), in which whites hostile to blacks make a reluctant exception for those of a more "pleasing shade, rather like eggnog." *The Human Stain* (New York: Houghton Mifflin, 2000), 122.

123 **"when she is fourteen"**: Harriet A. Jacobs, *Incidents in the Life of a Slave Girl, Written by Herself,* ed. Jean Fagan Yellin (Cambridge, Mass.: Harvard University Press, 1987), 51. It was, alas, a sound expectation. James Henry Hammond, for example, forced one of his slaves to become his mistress when she was eighteen, and when her daughter by another man reached the age of twelve, he took her too for the same purpose. There is no reason to regard Hammond's behavior as unusual. See Miller, *Arguing About Slavery,* 478.

123 *The Kidnapped Clergyman*: *The Kidnapped Clergyman* is excerpted in *Major Voices: The Drama of Slavery,* ed. Eric Gardner (New Milford, Conn.: Toby Press, 2005), 67–107.

124 **told the tale**: Lydia Maria Child, "The Quadroons," in *The Liberty Bell* (Boston: Anti-slavery Fair, 1842), 140. "The Quadroons" is printed on 115–41.

124 **"Her eyes were"**: Henry Wadsworth Longfellow, "The Quadroon Girl," in *Poems on Slavery* (Cambridge, Mass.: John Owen, 1842), 28, 29.

124 **"whose complexion was"**: Oliver Johnson, "Slatter's Slave Prison—Baltimore," *Signal of Liberty,* Jan. 5, 1842, 1.

125 **"her superb neck"**: Calvin Fairbank, *During Slavery Times: How He "Fought the Good Fight" to "Prepare the Way"* (Chicago: R. R. McCabe, 1890), 30.

125 **"Too white to keep"**: Johnson, "The White Slave, the Slave Trader, and the Politics of Racial Determination in the 1850s," 20. Johnson points out that "'fancy' was a transitive verb made noun," by which he means that it denoted the slave owner's fantasy as well as the girl's style (17).

125 **"awakened curiosity and indignation"**: *The Rev. J. W. Loguen, as a Slave and as a Freeman: A Narrative of Real Life* (Syracuse, N.Y.: J. G. K. Truair, 1859), 365. The case became famous in part because Gerrit Smith and his cousin the women's rights advocate Elizabeth Cady (not yet Elizabeth Cady Stanton) helped to publicize it.

126 *The Greek Slave*: For the exhibition history of Powers's sculpture, see Richard Wunder, *Hiram Powers: Vermont Sculptor, 1805–1873* (Cranbury, N.J.: Associated University Press, 1991), 1:207–74, 2:157–77. See also Maurie D. McInness, *Slaves Waiting for Sale: Abolitionist Art and the American Slave Trade* (Chicago: University of Chicago Press, 2011), and Joy S. Kasson, "Narratives of the Female Body," in *Marble Queens and Captives: Women and Nineteenth-Century American Sculpture* (New Haven, Conn.: Yale University Press, 1990), 46–72.

127 **"little sovereign nations"**: Alexis de Tocqueville, *Democracy in America,* trans. George Lawrence, ed. J. P. Mayer (New York: Harper Perennial, 1969), 61.

127 **"tranquility to the public mind"**: *Cong. Globe,* 24th Cong., 1st Sess., May 18, 1836, 469.

127 **"Am I gagged"**: *Cong. Globe,* 24th Cong., 1st Sess., May 25, 1836, 498. See also Miller, *Arguing About Slavery,* 204ff. and 480.

128 **"An Act to Regulate"**: Frank Uriah Quillin, *The Color Line in Ohio: A History of Race Prejudice in a Typical Northern State* (Ann Arbor, Mich.: George Wahr, 1913), 21. See also Stephen Middleton, *The Black Laws: Race and the Legal Process in Early Ohio* (Athens: Ohio University Press, 2005), 48–49.

128 **"not become a retreat"**: Elmer Gertz, "The Black Laws of Illinois," *Journal of the Illinois State Historical Society* 56, no. 3 (Autumn 1963): 463. As late as 1848, an Illinois referendum barring free blacks from entering the state received 70 percent of the popular vote. See Foner, *Fiery Trial,* 8.

128 **"free negroes and mulattoes"**: This clause of the Missouri Constitution infuriated northern congressmen and was in obvious violation of Article 4, Section 2 of the U.S. Constitution. The Missouri Constitution was only ratified upon the removal of the clause, a compromise engineered by Henry Clay. See Robert Remini, *At the Edge of the Precipice: Henry Clay and the Compromise That Saved the Union* (New York: Basic Books, 2010), 7. The 1820 Missouri Constitution is available online: press-pubs.uchicago.edu/founders/documents/a4_2_3s12.html.

128 **restricted the franchise**: William L. Andrews, introduction to *Life of William Grimes,* 7.

128 **whipping and expulsion**: Elizabeth McLagen, *A Peculiar Paradise: A History of Blacks in Oregon* (Portland, Ore.: Georgian Press, 1980), 26.

128 **"loathed slavery and feared emancipation"**: Laura L. Mitchell, "'Matters of Justice Between Man and Man': Northern Divines, the Bible, and the Fugitive Slave Act of 1850," in *Religion and the Antebellum Debate over Slavery,* John R. McKivigan and Mitchell Snay (Athens: University of Georgia Press, 1998), 138.

128 **"culpable in forcing"**: Samuel Sewall, *The Selling of Joseph: A Memorial,* ed. Sidney Kaplan (Amherst: University of Massachusetts Press, 1969), 10, 12.

128 **"If the gentlemen"**: Quoted in Richard B. Morris, *Government and Labor in Early America* (New York: Columbia University Press, 1946), 183.

129 **"be more false and heartless"**: John Quincy Adams, quoted in Miller, *Arguing About Slavery,* 189.

129 **"rude, unbleached African"**: John Quincy Adams, "Misconceptions of Shakspeare upon the Stage," *New England Magazine,* vol. 9 (Dec. 1835), 438.

129 **"race prejudice seems"**: Tocqueville, *Democracy in America,* 343.

129 as "more virulent": Watkins, editorial in *Frederick Douglass' Paper,* Feb. 10, 1854, in Ripley, *Black Abolitionist Papers,* 4:202, quoted in David Reynolds, "Our Ruinous Betrayal of Indians and Black Americans," *New York Review of Books,* Dec. 22, 2016, 90. See also Garrison, *Address at Park Street Church, Boston, July 4, 1829* (Directors of the Old South Work, 1907), 8.

129 "perhaps the first professional": George M. Fredrickson, *The Black Image in the White Mind: The Debate on Afro-American Character and Destiny, 1817–1914* (Middletown, Conn.: Wesleyan University Press, 1971), 92. Fredrickson further describes John H. Van Evrie as "not in any sense a scientist himself" and "blatantly and openly an anti-Negro propagandist" (92).

129 These observations appear: John H. van Evrie, *Negroes and Negro "Slavery": The First an Inferior Race; the Latter Its Normal Condition* (New York: Van Evrie, Horton, 1861), 227. The quoted text is from a much expanded 1861 edition, the first chapter of which was published as a pamphlet in 1853 in Baltimore. Van Evrie's sentiments evidently changed not at all in the intervening years.

129 "it cannot be maintained": Linda Allardt, ed., *The Journals and Miscellaneous Notebooks of Ralph Waldo Emerson* (Cambridge, Mass.: Harvard University Press, 1976), 12:152.

129 "at the bottom": Parker reserved his deepest contempt for Jews, whose "intellect was sadly pinched in those narrow foreheads," and who "were cruel also—always cruel," and who, he did not doubt, "did sometimes kill a Christian baby at the Passover." Parker to David A. Wasson, Dec. 12, 1857, in Octavius Brooks Frothingham, *Theodore Parker: A Biography* (New York: Putnam's, 1880), 327.

130 called "natural colorphobia": Thomas Wentworth Higginson, *Cheerful Yesterdays* (Cambridge, Mass.: Riverside Press, 1898), 174. Higginson claims that Emerson's "natural colorphobia" made him "one of that minority of anti-slavery men."

130 "The laws and usages": Smith to John G. Whittier, July 18, 1844, published in *Liberator,* Aug. 31, 1844.

130 "dragged from the cars": Frederick Douglass, *Life and Times of Frederick Douglass, Written by Himself* (New York: Collier Macmillan, 1962), 223.

130 When another refugee: Michelle Arnosky Sherburne, *Slavery and the Underground Railroad in New Hampshire* (Charleston, S.C.: History Press, 2016), 77–83.

130 "the slave is just as much": Brown, "I Have No Constitution, and No Country," published in *Liberator,* Nov. 2, 1849, reprinted in Philip Sheldon and Robert J. Branham, *Lift Every Voice: African American Oratory, 1787–1900* (Tuscaloosa: University of Alabama Press, 1998), 215.

130 After fleeing from: See Jean Fagan Yellin, *Harriet Jacobs: A Life* (New York: Basic Civitas Books, 2004), 128–29. See also Sarah Blackwood, "Fugitive Obscura: Runaway Slave Portraiture and Early Photographic Technology," *American Literature* 81, no. 1 (March 2009): 98.

130 "prejudice against color": William S. McFeely, *Frederick Douglass* (New York: W. W. Norton, 1991), 94.

131 a thousand antislavery societies: Nichols, *Many Thousand Gone,* 132.

131 "Opposing slavery and hating": Douglass, quoted in *The Slave's Narrative,* ed. Charles T. Davis and Henry Louis Gates Jr. (New York: Oxford University Press, 1985), xviii.

131 prospect of fully integrating: See John Stauffer, *The Black Hearts of Men: Radical Abolitionists and the Transformation of Race* (Cambridge, Mass.: Harvard University Press, 2002), 138–42.

131 The same newspapers: Murphy, *Jerry Rescue,* 8.

132 "deep interest manifested": *Liberator,* Oct. 8, 1841, quoted in Marion Wilson Starling, *The Slave Narrative: Its Place in American History* (Boston: G. K. Hall, 1981), 31.

132 "appearance and that of his family": Quoted in Marc M. Arkin, "A Convenient Seat in God's Temple: The Massachusetts General Colored Association and the Park Street Church Pew Controversy of 1830," *New England Quarterly* 79, no. 1 (March 2016): 17.

132 "preventive of amalgamation": Abraham Lincoln, "Speech at Springfield, Illinois," June 26, 1857, in *Collected Works of Lincoln,* 2:408, 409.

132 "wherever he has set down": Corwin, quoted in Marc Egnal, *Clash of Extremes: The Economic Origins of the Civil War* (New York: Hill and Wang, 2009), 91.

132 "negrophilic old ladies": Edgar Allan Poe, "The Little Longfellow War," *Aristidean,* April 1845, quoted in *Edgar Allan Poe: Literary Theory and Criticism,* ed. Leonard Cassuto (Mineola, N.Y.: Dover, 1999), 86.

Chapter 6: War of Words

134 thirty thousand copies: David B. Potts, *Liberal Education for a Land of Colleges: Yale's Reports of 1828* (New York: Palgrave Macmillan, 2010), 13, 55n11; Trent, introduction to *Narrative of James Williams,* x.

134 "the great enginery": Richard Henry Dana Jr., *The Journal of Richard Henry Dana Jr.,* ed. Robert F. Lucid (Cambridge, Mass.: Harvard University Press, 1968), 2:408.

134 black steamboat worker: Henry Boernstein, *Memoirs of a Nobody: The Missouri Years of an Austrian Radical, 1849–1866,* trans. Steven Rowan (St. Louis: Missouri Historical Society Press, 1997), 189.

135   **"seized in the street"**: Abraham Lincoln, "Address Before the Young Men's Lyceum of Springfield, Illinois," Jan. 27, 1838, in *Collected Works of Lincoln*, 1:110. For an account of the incident, see Paul Simon, *Freedom's Champion: Elijah Lovejoy* (Carbondale: Southern Illinois University Press, 1994), 45–50. Eight years later, the black abolitionist Charles Lenox Remond told of McIntosh's having "raised his dark, fettered hand" and being burned "in a slow fire!" "What was the Union to him?" Remond asked. Remond, July 18, 1844, in Ripley, *Black Abolitionist Papers*, 3:442–45.

135   **"most atrocious case"**: Adams, *Diaries, vol. 2, 1821–1848*, 419.

135   **"dark and threatening"**: The phrase is from New Jersey senator Garret Wall, who was responding to an attack on a petition submitted by Pennsylvania Quakers for the abolition of slavery in the District of Columbia. *Cong. Globe*, Senate, 24th Cong., 1st Sess., Feb. 29, 1836, 132.

135   **"await a more definite development"**: Quoted in Freehling, *Secessionists at Bay*, 188.

136   **"HAVE ye heard"**: Quoted in James G. Basker, ed., *American Antislavery Writings: Colonial Beginnings to Emancipation* (New York: Library of America, 2012), 278.

137   **"For the poor slaves"**: William Lloyd Garrison, "Sugar Plums," in *Juvenile Poems, for the Use of Free American Children, of Every Complexion* (Boston: Garrison and Knapp, 1835), 19.

137   **"as mere abstraction"**: Whittier, 1839, quoted in Harrold, *Border War*, 15.

137   **embossed on window blinds**: See Starling, *Slave Narrative*, 29; Ralph Waldo Emerson, "An Address . . . on . . . the Emancipation of the Negroes in the British West Indies, August 1, 1844," in *Emerson's Antislavery Writings*, 10.

138   **"sugar is excellent"**: Emerson, "Address . . . on . . . the Emancipation of the Negroes in the British West Indies, August 1, 1844," 20.

138   **Elizabeth Barrett Browning**: Sarah Brophy, "Elizabeth Barrett Browning's 'The Runaway Slave at Pilgrim's Point' and the Politics of Interpretation," *Victorian Poetry* 36, no. 3 (Fall 1998): 275.

138   **"How I love"**: *The Fugitives* was published in 1841 by the Massachusetts Female Emancipation Society. Quoted here from the reprint in Gardner, *Major Voices*, 117.

138   **"In the dark top"**: *The Anti-slavery Poems of John Pierpont* (Boston: Oliver Johnson, 1843), 31. The poem was not published until 1843. Pierpont was descended from the family of Sarah Pierpont, wife of Jonathan Edwards. Among his descendants was the financier John Pierpont Morgan, his grandson.

139   **"been left long enough"**: Quoted in Davis and Gates, *Slave's Narrative*, xvi.

139   **"have itching ears"**: Ripley, *Black Abolitionist Papers*, 3:28. It is unclear whether Collins intended an allusion to 2 Timothy 4:3–4, where the term "itching ears" is pejorative, signifying the desire to hear only what one wants to hear: "For the time will come when they will not endure sound doctrine; but after their own lusts shall they heap to themselves teachers, having itching ears; And they shall turn away their ears from the truth, and shall be turned unto fables."

139   **"if you give"**: Douglass, *Narrative*, ed. Quarles, 58.

140   **"black people in New York"**: Douglass, *My Bondage and My Freedom*, ed. Blight, 271.

140   **"on the wharves"**: Douglass, *Life and Times*, 211.

140   **"whisper in private"**: Douglass, *Life and Times*, 214.

140   **"Urgently solicited to become"**: Douglass, *Life and Times*, 216.

141   **"people doubted if"**: Douglass, *Life and Times*, 218.

141   **"tornado in a forest"**: Fairbank, *During Slavery Times*, 70. Long after Douglass's writing had made him famous, James Monroe Gregory reported that even in his diminished old age "the fire and action of the man could not be transferred to paper." James Monroe Gregory, *Frederick Douglass the Orator* (Springfield, Mass.: Willey, 1893), 92.

142   **"I did not run off"**: Sojourner Truth, quoted in Carleton Mabee and Susan Mabee Newhouse, *Sojourner Truth: Slave, Prophet, Legend* (New York: New York University Press, 1993), 13.

142   **"abolitionizing the free States"**: Bibb, quoted in Davis and Gates, *Slave's Narrative*, xvii.

143   **"the sinful system"**: Edward Beecher, "Dr. Beecher on Organic Sins—No. II," *Boston Recorder*, Oct. 23, 1845, 170. Beecher's idea of organic sin prompted an extensive debate in 1845 in the pages of the *Boston Recorder* in which Beecher tried to defend the concept against the suggestion by the theologian Calvin Stowe (husband of Harriet Beecher) that calling slavery an "organic sin" and attributing it to the organization of society as a whole exculpated southern slaveholders as individuals. See Charles A. Maxfield, "The 1845 Organic Sin Debate: Slavery, Sin, and the American Board of Commissioners for Foreign Missions," in *North American Foreign Missions, 1810–1914: Theology, Theory, and Policy*, ed. Wilbert R. Shenk (Grand Rapids, Mich.: William B. Eerdmans, 2004), 86–115.

143   **trace the growth**: See the chronological list of North American slave narratives available online at docsouth.unc.edu/neh/chronautobio.html.

144   **one who stowed away**: *Middlesex Standard*, Dec. 5, 1844. See also Bruce Laurie, *Beyond Garrison: Antislavery and Social Reform* (New York: Cambridge University Press, 2005), 77.

144   **pro-slavery thugs drove:** Robert Fogel, *Without Consent or Contract: The Rise and Fall of American Slavery* (New York: W. W. Norton, 1989), 345–46.

145   **"censorship by cudgel":** Frank Luther Mott, *American Journalism: A History of Newspapers in the United States Through 260 Years, 1690 to 1950* (New York: Macmillan, 1950), 309.

145   **"Jones will be here":** Quoted in Mott, *American Journalism,* 310.

145   **"Chronicle of Kidnappings":** *New York American Anti-slavery Reporter,* June 1834, 92.

146   **the local network:** Foner, *Gateway to Freedom,* 9.

146   **more than two hundred:** See the useful listing of antebellum newspapers and periodicals containing articles about fugitives in Starling, *Slave Narrative,* 351–54.

146   *Southern Quarterly Review:* The first number of the *Southern Quarterly Review* was published in New Orleans in January 1842, but it soon moved to Charleston, where it continued to be published until 1854.

147   **"freedom and equality":** Margaret Fuller, "The Great Lawsuit," *Dial,* July 1843. The article was revised and expanded in book form as *Woman in the Nineteenth Century* (Boston: John P. Jewett, 1855). The quotation is on p. 25.

147   **"would go home":** Quoted in George Dangerfield, *The Era of Good Feelings* (New York: Harcourt, Brace, and World, 1952), 220.

147   **"predominant love of sunshine":** John Pendleton Kennedy, *Swallow Barn* (1853; repr., New York: Hafner, 1971), 450–51. The defense of slavery was by no means limited to southern writers. In 1836, James Kirke Paulding, a New Yorker, warned that emancipation would lead to intermarriage, thereby "debasing the whites with a mixture of that blood, which, wherever it flows, carries with it the seeds of deterioration" (*Slavery in the United States,* 61). This kind of racist fearmongering was commonplace in the North as well as the South.

148   **"the slavery of sin":** Andrews, introduction to *Life of William Grimes,* 7.

149   **"Having lived some months":** Solomon Bayley, *Narrative of Some Remarkable Incidents in the Life of Solomon Bayley, Formerly a Slave in the State of Delaware, North America* (London: Harvey and Dalton, 1825), 1.

149   **dose of Christian piety:** There were exceptions. Venture Smith, for one, never mentions Christ or Christianity in his 1798 *Narrative of the Life and Adventures of Venture, a Native of Africa,* except to call out white people for professing the warmth of their faith while acting with cold cruelty toward blacks.

149   **"hungry for meat":** Grimes, *Life of William Grimes,* 41.

150   **"noise like one":** Grimes, *Life of William Grimes,* 34, 52.

150   **"bread, water, dried beef":** Grimes, *Life of William Grimes,* 82.

150   **"took the floor":** Grimes, *Life of William Grimes,* 94.

150   **to "northern regions":** *The Fugitives,* 114.

150   **"The more he reveals":** Andrews, introduction to *Life of William Grimes,* 23.

151   **the "liberty plot":** Laura Doyle, *Freedom's Empire: Race and the Rise of the Novel in Atlantic Modernity, 1640–1940* (Durham: Duke University Press, 2008), 15.

151   **"I bear no enmity":** Moses Roper, *Narrative of the Adventures and Escape of Moses Roper from American Slavery,* in *North Carolina Slave Narratives,* ed. William L. Andrews (Chapel Hill: University of North Carolina Press, 2003), 74.

151   **Josiah Henson writes:** See Sinha, *Slave's Cause,* 432; Josiah Henson, *The Life of Josiah Henson, Formerly a Slave, Now an Inhabitant of Canada, as Narrated by Himself* (Boston: Arthur D. Phelps, 1849), 42–43.

151   **a sentimental convention:** Cindy Weinstein, "The Slave Narrative and Sentimental Literature," in *The Cambridge Companion to the African American Slave Narrative,* ed. Audrey A. Fisch (Cambridge, U.K.: Cambridge University Press, 2007), 115–34.

151   **for the prey to get away:** On the slave narrative as captivity narrative and spiritual autobiography, see Yolanda Pierce, "Redeeming Bondage: The Captivity Narrative and the Spiritual Autobiography in the African American Slave Narrative Tradition," in Fisch, *Cambridge Companion to the African American Slave Narrative,* 83–98.

152   **novice courtroom witness:** See McFeely, *Frederick Douglass,* 115–16.

152   **"Tell your story":** Douglass, *Life and Times,* 217.

152   **promptly voted in favor:** See John W. Blassingame, "Using the Testimony of Ex-slaves: Approaches and Problems," in Davis and Gates, *Slave's Narrative,* 79–80. On Northup, see also Sue Eakin and Joseph Logsdon, introduction to *Twelve Years a Slave, by Solomon Northup* (Baton Rouge: Louisiana State University Press, 1968), xiii. Eakin and Logsdon write that "Wilson was not an abolitionist" and that "he merely became intrigued in the tragedy and recognized its publishing potential" (xiii). On Henson, see also Darryl Pinckney, introduction to *Uncle Tom's Cabin* (New York: Signet Classics, 1998), xvii–xix.

152   **assistance from other slaves:** Jeff Forret, *Slave Against Slave: Plantation Violence in the Old South* (Baton Rouge: Louisiana State University Press, 2015), 180–82.

152   **echo or anticipate other works:** Eakin and Logsdon write that "the prose style of [Northup's] narrative clearly belongs to Wilson" (xiv), while Pinckney calls Henson's narrative "ghostwritten" (introduction to *Uncle Tom's*

Cabin, xvii). In "Using the Testimony of Ex-slaves," the scholar John Blassingame argues for "the general reliability of the edited narratives" (81). Blassingame points out that their factual accuracy was rarely challenged by slave owners, though he notes that "certain literary devices that appear in the accounts were clearly beyond the ken of unlettered slaves" (82). There has been controversy about the originality of other widely noted African American texts including Hannah Crafts's *Bondswoman's Narrative* (1853–1861?; pub. 2002), which borrows liberally from Charles Dickens's novel *Bleak House*. See Hollis Robbins, "Blackening *Bleak House*: Hannah Crafts's *The Bondswoman's Narrative*," in *In Search of Hannah Crafts: Critical Essays on "The Bondswoman's Narrative*," ed. Henry Louis Gates Jr. and Hollis Robbins (New York: Basic Books, 2004), 71–86.

153   *"large stomach man"*: William Still, *The Underground Railroad: A Record of Facts, Authentic Narratives, Letters, etc.* (Philadelphia: Porter & Coates, 1872), 139.

153   **certain forced propriety:** In a discussion of several narratives including those of Box Brown and Moses Roper, Philip Gould writes that "editorial decisions continued to shape the rhetorical and thematic designs of the slave narrative." "The Rise, Development, and Circulation of the Slave Narrative," in Fisch, *Cambridge Companion to the African American Slave Narrative*, 24.

153   **"with trifling exceptions":** Lydia Maria Child, "Introduction by the Editor," in Jacobs, *Incidents in the Life of a Slave Girl*, 3.

153   **"jaws, heads, and feet":** *Narrative of James Williams*, 40; Henry Louis Gates Jr., "Did Dogs Eat Slaves, Like in '*Django*'?," concludes that "apparently, it sometimes did happen." theroot.com/articles/history/2013/01/how_accurate_is_django_unchained_on_riding_horses_mandingo_fighting_and_dogs_eating_slaves/. As for Williams's veracity, the scholar Hank Trent, in a valuable recent edition of the narrative, has painstakingly reconstructed Williams's life and distinguished between what was true (a lot) and what he wrote (a little) in order to throw slave hunters off his trail. See Trent's introduction and extensive notes in *Narrative of James Williams*.

153   **"foul fester of falsehood":** These were the words of J. B. Rittenhouse, editor of the *Alabama Beacon*, published on March 29, 1838, shortly after the book's publication. Quoted in Trent, *Narrative of James Williams*, xix.

154   **the interrogation continued:** My discussion of Williams's narrative is heavily indebted to the introduction and notes in Trent's excellent edition.

154   **"questions of identity":** Renata Adler, "Brontosaurs Whistling in the Dark," *Lapham's Quarterly* (Winter 2017), laphamsquarterly.org/home/brontosaurs-whistling-dark.

154   **new level of public trust:** Robert S. Levine, *The Lives of Frederick Douglass* (Cambridge, Mass.: Harvard University Press, 2016), 36–45.

154   **denounced Douglass's book:** A. C. C. Thompson, "Letter from a Former Slaveholder" (1845), in *Narrative of the Life of Frederick Douglass, an American Slave, Written by Himself*, ed. William L. Andrews and William S. McFeely (New York: W. W. Norton, 1997), 88–91. On Thompson's full name, see Levine, *Lives of Frederick Douglass*, 99.

154   **"have relieved me":** Douglass, "Reply to Thompson's Letter," in *Narrative*, ed. Andrews and McFeely, 93. See also Peter Ripley, "Autobiographical Writings of Frederick Douglass," *Southern Studies* 24, no. 1 (Spring 1985): 5–29.

155   **within five years:** McFeely, *Frederick Douglass*, 116–17.

155   **"refuge in monarchical England":** Douglass, *Life and Times*, 232.

155   **"it is quite an advantage":** Douglass to Francis Jackson, Jan. 29, 1846, quoted in McFeely, *Frederick Douglass*, 131.

155   **"Accounts of floggings":** McFeely, *Frederick Douglass*, 15.

155   **"I do not wish to dwell":** Douglass, *My Bondage and My Freedom*, ed. Blight, 331, 332, 334.

155   **"It was slavery":** Douglass, *My Bondage and My Freedom*, ed. Blight, 130.

156   **deed of manumission:** McFeely, *Frederick Douglass*, 144.

156   **"uncompromising antislavery friends":** Douglass, *Life and Times*, 255.

156   **"famous black exhibit":** Ross Posnock, *Color and Culture: Black Writers and the Making of the Modern Intellectual* (Cambridge, Mass.: Harvard University Press, 1998), 51.

156   **"I do not recollect":** Douglass, *Narrative*, ed. Quarles, 25.

156   **"theme of the hunted mother":** Northrop Frye, *Anatomy of Criticism* (New York: Atheneum, 1969), 199.

156   **"if they had lived":** Adams, *Diaries, vol. 2, 1821–1848*, 416.

156   **We meet her again:** Writing in 1861, Harriet Jacobs describes her anguish at having left her children in order to save herself. Elizabeth Keckley, who was able to buy her liberty with the help of loans from white employers and who worked as a seamstress first for Mrs. Jefferson Davis, then for Mary Todd Lincoln, writes after the Civil War about her struggle to go north without abandoning her son. Elizabeth Keckley, *Behind the Scenes; or, Thirty Years a Slave and Four Years in the White House* (1868; New York: Penguin Classics, 2005), 20–23.

157   **"Never having enjoyed":** Douglass, *Narrative*, ed. Quarles, 25.

NOTES

157 **"In coming to":** Douglass, *Narrative*, ed. Quarles, 118.
157 **"I found employment":** Douglass, *Narrative*, ed. Quarles, 151–52.
158 **a "glorious resurrection":** Douglass, *Narrative*, ed. Quarles, 105.
158 **"Representative American man":** Smith, introduction to Douglass, *My Bondage and My Freedom*, ed. Blight, 19.
158 **"the one portion":** Parker, quoted in Davis and Gates, *Slave's Narrative*, xxi.
158 **"literary flunkeyism towards England":** Herman Melville, "Hawthorne and His Mosses," in *The Piazza Tales and Other Prose Pieces, 1839–1860*, ed. Harrison Hayford et al. (Evanston, Ill.: Northwestern University Press, 1987), 245.
158 **a single line referring:** See Benjamin Friedlander, "Auctions of the Mind: Emily Dickinson and Abolition," *Arizona Quarterly* 54, no. 1 (Spring 1998): 1–26. In a book about the friendship between Emily Dickinson and Thomas Wentworth Higginson, Brenda Wineapple writes that "possibly she refers to emancipated slaves" in a poem (No. 754 in *The Poems of Emily Dickinson: Reading Edition*, ed. R. W. Franklin [Cambridge, Mass.: Harvard University Press, 1999], 336–37) that includes the following stanza: "Would'nt Dungeons sorer grate / On the Man—free— / Just long enough to taste— / Then—doomed new—." Wineapple, *White Heat: The Friendship of Emily Dickinson and Thomas Wentworth Higginson* (New York: Knopf, 2008), 151.
158 **"one of those evils":** Hawthorne, *Life of Franklin Pierce*, 417.
159 **"the shame of American literature":** Kenneth Lynn, introduction to *Uncle Tom's Cabin*, vii.
159 **a gingerbread cookie:** In Nathaniel Hawthorne, *The House of the Seven Gables* (1851; Cambridge, Mass.: Harvard University Press, 2009), 50–51.
159 **"whale would sell":** Melville, *Moby-Dick*, 413.
159 **naive point of view:** For an elaboration of this reading, see my *Melville: His World and Work* (New York: Knopf, 2005), 229–43.
160 **"flood of evidence":** Marcus Wood, *Blind Memory: Visual Representations of Slavery in England and America, 1780–1865* (Manchester: Manchester University Press, 2000), 83.
160 **"My friends call me Fred":** McBride, *Good Lord Bird*, 223, 225–26.
161 **one putative friend complained:** Richard Webb to Maria Weston Chapman, May 16, 1846, quoted in Levine, *Lives of Frederick Douglass*, 86.
162 **"rather breathlessly review":** Robin W. Winks, "The Making of a Fugitive Slave Narrative: Josiah Henson and Uncle Tom—a Case Study," in Davis and Gates, *Slave's Narrative*, 114.
163 **"slavery can never be":** *Narrative of William W. Brown*, in Andrews and Gates, *Slave Narratives*, 391.
163 **"Turning to me":** Northup, *Twelve Years a Slave*, 196.

Chapter 7: Into the Courts

164 **"this fugitive slave literature":** Quoted from Wright's weekly paper *Chronotype*, in Bibb, *Narrative*, 207.
164 **"warm halls of the heart":** Melville, *Pierre*, 71.
164–65 **"You know full well":** Quoted from letter to Hon. Ezekiel Bacon, Nov. 19, 1842, in *Life and Letters of Joseph Story*, ed. William W. Story (Boston: Little, Brown, 1851), 2:431.
165 **"object" of that clause:** *Prigg v. Commonwealth of Pennsylvania*, in *Report of Cases Argued and Adjudged in the Supreme Court of the United States* (Boston: Charles C. Little, 1842), 16:540.
165 **"At the adoption":** *In the Court for the Correction of Errors. Jack a Negro Man, Plaintiff in Error, Against Mary Martin, Defendant in Error. Case on the Part of the Plaintiff in Error*, in *Fugitive Slaves and American Courts: The Pamphlet Literature, series 3*, ed. Paul Finkelman (Clark, N.J.: Lawbook Exchange, 1988), 1:27.
166 **"The right of the owner":** *In the Court for the Correction of Errors*, ed. Finkelman, 29.
166 **"It being my duty":** Nathaniel Read, in the case of *State v. Hoppess*, quoted in Charles R. McKirdy, *Lincoln Apostate: The Matson Slave Trial* (Jackson: University Press of Mississippi, 2011), 59.
166 **"living, breathing fact":** Douglass, quoted in Morris, *Free Men All*, 128.
167 **"A sacred compact":** *Liberator*, Dec. 29, 1832.
167 **"It does very well":** Remond, *National Anti-slavery Standard*, July 18, 1844, reprinted in Ripley, *Black Abolitionist Papers*, 3:442, 443.
168 **Until such time:** See Eisgruber, "Justice Story, Slavery, and the Natural Law Foundations of American Constitutionalism," 296.
169 **"The person may be":** Joseph Varnum, Jan. 30, 1797, quoted in Morris, *Free Men All*, 31.
170 **"claim to a runaway":** William R. Leslie, "The Pennsylvania Fugitive Slave Act of 1826," *Journal of Southern History* 18, no. 4 (Nov. 1952): 443.
171 **The substantive issue:** Leonard W. Levy, *The Law of the Commonwealth and Chief Justice Shaw* (New York: Oxford University Press, 1957), 63.

171   **"qualified extent slavery"**: Judge Nelson, in *In the Court for the Correction of Errors. Jack a Negro Man, Plain-tiff in Error, Against Mary Martin, Defendant in Error. Case on the Part of the Plaintiff in Error*, 25.

171   **principle of "voluntary comity"**: Quoted in Finkelman, *Imperfect Union*, 106.

172   **Louisiana was known**: Finkelman, *Imperfect Union*, 109.

172   **"only to those commodities"**: Quoted in Levy, *Law of the Commonwealth and Chief Justice Shaw*, 65.

172   **sent to an orphanage**: Finkelman, "Commonwealth v. Aves," in *Abolition and Antislavery: An Historical Encyclopedia of the American Mosaic*, ed. Peter Hinks and John McKivigan (Santa Barbara, Calif.: Greenwood, 2015), 87.

172   **New York repealed**: Scott Gac, "Slave or Free? White or Black? The Representation of George Latimer," *New England Quarterly* 88, no. 1 (March 2015): 76.

172   **"Although such persons"**: *Report of the Arguments of Counsel and of the Opinion of the Court in the Case of Commonwealth v. Aves* (Boston, 1836), 38.

173   **"The claimant of a slave"**: *Commonwealth v. Aves*, 39. Fifteen years later, Shaw paraphrased his own opinion in the *Aves* case in order to make clear that it did not apply to the explosive case of the fugitive slave Thomas Sims: "If a slave is brought into this state by his master, or comes here in the course of his occupation or employment without having *escaped*, he is not within the case provided for by the constitution." *Reports of Cases Argued and Determined in the Supreme Judicial Court of Massachusetts*, ed. Luther S. Cushing (Boston: Little, Brown, 1853), 7:298.

173   **called him "rational"**: Levy, *Law of the Commonwealth and Chief Justice Shaw*, 67.

173   **"If the master"**: Judge Harrington, quoted in Levy, *Law of the Commonwealth and Chief Justice Shaw*, 83.

173   **convictions were the norm**: Beginning in the early republic, judicial decisions on slavery—by no means limited to fugitive slave cases—were replete with examples of judges' lamenting that the law compelled them to render verdicts in conflict with their own conscience. Many judges, including some in the South, privately believed that slavery was a crime against humanity—or, in the language of the day, a violation of natural law. John Marshall of Virginia, chief justice of the United States from 1801 to 1835, somehow managed to reconcile the fact that he himself was a slave owner with his firm conviction ("it can scarcely be denied") that slavery was "contrary to the law of nature" (*The Antelope*, 10 Wheat. 66 1825). Yet in 1825, when the case came before him of the *Antelope*—a Spanish slave ship seized by the U.S. Coast Guard on suspicion of planning to sell its human cargo in the United States despite the congressional ban on the Atlantic slave trade—he ruled that slaves aboard the vessel who had been lawfully purchased by the kings of Spain and Portugal for transport to Cuba must be returned to their regal owners.
        Another judge beset by conflicting convictions was Thomas Ruffin, chief justice of the North Carolina Supreme Court. In 1829, a lower court found a North Carolina man guilty of assault against a female slave who had been leased to him by her owner. The defendant, John Mann, whose punishment was a five-dollar fine, had shot and wounded her as she ran off when he tried to beat her. When the case reached the state supreme court on appeal, Ruffin expressed his personal disgust at the ungentlemanly conduct of the defendant and asked the public to sympathize with his own predicament—"the struggle" within his "own breast between the feelings of the man, and the duty of the magistrate." But on the grounds that the "power of the master must be absolute to render the submission of the slave perfect," Ruffin reversed Mann's conviction. *State v. John Mann*, 13 N.C. 263 (1829). See Tushnet, *Slave Law in the American South*, and Eric L. Muller, "Judging Thomas Ruffin and the Hindsight Defense," *North Carolina Law Review* 87 (2009): 757–98.

174   **"Stop the thief"**: *Report of the Case of Charles Brown, a Fugitive Slave*, in Finkelman, *Fugitive Slaves and American Courts: The Pamphlet Literature*, series 2, 1:47, 61–62.

175   **"the golden scales"**: *Speech of Salmon P. Chase in the Case of the Colored Woman, Matilda: Who Was Brought Before the Court of Common Pleas of Hamilton County, Ohio, by Writ of Habeas Corpus, March 11, 1837*.

175   **"in the course"**: Quoted in Lubet, *Fugitive Justice*, 29.

176   **What became of her**: See Lubet, *Fugitive Justice*, 26.

176   **Eight were returned**: See Finkelman, *Imperfect Union*, 245–48.

177   **Chase then launched**: Finkelman, *Fugitive Slaves and American Courts: The Pamphlet Literature*, series 2, 1: 387, 464.

177   **"Vigilance committees" formed**: For a good brief survey of vigilance committee activity, see Jane H. Pease and William H. Pease, *They Would Be Free: Blacks' Search for Freedom, 1830–1861* (Urbana: University of Illinois Press, 1990), 206*ff*.

178   **Pennsylvania law granted**: Mark Mikula and L. Mpho Mabunda, eds., *Great American Court Cases* (Detroit: Gale, 1999), 4:117.

178   **"to seize and arrest"**: *Prigg v. Commonwealth of Pennsylvania*, 556.

178   **"have declared free"**: *Prigg v. Commonwealth of Pennsylvania*, 612.

179   **"One-half of the nation"**: Don E. Fehrenbacher, *The Dred Scott Case: Its Significance in American Law and Politics* (New York: Oxford University Press, 1978), 44.

179   **"The provisions of the act"**: *Report of the Case of Edward Prigg Against the Commonwealth of Pennsylvania Argued and Adjudged by the Supreme Court of the United States* (Philadelphia, 1842), 542.

180   **"triumph of freedom"**: Quoted in Lubet, *Fugitive Justice*, 332n19.

181   **"He probably felt"**: Garrison, quoted in Levy, *Law of the Commonwealth and Chief Justice Shaw*, 81.

181   **"the part of Pilate"**: Garrison, quoted in Levy, *Law of the Commonwealth and Chief Justice Shaw*, 82.

181   **"Fire and bloodshed"**: *The Latimer Case*, in Finkelman, *Fugitive Slaves and American Courts: The Pamphlet Literature*, series 3, 1:169.

182   **"subject to my bounden duty"**: Quoted in Ripley, *Black Abolitionist Papers*, 3:445n2. See also Adams, *Diaries, vol. 2, 1821–1848*, 578.

182   **"The slave shall never"**: Quoted in Levy, *Law of the Commonwealth and Chief Justice Shaw*, 84.

183   **similar statutes were adopted**: Morris, *Free Men All*, 114; Lubet, *Fugitive Justice*, 34.

183   **"No slave-hunt in our borders"**: John Greenleaf Whittier, "Massachusetts to Virginia" (1843), in *Antislavery Poems: Songs of Labor and Reform* (Cambridge, Mass.: Riverside Press, 1888), 86.

184   **"any jail or prison"**: Morris, *Free Men All*, 118.

184   **"to destroy the force"**: *Niles' Register*, March 20, 1847, quoted in Morris, *Free Men All*, 119.

184   **"seeing their fellows"**: Quoted in George R. Crooks, *Life and Letters of Rev. John M'Clintock* (New York: Nelson and Phillips, 1876), 158.

184   **were arrested on charges**: See Martha C. Slotten, "The McClintock Slave Riot of 1847," *Cumberland County History* 17 (2000): 14–35.

185   **"probably not an abolitionist"**: Quoted in Slotten, "McClintock Slave Riot of 1847," 18.

185   **"the Abolition fanatics"**: *American Volunteer*, June 28, 1847, quoted in Slotten, "McClintock Slave Riot of 1847," 26.

186   **"one of the most fatal blows"**: Calhoun and Garrison, quoted in Lubet, *Fugitive Justice*, 32, 33.

186   **"This decision of the Supreme Court"**: Benton, *Thirty Years' View*, 2:778.

Chapter 8: To the Brink

190   **The slave population was growing**: Howe, *What Hath God Wrought*, 659–60; Randolph B. Campbell, "Slavery," in *Handbook of Texas Online*, accessed Feb. 22, 2018, tshaonline.org/handbook/online/articles/yps01.

190   **"put an inch or two"**: Joseph G. Baldwin, *The Flush Times of Alabama and Mississippi* (1853; repr., Baton Rouge: Louisiana State University Press, 1987), 307–8.

190   **who "are imitating"**: Walker, quoted in James P. Shenton, *Robert John Walker: A Politician from Jackson to Lincoln* (New York: Columbia University Press, 1961), 22.

190   **"a race war"**: Howe, *What Hath God Wrought*, 666.

191   **pressuring slavery out of existence**: Brown, *Moral Capital*, 94, 11–13.

191   **"an asylum for all"**: Jackson, quoted in Freehling, *Secessionists at Bay*, 416. Historians are still arguing over whether there was ever much chance that such a deal would be reached, or whether it was merely a scare promoted by pro-slavery advocates.

191   **"to overspread the continent"**: "Annexation," *Democratic Review*, July 1845, 5. The famous phrase was probably coined by the editor, John L. O'Sullivan, though one recent scholar has attributed it to Jane Storm, a journalist who wrote for the magazine under various pseudonyms. See Linda Hudson, *Mistress of Manifest Destiny* (Austin: University of Texas Press, 2001), 60–62.

191   **"The cry of Free Men"**: Douglass, quoted in Michael F. Holt, *The Political Crisis of the 1850s* (New York: W. W. Norton, 1978), 191.

192   **grow cotton profitably**: Beckert, *Empire of Cotton*, 103.

192   **"I skirt sierras"**: Walt Whitman, "Song of Myself," in *Complete Poetry and Collected Prose* (New York: Library of America, 1982), 219.

192   **"Is not America"**: Walt Whitman, "Prohibition of Colored Persons," *Brooklyn Daily Times*, May 6, 1858, quoted in *A House Divided: The Antebellum Slavery Debates in America, 1776–1865*, ed. Mason I. Lowance Jr. (Princeton, N.J.: Princeton University Press, 2003), 201.

192   **"the proof of a poet"**: Walt Whitman, preface to *Leaves of Grass* (1885), in *Complete Poetry and Collected Prose*, 26.

192   **"masked its intentions"**: Boernstein, *Memoirs of a Nobody*, 139. Cuba was regarded by southern propagandists as an ideal slave society threatened by British efforts to foment slave rebellion. In 1844, Charleston physician J. G. F. Wurdemann warned that Britain was plotting to overthrow slavery in Cuba just as it was doing in Texas, in order "to form around our southern shores a cordon of free negroes." Wurdemann, quoted in Matthew Karp, *This Vast Southern Empire*, 61. Fearful that the Spanish government would lose its grip on Cuba, which, like Haiti, would then fall under the rule of self-emancipated slaves, the U.S. government—whose foreign policy, Karp argues, was largely controlled by pro-slavery interests—made repeated offers to purchase the island. See Karp, *This Vast Southern Empire*, 57–69, 229–30.

194 **"funnel through which"**: Shenton, *Robert John Walker,* 2.
194 **"what color you was"**: These are the words of Felix Haywood, a former slave interviewed in 1937 at the age of ninety-two. See George P. Rawick, *The American Slave: A Composite Autobiography* (Westport, Conn.: Greenwood Press, 1972), 4:132. As early as 1827, the U.S. Congress had proposed a treaty to the Mexican government requiring the return of fugitive slaves. See Samuel Gridley Howe, *Report to the Freedmen's Commission: The Refugees from Slavery in Canada West* (Boston, 1864), 12.
194 **"had ceased to distinguish"**: Baldwin, *Flush Times of Alabama and Mississippi,* 4. In fact, Walker was not alone in imagining that racially mixed Mexico could solve America's race problem. In 1833, the Quaker abolitionist Benjamin Lundy had traveled to San Antonio (still under Mexican rule at the time) on a mission to buy land on which he hoped to relocate emancipated American slaves. There he recalled meeting a "jet-black" man who told him that "the Mexicans pay him the same respect as to other laboring people, there being no difference made here on account of colour." See Benjamin Lundy, *The Life, Travels, and Opinions of Benjamin Lundy* (Philadelphia: William D. Parrish, 1847), 48. See also Ronnie C. Tyler, "Fugitive Slaves in Mexico," *Journal of Negro History* 57, no. 1 (Jan. 1972): 1–12.
194 **"crowding into the far South"**: Tocqueville, *Democracy in America,* 357. By 1860, slaves had risen to 47.5 percent of the population in the first seven states to secede from the Union following Lincoln's election. See Holt, *Political Crisis of the 1850s,* 224.
194 **the "Negro pens"**: Boernstein, *Memoirs of a Nobody,* 263.
194 **sight of a Maryland slave:** George Wilson Pierson, *Tocqueville in America* (Baltimore: Johns Hopkins University Press, 1938), 491.
194 **slave could be whipped:** Grimes, *Life of William Grimes,* 41.
195 **"coffle" of seventy-five slaves:** Harrold, *Border War,* 17.
196 **as "retaliatory measures"**: Sinha, *Slave's Cause,* 64, 201.
196 **"that one good black"**: David Walker, *Walker's Appeal in Four Articles; Together with a Preamble to the Coloured Citizens of the World, but in Particular, and Very Expressly, to Those of the United States of America* (Boston, 1830), 29.
196 **"reach the slaveholder's conscience"**: Douglass, Dec. 1860, quoted in Levine, *Lives of Frederick Douglass,* 192.
196 **"the insurrection of Nathaniel Turner"**: Douglass, *My Bondage and My Freedom,* ed. Blight, 134.
196 **"rejoice in every uprising"**: Frederick Douglass, Speech of Dec. 3, 1860, quoted in Harold Holzer and Norton Garfinkle, *A Just and Generous Nation: Abraham Lincoln and the Fight for American Opportunity* (New York: Basic Books, 2015), 59.
196 **"with clubs, handspikes, and knives"**: The newspaper account was reprinted in the *Liberator,* Dec. 31, 1841, quoted in Levine, *Lives of Frederick Douglass,* 129.
197 **Fathers could be flogged:** William Goodell, *The American Slave Code in Theory and Practice* (New York: American and Foreign Anti-slavery Society, 1853), 321–22.
197 **"forbidden on pain"**: Boernstein, *Memoirs of a Nobody,* 263.
197 **"every negro house"**: Theodore D. Weld, *American Slavery as It Is: Testimony of a Thousand Witnesses* (New York: American Anti-slavery Society, 1839), 51.
197 **Every "slaveholding community"**: Douglass, *My Bondage and My Freedom,* ed. Blight, 256.
197 **"knowledge of letters"**: Charles Colcock Jones, *The Religious Instruction of the Negroes in the United States* (Savannah, Ga.: Thomas Purse, 1842), 115.
197 **"took an almost malicious satisfaction"**: Quoted in Gerda Lerner, *The Grimké Sisters from South Carolina: Pioneers for Women's Rights and Abolition* (Chapel Hill: University of North Carolina Press, 2004), 18.
198 **"not *one* city"**: Angelina Grimké, *Appeal to the Christian Women of the South* (New York, 1836), 10.
198 **"two terrors were constantly"**: James Freeman Clarke, *Anti-slavery Days* (New York: R. Worthington, 1884), 19.
198 **"servants knowing that"**: St. George Tucker to Lelia Tucker, Jan. 19, 1813, quoted in Taylor, *Internal Enemy,* 230.
198 **lived in fear:** Irving H. Bartlett, *John C. Calhoun* (New York: W. W. Norton, 1993), 281. One of the accused conspirators was hanged; two were lashed and branded.
198 **Arson, suspected in every fire:** Steven Channing, *Crisis of Fear: Secession in South Carolina* (New York: W. W. Norton, 1970), 43–44.
198 **A slave's "impudence"**: Bertram Wyatt-Brown, *Honor and Violence in the Old South* (New York: Oxford University Press, 1986), 158.
199 **"only living *white* men"**: Edgar Allan Poe, *The Narrative of Arthur Gordon Pym,* in *Poe: Poetry, Tales, and Selected Essays* (New York: Library of America, 1984), 1156, italics added.
199 **"Whatever liberty is worth"**: Martin R. Delany, *Blake; or, The Huts of America,* ed. Floyd J. Miller (Boston: Beacon Press, 1970), 192. Delany's novel was first published in *The Weekly Anglo-African,* between November 1861 and May 1862.

199   **outbreak of slave rebellion:** Jefferson, "Query XVIII," *Notes on the State of Virginia*, 289.

199   **"the most horrible of civil wars":** Tocqueville, *Democracy in America*, 360.

199   **"Union at hazard":** Adams, quoted in Miller, *Arguing About Slavery*, 190.

199   **the gag rule:** For an account of the introduction and persistence of the gag rule, see Miller, *Arguing About Slavery*, 204–10.

200   **"as near the boundary line":** Quoted in Howe, *What Hath God Wrought*, 734.

201   **"mischievous, but wicked":** Polk, April 6, 1847, in *The Diary of a President, 1845–1849*, ed. Allan Nevins (New York: Longmans, Green, 1952), 210.

201   **"It is to be doubted":** Speech of Alexander H. Stephens of Georgia in the House of Representatives, Feb. 12, 1847, *Cong. Globe*, 29th Cong., 2nd Sess., app., 352, 351.

201   **"the best speech":** Lincoln to William H. Herndon, Feb. 2, 1848, in *Collected Works of Lincoln*, 1:448.

201   **"joined the contemptible hordes":** William L. Yancey, quoted in Thomas E. Schott, *Alexander H. Stephens of Georgia: A Biography* (Baton Rouge: Louisiana State University Press, 1988), 72.

202   **"I would not care":** *North Star*, June 15, 1849, quoted in Fergus M. Bordewich, *America's Great Debate: Henry Clay, Stephen A. Douglas, and the Compromise That Preserved the Union* (New York: Simon & Schuster, 2012), 10. Douglass delivered these lines at the New England Convention, May 31, 1849.

202   **remembers the Vietnam years:** One limit to the analogy is that in the case of the Mexican War the division in public opinion was largely partisan, with most Democrats supportive and most Whigs opposed.

202   **a staggering expansion:** This figure includes Texas and the territorial transfer from Mexico that was completed by the Gadsden Purchase in 1853; the size of Mexico was reduced by more than half.

203   **"Mexico will poison us":** Emerson, quoted in Porte, *Emerson in His Journals*, 275.

203   **"little about Mexico":** Robert Montgomery Bird, quoted in Clement Edgar Foust, *The Life and Dramatic Works of Robert Montgomery Bird* (New York: Knickerbocker Press, 1919), 89–90.

203   **"the large acquisition":** Benton, *Thirty Years' View*, 2:724.

203   **"Before I vote":** Horace Greeley, *Recollections of a Busy Life* (New York: J. B. Ford, 1868), 252.

204   **soft on defending slavery:** See John S. D. Eisenhower, *Zachary Taylor* (New York: Holt, 2008), 102.

205   **"a cockpit in which":** Potter, *Impending Crisis*, 67.

206   **"the slave power must":** Douglass, "Anti-slavery Movement," 394.

206   **dozen richest counties:** James Oakes, *The Ruling Race: A History of American Slaveholders* (New York: W. W. Norton, 1998), 39. Karp, *This Vast Empire*, 226, points out that while the southern "share of slave-state representatives in Congress had grown smaller with each election . . . in the executive branch southern power and southern influence were never overthrown" until the election of 1860.

206   **the "Saudi Arabia":** Beckert, *Empire of Cotton*, 113.

206–7 **"*lie down* pleasantly dreaming":** Abraham Lincoln, "House Divided Speech," June 16, 1858, in *Collected Works of Lincoln*, 2:467.

207   **"living up here":** Miller, *Arguing About Slavery*, 187.

207   **Slaves running north:** Joshua Giddings, *Speeches in Congress* (Boston: John P. Jewett, 1853), 175. See also p. 395.

207   **cascade of panic sales:** Robert A. Burt, *The Constitution in Conflict* (Cambridge, Mass.: Harvard University Press, 1992), 180. See also Oakes, *Scorpion's Sting*, 35.

207   **"growing more hostile":** Freehling, *Secessionists at Bay*, 473.

207   **"day of its doom":** John Stuart Mill, *Contest in America* (1862), quoted in Holzer and Garfinkle, *Just and Generous Nation*, 72. The historian Walter Johnson puts the matter even more briefly: "In order to survive, slave-holders had to expand." *River of Dark Dreams*, 14.

207   **"Confined to prescribed limits":** Governor William Smith of Virginia, quoted by J. A. Rockwell of Connecticut, Feb. 17, 1849, *Cong. Globe*, 30th Cong., 2nd Sess., app., 232. See also Potter, *Impending Crisis*, 93.

208   **"predominance in every department":** John C. Calhoun, "On the Slavery Question, Delivered in the Senate, March 4th, 1850," in *Works*, 4:545.

208   **"Ostensibly," he wrote:** Benton, *Thirty Years' View*, 2:696.

208   **Connecticut Supreme Court:** Finkelman, *Imperfect Union*, 127–30.

208   **were free regardless:** McKirdy, *Lincoln Apostate*, 68.

208   **"shall not give":** *The Acts of the General Assembly of the Commonwealth of Pennsylvania* (Philadelphia: Francis Bailey, 1782), 286.

209   **"By the laws of this country":** Justice Alexander Porter, quoted in Morris, *Free Men All*, 14.

209   **"Better disunion, better a civil":** *Cong. Globe*, House of Representatives, 31st Cong., 1st Sess., Feb. 15, 1850, app., 224.

210   **"the paradox of the 1850s":** Karp, *This Vast Southern Empire*, 9.

210   **"Evils which are":** Alexis de Tocqueville, *The Old Regime and the Revolution*, trans. John Bonner (New York: Harper and Brothers, 1856), 214.

210 **"revolution of rising expectations":** Now conventional in sociological literature, the concept is often traced to Tocqueville.

210 **"bitterness and anxiety":** Barrington Moore Jr., *Social Origins of Dictatorship and Democracy* (Boston: Beacon Press, 1966), 122.

211 **"agitating our country":** David Rorer (attorney for the plaintiff in the Iowa case of *Daggs v. Frazier*), "An Iowa Fugitive Slave Case—1850," *Annals of Iowa* 6, no. 1 (1903): 37.

211 **marking him forever:** For excellent summaries of these cases as well as excerpts from the legal documents, see Finkelman, *Slavery in the Courtroom*, 161–72.

211 **"deny the right":** Finkelman, *Imperfect Union*, 167–71.

212 **"was law, not morality":** David Herbert Donald, *Lincoln* (London: Jonathan Cape, 1995), 104.

212 **He ruled against:** See Foner, *Fiery Trial*, 47–49, and for a full study of the *Matson* case, see McKirdy, *Lincoln Apostate*.

212 **"You may go up":** *The History of Henry County, Iowa* (Chicago: Western Historical Company, 1879), 543.

213 **sued six Iowans:** See Finkelman, *Slavery in the Courtroom*, 79–80.

213 **"the age of tyrants":** Daniel Drayton, *Personal Memoir of Daniel Drayton* (Boston: American and Foreign Anti-slavery Society, 1853), 27.

213 **remained enslaved in neighboring states:** Ricks, *Escape on the Pearl*, 259.

213 **"gentleman of Washington":** Ricks, *Escape on the* Pearl, 23.

214 **"Breakfasts were not ready":** Pacheco, *The Pearl*, 57.

214 **"any riotous or tumultuous":** Fehrenbacher, *Slaveholding Republic*, 51.

215 **a "double-distilled devil":** Quoted in Pacheco, *The Pearl*, 95.

215 **fending off relatives:** Pacheco, *The Pearl*, 92.

216 **abandon their slaves:** Bordewich, *America's Great Debate*, 51.

216 **"all causes of uneasiness":** Zachary Taylor, "Annual Message," Dec. 4, 1849. Online by Gerhard Peters and John T. Woolley, *The American Presidency Project*, presidency.ucsb.edu/ws/?pid=29490.

217 **alienated southern supporters:** Walter Stahr, *Seward: Lincoln's Indispensable Man* (New York: Simon & Schuster, 2012), 69.

217 **confront "disquieting issues":** Freehling, *Secessionists at Bay*, 491.

217 **"avow themselves disunionists":** Calhoun, quoted in Potter, *Impending Crisis*, 94.

217 **"The value of the Union":** Hammond and Crallé, quoted in Egnal, *Clash of Extremes*, 92.

217 **meetings were called:** Potter, *Impending Crisis*, 94. See also Melvin J. White, *The Secession Movement in the United States, 1847–1852* (New Orleans, 1910), 59.

217 **"if this Union":** Hale, quoted in Potter, *Impending Crisis*, 45.

218 **"Thou too, sail on":** Henry Wadsworth Longfellow, "The Building of the Ship," in *Henry Wadsworth Longfellow: Poems and Other Writings* (New York: Library of America, 2000), 126.

218 **"prostituted his fine genius":** *Annual Report Presented to the Massachusetts Anti-slavery Society, January 23, 1850*, 99, 100.

218 **for "IMMEDIATE DISSOLUTION":** *Annual Report Presented to the Massachusetts Anti-slavery Society, January 24, 1849*, 86.

219 **flaunting his "wages":** *Annual Report Presented to the Massachusetts Anti-slavery Society, January 26, 1848*, 86.

219 **"I do not hesitate":** *Cong. Globe*, 31st Cong., 1st Sess., Dec. 13, 1849, 27–28, quoted in Potter, *Impending Crisis*, 94.

219 **"we talk flippantly":** *Cong. Globe*, Senate, 31st Cong., 1st Sess., Feb. 11, 1850, 331.

Chapter 9: State of the Union

220 **idea of secession:** For recent variations on the theme, see Richard Striner, "A Brief History of Secession: Why Calexit Might Not Be as Crazy as You Think," *American Scholar*, March 6, 2017, and Kevin Baker, "Bluexit: A Modest Proposal for Separating Blue States from Red," *New Republic*, March 9, 2017, newrepublic.com/article/140948/bluexit-blue-states-exit-trump-red-america. Baker makes a tongue-in-cheek argument that "blue states" should cease subsidizing "red states" by withholding tax revenue from the federal government. One measure of how long it has been since the idea of secession had any real currency in American life is the work of the distinguished émigré social scientist Albert O. Hirschman. Writing in the mid-twentieth century about America's "national love affair with exit" (by which he meant that the United States was settled by people who left their native lands rather than remain under some form of tyranny), Hirschman never mentions the largest instance of collective exit in American history, the secession of eleven states in 1861. *Exit, Voice, and Loyalty: Responses to Decline in Firms, Organizations, and States* (Cambridge, Mass.: Harvard University Press, 1970), 112.

221   **as "living history":** Lincoln, "Address Before the Young Men's Lyceum of Springfield, Illinois," Jan. 27, 1838, *Collected Works of Lincoln*, 1:115.
221   **"a secessionist ethos":** Jay Winik, *April 1865: The Month That Saved America* (New York: HarperCollins, 2001), 16.
221   **"who was born":** Calhoun, "On the Slavery Question, Delivered in the Senate, March 4th, 1850," 561–62.
221   **"implied, if not expressed":** Lincoln, "First Inaugural Address," March 4, 1861, in *Collected Works of Lincoln*, 4:252.
221   **they were deferred:** See Kenneth Stampp, "The Concept of a Perpetual Union," in *Imperiled Union*, 3–36.
221   **threatened secession if:** Sinha, *Slave's Cause*, 69.
221   **"I love the Union":** Adams to William Vans Murray, April 7, 1801, in *Writings of John Quincy Adams*, ed. Worthington C. Ford, 7 vols. (New York, 1913), 2:526.
222   **meeting at Hartford:** Richard Buel Jr., *America on the Brink: How the Political Struggle over the War of 1812 Almost Destroyed the Young Republic* (New York: Palgrave Macmillan, 2005), 220. For a full discussion of the debate, see *America on the Brink*, chaps. 7–8.
222   **"no magic in":** Pickering, quoted in Stampp, *Imperiled Union*, 24. Pickering had been a leader of the secessionist faction in 1804.
222   **"if the Union":** *Memoirs of John Quincy Adams Comprising Portions of His Diary from 1795 to 1848*, 12 vols. (Philadelphia, 1874–76), 5:12, quoted in Stampp, *Imperiled Union*, 27.
222   **"this government is the breath":** Quoted in Adams, *John Randolph*, 180.
222   **"federated along one keel":** Melville, *Moby-Dick*, 121.
223   **"right to impose":** Calhoun, "Speech on the Revenue Collection Bill (Commonly Called the Force Bill), in Reference to the Ordinance of the South Carolina Convention, Delivered in the Senate, February 15th and 16th, 1833," 198.
223   **"a miracle of mercy":** John Witherspoon, quoted in Oakes, *Ruling Race*, 110.
223   **"It was formed":** Madison to Everett, Aug. 28, 1830, in *James Madison: Writings* (New York: Library of America, 1999), 843, 848.
224   **"essence of anarchy":** Abraham Lincoln, "First Inaugural Address," *Collected Works of Lincoln*, 4:253, 256.
224   **"any people anywhere":** Abraham Lincoln, "Speech in United States House of Representatives: The War with Mexico," Jan. 12, 1848, in *Collected Works of Lincoln*, 1:438. See also Thomas J. Pressly, "Bullets and Ballots: Lincoln and the 'Right of Revolution,'" *American Historical Review* 67, no. 3 (April 1962): 647–62.
225   **doctrine were adopted:** Remini, *At the Edge of the Precipice*, 52, 56.
225   **"conglomerated mass of gold-hunters":** *Cong. Globe*, Senate, 31st Cong., 1st Sess., Feb. 13, 1850, app., 151.
226   **doctrine of popular sovereignty:** Elbert B. Smith, *The Presidencies of Zachary Taylor and Millard Fillmore* (Lawrence: University Press of Kansas, 1988), 102.
226   **a stymied Texas:** Remini, *At the Edge of the Precipice*, 59.
226   **one thousand fugitives:** Campbell, *Slave Catchers*, 6.
226   **had "greatly magnified":** Craven, *Coming of the Civil War*, 246.
227   **Two weeks later:** Campbell, *Slave Catchers*, 15.
227   **commissioners were corrupt police:** Samuel J. May, *Some Recollections of Our Anti-slavery Conflict* (Boston, 1869), 346–47; Lubet, *Fugitive Justice*, 42–44.
227   **"forts, arsenals, and dockyards":** Solomon Downs of Louisiana, *Cong. Globe*, 31st Cong., 1st Sess., June 8, 1850, app., 795.
228   **"meet with no resistance":** *Cong. Globe*, Senate, 31st Cong., 1st Sess., Jan. 4, 1850, 103.
228   **"I have little hope":** *Cong. Globe*, Senate, 31st Cong., 1st Sess., Jan. 28, 1850, 233.
228   **"no very great confidence":** *Cong. Globe*, 31st Cong., 1st Sess., Jan. 24, 1850, app., 79. For the earlier bill, see Harrold, *Border War*, 142.
228   **"as well enforced":** Lincoln, "First Inaugural Address," March 4, 1861, in *Collected Works of Lincoln*, 4:269.
229   **"the feeling of disunion":** Quoted in Remini, *At the Edge of the Precipice*, 56.
229   **spent the summer:** Merrill D. Peterson, *The Great Triumvirate: Webster, Clay, and Calhoun* (New York: Oxford University Press, 1987), 452.
229   **transportation to Liberia:** Daniel Walker Howe, *The Political Culture of the American Whigs* (Chicago: University of Chicago Press, 1979), 133.
229   **The colonization movement:** David Brion Davis, *The Problem of Slavery in the Age of Emancipation* (New York: Knopf, 2014), 107–8.
230   **"What do I know":** Quarles, *Black Abolitionists*, 219.
230   **"I would rather":** Quarles, *Black Abolitionists*, 216. Garnet was more interested in the idea that blacks could develop independent communities located somewhere in the expanding territories of the United States.
230   **"to their political elevation":** Delany, quoted in Quarles, *Black Abolitionists*, 215.
230   **"would become proprietors":** Harper, quoted in Davis, *Problem of Slavery in the Age of Emancipation*, 108.

230 **"Reduce the supply":** Lincoln, "Annual Message to Congress," Dec. 1, 1862, in *Collected Works of Lincoln*, 5:535.

231 **"ultimate redemption of the African":** Abraham Lincoln, "Eulogy on Henry Clay," July 6, 1852, in *Collected Works of Lincoln*, 2:132.

231 **"the brooding indolence":** Henry Adams, *The Education of Henry Adams* (1918; repr., New York: Library of America, 1990), 46.

231 **"ideologue of the center":** Howe, *Political Culture of the American Whigs*, 125.

232 **"reproaches came thick":** Frederick Douglass, "Oration in Memory of Abraham Lincoln," April 14, 1876, in *The Lincoln Anthology: Great Writers on His Life and Legacy from 1860 to Now*, ed. Harold Holzer (New York: Library of America, 2009), 231.

232 **Clay brandished it:** *Cong. Globe*, Senate, 31st Cong., 1st Sess., Jan. 29, 1850, 246.

233 **"What a squeeze":** *New-York Tribune*, Feb. 8, 1850, quoted in Peterson, *Great Triumvirate*, 457.

234 **"he had to unwind":** Kate Chase, quoted in David S. Heidler and Jeanne T. Heidler, *Henry Clay: The Essential American* (New York: Random House, 2010), 463.

234 **"of all the States":** *Cong. Globe*, Senate, 31st Cong., 1st Sess., Feb. 6, 1850, app., 123.

235 **"most cordially and willingly":** *Cong. Globe*, Senate, 31st Cong., 1st Sess., Feb. 6, 1850, app., 124, 123.

235 **"The Supreme Court":** *Cong. Globe*, Senate, 31st Cong., 1st Sess., Feb. 6, 1850, app., 123.

236 **"you may as well":** Quoted in Freehling, *Secessionists at Bay*, 501.

236 **"I do not say":** *Cong. Globe*, Senate, 31st Cong., 1st Sess., Feb. 6, 1850, app., 122.

236 **"posterity, undefined, unlimited":** *Cong. Globe*, Senate, 31st Cong., 1st Sess., Feb. 6, 1850, app., 127.

Chapter 10: The Last Truce

237 **"there will be no disunion":** Webster to Peter Harvey, Feb. 13, 1850, in *The Letters of Daniel Webster*, ed. C. H. Van Tyne (1902; repr., New York: Greenwood Press, 1968), 392.

237 **"there are two incompatible":** Henry Ward Beecher, "Shall We Compromise?," *Independent*, Feb. 21, 1850, reprinted in Henry Ward Beecher, *Patriotic Addresses*, ed. John R. Howard (New York: Fords, Howard, and Hulbert, 1887), 167; Calhoun, quoted in Peterson, *Great Triumvirate*, 460.

237–38 **"cadaverous, ghost-like man":** Herman Melville, *Mardi, and a Voyage Thither* (1849; repr., Evanston, Ill.: Northwestern University Press, 1970), 532.

238 **a "small potato":** Scoville to James G. Bennett, April 30, 1850, *New York Herald*, May 5, 1850.

238 **"he was evidently approaching":** William T. Sherman, *Memoirs of General W. T. Sherman* (New York: Library of America, 1990), 107.

238 **"Mr. Calhoun, in his earlier days":** Francis Lieber, "Address Read at the Inaugural Meeting of the Loyal National League, by the Request of the League, in Union Square, New York, on the 11th of April, 1863," in *The Civil War: The Third Year Told by Those Who Lived It*, ed. Brooks D. Simpson (New York: Library of America, 2013), 142.

239 **a "positive good":** John C. Calhoun, "Speech on the Reception of Abolition Petitions," Feb. 6, 1837, in *Works*, 2:631–32.

240 **"In all social systems":** "Speech of Hon. J. H. Hammond of South Carolina, Mar. 4, 1858," in Cong. Globe, 35th Cong., 1st Sess., app., 71.

240 **He was a sexual predator:** Carol Bleser, *The Hammonds of Redcliffe* (New York: Oxford University Press, 1981), 10; Carol Bleser, ed., *Secret and Sacred: The Diaries of James Henry Hammond, a Southern Slaveholder* (New York: Oxford University Press, 1988), 18.

240 **"I am averse":** Quoted in Drew Gilpin Faust, *James Henry Hammond and the Old South: A Design for Mastery* (Baton Rouge: Louisiana State University Press, 1982), 315.

240 **calls "caste pride":** Eugene Genovese, *The World the Slaveholders Made* (New York: Vintage Books, 1969), 208.

241 **"no social state":** Iveson Brookes, *A Defence of Southern Slavery* (Hamburg, S.C.: Robinson and Carlisle, 1851), quoted in Lacy K. Ford Jr., *Origins of Southern Radicalism: The South Carolina Upcountry, 1800–1860* (New York: Oxford University Press, 1988), 351.

241 **"Virginians," Foster wrote:** Quoted in Edmund S. Morgan, *American Slavery, American Freedom: The Ordeal of Colonial Virginia* (New York: W. W. Norton, 1975), 380.

241 **higher rates of insanity:** Peterson, *Great Triumvirate*, 346–47. For a discussion of Calhoun's letters to Pakenham, and the spurious census evidence on which he based his conclusions, see Bartlett, *John C. Calhoun*, 310–14.

242 **"the most odious and dangerous":** Quoted in Bartlett, *John C. Calhoun*, 222.

242 **"I never heard":** Bartlett, *John C. Calhoun*, 282–83.

242 **"in the double capacity":** Quoted in Richard Hofstadter, *The American Political Tradition and the Men Who Made It* (New York: Vintage, 1948), 77.

242   "the place of a Charleston gentleman": Bartlett, *John C. Calhoun*, 53.

242   "of fair and candid mind": Quoted in Miller, *Arguing About Slavery*, 185.

243   "eyes, bright as coals": Nathaniel Parker Willis, *Hurry-Graphs; or, Sketches of Scenery, Celebrities, and Society* (New York, 1851), 181. Willis, a friend of Edgar Allan Poe, employed the fugitive slave Harriet Jacobs in his home in New York City. In 1852, Willis's wife, Cornelia, bought Jacobs's freedom for $300, half of which she paid from her own funds and half of which she raised from friends, to whom she described Harriet as a "most legitimate charity." *The Harriet Jacobs Family Papers* (Chapel Hill: University of North Carolina Press, 2008), 2 vols., ed. Jean Fagan Yellin et al., 1:180.

243   "the very incarnation": *Seventeenth Annual Report Presented to the Massachusetts Anti-slavery Society by Its Board of Managers, January 24, 1849* (Boston: Andrews and Prentiss, 1849), 7.

243   "incomparably to be preferred": *Seventeenth Annual Report Presented to the Massachusetts Anti-slavery Society*, 86.

243   "such men as Mr. Clay": *Eighteenth Annual Report Presented to the Massachusetts Anti-slavery Society by Its Board of Managers, January 23, 1850* (Boston: Andrews and Prentiss, 1850), 30.

244   "absolutely right and absolutely wrong": Daniel Webster used this phrase to describe abolitionists in his speech of March 7, 1850.

244   "Even the sight of Satan": *Eighteenth Annual Report Presented to the Massachusetts Anti-slavery Society*, 30–31.

244   the "social organization": Calhoun, "On the Slavery Question, Delivered in the Senate, March 4th, 1850," 552.

244   "be saved by eulogies": Calhoun, "On the Slavery Question, Delivered in the Senate, March 4th, 1850," 559.

244   the "perfect equilibrium": Calhoun, "On the Slavery Question, Delivered in the Senate, March 4th, 1850," 544.

244   "to give the northern section": Calhoun, "On the Slavery Question, Delivered in the Senate, March 4th, 1850," 545.

244   government had "changed": Calhoun, "On the Slavery Question, Delivered in the Senate, March 4th, 1850," 551.

245   "what they call the Nation": Calhoun, "On the Slavery Question, Delivered in the Senate, March 4th, 1850," 552.

245   "the great exporting portion": Calhoun, "On the Slavery Question, Delivered in the Senate, March 4th, 1850," 549.

245   Fewer than one in thirty: Egnal, *Clash of Extremes*, 59.

245   had only three towns: Elizabeth Fox-Genovese, *Within the Plantation Household: Black and White Women of the Old South* (Chapel Hill: University of North Carolina Press, 1988), 78.

245   "honored violence as a sign": Howe, *Political Culture of the American Whigs*, 129.

246   "depopulated and impoverished": Hinton Rowan Helper, *The Impending Crisis of the South: How to Meet It* (1857), in *Ante-bellum: Three Classic Works on Slavery in the Old South*, ed. Harvey Wish (New York: Capricorn Books, 1960), 171–72.

246   "no government, based": John C. Calhoun, "Original Draft of the South Carolina Exposition, Prepared for the Special Committee on the Tariff, and, with Considerable Alterations, Adopted by the Legislature of South Carolina," Dec. 1828, in *Works*, 6:33, quoted in Hofstadter, *American Political Tradition*, 71.

246   "knows nothing of the human heart": John C. Calhoun, "Speech on the Amendment Proposed to Mr. Webster's Bill in Regard to the Public Deposits," June 28, 1838, in *Works*, 3:357.

246   "the last American statesman": Hofstadter, *American Political Tradition*, 69.

247   some northern conservatives: George Ticknor was one prominent example. See David B. Tyack, *George Ticknor and the Boston Brahmins* (Cambridge, Mass.: Harvard University Press, 1967), 229–30.

247   "we of the South": John C. Calhoun, "Speech on the Oregon Bill," June 27, 1848, in *Works*, 4:501.

247   must be "vested": Calhoun, "On the Slavery Question, Delivered in the Senate, March 4th, 1850," 564.

247   equilibrium between the sections: John C. Calhoun, *A Disquisition on Government*, in *Works*, 1:392–95.

247   "Mr. Calhoun, intent": Benton, *Thirty Years' View*, 2:741.

248   "most vital of all questions": *Cong. Globe*, 30th Cong., 1st Sess., April 20, 1848, app., 501.

248   "sophistry and subterfuges": John C. Calhoun, "Address to the Southern Delegates in Congress," in *Works*, 6:293.

248   "the North must do her duty": Calhoun, "On the Slavery Question, Delivered in the Senate, March 4th, 1850," 572.

248   "The cast-iron man": The phrase is Harriet Martineau's, quoted in Alan Heimert, "*Moby-Dick* and American Political Symbolism," *American Quarterly* 15, no. 4 (Winter 1963): 523.

248   "He is not dead": Quoted in Smith, *Presidencies of Zachary Taylor and Millard Fillmore*, 118.

249   "all this agitation": Remini, *At the Edge of the Precipice*, 63–64.

249 **"I am nearly broken down":** Webster to Daniel Fletcher Webster, Feb. 24, 1850, in *Papers of Webster: Correspondence,* 7:16.

249 **"I mean to make an honest":** Webster to Charles Henry Warren, March 1, 1850, in *Papers of Webster: Correspondence,* 7:20.

249 **"Liberty and Union":** "Second Reply to Hayne, Jan. 26–27, 1830: Published Version," in *The Papers of Daniel Webster: Speeches and Formal Writings, vol. 1, 1800–1830,* ed. Charles M. Wiltse and Michael J. Birkner (Hanover, N.H.: University Press of New England, 1986), 348.

249 **"from my earliest youth":** Webster to Furness, Feb. 15, 1850, in *Papers of Webster: Correspondence,* 7:11.

249 **"give yourself utterly":** Furness to Webster, Jan. 9, 1850, in Van Tyne, *Letters of Daniel Webster,* 390.

249 **"a good deal moved":** Webster to Furness, Feb. 15, 1850, 11.

250 **as "peaceable secession":** Webster to Furness, Feb. 15, 1850, 12.

250 **"I am for the abolition of slavery":** Garrison to May, Jan. 13, 1850, in *Letters of William Lloyd Garrison,* ed. Louis Ruchames (Cambridge, Mass.: Harvard University Press, 1975), 4:4. With the thinker's condescension for the doer, Emerson called May "God's chore-boy" (quoted in Von Frank, *Trials of Anthony Burns,* 21).

250 **"attained the preponderance of strength":** Potter, *Impending Crisis,* 95.

250 **"dreaming of a new empire":** Margaret Leech, *Reveille in Washington* (1941; New York: New York Review of Books, 2011), 25.

251 **"an honorable member":** Webster, "Constitution and the Union, March 7, 1850," 525.

251 **"south of the line":** Webster, "Constitution and the Union, March 7, 1850," 518–19.

252 **"view things as they are":** Webster, "Constitution and the Union, March 7, 1850," 526, 522.

252 **"compromises or modifications":** Webster, "Constitution and the Union, March 7, 1850," 521.

252 **"I will allude":** Webster, "Constitution and the Union, March 7, 1850," 540.

253 **the word "compromise":** Stahr, *Seward,* 123.

254 **"heavy in the extreme":** Sherman, *Memoirs,* 109.

255 **"wandering and vagrant philanthropy":** Webster to Edward Sprague Rand et al., May 15, 1850, in *Papers of Webster: Correspondence,* 7:93. See also Richard N. Current, *Daniel Webster and the Rise of National Conservatism* (Boston: Little, Brown, 1955), 167.

255 **a "tranquillizing effect":** *Boston Advertiser,* April 3, 1850. See Maurice G. Baxter, *One and Inseparable: Daniel Webster and the Union* (Cambridge, Mass.: Harvard University Press, 1984), 417.

255 **"'Liberty! liberty!' Pho!":** *Journals of Ralph Waldo Emerson,* ed. Ralph H. Orth and A. R. Ferguson (Cambridge, Mass.: Harvard University Press, 1971), 11:345–46, quoted in Peterson, *Great Triumvirate,* 465.

255 **"All the arguments of Mr. Webster":** Emerson, "Address to the Citizens of Concord on the Fugitive Slave Law," May 3, 1851, 60.

256 **"So fallen! so lost!":** John Greenleaf Whitter, "Ichabod," *National Era,* May 2, 1850, quoted in Peterson, *Great Triumvirate,* 466. Satan's first lines in book 1 are "If thou beest he; but O how fallen! how changed / From him, who in the happy realms of light / Clothed with transcendent brightness didst outshine / Myriads though bright" (lines 84–87). *Paradise Lost* (New York: Oxford University Press, 2005), 20. Whittier's poem contains many other echoes of Milton's language and compares Webster to the fallen angel.

256 **of "fatal apostasy":** Joseph Howard Jr., *Life of Henry Ward Beecher* (Philadelphia: Hubbard Brothers, 1887), 493.

256 **city council of Chicago:** James F. Rhodes, *History of the United States: From the Compromise of 1850 to the McKinley-Bryan Campaign of 1896* (New York: Macmillan, 1920), 1:197.

256 **"Webster's intellectual life":** Horace Mann to Mary Mann, March 8, 1850, quoted in Peterson, *Great Triumvirate,* 465.

256 **In a letter:** See Webster to Rand et al., May 15, 1850, 88–91.

257 **"enthusiasm for self":** Edward Allen Tanner, *Baccalaureate and Other Sermons and Addresses* (Chicago: F. H. Revell, 1892), 201.

257 **accepted "political crucifixion":** John F. Kennedy, *Profiles in Courage* (New York: Harper and Row, 1964), 56.

257 **March 7 speech abject appeasement:** See Paul Finkelman, "The Appeasement of 1850," in *Congress and the Crisis of the 1850s,* ed. Paul Finkelman and Donald R. Kennon (Athens: Ohio University Press, 2012), 36–79.

257 **an agonistic figure:** See Scott M. Reznick, "On Liberty and Union: Moral Imagination and Its Limits in Daniel Webster's Seventh of March Speech," *American Political Thought* 6, no. 3 (Summer 2017): 371–95.

257 **"the calm and cruel confidence":** Craven, *Coming of the Civil War,* 255.

257 **"to enforce upon":** *Cong. Globe,* 31st Cong., 2nd Sess., Feb. 17, 1851, app., 575.

258 **"the Constitution contains":** *Cong. Globe,* 31st Cong., 1st Sess., March 11, 1850, app., 263.

258 **"alter the Constitution":** *Cong. Globe,* 31st Cong., 1st Sess., March 11, 1850, app., 263.

258 **"There is a higher law"**: *Cong. Globe*, 31st Cong., 1st Sess., March 11, 1850, app., 265. See Glyndon G. Van Deusen, *William Henry Seward* (New York: Oxford University Press, 1967), 127–28, for useful commentary on how relatively conventional was the phrase "higher law."

258 **no constitutional basis**: Seward also introduced an amendment to the compromise bill on September 10, 1850, that would abolish slavery outright in the District of Columbia (Cong. Globe, 31st Cong., 1st Sess., Sept. 10, 1850, app., 1642). The amendment provoked much heated debate and was voted down. See Stahr, *Seward,* 131.

258 **"all legislative compromises"**: *Cong. Globe*, 31st Cong., 1st Sess., March 11, 1850, app., 262.

260 **"adjudicating the facts"**: Quoted in Campbell, *Slave Catchers,* 19.

260 **right to a jury trial**: This was an amendment by Stephen A. Douglas to Seward's proposed amendments. See Robert W. Johannsen, *Stephen A. Douglas* (Urbana: University of Illinois Press, 1997), 818.

260 **"the fugitive shall deny"**: *Cong. Globe*, 31st Cong., 1st Sess., June 3, 1850, 1111. See also "Fugitive Slave Bill," June 3, 1850, in *Papers of Webster: Correspondence,* 7:111.

261 **only four senators voted**: Walter A. McDougall, *Throes of Democracy: The American Civil War Era, 1829–1877* (New York: HarperCollins, 2008), 319.

261 **"Looked on merely"**: Rhodes, *History of the United States,* 1:193. Recent scholars tend to agree: "The Compromise gave the North ten years to build its industrial strength and enable it to overpower the South when war finally broke out." Remini, *At the Edge of the Precipice,* xiii.

261 **"should be sustained"**: Calhoun to Clemson, March 10, 1850, in *Correspondence of John C. Calhoun,* ed. J. Franklin Jameson (Washington, D.C.: Government Printing Office, 1900), 2:784.

Chapter 11: Explosion

262 **"howling and hurrahing"**: *The Diary of George Templeton Strong: The Turbulent Fifties, 1850–1859,* ed. Allan Nevins and Milton Halsey Thomas (New York: Macmillan, 1952), 2:24.

262 **"upon a faithful execution"**: *Debates and Proceedings of the Georgia Convention, 1850,* 9.

262 **Secessionist sentiment seemed**: See Campbell, *Slave Catchers,* 72. See also Potter, *Impending Crisis,* 126–29.

262 **crack and boom**: Johannsen, *Stephen A. Douglas,* 297.

262 **"between twenty and thirty"**: "Artful Dodgers," *Concord New Hampshire Patriot & State Gazette,* Nov. 7, 1850, 3.

263 **considered it "injudicious"**: "Senator Benton's Speech," *Brattleboro (Vt.) Semi-weekly Eagle,* Nov. 21, 1850, 2.

263 **"to stand neuter"**: "Benton and Douglas," *New Orleans Daily Picayune,* Sept. 20, 1850, 2. Some predicted that "the South will be the first to pray for its repeal, and that it is now a most effective instrument for working out emancipation. It is the means of carrying back many to slavery, who for a period have tasted the sweets of liberty. They will preach abolition." James J. Robbins, *Report of the Trial of Castner Hanway for Treason, in the Resistance of the Execution of the Fugitive Slave Law of September, 1850* (Philadelphia: King and Baird, 1852), 185.

263 **"noise and confusion"**: "The Fugitive Slave Bill—Absent, Stepped Out, or Not Voting," *Charleston (N.C.) Mercury,* Nov. 21, 1850, 2. Ever since Cass used the phrase "noise and confusion" to excuse a noncommittal speech on internal improvements he delivered in Cleveland during the 1848 presidential campaign, the phrase was used by his critics to mock him. See John Clark Ridpath, *The New Complete History of the United States of America,* vol. 9, *Slavery and the Territories* (Washington, D.C.: Ridpath History Company, 1905), 426.

263 **never cast a vote**: Johannsen, *Stephen A. Douglas,* 296. See also Potter, *Impending Crisis,* 113, who writes that "Northern abstainers skulked in the corridors while every Southern congressman who voted cast his vote in favor."

263 **"has turned Whigs"**: *New York Herald,* reprinted in "Fugitive Slave Bill—Absent, Stepped Out, or Not Voting," 2.

263 **on "law-abiding men"**: Jonathan Blanchard, *Western Citizen,* Nov. 18, 1850, 2.

263 **Douglas responded by saying**: Johannsen, *Stephen A. Douglas,* 302.

263 **"Webster's fugitive-slave bill"**: Thoreau, *Walden, Civil Disobedience, and Other Writings,* 157.

264 **"see him in hell first"**: Quoted in Collison, *Shadrach Minkins,* 89.

264 **"if we would avoid"**: Webster to Thomas B. Curtis, March 21, 1850, in *Papers of Webster: Correspondence,* 7:38.

264 **Hamlet tried to dispute**: Finkelman, *Slavery in the Courtroom,* 85.

264 **was ruled inadmissible**: Quarles, *Black Abolitionists,* 197.

264 **by "two men"**: *The Fugitive Slave Bill; Its History and Unconstitutionality; with an Account of the Seizure and Enslavement of James Hamlet, and His Subsequent Restoration to Liberty* (New York: William Harned, 1850), 5. This pamphlet is reprinted in Finkelman, *Fugitive Slaves and American Courts: The Pamphlet Literature,* series 2, 1:535–72.

265 **"He is a free man":** Quarles, *Black Abolitionists*, 198.

265 **"every colored person":** Jacobs, *Incidents in the Life of a Slave Girl*, 191.

265 **"A fugitive," he wrote:** Theodore Parker, "The Function and Place of Conscience in Relation to the Laws of Men, Sermon Preached on September 22, 1850," in *Collected Works of Theodore Parker*, ed. F. P. Cobbe (London: Trübner, 1863), 5:148.

266 **"fugitive slaves ought not":** Quoted in Dean Grodzins, "'Slave Law' Versus 'Lynch Law' in Boston: Benjamin Robbins Curtis, Theodore Parker, and the Fugitive Slave Crisis, 1850–1855," *Massachusetts Historical Review* 12 (2010): 10.

266 **three were released:** Campbell, *Slave Catchers*, 207.

266 **duty to "surrender":** *The Proceedings of the Union Meeting, Held at Castle Garden, October 30, 1850* (New York: Union Safety Committee, 1850), 24.

266 **"Union safety" committees:** *Proceedings of the Union Meeting, Held at Castle Garden, October 30, 1850*, 25.

267 **the "peace measures":** "Peace measures" was the term used by Webster in his letter to the Union Meeting held at New York's Castle Garden on October 30, 1850, and it came into wide use by compromise advocates and opponents alike. Webster referred to "peace measures" in his letter to Benjamin Franklin Ayer, Nov. 16, 1850, published in the *Boston Daily Advertiser*, Nov. 25, 1850. Webster to Ayer, Nov. 16, 1850, in *Papers of Webster: Correspondence*, 7:183.

267 **"null and void":** Harmon Kingsbury, *The Fugitive Slave Law* (sermon delivered in Cleveland, Oct. 5, 1850), in *Thoughts on the Fugitive Slave Law and the Nebraska Bill* (New York, 1855), 5.

267 **"the vilest law":** May, *Some Recollections of Our Anti-slavery Conflict*, 367, 351. The ministers were, respectively, Orville Dewey and Charles B. Sedgwick. By making vividly credible William Wells Brown's description of America as a vast "hunting ground," the fugitive slave law also deepened the sense of solidarity among antislavery activists throughout the free states. When Henry Long, who had recently escaped from Virginia, was captured in New York on January 8, *the Anti-slavery Bugle*, published in Ohio, reported on his case at length. With the help of a slave hunter named Henry Western, Long was remanded to his owner, Dr. John Smith, of Virginia, who promptly sold him to a buyer in Georgia. The *Bugle* article, titled "That's a Good Dog," showered Western with mock praise as if he were a dog lapping up his master's spit:

> The slave holders understand the management of the canine species, and all those puppies among us who can screw their courage up to the mark of catching a negro and holding on to him, may be sure of something nice from their grateful masters. The *New York Express* contains a correspondence between F. S. Lathrop, Esq., and Henry M. Western, Esq., of New York, which illustrates this. Lathrop writes that his friend Parker, of Richmond, assigned to him "The pleasing duty of presenting the accompanying piece of Plate, in the name, and in behalf of Dr. John D. Smith, of Virginia, as a small testimonial of his appreciation of the eminent and valuable profession services rendered by you in the recovery of his slave Henry Long, and in the vindication of the laws of the United States." The dog Western proudly accepts the plate, and acknowledges his own valuable services in "preserving this glorious Union," but says nothing of the "slave Henry Long." He ought to have added that he would feel proud to lick any Southern expectoration from that platter.

267 **made them celebrities:** An article of April 27, 1849, in the *Liberator*, 67, reported Ellen Craft speaking to an audience of eight to nine hundred people in Newburyport, Massachusetts.

267 **"the most thrilling":** Phillips, quoted in Barker, *Fugitive Slaves and the Unfinished American Revolution*, 26.

267 **"It occurred to me":** William Craft and Ellen Craft, *Running a Thousand Miles for Freedom*, ed. Barbara McCaskill (Athens: University of Georgia Press, 1999), 20–21.

267 **As the Crafts later recalled:** Craft and Craft, *Running a Thousand Miles for Freedom*, 34.

268 **Ellen's disguise was so convincing:** Craft and Craft, *Running a Thousand Miles for Freedom*, 38–39.

268 **"Probably not a church":** Stone, quoted in Barker, *Fugitive Slaves and the Unfinished American Revolution*, 32–33.

269 **get them back:** Barker, *Fugitive Slaves and the Unfinished American Revolution*, 31.

269 **hid the Crafts:** Jeffrey L. Amestoy, *Slavish Shore: The Odyssey of Richard Henry Dana Jr.* (Cambridge, Mass.: Harvard University Press, 2015), 119.

269 **"I have had to arm myself":** Barker, *Fugitive Slaves and the Unfinished American Revolution*, 11.

269 **"Weightier than the Constitution":** Quoted in Barker, *Fugitive Slaves and the Unfinished American Revolution*, 30, 31.

270 **"a piece of friendly advice":** Hughes's account, dated November 21, 1850, and published in the *Georgia Constitutionalist*, was reprinted in the *Liberator*, Dec. 6, 1850, 196.

270 **Shadrach had escaped:** Finkelman, *Slavery in the Courtroom*, 86.

270 **"with his waiter's apron":** Quoted in Barker, *Fugitive Slaves and the Unfinished American Revolution*, 43.

270 **writ of habeas corpus:** Lubet, *Fugitive Justice*, 138; Amestoy, *Slavish Shore*, 121, 321n44.

270   "**This won't do**": Dana, *Journal*, 2:411.

270   the "**kidnapper's jackal**": Grodzins, "'Slave Law' Versus 'Lynch Law,'" 2.

271   "**leading negro in Boston**": Higginson, *Cheerful Yesterdays*, 140.

271   a "**black squall**": Dana, *Journal*, 2:412.

271   **settling in Montreal**: Barker, *Fugitive Slaves and the Unfinished American Revolution*, 43–44; Lubet, *Fugitive Justice*, 140.

271   "**writ of Deliverance**": Quoted in Collison, *Shadrach Minkins*, 135.

271   "**take him out**": Collison, *Shadrach Minkins*, 144, 194. See also Barker, *Fugitive Slaves and the Unfinished American Revolution*, 39.

271   "**this law was constitutionally passed**": *United States v. Charles G. Davis*, in Finkelman, *Fugitive Slaves and American Courts: The Pamphlet Literature*, series 2, 1:599–600.

272   **all of whose cases**: Paul Finkelman, *Millard Fillmore* (New York: Times Books, 2011), 116–19.

272   "**TE DEUM LAUDAMUS**": Collison, *Shadrach Minkins*, 136.

272   "**whether the government**": *Liberator*, Feb. 28, 1851, 34. Clay's language as quoted in the *Congressional Globe*, Feb. 21, 1851, 597, was slightly different: "whether we shall have a Government of white men or black men in the cities of this country."

272   **committed "by negroes"**: Conway and Clay, quoted in Collison, *Shadrach Minkins*, 139.

272   "**the day for dissolution**": Senator Jeremiah Clemens, *Liberator*, March 7, 1851, 38.

273   "**calling on all well-disposed citizens**": Millard Fillmore, "Proclamation 56—Calling On Citizens to Assist in the Recapture of a Fugitive Slave Arrested in Boston, Massachusetts," Feb. 18, 1851. Online by Gerhard Peters and John T. Woolley, *The American Presidency Project*, presidency.ucsb.edu/ws/?pid=68154.

273   **prepare for action**: Robert W. Coakley, *The Role of Federal Military Forces in Domestic Disorders, 1789–1860* (Washington, D.C.: Center of Military History, 1988), 129.

273   were "**deeply mortified**": Lawrence, quoted in Collison, *Shadrach Minkins*, 140.

273   "**a naval and military force**": Quoted in Barker, *Fugitive Slaves and the Unfinished American Revolution*, 48.

273   "**the spirit which resisted**": Quoted in Barker, *Fugitive Slaves and the Unfinished American Revolution*, 53.

274   "**low-bred, dissolute, degraded beings**": Dana, *Journal*, 2:420.

274   "**In the name of the President**": Quoted in Barker, *Fugitive Slaves and the Unfinished American Revolution*, 56.

275   "**a most unlucky knife**": Theodore Parker, *The Boston Kidnapping: A Discourse to Commemorate the Rendition of Thomas Sims, Delivered on the First Anniversary Thereof, April 12, 1852, Before the Committee of Vigilance at the Melodeon in Boston* (Boston: Crosby, Nichols, 1852), 36.

275   "**how really weak**": Higginson, *Cheerful Yesterdays*, 140.

275   **losing their jobs**: Albert J. Von Frank, *The Trials of Anthony Burns: Freedom and Slavery in Emerson's Boston* (Cambridge, Mass.: Harvard University Press, 1998), 38.

275   "**Your Coat came to me**": Weeden to Freeman, Dec. 4, 1850, Gilder Lehrman Collection #09028.01, gilderlehrman.org/mweb/search?needle=Henry%20Weeden.

276   "**The authorities of the City**": Quoted in Barker, *Fugitive Slaves and the Unfinished American Revolution*, 58.

276   "**a critical test**": Quoted in Barker, *Fugitive Slaves and the Unfinished American Revolution*, 58.

276   a "**singular devotion**": Amestoy, *Slavish Shore*, 136.

276   **Boston resisters "insane"**: Webster to Fillmore, April 13, 1851, in *Papers of Webster: Correspondence*, 7:232.

276   "**Bastille of the Slavocracy**": Quoted in Barker, *Fugitive Slaves and the Unfinished American Revolution*, 60.

276–77 "**Minister-at-Large for Fugitive Slaves**": Grodzins, "'Slave Law' Versus 'Lynch Law,'" 4.

277   "**mounted guard at the entrance**": Theodore Parker, *The Trial of Theodore Parker for the "Misdemeanor" of a Speech in Faneuil Hall Against Kidnapping, Before the Circuit Court of the United States, at Boston, April 2, 1855* (Boston, 1855), 5.

277   "**counseled every colored man**": Barker, *Fugitive Slaves and the Unfinished American Revolution*, 62.

277   **speech so "vehement"**: Higginson, *Cheerful Yesterdays*, 142.

277   "**O city without a soul!**": Quoted in Barker, *Fugitive Slaves and the Unfinished American Revolution*, 63.

277   **Bronson Alcott, writing**: Quoted in Barker, *Fugitive Slaves and the Unfinished American Revolution*, 62.

277   "**the legal pimp**": Quoted in Barker, *Fugitive Slaves and the Unfinished American Revolution*, 64.

277   "**never knew such a person**": Quoted in Barker, *Fugitive Slaves and the Unfinished American Revolution*, 65.

277   "**Think of old stiff-necked Lemuel**": Quoted in Levy, *Law of the Commonwealth and Chief Justice Shaw*, 102.

278   "**so odious, that nothing**": *Reports of Cases Argued and Determined in the Supreme Judicial Court of Massachusetts*, ed. Luther Cushing (Boston: Little, Brown, 1855), 7:313.

278   **prohibition of "states"**: *Reports of Cases Argued and Determined in the Supreme Judicial Court of Massachusetts*, 7:319.

278   "**It seems, therefore**": *Reports of Cases Argued and Determined in the Supreme Judicial Court of Massachusetts*, 7:315.

278   positive law must be "acted upon": *Reports of Cases Argued and Determined in the Supreme Judicial Court of Massachusetts*, 7:313.

279   "actually occupying the judge's seat": Dana, *Journal*, 2:410.

279   challenged the validity: Barker, *Fugitive Slaves and the Unfinished American Revolution*, 65–66.

279   made him an interested party: Cover, *Justice Accused*, 177.

280   "not be surrendered": Quoted in Barker, *Fugitive Slaves and the Unfinished American Revolution*, 66. Sympathy in the senate was sufficient to appoint a committee for investigating whether "the freedom of any inhabitant of this Commonwealth is in danger" and whether "any law for the security of personal freedom" had been broken. Quoted in Barker, *Fugitive Slaves and the Unfinished American Revolution*, 66–67.

280   "an impudence unparalleled": Quoted in Barker, *Fugitive Slaves and the Unfinished American Revolution*, 65.

280   "a physical assault on the courthouse": Quoted in Barker, *Fugitive Slaves and the Unfinished American Revolution*, 67.

280   got wind of the plan: Another plan devised by Theodore Parker, Austin Bearse, and others involved intercepting, boarding, and hijacking the ship on which Sims was to be returned to Georgia. The plan was not attempted, though abolitionists did attempt to bribe the captain of the ship—which also failed. See Barker, *Fugitive Slaves and the Unfinished American Revolution*, 68.

280   "Our Temple of Justice": Dana, *Journal*, 2:424.

281   "was to prevent State legislation": Quoted in Barker, *Fugitive Slaves and the Unfinished American Revolution*, 69.

281   "I will not go back to Slavery": Quoted in Barker, *Fugitive Slaves and the Unfinished American Revolution*, 69.

281   "the Boston of 1851": Quoted in Barker, *Fugitive Slaves and the Unfinished American Revolution*, 69.

281   was led, "his sable cheeks": Austin Bearse, quoted in Barker, *Fugitive Slaves and the Unfinished American Revolution*, 69–70.

281   "Sims! preach liberty": Quoted in Leonard W. Levy, "The Fugitive Slave Law in Boston in 1851," *Journal of Negro History* 35, no. 1 (Jan. 1950): 71.

281   "Goodbye to you too": Herman Melville, *Billy Budd, Sailor (an Inside Narrative)*, ed. Harrison Hayford and Merton M. Sealts Jr. (Chicago: University of Chicago Press, 1962), 49.

282   "I congratulate you": Fillmore to Webster, April 16, 1851, in *Papers of Webster: Correspondence*, 7:237.

282   "The whole land": Pennington to unknown recipient, April 29, 1851, Gilder Lehrman Collection #09088, gilderlehrman.org/content/runaway-slave.

282   "the most noble deed": Quoted in Collison, *Shadrach Minkins*, 134.

282   the "Anti-man-hunting League": Daniel Bever, "'The Higher Court of Heaven': Dr. Henry Ingersoll Bowditch and Violent Abolition" (undergraduate thesis, College of William and Mary, 2011), 80, publish .wm.edu/cgi/viewcontent.cgi?article=1378&context=honorstheses.

282   "no sacrifice of blood": Charles B. Sedgwick to Dora Sedgwick, April 11, 1851, Special Collections Research Center, Syracuse University Library, library.syr.edu/digital/exhibits/u/undergroundrr/case2.htm.

283   "Mr. Nathan Brooks": Quoted in Collison, *Shadrach Minkins*, 151.

283   "a statute which enacts": Emerson, "Address to the Citizens of Concord on the Fugitive Slave Law," May 3, 1851, 57, 68. When his children brought home a school assignment to design a house, Emerson instructed them, "You must be sure to say that no house nowadays is perfect without having a nook where a fugitive slave can be safely hidden away." Edward Waldo Emerson, *Emerson in Concord: A Memoir* (Boston: Houghton, Mifflin, 1889), 77.

283   "since you have access to many": Sumner to Emerson, May 7, 1851, in *The Selected Letters of Charles Sumner*, ed. Beverly Wilson Palmer (Boston: Northeastern University Press, 1990), 1:333.

283   "walk over corpses": Samuel May Jr., *The Fugitive Slave Law and Its Victims* (New York: American Anti-slavery Society, 1856), 13. See also Barker, *Fugitive Slaves and the Unfinished American Revolution*, 101.

283   "the bludgeon process": *Buffalo Morning Express*, Aug. 30, 1851.

283   called "compromise politicians": *Buffalo Morning Express*, Aug. 30, 1851.

283   and "lower-law co-laborers": *New-York Daily Tribune*, Sept. 2, 1851.

283–84 "a fine, athletic negro": *Buffalo Commercial Advertiser*, Aug. 16, 1851.

284   "Daniel in the Den and Out": See *Buffalo Morning Express*, Aug. 30, 1851; *New-York Daily Tribune*, Sept. 2, 1851. That same month, more than three hundred miles to the southeast, a black tailor named John Bolding was recognized in Poughkeepsie, New York, by his former owner, a woman from South Carolina who might have had a ransom scheme in mind rather than a serious attempt to get him back. After spotting Bolding on the street, she sold her interest in him for eight hundred dollars to another Carolinian, who arranged for a commissioner from New York City to come the eighty miles up the Hudson to seize him and take him back downriver, presumably to be shipped south. A group of Hudson valley gentry, led by Matthew Vassar, founder of the college that bears his name, raised two thousand dollars to purchase Bolding's liberty,

enabling him to return to his tailor shop. The transaction was nicely profitable for Bolding's original owner and downright lucrative for the man to whom she sold him, who more than doubled his short-term investment.

284 "decrepit old man": *Liberator,* June 6, 1851, 89.

284 "I do not say the law is perfect": "Speech at Syracuse," *Mr. Webster's Speeches at Buffalo, Syracuse, and Albany, May, 1851* (New York: Mirror Office, 1851), 36–37.

285 "Down with the Traitors": *Liberator,* Nov. 21, 1851, 185.

Chapter 12: Trials of Conscience

286 history of conflict: Barker, *Fugitive Slaves and the Unfinished American Revolution,* 81.

287 "secret black militia": Bordewich, *Bound for Canaan,* 327, quoted in Barker, *Fugitive Slaves and the Unfinished American Revolution,* 82.

287 "sitting on a sorrel horse": Robbins, *Report of the Trial of Castner Hanway for Treason,* 58–59, 62.

288 "It is cowardly": Quoted in Murphy, *Jerry Rescue,* 28.

289 "made me ashamed": *Autobiography of Edward Austin Sheldon,* ed. Mary Sheldon Barnes (New York: Ives-Butler, 1911), 96.

289 "the moral effect": Quoted in Barker, *Fugitive Slaves and the Unfinished American Revolution,* 106.

289 he stopped the hearing: Barker, *Fugitive Slaves and the Unfinished American Revolution,* 108 *ff.*

289 first slate of indictments: Barker, *Fugitive Slaves and the Unfinished American Revolution,* 90.

290 "This man deserves": Quoted in Barker, *Fugitive Slaves and the Unfinished American Revolution,* 15.

290 congressman Thaddeus Stevens: Trefousse, *Thaddeus Stevens,* 14. Stevens carried the case all the way to the state supreme court, where he won a judgment in favor of the plaintiff.

290 "My disease is *angina pectoris*": Robbins, *Report of the Trial of Castner Hanway for Treason,* 10.

291 "I am hard of hearing": Robbins, *Report of the Trial of Castner Hanway for Treason,* 11.

291 "It may not be said": Robbins, *Report of the Trial of Castner Hanway for Treason,* 243.

291 "The resistance of the execution": Robbins, *Report of the Trial of Castner Hanway for Treason,* 247.

292 "Individuals without any authority": Robbins, *Report of the Trial of Castner Hanway for Treason,* 248.

292–93 "compared with the number": Campbell, *Slave Catchers,* 148.

293 exclusion of testimony: Lubet, *Fugitive Justice,* 42–43. For a detailed account of the rise and fall of "competency rules" governing the admission of witness testimony, see George Fisher, "The Jury's Rise as Lie Detector," *Yale Law Journal* 107 (1997): 575–713, esp. 659, 668.

293 "new discovery in ethics": The U.S. district judge Thomas Irwin, in a June 1851 charge to a grand jury in Williamsport, Pennsylvania, quoted in Finkelman, *Fugitive Slaves and American Courts: The Pamphlet Literature, series 2,* 1:679.

293 "the only obligation": Henry David Thoreau, "Resistance to Civil Government," in *Walden, Civil Disobedience, and Other Writings,* 228.

293 "if the compromises": Beecher, "Shall We Compromise?," 173.

294 torment at "participating": John Codman Ropes, "Memoir," in *Charles Devens: Orations and Addresses on Various Occasions Civil and Military,* ed. Arthur Lithgow Devens (Boston: Little, Brown, 1891), 4.

294 "thought the Law": Quoted in Matthew J. Grow, *"Liberty to the Downtrodden": Thomas L. Kane, Romantic Reformer* (New Haven, Conn.: Yale University Press, 2009), 126–27.

294 contempt of court: During the Christiana case, Tom gave the prisoners "six superior turkeys, two of them extra size, together with a pound cake." Grow, *"Liberty to the Downtrodden,"* chap. 7.

294 "naturally tender heart": Quoted in Grow, *"Liberty to the Downtrodden,"* 127.

295 "the great body": Lincoln, letter to Joshua F. Speed, Aug. 24, 1855, in *Collected Works of Lincoln,* 2:320.

295 a "committed conscience": John Jay Chapman, "Emerson," in *Emerson, and Other Essays* (New York: Moffat, Yard, 1909), 7.

295 "inner civil war": George M. Fredrickson, *The Inner Civil War: Northern Intellectuals and the Crisis of the Union* (New York: Harper & Row, 1965).

296 "in face of the unpopularity": Ropes, "Memoir," 4.

296 "a handsome congratulatory letter": Dana, *Journal,* 2:415.

297 "Saint of the West": Emerson to Lidian Emerson, Dec. 31, 1852, in *The Letters of Ralph Waldo Emerson,* ed. Ralph L. Rusk (New York: Columbia University Press, 1939), 4:338.

297 "Over the best": Eliot, *Archer Alexander,* 28–29.

297 "Upon no other" subject: Quoted in Earl K. Holt III, *William Greenleaf Eliot: Conservative Radical* (St. Louis: First Unitarian Church of St. Louis), 40.

298 "he himself once bought": Joseph Shippen, "Tribute Delivered Before the Channing Club of Chicago," published in the Unitarian periodical *Our Best Words,* April 15, 1887, 8.

298   **worked to persuade:** Holt, *William Greenleaf Eliot*, 66.

298   **Eliot sided with the general:** Writing to his abolitionist friend Clarke on November 14, 1861, soon after Lincoln relieved Frémont of his command, Eliot protested that "the leading measures of his administration were good, & for the incidental errors, mistakes, and mishaps, he was either not at all or only partly responsible." MS letter, Missouri Historical Museum.

299   **"is the more dangerous":** William Greenleaf Eliot Personal Papers, Series 1, Notebook 5 (March 1860–March 1861), 164–65, University Archives, Department of Special Collections, Washington University Libraries, St. Louis.

299   **"the most dangerous":** William Greenleaf Eliot Personal Papers, Series 1, Notebook 5 (March 1860–March 1861), 164.

299   **"had set me rather":** "A Tribute from Robert Collyer," *Our Best Words*, March 22, 1887, 5.

299   **"a man of sorrows":** "Tribute from Robert Collyer," 5.

299   **"in the days of slavery":** Shippen, "Tribute Delivered Before the Channing Club of Chicago," 8.

300   **"A true history":** Eliot, *Archer Alexander*, 44.

299–300 **putting "the law":** Robbins, *Report of the Trial of Castner Hanway for Treason*, 185.

301   **asking newspaper editors to refrain:** See, for example, Emerson to Evert Duyckinck, Dec. 21, 1851, in Rusk, *Letters*, 4:267–68.

301   **"Delight is to him":** Melville, *Moby-Dick*, 48.

301   **"In heaven's name":** Melville, *Pierre*, 162–63.

301   **"We pity the restored fugitive":** Moses Stuart, *Conscience and the Constitution, with Remarks on the Recent Speech by the Hon. Daniel Webster on the Subject of Slavery* (Boston: Crocker and Brewster, 1850), 32.

302   **"Shaw faced the same":** Brook Thomas, *Cross-examinations of Law and Literature: Cooper, Hawthorne, Stowe, and Melville* (New York: Cambridge University Press, 1987), 226.

302   **"this Fugitive Law":** Quoted in Larry J. Reynolds, *Devils and Rebels: The Making of Hawthorne's Damned Politics* (Ann Arbor: University of Michigan Press, 2008), 183.

302   **"by a blindness":** Moncure D. Conway, *Life of Nathaniel Hawthorne* (New York: Scribner and Welford, 1890), 147.

302   **help from Thoreau:** Laura Dassow Walls, *Henry David Thoreau: A Life* (Chicago: University of Chicago Press, 2017), 215–16.

302   **"I have not, as you suggest":** Hawthorne to Zachariah Burchmore, quoted in Reynolds, *Devils and Rebels*, 183.

303   **"the time is come":** Quoted in Joan D. Hedrick, *Harriet Beecher Stowe: A Life* (New York: Oxford University Press, 1994), 208.

303   **sold 300,000 copies:** David S. Reynolds, *Mightier Than the Sword: "Uncle Tom's Cabin" and the Battle for America* (New York: W. W. Norton, 2011), 128. See also Gail K. Smith, "The Sentimental Novel: The Example of Harriet Beecher Stowe," in *The Cambridge Companion to Nineteenth-Century American Women's Writing*, ed. Dale M. Bauer and Philip Gould (Cambridge, U.K.: Cambridge University Press, 2001), 221.

304   **"the history of literature":** Quoted in Reynolds, *Mightier Than the Sword*, 128.

304   **Stowe had "baptized":** Douglass, quoted in Reynolds, *Mightier Than the Sword*, 128–29.

305   **"the normal condition":** William Grayson, *The Hireling and the Slave, Chicora, and Other Poems* (Charleston, S.C.: McCarter, 1856), v, 41.

305   **a severed human ear:** George Parsons Lathrop, "A Model State Capital," *Harper's New Monthly Magazine*, Oct. 1885, 730.

305   **"whose idea of a fugitive":** Stowe, *Uncle Tom's Cabin*, ed. Lynn, 93.

305   **"great public interests":** Stowe, *Uncle Tom's Cabin*, ed. Lynn, 84.

305   **"cut and bleeding":** Stowe, *Uncle Tom's Cabin*, ed. Lynn, 86.

305   **"my vocation is simply":** Quoted in Michael Winship, "'The Greatest Book of Its Kind': A Publishing History of 'Uncle Tom's Cabin,'" *Proceedings of the American Antiquarian Society* (2002): 312.

305   **"less a book":** Henry James, *A Small Boy and Others* (New York: Charles Scribner's Sons, 1913), 139.

306   **"the real presence":** Stowe, *Uncle Tom's Cabin*, ed. Lynn, 93.

306   **the "picture passion":** Frederick Douglass, "Lecture on Pictures," Dec. 3, 1861, in *Picturing Frederick Douglass: An Illustrated Biography of the Nineteenth Century's Most Photographed American*, ed. John Stauffer, Zoe Trodd, and Celeste-Marie Bernier (New York: Liveright, 2015), 133.

306   **"In the last judgment":** Harriet Beecher Stowe, *A Key to "Uncle Tom's Cabin"* (Boston: John P. Jewett, 1853), 256.

307   **"Now, when any one":** Stowe, *Uncle Tom's Cabin*, ed. Lynn, 190. It is tempting to speculate that the name is meant to convey the clarity (St. Clare) of his conviction that human beings are motivated by the sin of self-interest (Saint Augustine).

308   **On June 2:** Quoted in Von Frank, *The Trials of Anthony Burns*, 202.

308   **"wicked and cruel":** Quoted in Von Frank, *The Trials of Anthony Burns*, 202.

308   and "taken chiefly": May, *Fugitive Slave Law and Its Victims*, 35.

309   "a piteous object": Quoted in Von Frank, *Trials of Anthony Burns*, 2, 4.

309   Burns asked him, "Mr. Phillips": Austin Bearse, *Reminiscences of Fugitive-Slave Law Days in Boston* (Boston: Warren Richardson, 1880), 12–13.

309   "a comely coloured girl": Quoted in Von Frank, *Trials of Anthony Burns*, 216.

310   "solid men of Boston": Von Frank, *Trials of Anthony Burns*, 53.

310   "in the execution": Quoted in Von Frank, *Trials of Anthony Burns*, 206.

310   "We went to bed": Quoted in Jane Pease and William Pease, *The Fugitive Slave Law and Anthony Burns: A Problem in Law Enforcement* (Philadelphia: Lippincott, 1975), 43.

311   "no one during that week": Parkman, quoted in William C. Gannett, *Ezra Stiles Gannett: Unitarian Minister in Boston, 1824–1871: A Memoir* (Boston: Roberts Brothers, 1875), 289.

311   preached a sermon: Ezra Stiles Gannett, *Relation of the North to Slavery: A Discourse Preached in the Federal Meetinghouse in Boston, June 11, 1854* (Boston: Crosby, Nichols, 1854).

311   "Loyalty to the Law": Gannett, *Memoir*, 291.

311   "struggle between opposing": Gannett, *Memoir*, 289.

311   calls "psychic violence": Von Frank, *Trials of Anthony Burns*, 271.

311   "the Abolitionists could not": Gannett, *Memoir*, 286. Gannett's daughter also remembered her father's anguish. When she asked him after the Burns affair what he would do if a fugitive were to come personally to his door, he replied, "I should shelter him and aid him to go further on to Canada, and then I should go and give myself up to prison, and insist on being made a prisoner, [and] accept of no release." His daughter recalls that "his manner of speaking" his pledge "could never be forgotten. It was intensely quiet and determined, his hands clenched, and he set his teeth each time" (Gannett, *Memoir*, 290–91). The risk of such a pledge, however, was low. As in the Shadrach and Christiana cases, no one in the Burns case was ever convicted of anything.

311   "contemptible moderates," in the words: Berlin to Jean Floud, July 7, 1968, in *Isaiah Berlin, Building: Letters, 1960–1975*, ed. Henry Hardy and Mark Pottle (London: Penguin, 2016), 355.

311   "as mediocre, timid": Daniel Kahneman, *Thinking Fast and Slow* (New York: Farrar, Straus & Giroux, 2011), 204.

311   "The problem for Americans": Potter, *Impending Crisis*, 44–45.

312   "And, as I thought of Liberty": Whittier, "The Rendition," in *Anti-slavery Poems*, 170.

312   "perhaps a million slaves": Henry David Thoreau, "Slavery in Massachusetts" (1854), in *Walden, Civil Disobedience, and Other Writings*, 247.

312   "The framers of the constitution": Theodore Parker, "The New Crime Against Humanity," in *Collected Works of Theodore Parker*, ed. F. P. Cobbe (London: Trübner, 1864), 2:102.

313   "None of his abolition friends": Quoted in Von Frank, *Trials of Anthony Burns*, 234.

313   "I am yet Bound": Burns to Dana, quoted in Von Frank, *Trials of Anthony Burns*, 287–88.

314   "university to the people": Emerson, "Address to the Citizens of Concord on the Fugitive Slave Law," May 3, 1851, 64.

314   "Beyond all such": Walt Whitman, "Song for Certain Congressmen," *New York Evening Post*, March 2, 1850, 2. Whitman later retitled it "Dough-Face Song," in *Complete Poetry and Collected Prose*, 1076–78. See John Frederick Bell, "Poetry's Place in the Crisis and Compromise of 1850," *Journal of the Civil War Era* 5, no. 3 (Sept. 2015): 399–421.

314   "there are always compromisers": Quoted in Tilden G. Edelstein, *Strange Enthusiasm: A Life of Thomas Wentworth Higginson* (New Haven, Conn.: Yale University Press, 1968), 104.

314   "From the beginning": Sumner, quoted in Amanda Foreman, *A World on Fire: Britain's Crucial Role in the American Civil War* (New York: Random House, 2010), 33.

315   "I am just as much": *Middlesex Standard*, Jan. 9, 1845.

315   "by what an infinite complexity": Stowe to Lord Carlisle, quoted in Charles Edward Stowe, *Life of Harriet Beecher Stowe, Compiled from Her Letters and Journals* (Boston: Riverside Press, 1891), 165.

315   "Lidian grieves aloud": Oct. 1, 1837, in Porte, *Emerson in His Journals*, 169.

316   "You have just dined": Ralph Waldo Emerson, "Fate," in *The Collected Works of Ralph Waldo Emerson, vol. 6, The Conduct of Life* (Cambridge, Mass.: Harvard University Press, 2003), 4.

316   "we have no responsibility": Quoted in Von Frank, *Trials of Anthony Burns*, 275.

316   "So long as slavery exists": Kingsbury, *Thoughts on the Fugitive Slave Law and Nebraska Bill*, 4.

Chapter 13: The End of Compromise

317   "it is a terrible fact": Dwight Macdonald, "The Responsibility of Peoples," in *Politics Past: Essays in Political Criticism* (New York: Viking, 1970), 65.

318   the 1853 attack: May, *Fugitive Slave Law and Its Victims*, 21–22.

318   remembered, "twenty strong": C. C. Olin, *The Olin Album* (Indianapolis: Baker-Randolph, 1893), lvi–lvii.
      The Glover story appears in that portion of *The Olin Album* called "Reminiscences of the Busy Life of C. C.
      Olin," liii–lx. For May's account of the Glover incident, see *Fugitive Slave Law and Its Victims,* 23–24.

318   "mercenary, lustful, and diabolical": Samuel May Jr., *The Fugitive Slave Law and Its Victims, rev. ed.* (New
      York: American Anti-slavery Society, 1861), 78.

318   "I am a Kentuckian": May, *Fugitive Slave Law and Its Victims,* 85.

319   Pregnant—possibly by her master: See Nikki M. Taylor, *Driven Toward Madness: The Fugitive Slave Mar-
      garet Garner and Tragedy on the Ohio* (Athens: Ohio University Press, 2016), 96-106.

319   "If in her deep": Quoted in Mark Reinhardt, *Who Speaks for Margaret Garner?* (Minneapolis: University of
      Minnesota Press, 2010), 112.

320   new personal liberty laws: Potter, *Impending Crisis,* 139.

320   "She is a mother": Frances Ellen Watkins [Harper], *Poems on Miscellaneous Subjects* (Philadelphia: Merri-
      hew & Thompson, 1857), 7–8.

321   *The Modern Medea*: On Noble's painting, see Leslie Furth, "'The Modern Medea' and Race Matters:
      Thomas Satterwhite Noble's *Margaret Garner,*" *American Art* 12, no. 2 (Summer 1998): 36–67.

321   1857 fugitive slave hearing: Patrick W. Riddleberger, *George Washington Julian: Radical Republican* (India-
      napolis: Indiana Historical Bureau, 1966), 119.

321   "Fugitive Slave *Bill*": Oliver Wendell Holmes, *Ralph Waldo Emerson,* in *The Works of Oliver Wendell Holmes,*
      13 vols. (Cambridge, Mass.: Riverside Press, 1892), 11:234.

321   "It is an old saying": "The Duty of the North, Lecture of the Rev. Theodore Parker at the Tabernacle,"
      New-York Daily Tribune, March 7, 1856, quoted in Reinhardt, *Who Speaks for Margaret Garner?,* 212.

322   "The runaway slave came": Whitman, *"Song of Myself,"* 197.

324   "great principle of self-government": Johannsen, *Stephen A. Douglas,* 421.

324   by professing "indifference": "First Debate with Stephen A. Douglas, at Ottawa, Illinois, Aug. 21, 1858,"
      in *Collected Works of Lincoln,* 3:14. This charge was either a politically calculated exaggeration or a confusion
      of what Lincoln feared would be the result of Douglas's policy with the motives that led him to promote it.
      Lincoln is reading from his own earlier speech at Peoria from October 16, 1854 (2:255).

324   become "slave-holding country": Johannsen, *Stephen A. Douglas,* 421.

325   "the greatest railroad": Johannsen, *Stephen A. Douglas,* 436.

325   the "Nebraska swindle": William J. Watkins, editorial, March 3, 1854, in Ripley, *Black Abolitionist Papers,*
      4:208.

326   "within a stone's throw": Lincoln, "Speech at Peoria, Illinois," Oct. 16, 1854, in *Collected Works of Lincoln,*
      2:271, 262.

326   a raft of slave codes: McPherson, *Battle Cry of Freedom,* 147.

327   were "walking arsenals": McPherson, *Battle Cry of Freedom,* 148.

327   reading "the Bible to Buffaloes": Edelstein, *Strange Enthusiasm,* 182.

327   "ever since the rendition": *New-York Tribune,* Oct. 4, 1856, in *The Magnificent Activist: The Writings of
      Thomas Wentworth Higginson,* ed. Howard N. Meyer (New York: Da Capo Press, 2000), 88.

327   that "certain rifles": Higginson, *Cheerful Yesterdays,* 206.

328   "the carcasses of the Abolitionists": B. F. Stringfellow, quoted in David S. Reynolds, *John Brown, Aboli-
      tionist: The Man Who Killed Slavery, Sparked the Civil War, and Seeded Civil Rights* (New York: Random
      House, 2005), 162.

328   the only casualty: Nicole Etcheson, *Bleeding Kansas: Contested Liberty in the Civil War Era* (Lawrence:
      University of Kansas Press, 2004), 105.

328   dragged five men: Potter, *Impending Crisis,* 212; Evan Carton, *Patriotic Treason: John Brown and the Soul of
      America* (New York: Free Press, 2006), 179.

328   "a machine of torture": Charles Sumner, "Freedom National; Slavery Sectional: Speech in the Senate of
      the United States, Aug. 26, 1852, on His Motion to Repeal the Fugitive Slave Bill," in *Recent Speeches and
      Addresses of Charles Sumner* (Boston: Higgins and Bradley, 1856), 120.

328   as "murderous robbers": Charles Sumner, *The Crime Against Kansas: The Apologies for This Crime: The True
      Remedy: Speech in the Senate of the United States, 19th and 20th May, 1856* (Boston: Higgins and Bradley,
      1856), 621.

328   taking "the harlot, slavery": Sumner, *Crime Against Kansas,* 595.

329   "That damn fool": Johannsen, *Stephen A. Douglas,* 503.

330   a discouraging panel of judges: Collison, *Shadrach Minkins,* 195, 266–67n56.

331   "small & second rate": Dana, *Journal,* 2:466. Dana's complaint concerned Curtis's ruling that in order to
      prove Shadrach's status as a slave, the claimant did not have to show that he was descended through the
      female line from persons held as slaves (as prescribed by Virginia law), but that his having been "held and
      treated as a slave in Virginia" was sufficient. Elsewhere in his journal, Dana conceded that Curtis conducted
      himself "well & fairly—very fairly." Dana, *Journal,* 2:511.

332   **chief justice further denied:** Kenneth M. Stampp, *America in 1857: A Nation on the Brink* (New York: Oxford University Press, 1990), 96.

333   **"perpetuity and nationalization":** "First Debate with Stephen A. Douglas, at Ottawa, Illinois, Aug. 21, 1858," in *Collected Works of Lincoln*, 3:18, 27.

333   **made contingency plans:** David Hunter, a major and future general, reported Wise's plan to Lincoln in a letter of Dec. 22, 1860. *Collected Works of Lincoln*, 4:159.

334   **"aroused" by the Kansas-Nebraska Act:** Abraham Lincoln, "Autobiography Written for John L. Scripps," June 1860, in *Collected Works of Lincoln*, 4:67.

334   **"the whole nation":** Lincoln, "Speech at Peoria, Illinois," Oct. 16, 1854, in *Collected Works of Lincoln*, 2:268.

334   **"dissolve into one another":** Eric Foner, *Free Soil, Free Labor, Free Men: The Ideology of the Republican Party Before the Civil War* (New York: Oxford University Press, 1995), 310.

335   **"All the powers":** Lincoln, "Speech at Springfield, Illinois," June 26, 1857, in *Collected Works of Lincoln*, 2:404.

335   **won election to Congress:** Stampp, *America in 1857*, 141; Elbert B. Smith, *Francis Preston Blair* (New York: Free Press, 1980), 235.

336   **"What will be done":** Quoted in Stampp, *America in 1857*, 141.

336   **"so only to denounce":** Abraham Lincoln, "Address at Cooper Institute, New York City," Feb. 27, 1860, in *Collected Works of Lincoln*, 3:536.

336   **no cause to complain:** Andrew Wender Cohen, *Contraband: Smuggling and the Birth of the American Century* (New York: W. W. Norton, 2015), 65. See also Potter, *Impending Crisis*, 395–98.

336   **"sloth and error":** Grayson, *The Hireling and the Slave*, 31.

336   **reviving the Atlantic slave trade:** Manisha Sinha, *The Counter-revolution of Slavery: Politics and Ideology in Antebellum South Carolina* (Chapel Hill: University of North Carolina Press, 2006), 131, 163–64.

336   **prefix "gur-reat pur-rinciple":** See Lincoln, "Address at Cooper Institute, New York City," in *Collected Works of Lincoln*, 3:538.

336   **"If it is a sacred right":** Lincoln, "Speech at Peoria, Illinois," Oct. 16, 1854, in *Collected Works of Lincoln*, 2:267.

337   **"one of the best and bravest":** Wendell Phillips's recollection of John Brown's words, quoted in Catherine Clinton, *Harriet Tubman: The Road to Freedom* (Boston: Little, Brown, 2004), 130.

337   **"rivet the fetters":** Douglass, *Life and Times*, 320.

338   **"will make the gallows":** Quoted in Robert D. Richardson Jr., *Emerson: The Mind on Fire* (Berkeley: University of California Press, 1995), 545. Emerson spoke this memorable and polarizing phrase during a lecture provocatively titled "Courage" at the Music Hall in Boston on November 8, and it was widely quoted in newspapers around the nation. Emerson had evidently lifted the phrase from the abolitionist writer Mattie Griffith. See Reynolds, *John Brown, Abolitionist*, 366–67.

338   **"so justly hanged":** Nathaniel Hawthorne, "Chiefly About War Matters," in *Tales, Sketches, and Other Papers*, 327.

338   **"John Brown was no Republican":** Lincoln, "Address at Cooper Institute, New York City," in *Collected Works of Lincoln*, 3:538, 541.

338   **tried to dissociate himself:** Van Deusen, *William Henry Seward*, 226, 245.

338   **"an Abolition party":** Stephen A. Douglas, "First Debate with Stephen A. Douglas, at Ottawa, Illinois, Aug. 21, 1858," in *Collected Works of Lincoln*, 3:3.

339   **"question of American slavery":** William Wells Brown, "Speech at Horticultural Hall, West Chester, PA, October 23, 1854," in Ripley, *Black Abolitionist Papers*, 4:250.

339   **always been equivocal:** For discussion of southern doubts about whether "squatter sovereignty" would serve the cause of slavery expansion, see Johannsen, *Stephen A. Douglas*, 423.

339   **"slavery was safer":** Herschel V. Johnson, quoted in Potter, *Impending Crisis*, 475.

340   **"The policy of the one wing":** Henry Adams, "The Great Secession Winter of 1860–61," in *The Great Secession Winter of 1860–61, and Other Essays*, ed. George E. Hochfield (New York: A. S. Barnes, 1963), 20.

340   **"those who deny":** "Speech at Peoria, Illinois," Oct. 16, 1854, in *Collected Works of Lincoln*, 2:265. The specific context of this remark was a discussion of the possible revival of the African slave trade.

341   **"We offer no resistance":** Lincoln, "Speech at Springfield, Illinois," June 26, 1857, in *Collected Work of Lincoln*, 2:401.

341   **the Republican plan:** A clear exposition of Republican policy is Oakes, *Scorpion's Sting*.

341   **"a house divided":** Lincoln, "House Divided," June 16, 1858, in *Collected Works of Lincoln*, 2:461.

342   **"rose to the sublimity":** Alexander Stephens, *Recollections of Alexander H. Stephens*, ed. Myrta Lockett Avary (1910; repr., Baton Rouge: Louisiana State University Press, 1998), 62.

342   **"not hold the black man":** Lincoln to Raymond, Dec. 18, 1860, in *Collected Works of Lincoln*, 4:156.

342   **"Do the people of the South":** Lincoln to Stephens, Dec. 22, 1860, in *Collected Works of Lincoln*, 4:160.

342   **been "fundamentally wrong":** Alexander H. Stephens, "African Slavery: The Corner-Stone of the Southern Confederacy," March 22, 1861, in *The Confederate and Neo-Confederate Reader: The "Great Truth" About*

the *"Lost Cause,"* ed. James W. Loewen and Edward H. Sebesta (Jackson: University of Mississippi Press, 2010), 188.

343 **"in the path of ultimate extinction":** Lincoln, "House Divided," in *Collected Works of Lincoln,* 2:461.

343 **the "irrepressible conflict":** The phrase was the title of a speech given by Seward in Rochester, New York, on Oct. 25, 1858.

343 **"Stand WITH the abolitionist":** Lincoln, "Speech at Peoria, Illinois," Oct. 16, 1854, in *Collected Works of Lincoln,* 2:273.

343 **vigorously denied it:** Lincoln, "First Debate with Stephen A. Douglas, at Ottawa, Illinois," Aug. 21, 1858, in *Collected Works of Lincoln,* 3:14.

343 **"I would give them":** Lincoln, "Speech at Peoria, Illinois," Oct. 16, 1854, in *Collected Works of Lincoln,* 2:256.

343 **he was willing to pursue":** Douglass, "Oration in Memory of Abraham Lincoln," in *The Lincoln Anthology,* ed. Holzer, 226.

343 **"arrest and return":** Lincoln, "Address at Cooper Institute, New York City," in *Collected Works of Lincoln,* 3:548.

344 **"there is much controversy":** Lincoln, "First Inaugural Address," in *Collected Works of Lincoln,* 4:251.

344 **"I take the official":** Lincoln, "First Inaugural Address," in *Collected Works of Lincoln,* 4:252.

344 **denounced "palpable violations":** James Buchanan, "Annual Message to Congress," Dec. 3, 1860, in George Ticknor Curtis, *The Life of James Buchanan: Fifteenth President of the United States* (New York: Harper and Brothers, 1883), 2:340–41.

345 **Incidents were still reported:** Campbell, *Slave Catchers,* 161–64.

345 **ended in a deal:** Campbell, *Slave Catchers,* 64–67.

346 **"enactments conceived in a spirit":** Virginia Legislature, "Report of the Joint Committee on the Harpers Ferry Outrages," Jan. 26, 1860, in *Virginia Documents,* No. 57, 24.

346 **free states should compensate:** *New York Times,* Nov. 14, 1860; see Russell McClintock, *Lincoln and the Decision for War: The Northern Response to Secession* (Chapel Hill: University of North Carolina Press, 2008), 56–57.

346 **"to be divested":** "Report of the Committee of Thirteen," in *Index to the Reports of the Committees of the Senate of the United States for the Second Session of the Thirty-sixth Congress* (Washington, D.C.: George W. Bowman, 1861), 3.

346 **"plan of adjustment":** "Report of the Committee of Thirteen," 1.

347 **"prepared the way":** Davis, *Problem of Slavery in the Age of Emancipation,* 250.

347 **"the primarily pejorative meaning":** Sacvan Bercovitch, *The Office of the Scarlet Letter* (Baltimore: Johns Hopkins University Press, 1991), 100.

347 **"there is no term":** Samuel Ringgold Ward, "Speech at Faneuil Hall," March 25, 1850, in Ripley, *Black Abolitionist Papers,* 4:49.

347 **"that nothing is good":** Webster, "Constitution and the Union, March 7, 1850," 521.

347 **"every compromise which":** Jacob D. Green, *Narrative of the Life of J. D. Green, a Runaway Slave from Kentucky* (1864), in Andrews and Gates, *Slave Narratives,* 988.

348 **"the crusade for Southern independence":** Holt, *Political Crisis of the 1850s,* 220.

348 **"Fourteen of the States":** South Carolina Secession Convention, *Declaration of the Immediate Causes Which Induce and Justify the Secession of South Carolina from the Federal Union,* Dec. 24, 1860, in Loewen and Sebesta, *Confederate and Neo-Confederate Reader,* 114.

348 **"In the State of New York":** Loewen and Sebesta, *Confederate and Neo-Confederate Reader,* 115.

348 **"slavery was without doubt":** Stephens, *Recollections of Alexander H. Stephens,* 173.

348 **"basic minimal regard":** Hofstadter, *Progressive Historians,* 454.

348 **In December 1860:** Foner, *The Fiery Trial,* 148–50. Matthew Karp, in *This Vast Southern Empire,* argues that from the slaveholders' point of view, keeping alive the prospect of expanding slavery into territories "hereafter acquired" was imperative if they were to stay in the union (230–31).

349 **"The veriest spawn":** "Compromise," *Vanity Fair,* July 6, 1861, 6.

349 **"You are of your father the devil":** English Standard Version.

Chapter 14: "And the War Came"

351 **"After all that noise":** Chesnut, *Mary Chesnut's Civil War,* 47. For the note informing Anderson of the impending attack, see Adam Goodheart, "The Defenders," in *Disunion: Modern Historians Revisit and Reconsider the Civil War,* ed. Ted Widmer (New York: Black Dog & Leventhal, 2013), 104.

351 **"orators of the South":** Sherman, *Memoirs,* 184.

351 **"all talk about putting down":** Quoted in James M. McPherson, *The Struggle for Equality: Abolitionists and the Negro in the Civil War and Reconstruction* (Princeton, N.J.: Princeton University Press, 1964), 46.

352 **"the guns are firing":** George Lovell Austin, *Life and Times of Wendell Phillips* (Boston: Lee and Shepard, 1893), 206. I owe this reference to David Marcus.

352   **"One noonday, at my window"**: Herman Melville, "Ball's Bluff: A Reverie," in *Battle-Pieces and Aspects of the War*, ed. Sidney Kaplan (Boston: University of Massachusetts Press, 1972), 28. Note that the poem was written in retrospect.

352   **bits of knotted rope**: Robert Roper, *Now the Drum of War: Walt Whitman and His Brothers in the Civil War* (New York: Walker, 2008), 7.

352   **a capital city rife**: Kenneth J. Winkle, *Lincoln's Citadel: The Civil War in Washington, DC* (New York: W. W. Norton, 2013), 148.

353   **"we have manufactured"**: *Cong. Globe*, House of Representatives, 37th Cong., 1st Sess., July 19, 1861, 212.

353   **as "jocund levity"**: Sunset Cox, quoted in Leech, *Reveille in Washington*, 122.

353   **"tiptoe of expectation"**: Elizabeth Blair Lee to Samuel Phillips Lee, July 19, 1861, in *Wartime in Washington: The Civil War Letters of Elizabeth Blair Lee*, ed. Virginia Jeans Laas (Urbana: University of Illinois Press, 1991), 64.

353   **large-scale "Negro *Deportation*"**: Elizabeth Blair Lee to Samuel Phillips Lee, June 1, 1861, in Laas, *Wartime in Washington*, 40–41.

353   **"the belchings of the Cannon"**: Elizabeth Blair Lee to Samuel Phillips Lee, July 21, 1861, in Laas, *Wartime in Washington*, 65.

353   **"*debris*" of an army**: William Howard Russell, quoted in Leech, *Reveille in Washington*, 128.

353   **"half" the "lookers-on"**: Whitman, *Specimen Days*, in *Complete Poetry and Collected Prose*, 709.

354   **"The vaunted Union"**: Whitman, *Specimen Days*, in *Complete Poetry and Collected Prose*, 710.

354   **"the battles which are"**: *Cong. Globe*, Senate, 37th Cong., 1st Sess., July 24, 1861, 251.

354   **"fire-eaters would commit"**: Whitman, *Specimen Days*, 707. Brooklyn was not yet a borough of New York.

354   **been "insolently attack'd"**: Walt Whitman, "Democratic Vistas," in *Complete Poetry and Collected Prose*, 944.

354   **"war has flung"**: Higginson, quoted in Brenda Wineapple, *Ecstatic Nation: Confidence, Crisis, and Compromise, 1848–1877* (New York: HarperCollins, 2013), 233.

354   **"the sole object"**: *Cong. Globe*, House of Representatives, 37th Cong., 1st Sess., July 13, 1861, 117.

355   **no "purpose of overthrowing"**: *Cong. Globe*, House of Representatives, 37th Cong., 1st Sess., July 25, 1861, 259. See Oakes, *Freedom National*, 128.

355   **"drop the nigger"**: Quoted in James McPherson, *The Negro's Civil War* (New York: Vintage, 1965), 22. A federal statute dating back to 1792 prohibited blacks from militia service. See Foner, *Fiery Trial*, 187.

355   **"overthrow of slavery"**: Quoted in McPherson, *Struggle for Equality*, 77.

355   **"degenerate into a violent"**: Abraham Lincoln, "Annual Message to Congress," Dec. 3, 1861, in *Collected Works of Lincoln*, 5:49.

356   **"For our homes"**: Oliver Wendell Holmes, "My Hunt After 'The Captain,'" *Atlantic Monthly*, Dec. 1862, 757.

356   **"the first movement"**: John George Nicolay and John Hay, *Abraham Lincoln: A History, 8 vols.* (New York: Century, 1904), 4:385.

357   **mollified by assurances**: Leech, *Reveille in Washington*, 98.

357   **the first shipment**: See Adam Goodheart, *1861: The Civil War Awakening* (New York: Alfred A. Knopf, 2012), 295.

357   **"rigorous military impressment"**: Nicolay and Hay, *Abraham Lincoln*, 4:386.

358   **"us piling up sandbags"**: Benjamin Franklin Butler, *Autobiography and Personal Reminiscences of Major-General Benjamin F. Butler: Butler's Book* (Boston: A. M. Thayer, 1892), 256.

358   **"one of the most sudden"**: Nicolay and Hay, *Abraham Lincoln*, 4:387.

358   **"I am informed"**: Butler, *Autobiography*, 257–58.

360   **"became to the discontented blacks"**: Nicolay and Hay, *Abraham Lincoln*, 4:387.

360   **abandoning their homes**: Goodheart, *1861*, 328.

360   **Among those who tended**: See Clinton, *Harriet Tubman*, 147–49.

360   **"even old men and women"**: Lewis Lockwood, "Dear Brethren," quoted in Goodheart, *1861*, 334.

360   **Butler reported the situation**: Butler to Scott, May 27, 1861, in Ira Berlin et al., *Free at Last: A Documentary History of Slavery, Freedom, and the Civil War* (New York: New Press, 1992), 10.

361   **"*Where* we are drifting"**: Child, quoted in Foner, *Fiery Trial*, 171.

361   **"I have no doubt"**: Quoted in Goodheart, *1861*, 333.

362   **Some who hoped**: Louis S. Gerteis, *From Contraband to Freedman: Federal Policy Toward Southern Blacks, 1861–1865* (Westport, Conn.: Greenwood Press, 1973), 17, attributes these views to James Redpath and Lewis Tappan, respectively.

362   **"Black People should have"**: Wool, quoted in Chandra Manning, *Troubled Refuge: Struggling for Freedom in the Civil War* (New York: Knopf, 2016), 55.

362   **not materially different**: Gerteis, *From Contraband to Freedman*, 19–20.

362   **"patently contradictory" nature**: Foner, *Fiery Trial*, 173.

362 **"it is no part of the duty"**: Cong. Globe, House of Representatives, 37th Cong., 1st Sess., July 8–9, 1861, 24, 32. See also Gerteis, *From Contraband to Freedman*, 16.

362 **that "secession niggers"**: Quoted in Gerteis, *From Contraband to Freedman*, 14.

362 **passed the House**: Foner, *Fiery Trial*, 173.

362 **approved another resolution**: Foner, *Fiery Trial*, 174.

362 **First Confiscation Act**: See Oakes, *Freedom National*, 120.

363 **"giving an anti-slavery character"**: Crittenden, quoted in Foner, *Fiery Trial*, 175.

364 **"a hero, every inch"**: Dana, quoted in Kevin Starr, *Americans and the California Dream, 1850–1915* (New York: Oxford University Press, 1973), 370.

364 **"without first having my approbation"**: Lincoln to Frémont, Sept. 2, 1861, in *Collected Works of Lincoln*, 4:506.

365 **"If any of the Border States"**: Oakes, *Freedom National*, 161. Oakes describes Frémont as surrounding "himself with a protective coterie of sycophants" (155).

365 **"openly direct me"**: Frémont's response quoted in *Collected Works of Lincoln*, 4:507n3.

365 **cold and noncommittal**: Donald, *Lincoln*, 315.

365 **Lincoln "very cheerfully"**: Lincoln to Frémont, Sept. 11, 1861, in *Collected Works of Lincoln*, 4:518. See Michael Fellman, "The First Emancipation Proclamation," in Widmer, *Disunion*, 194–98.

365 **the "vacillating policy"**: Thomas Wentworth Higginson, *Army Life in a Black Regiment* (1869; Boston: Beacon Press, 1962), 266–67.

365 **issued an order**: Ira Berlin et al., *Freedom: A Documentary History of Emancipation*, series 1 (Cambridge, U.K.: Cambridge University Press, 1985), 1:399.

366 **"much valuable information"**: "Commander of the Missouri State Militia to the Headquarters of the Department of the Missouri," March 3, 1862, in Berlin et al., *Freedom*, 429.

366 **"To drive them from camp"**: "Commander of the Department of the Missouri to the Commander of the 4th Division of the Department," Dec. 26, 1861, in Berlin et al., *Freedom*, 423.

366 **one documented case**: See Berlin et al., *Free at Last*, 11–12.

366 **"terror must be made"**: Quoted in Leon F. Litwack, *Been in the Storm So Long: The Aftermath of Slavery* (New York: Vintage Books, 1979), 55.

366 **"every negro returned"**: John M. Richardson to Cameron, Dec. 1, 1861, in Berlin et al., *Freedom*, 1:418.

366 **loath to lose them**: See Berlin et al., *Freedom*, 400, who write that if "high principle did not move Yankee soldiers to harbor fugitive slaves, low expediency often did."

366 **"every excursion and raid"**: Gerteis, *From Contraband to Freedman*, 120.

367 **to the slaveholders of Delaware**: See Foner, *Fiery Trial*, 181–84.

367 **"the most diluted"**: Stevens, quoted in Louis P. Masur, *Lincoln's Hundred Days: The Emancipation Proclamation and the War for the Union* (Cambridge, Mass.: Harvard University Press, 2012), 45.

367 **"a brave man trying"**: Douglass, quoted in Masur, *Lincoln's Hundred Days*, 41.

367 **prescribing the penalty**: Foner, *Fiery Trial*, 195.

367 **"a fine regiment"**: Hunter to Stanton, June 23, 1862, in *The Civil War: The Second Year Told by Those Who Lived It*, ed. Stephen W. Sears (New York: Library of America, 2013), 239.

367 **"negro freeing machine"**: Quoted in Berlin et al., *Free at Last*, 82.

367 **"negroes [were] wild"**: Burnside to Stanton, in Berlin et al., *Free at Last*, 35.

368 **abolishing slavery in the District of Columbia**: Foner, *Fiery Trial*, 199.

368 **limited abolition act**: Foner, *Fiery Trial*, 198.

368 **defended by federal troops**: Foner, *Fiery Trial*, 201.

368 **Congress banned slavery**: Foner, *Fiery Trial*, 204.

368 **slavery "will be extinguished"**: Abraham Lincoln, "Appeal to Border State Representatives to Favor Compensated Emancipation," July 12, 1862, in *Collected Works of Lincoln*, 5:318.

368 **Second Confiscation Act**: Gerteis, *From Contraband to Freedman*, 23.

368 **Confiscation Act and the Militia Act**: See Berlin et al., *Free at Last*, 60. Technically, this last provision applied to family members owned by disloyal owners, but the technicalities were increasingly lost in the widening sphere of freedom.

369 **"both the worst event"**: Quoted in Gary W. Gallagher, *The Union War* (Cambridge, Mass.: Harvard University Press, 2011), 90.

369 **"the war might have ended"**: Foner, *Fiery Trial*, 205.

369 **new technologies of killing**: Roper, *Now the Drum of War*, 75.

369 **became almost "spreelike"**: Roper, *Now the Drum of War*, 233.

369 **science of healing**: See Margaret Humphreys, *Marrow of Tragedy: The Health Crisis of the American Civil War* (Baltimore: Johns Hopkins University Press, 2013), esp. 88–89.

370 **"over which the Confederates"**: Ulysses S. Grant, *Personal Memoirs of U. S. Grant* (New York: Century, 1895), 1:293.

370   **"blackened bloated corpses":** Quoted in Drew Gilpin Faust, *This Republic of Suffering: Death and the American Civil War* (New York: Knopf, 2008), 66–67.

371   **"six million pounds":** Faust, *This Republic of Suffering*, 69.

371   **picked through the dung:** Winik, *April 1865*, 33.

371   **rioting that engulfed New York City:** For a thorough account of the draft riots, see Iver Bernstein, *The New York City Draft Riots: Their Significance for American Society and Politics in the Age of the Civil War* (New York: Oxford University Press, 1990).

372   **"abolitionizing the whole army":** Soldier in the Third Wisconsin Volunteers, quoted in Masur, *Lincoln's Hundred Days*, 35.

372   **"This must never see daylight":** Quoted in Foner, *Fiery Trial*, 230.

372   **"General who takes":** Quoted in Ron Chernow, *Grant* (New York: Penguin Press, 2017), 223.

373   **nearly 200,000 black soldiers:** Foner, *Fiery Trial*, 252.

373   **"their demeanor under arms":** Higginson, *Army Life in a Black Regiment*, 267.

373   **"we had about played":** Quoted in Masur, *Lincoln's Hundred Days*, 80.

373   **"all persons held as slaves":** Abraham Lincoln, "Emancipation Proclamation—First Draft," July 22, 1862, in *Collected Works of Lincoln*, 5:337.

373   **"cost the Administration":** Quoted in Masur, *Lincoln's Hundred Days, 151.*

373   **public announcement should be postponed:** Masur, *Lincoln's Hundred Days*, 81–82.

374   **"the councils, the representations":** Horace Greeley, "The Prayer of Twenty Millions," *New-York Tribune*, Aug. 19, 1862.

374   **"I have just read yours":** Lincoln to Greeley, Aug. 22, 1862, in *Collected Works of Lincoln*, 5:388–89.

375   **"under the Presidents proclamation":** Letter of Colonel S. D. Atkins, in Berlin et al., *Free at Last*, 75.

375   **"The dogmas of the quiet past":** Lincoln, "Annual Message to Congress," Dec. 1, 1862, in *Collected Works of Lincoln*, 5:537.

375   **his hand trembled:** Foner, *Fiery Trial*, 240; Allen C. Guelzo, *Lincoln's Emancipation Proclamation: The End of Slavery in America* (New York: Simon & Schuster, 2006), 182; and see Harold Holzer et al., *The Emancipation Proclamation: Three Views* (Baton Rouge: Louisiana State University Press, 2006), x.

376   **"The proclamation," he wrote:** Douglass, *Life and Times*, 352.

376   **"a mere strife for territory":** Douglass, *Life and Times*, 354–55.

376   **"It is the policy":** Halleck to Grant, March 31, 1863, in Simpson, *Civil War*, 105.

376   **His allusion to it:** "No one could mistake the meaning," Eric Foner writes, when he said that "this nation, under God, shall have a new birth of freedom." Foner, *Fiery Trial*, 268.

377   **"why," if slavery:** Quoted in Litwack, *Been in the Storm So Long*, 53–54.

377   **fleeing every week:** Litwack, *Been in the Storm So Long*, 52.

377   **"go out in any direction":** Thomas Calahan, quoted in McPherson, *Negro's Civil War*, 111.

378   **"the greatest slave revolt":** Steven Hahn, *The Political Worlds of Slavery and Freedom*, pp. 55-114.

378   **"lying in a little ice house":** Berlin et al., *Free at Last*, 359–60.

378   **shackled, whipped, and locked up:** Litwack, *Been in the Storm So Long*, 55–56.

378   **the "damned Yankees":** Berlin et al., *Free at Last*, 54.

378   **"Organized Bands Prowling":** These are the words of a semiliterate white Annapolis lighthouse keeper (Thomas B. Davis) who professed his consternation in a letter to a local antislavery judge, Hugh L. Bond. Davis to Bond, Nov. 6, 1864, in Berlin et al., *Free at Last*, 370–71.

378   **"roads Northward for hours":** *Franklin Repository*, July 8, 1863, quoted in Edward L. Ayers, *The Thin Light of Freedom: The Civil War and Emancipation in the Heart of America* (New York: W. W. Norton, 2017), 46.

378   **Mounted soldiers snatched up:** Ayers, *Thin Light of Freedom*, 46.

379   **captives were executed:** Manning, *Troubled Refuge*, 63–64.

379   **Some were decapitated:** Manning, *Troubled Refuge*, 77.

379   **"arrived to the Union camp":** Quoted in Jim Downs, *Sick from Freedom: African-American Illness and Suffering During the Civil War and Reconstruction* (New York: Oxford University Press, 2012), 22.

379   **"workers who carried":** Downs, *Sick from Freedom*, 35.

379   **"instant recruiting stations":** Manning, *Troubled Refuge*, 35.

379   **to prostitute themselves:** Gerteis, *From Contraband to Freedman*, 121.

379   **burying the Union dead:** Manning, *Troubled Refuge*, 51.

380   **volunteered to teach:** Manning, *Troubled Refuge*, 47.

380   **sell fugitive slaves:** Manning, *Troubled Refuge*, 62.

380   **risk of kidnapping:** Manning, *Troubled Refuge*, 91.

380   **"enlistment practices so coercive":** Manning, *Troubled Refuge*, 92.

380   **"everything unexpected in its own time":** Philip Roth, *The Plot Against America* (Boston: Houghton Mifflin, 2004), 114. Roth was writing not about the Civil War but about World War II, but the point is transportable.

381   sense of "*contingency*": McPherson, *Battle Cry of Freedom*, 858.

381   "**I have never claimed**": Lincoln to Albert G. Hodges, April 4, 1864, in *Collected Works of Lincoln*, 7:282.

381   **We helped bring off:** Sam R. Watkins, *Co. Aytch*, in Sears, *Civil War*, 598.

381   "**the fallacy of imagining**": Gallagher, *Union War*, 88–89.

381   "**with different battlefield accidents**": Mark A. Graber, *Dred Scott and the Problem of Constitutional Evil* (New York: Cambridge University Press, 2006), 14.

381   **overshot their targets:** James M. McPherson, *Hallowed Ground: A Walk at Gettysburg* (New York: Crown, 2003), 108.

382   "**You stood**," **he said:** Lincoln to Meade, July 14, 1863, in *Collected Works of Lincoln*, 6:327–28.

382   "**we might have won**": Ward Moore, *Bring the Jubilee* (Rockville, Md.: Wildside Press, 1955), 42.

383   "**saw the danger of premature peace**": Douglass, *Life and Times*, 358–59.

383   **vulnerable to revision:** In his last annual message, delivered on December 6, 1864, he told Congress that "should, by whatever mode or means, make it an Executive duty to re-enslave such persons" who had risked their lives for the Union, "another, and not I, must be their instrument to perform it." *Collected Works of Lincoln*, 8:152. The "peace candidate," George McClellan, who had mounted a serious challenge in the recent election, never endorsed the proclamation as settled policy.

384   "**the abolition Pharisees**": Letter to his mother, Dec. 20, 1862, in Eliot Personal Papers.

384   "**mighty scourge of war**": Abraham Lincoln, "Second Inaugural Address," March 4, 1865, in *Collected Works of Lincoln*, 8:333.

384   "**Americans, let us remember**": "Serious Thoughts," *Freedom's Journal*, June 29, 1827.

385   **new kind of limbo:** For a brief but powerful elaboration of this point, see Frank Tannenbaum, *Slave and Citizen: The Negro in the Americas* (New York: Vintage Books, 1946), esp. 111–12.

385   "**Poor dusky children**": Quoted in Downs, *Sick from Freedom*, 23.

385   **found guilty of "crimes"**: Douglas A. Blackmon, *Slavery by Another Name: The Re-enslavement of Black Americans from the Civil War to World War II* (New York: Anchor Books, 2008), 6–7.

385   **excluded from the social welfare programs:** See Ira Katznelson, *When Affirmative Action Was White: An Untold History of Racial Inequality in Twentieth-Century America* (New York: W. W. Norton, 2005); and Ira Katznelson, *Fear Itself: The New Deal and the Origins of Our Time* (New York: Liveright, 2013), 156–94. Katznelson points out that as the price of southern support, predominantly black "farm workers and maids" were "deliberately left out" of the Fair Labor Standards Act of 1937, which established a minimum hourly wage of 25 cents (171).

386   "**anything more helpless**": Edward Dicey, quoted in James R. Mellow, *Nathaniel Hawthorne in His Times* (Boston: Houghton Mifflin, 1980), 553.

386   "**One very pregnant token**": Hawthorne, "Chiefly About War Matters," 318–19.

386   "**many thoughtful and patriotic men**": Douglass, "Address at Cooper Union," in *Lincoln Assassinated!!: The Firsthand Story of the Murder, Manhunt, Trial, and Mourning*, ed. Harold Holzer (New York: Library of America, 2014), 313.

386   "**Let the conflict come**": Frederick Douglass, "The New President," in *The Civil War: The First Year Told by Those Who Lived It*, ed. Brooks D. Simpson, Stephen W. Sears, and Aaron Sheehan-Dean (New York: Library of America, 2012), 209.

386   "**The cost of the experiment**": Douglass, "Address at Cooper Union," 313.

387   **repealed the fugitive slave law:** Foner writes that the fugitive slave law had "incongruously remained on the books despite emancipation." *Fiery Trial*, 295.

INDEX

Page numbers in *italics* refer to illustrations.